LIGHT FOR THE ROAD

LIGHT
for the
ROAD

EDITED BY

Samuel and Kathryn

Rapport

HARPER & BROTHERS, PUBLISHERS, NEW YORK

Grateful acknowledgment is made to the following for permission to reprint selections included in this book:

"The Moments That Educate" and "The Miracle of an Artist" from *The Courage to Be Happy* by Dorothy Thompson; by permission of Houghton Mifflin Company.

"A Great Lesson from a Great Man" by Stefan Zweig; by permission of *The Catholic World*.

"Have You an Educated Heart?" from *The Bromide and other Theories* by Gelett Burgess, copyright 1933 by Gelett Burgess; by permission of The Viking Press, Inc. and *The Reader's Digest*.

"Why Laughter Has Power" by Bob Hope, copyright 1952 by Guideposts Associates, Inc.; permission of *Guideposts* and the author.

"Love" and "Beauty" from *The Prophet* by Kahlil Gibran, copyright 1923 by Kahlil Gibran, renewal copyright 1951 by Administrators C.T.A. of Kahlil Gibran Estate, and Mary G. Gibran; by permission of Alfred A. Knopf, Inc.

Selection from *Happiness* by William Lyon Phelps, copyright 1927 by E. P. Dutton & Co., Inc., renewal 1955 by Dryden L. Phelps; by permission of E. P. Dutton & Co., Inc.

Selection from *Witness to the Truth* by Edith Hamilton, copyright 1948 by W. W. Norton & Company, Inc.; by permission of W. W. Norton & Company, Inc.

"Pattern of a Life" from *R. E. Lee*, Volume IV, by Douglas Southall Freeman, copyright 1935 by Charles Scribner's Sons; by permission of Charles Scribner's Sons.

CONTENTS

Part Two. Art

VI. *The Gifts of Religion and God*

INTRODUCTION

To every one of us—even the most fortunate—there come periods of bewilderment and frustration, and on occasion deep sorrow. As we think of our own lives or the lives of others, we realize that in spite of all the woes such periods bring, in the end they mean enrichment of our lives. After them come peace and understanding, and a quality we describe as wisdom. Its growth is slow. It comes only by a process of accretion—born out of the ordeals of life. Persons who have experienced the heights and the depths are apt to have it in greatest measure. For those who are unable to achieve it, we instinctively have little respect.

Yet even the wisest are baffled by the problems that mankind must face. To use a homely but expressive phrase, they often "do not know which way to turn." In such situations, they lay their burdens before a higher power. "I will lift up mine eyes unto the hills, from whence cometh my help," says the Bible. And from no other source will they obtain comparable assistance. Yet there is help also to be found in human experience; for whatever our problems, others have faced them. The weak have fallen by the wayside—the strong have survived and been the richer for it. And among the latter have been those gifted with the talent of passing on to others the fruits of their ordeals. Sometimes, if we are fortunate, they are to be found among our friends. Often they are men of God, or men of medicine, or others whom we seek out instinctively. Yet many of us feel the need for impersonal communion with these wise spirits. There is only one way to do so—through books, the written word.

It is with this deep need in mind that the present volume has been prepared. The selections have not been chosen to illuminate any specific creed or faith—that is the function of those whose training fits them for the task. Yet they are here presented in the hope that they will offer guidance and comfort to those who stand in need. They are written, the Editors feel, with a deep sense of sincerity and purpose. They are, in the words of a famous quotation, the precious life blood of master spirits.

Our primary spiritual need is a philosophy of life—a goal for the daily round of life. Without such philosophy, without some notion of the meaning of existence, our activities are without direction and our lives empty. Even the most cynical among us feels the void; and it is the purpose of our first section, "For a Way of Life," to suggest some of the necessary standards. Are we to exist for the moment? Are we to strive for insubstantial and unimportant things? Are we to face the world in solemn or in joyous mood? Are we to live for ourselves alone? In actual practice these are questions more easily asked than answered. Some of the writers who have considered them tell us what they think.

Daily life is often interspersed with times of stress when problems rise to crescendo, when we have need for greater courage and deeper understanding than during the ordinary round. For those less fortunate, the need can be ever-present. A hostile environment must be faced. Physical handicaps are present, through accident or heredity. The necessity to "stand up and be counted," sometimes in the presence of the hostile mob, arises. These are the times when we feel the need for courage. And our section, "For the Struggle Against Odds," tells us how to face such crises. In this section, also, are inspiring accounts of individuals who, in such situations, have been able to call on their own resources, and on those offered by a greater Power—if indeed the two be not the same. Some of these brave ones have been among the greatest, like Joan of Arc. Some have been unknown and by the world's standards unimportant, like the little girl whose name was Hannah.

To all of us there comes a period of lessening power. Our bodies become feeble or ill, our minds begin to lack that alertness which we had when young. For many, the change is hard to bear. The road appears to roughen and there seems no future in store but declining ability to face the world. Yet if this be our attitude, there is no hope for us. It is a period of life that has its own values, its own pathways to contentment, and others before us have pointed the way. It is a way of serenity, filled with satisfactions which lie within our grasp and which are no less important because they lack the savage intensity of youth. And when the final adventure draws closer—as it must—it should be faced as the greatest experience of all, to be awaited without dread, a rounding out of the fullness and richness that have preceded it. These are the messages of our section, "For the Lengthening Shadows."

The time of tragedy, when a loved one goes, is the time when our resources are called on to the utmost. How is it possible to offer consolation to those who are desolated by loss? The human instinct is to ask the question, "Why?," and often it seems impossible to find an answer. Yet even in this darkest hour, the answer does exist; and in the section, "For the Time of Sorrow," are thoughts which have proved their helpfulness to others. Is the life that is gone wasted on that account? Impossible, we say. Is there hope for another—a different meeting? Some of the profoundest thinkers offer more than hope. And in these two ideas—the goodness which remains of a life now past, the concept of a life to come—can be found the strength to face the inescapable.

So far in *Light for the Road*, the emphasis has been on basic needs —for a philosophy of living, for courage in adversity, for times of aging and of sorrow. We turn now to some ever-present sources of strength and inspiration. The first of these is Nature, the second Art, the third Religion and God. The man or woman is rare who cannot find deep satisfaction in the world around us. The sight of a towering mountain, or a peaceful meadow at sundown, or even a single beautiful tree or flower, arouses almost indefinable sentiments. To some the feeling is almost unconscious. To others it is identified with simple happiness. To yet a third group, it is a feeling akin to religion itself. In the selections offered in "The Gifts of Nature and Art" and in "The Gifts of Religion and God," are examples of each of these reactions. They offer us experiences which we cannot neglect without grave loss to ourselves.

It is thus also with Art and Beauty, which can perform a twofold function in our lives. We may find deep enrichment in the thunderous music of Beethoven or the chiselled cadences of Shelley. This is the joy of appreciation. Or we ourselves may learn to play the violin or paint a landscape. This, in however humble a fashion, is the joy of creation. Both, in Walter Russell Bowie's phrase, help us "to be alive"—to savor more intensely the world around us.

And finally there is the helpfulness which lies in Religion and God. "There are no atheists in foxholes" was a wartime slogan. It is a slogan which applies to all of us in time of need. Instinctively we turn to God. Instinctively we pray. Even a Tolstoy, unwilling to accept the tenets of his church, was forced by his deepest needs to turn in the end to a higher Power. These are feelings which are intuitive and fundamental. By satisfying them, we satisfy our deepest necessities.

Light for the Road is not a book to read at a sitting. It is a browsing book, a bedside book, a book to turn to from time to time according to the reader's mood. Its purpose is to offer help in the words of those who themselves have found it. It is hoped that the reader will find satisfaction in its pages.

Because of limitations of space, some of the selections have been abridged, omitting material which is not relevant to the purpose of the book.

THE EDITORS

LIGHT FOR THE ROAD

I. For a Way of Life

PART ONE

THE WHISTLE

Benjamin Franklin

We all think of Benjamin Franklin as almost the epitome of the American dream—the poor boy who comes to a strange city, a loaf of bread under his arm, owning nothing but his ability and his integrity, who with them reaches the highest position. He became famous as a printer, author, inventor, scientist and statesman. It was his inspired common sense which made Poor Richard's Almanac one of the most successful publications of Colonial times. This quality was perhaps never shown to better effect than in his famous letter to Madame Brillon which is printed below. The Whistle of the child becomes the false gods and worldly success of the adult. The choice of wisdom is to avoid them.

WHEN I was a child of seven years old, my friends, on a holiday, filled my pockets with coppers. I went directly to a shop where they sold toys for children; and, being charmed with the sound of a *whistle*, that I met by the way in the hands of another boy, I voluntarily offered and gave all my money for one. I then came home, and went whistling all over the house, much pleased with my *whistle*, but disturbing all the family. My brothers, and sisters, and cousins, understanding the bargain I had made, told me I had given four times as much for it as it was worth; put me in mind what good things I might have bought with the rest of the money; and laughed at me so much for my folly, that I cried with vexation; and the reflection gave me more chagrin than the *whistle* gave me pleasure.

This however was afterwards of use to me, the impression continuing on my mind; so that often, when I was tempted to buy some unnecessary thing, I said to myself, *Don't give too much for the whistle;* and I saved my money.

As I grew up, came into the world, and observed the actions of men, I thought I met with many, very many, who *gave too much for the whistle.*

When I saw one too ambitious of court favour, sacrificing his time in attendance on levees, his repose, his liberty, his virtue, and perhaps his friends, to attain it, I have said to myself, *This man gives too much for his whistle.*

When I saw another fond of popularity, constantly employing himself in political bustles, neglecting his own affairs, and ruining them by that neglect, *He pays, indeed,* said I, *too much for his whistle.*

If I knew a miser, who gave up every kind of comfortable living, all the pleasure of doing good to others, all the esteem of his fellow-citizens, and the joys of benevolent friendship, for the sake of accumulating wealth, *Poor man,* said I, *you pay too much for your whistle.*

When I met with a man of pleasure, sacrificing every laudable improvement of the mind, or of his fortune, to mere corporeal sensations, and ruining his health in their pursuit, *Mistaken man,* said I, *you are providing pain for yourself, instead of pleasure; you give too much for your whistle.*

If I see one fond of appearance, or fine clothes, fine houses, fine furniture, fine equipages, all above his fortune, for which he contracts debts, and ends his career in a prison, *Alas!* say I, *he has paid dear, very dear, for his whistle.*

When I see a beautiful, sweet-tempered girl married to an ill-natured brute of a husband, *What a pity,* say I, *that she should pay so much for a whistle!*

In short, I conceive that great part of the miseries of mankind are brought upon them by the false estimates they have made of the value of things, and by their *giving too much for their whistles.*

Yet I ought to have charity for these unhappy people, when I consider, that, with all this wisdom of which I am boasting, there are certain things in this world so tempting, for example, the apples of King John, which happily are not to be bought; for if they were put to sale by auction, I might very easily be led to ruin myself in the purchase, and find that I had once more given too much for the *whistle.*

THE MOMENTS THAT EDUCATE

———— *Dorothy Thompson* ————

Benjamin Franklin wrote about a small boy with a whistle. Dorothy Thompson writes about a little girl who envied bitterly the great house, the servants and the elegant clothes of a rich acquaintance. It was her father, a minister, who was able to show her the falsity of such goals, and to provide her with the solid background which was to carry her so far in later life. Dorothy Thompson was to become a world-renowned journalist. Heads of states were to welcome her, take her into their confidence, seek her advice. In such surroundings she must often have thought of the moment which educated her and which she here describes.

ᝌ

Many seeds fall into the mind of a child or adolescent, some to take root and others to perish, and it is hard to say just why. In every young person's life, also, there are crises—moral or intellectual—and how they are responded to often depends upon the guidance on hand at the given moment.

I know, for instance, exactly when and where I first became aware of the existence of social classes, an awareness initially accompanied by shock, envy, grief, shame, and resentment. Had these reactions, however repressed, continued to fester, they would, I am inclined to think, have influenced my life and attitudes and not for my future contentment or happiness. But an immediate intervention prevented that. The instrument was my father.

When I was a little over ten, the "Conference" to which my Methodist minister father belonged—"the faith," as he used to quip, "which moves parsons"—transferred him to a new parish, or "charge."

Hitherto, from the time I had begun to notice things at all, our successive parsonage homes had been in villages of two to four thousand people, all of them serving surrounding agricultural communities. Each contained families who were well or less well off, a status reflected in whether they lived in larger or smaller houses, with wider or narrower yards, or whether (which in those days was rare) they owned an automobile.

But the differences were in degree, not in kind. The presidents of the creamery and the local bank, the owner of the biggest hardware, "drygoods," or grocery stores, the man who did the largest insurance business, and often the most popular doctor lived in the larger houses, their children had more nickels to spend on licorice whips, horehound drops, and milk chocolate, and had shinier bicycles, and their small daughters (I don't remember about the sons) had several "best dresses" instead of one. But we all wore the same kind of clothes, every kid's spending money was in nickels—I never saw one flash a dollar bill—and our mothers did all of their housework, or were aided by a "hired girl," a farmer's daughter who lived as part of the family, or by neighbors who came to "help out" for an hourly fee, none of them regarded by themselves or their employers as servants, and often, like the older persons working in the stores, calling their employers by their first names.

In these villages my father, as an educated man and a clergyman, was definitely among the "leading citizens," and although we lived austerely, not to say penuriously, I never had any feeling of inferiority.

My father's new parish was different. Its backbone occupations were still services to the surrounding farmers, but it was a larger town, with several prosperous mills. These were largely family concerns with financial cross-pollination. They also did their banking locally, and the bank president was one of them. So a few families were rich, not just "well off." They lived in homes surrounded not by "yards," however pretty, but by expansive, beautifully kept gardens.

Still, the new two-story parsonage was the finest and most commodious house we had ever occupied, with a parlor, sitting room, dining room, study, and large, if old-fashioned kitchen on the first floor and four bedrooms, a bathroom, and a small unfinished attic on the second. For the first time I lived in a house with a full bathroom, and had a room of my own!

If its furniture, collected by the parsonage committee, was heterogeneous and ill-matched—Victorian sofas upholstered in horsehair, a "patent" rocking chair covered with worn Brussels carpeting, a remarkable combination writing desk, bookcase, and chest of drawers of "golden oak" with an oval mirror set in one side of the upper cabinet, giving the piece the look of a one-eyed monster—it was the kind of furniture to which I was accustomed, and not only in parsonages furnished by lady committees. Altogether, it seemed to my childish eyes palatial!

Of course I had no knowledge of the economic structure of the town, nor was yet aware that the local rich never sent their offspring to the town's high school, but East, to private boarding schools, and thence to Harvard, Yale, or Dartmouth. None of them was a member of my father's church; they were Episcopalians or Presbyterians, and their ministers did not wear Prince Alberts on weekdays, as did my father, for he had no other, but business suits, or tweed jackets— all of which I was only later to observe.

But the "hill set" did send their children to grade school, where I promptly made a friend, who asked me to "luncheon" the following Saturday.

Her home, set in a professionally landscaped garden, was impressive from the outside, and when I rang the bell the door was opened by a gentleman in a striped waistcoat and a funny little jacket, who announced that "Miss" Fanny was expecting me and would I please go upstairs—up a very wide winding staircase with a delicate rail, the like of which I had never seen, sweeping up from an enormous lounge-hall in which I stood completely overcome. The floor was so polished that I glanced for my own reflection as in a pool, and on it lay silky rugs of jewel colors, like islands of enamel. Deep-cushioned chairs were covered with ruby damask-silk, of which the draperies at the long windows were also made, and along the pale high walls were delicate chairs with fretted backs and small pedestaled tables, on which were enormous bowls of autumn roses and chrysanthemums. At the right, through a wide-open door, I saw the gleaming dark wood of a dining table, set with no tablecloth but lacy mats and twinkling silver, and at the left, through a similar doorway, a room even larger than the one where I stood, with walls of palest green, silken curtains of darker jade, a rug all rubies, emeralds, topazes, turquoises covering the whole floor, more chairs surely not designed to be sat on, flowers again, and everywhere the most wonderful smell, of roses, lavender, I knew not what.

A devouring bookworm, I had read of castles and palaces, but they were just in books, in stories, made up, not real.

A voice from the stairtop called "Miss" Dorothy, in an odd accent, and slowly I mounted the stairs, which again opened into a wide hall with many doors. One was open to a room in which sat my classmate, before a mirrored table. She wore a slip with a round neck, white and fine as silk, edged top and bottom with delicate lace, and a lady in a beautiful black silk dress, frilly apron, and tiny lace cap was brushing her long hair. "Good morning, miss," she said to me, and Fanny, leaping up said, "Goody! You've come! This is Marie. She's Ma's maid but she takes care of me, too."

What a strange house where grownups called children "Miss" and children called grownups by their first names! And Fanny's room! Why it was bigger than our parlor and sitting room together, with pale gold-colored furniture all matching, a long bookcase, the color of the pale blue walls, frilly curtains, and draperies and chairs sprinkled all over with roses.

I stood in a "Peter Thompson" sailor suit, conscious for the first time in my life that its blue serge cloth was coarse, that the let-down skirt had a faint line from the earlier hem, that my shoes, though vigorously polished, were scuffed.

Fanny chattered gaily, her dressing being completed, while I, with my heart burning in me like a fire, surveyed the books, remarking superiorly that I had read them all, didn't she think they were "childish"? —I was reading *The Outcasts* by Victor Hugo, who was French. Marie having left the room, Fanny explained that she was French, Ma had brought her from Paris and Ma spoke French, too. I announced my pahpie spoke Latin—a gross exaggeration, but greatly impressive to Fanny—and that I contemplated learning all the languages in the world, including Chinee, to which the wide-eyed Fanny asked "Whyever *for?*" regretting, "I'll *have to* learn French but I don't want to."

I flaunted my intellectual interests (hitherto nonexistent or unconscious), with Fanny listening admiringly all through lunch, which was dinner to me, with clear soup in cups, and fresh meat (our Sunday treat) and ice cream, all served from silver dishes on gold-edged plates by the gentleman in the striped vest. We were alone—Ma, Fanny explained, having gone riding. I made another mental memo that Fanny's mother had nothing more to do than ride a horse, while my auntie at that moment was doubtless baking bread.

I broke away then, as quickly as I could, and when I was beyond the grounds, burst into bitter tears. It was so *beautiful*—a house one lived in could be *beautiful*—and I hated it, hated Fanny, hated myself. I was ashamed, and worst of all, a feeling accompanied by a crushing sense of guilt, I was ashamed of my father! Like being ashamed of God! I did not see him as a face but as a suit of clothes walking, clothes no one else wore, shiny and greenish at the elbows.

As I approached the parsonage I saw for the first time its skimpy windows, which seemed to be making mean faces at me. Its narrow hall closed like prison walls, and looking into the sitting room I saw the threadbare patch before the sofa, discouraging as a sigh.

I crept up to my bedroom, whose privacy only that morning had delighted me. Now it appeared as a narrow box papered hideously, its iron brass-trimmed bed, with a plain white spread, the chest of drawers, from which a shred of paint hung like loose skin, and one straight "golden oak" chair filling it but for a narrow passage between bed and wall and bed and chest, on which lay two small rag mats. I guessed that even the servants in the big house had better rooms. And lying on the bed, under the spread, I cried silently, hopelessly, in furious revolt against all this ugliness.

My aunt, looking for me at suppertime, thought I slept, though I was feigning it, not wanting among other things to see her apron, and reported to my father her anxiety that I must be sick because I'd never gone to bed in my life without being urged.

But my father, who knew me best, came up after supper, turned on the gas light, sat on the edge of the bed, felt my pulse, saw it was normal, and regarded my smeared cheeks and red eyes. He went right to the heart of the matter. "You were at Fanny's today, and saw a beautiful home, and are envious and discontented." It was not an accusation. I turned my eyes from him for the treason in my heart, but nodded.

"Get up," he said, "and come downstairs. You should eat some supper." I murmured that I was not hungry—though I had only picked at the fine luncheon—but I got up, being unaccustomed to disobey, and we went downstairs together, through the kitchen, where Auntie, buttering bread, said nothing, and into the garden. Night falls early and swiftly in the autumn, the stars were out and a sickle moon, and trees and shrubbery only faint dark masses. We sat on a wooden bench.

"Do you wish on the first star you see?" asked my father's voice lightly. "Then wish to learn how to be happy."

"Star-light, star-bright, first star I've seen tonight," I murmured obediently, not making any wish aloud.

"Where Fanny lives is so lovely—like in a story—and it gives me a pain here," I opened up with my hand on my heart.

"Is it more lovely than the stars?" I heard a voice with humor in it.

"Different from the stars," I said.

"If we sit here more and more will come out. You know how they make pictures in the sky, each in its own constellation: Andromeda, Cassiopeia, Lyra, the Bear. (Lovely words: Andromeda, Cassiopeia.) The astronomers say each great star is a world, each has its place in the scheme of the universe. Look how they differ from each other. Follow along from the handle of the Dipper—that big, blue, sparkling star is Arcturus. They say it is the star that guided the wise men to Bethlehem. But Sirius is brightest. And Antares is red. See?

"The universe is greater than the greatest mind can comprehend," the voice from the dimness went on. "Even our whole wide world within it is but a tiny part. And in that small world the largest, grandest house ever built is—like an almost invisible speck."

"Yes, but some people *do* have big beautiful houses and some littler and ugly ones."

"Everybody born has something more and something less than others. Some have food but no appetite. Some own beauty but have no eyes to see. Some see beauty all around them without wanting to own it. Some have clever hands and some clever heads."

"Who are the richest?"

"Those who have love"—the words came lightly.

After a pause he asked, "What is the nicest taste?"

"Ice cream," I replied promptly.

"Are you sure? Is it better than the taste of an apple? How does an apple taste?"

This was a game we often played at home, describing the tastes, sounds, smells, and touch of things.

"It tastes like autumn," I said, "like frost and red leaves. It is cool and wet and crunchy, like when you walk in snow. You taste it in your teeth, too."

"Is ice cream better than the taste of bread?"

"With butter on it?"

"Bread and butter," my father agreed.

"Bread tastes brown and white and hard and soft," I attempted. "It tastes chewy, like butternuts, and smooth like cream. Like cream and nuts."

"If you were very, very hungry?"

"Like when your stomach feels squeaky?"

"Yes, like that. Then what would taste better, bread or ice cream?"

Ice cream, I thought, would taste cold—all the way down into the rattle. "I think for a shivery stomach bread would be more—cozy."

"I think so too," my father laughed. "Definitely more cozy."

"So, you see, between big and little, great and small, rich and poor, bread and butter and ice cream, there is proportion. To see things in proportion helps us to be happy. Those who have milk and bread and butter, a snug shelter, a bed for sleep, a fire when it is cold, a breeze when it is warm, have all they really need of such things. And if not everyone has even these, it means people are not helping God answer the prayer they pray. God intends everyone to have his daily bread, and earn it for himself, unless of course he is sick or old, and then his neighbors must furnish it, with love. But if that sort of thing were all we had, we would be poor indeed."

"What else do we have, anyhow?"

"Beauty, my child, beauty!" Now the voice was impatient. "Beauty everywhere—in the sky, in people's faces, in books, in pictures, in poems, in a tree. Have you read *Walden* yet?"

"No, but I will, Pahpie."

He changed the subject. "I hope you and Fanny will be friends," he said. "People say she is lonely. She is an only child, you know, and her mother is busy with other things."

"She rides a horse," I confided. "Every single day. She wasn't home for lunch."

"She travels a great deal," said my father, "and leaves Fanny to the servants."

"The man at lunch didn't even talk," I said. "Just passed things."

"And I suspect some of the other village children feel the way you once did," said my father blandly, referring to the distant past of a previous hour.

Pity for Fanny overwhelmed my highly susceptible nature. No brother to romp with, no little sister to pet or scold, no games at the table, no Auntie!

"Is envy a very bad sin?" I inquired. "Do I get punished?"

"Envy is its own punishment," replied my father. "But I will sentence you to learn a Psalm:

The heavens declare the glory of God, and the firmament showeth his handiwork.

Readers will protest that I cannot possibly recall such a conversation verbatim after many years. Of course they are right. What I recall are all my feelings, my father's reaction to them, and the gist of our conversation. I have recalled them again, and again, throughout my life, in similar circumstances of frustrated desires and ambitions.

We went into the house, finally, for it had grown chilly outside. Auntie had laid a clean napkin on the corner of the kitchen table. The gas cast a yellow gleam and the wood range filled the room with warmth. The other children must have gone to bed. At the place laid for me there were soft-boiled eggs in a cup, a glass of milk, fresh homemade buttered bread, a dish of apple sauce. I was ravenous.

"It tastes good, Auntie," I said shyly. "I like it here."

"To be sure it does," she said. "To be sure you do."

A WAY OF LIFE
An Address Delivered to Students at Yale

William Osler

It is the physician, as well as the man of God, to whom we turn in time of trouble. Even when our bodies are well, we feel that these dedicated men, who have witnessed so much suffering, will have the wisdom to help us in our dilemmas. Perhaps the best-known of these great modern physicians was William Osler, later to be knighted by the King of England. As he relates, he was born in a poor country parsonage, but went on to honors innumerable, including the Regius Professorship of Medicine at Oxford. He was the author of the world-famous Principles and Practices of Medicine, and it was as a practicing physician, a man wise not only in the ways of disease but of suffering humanity, that he was best known and loved. His little talks to young people were recognized by them, as well as by their elders, as rare gems of wisdom. It is one of the most popular of these talks, which teaches us how to look backward without regret and forward without fear, that we here reprint.

ᕦ

A FEW years ago a Christmas card went the rounds, with the legend "Life is just one 'derned' thing after another," which, in more refined language, is the same saying "Life is a habit," a succession of actions that become more or less automatic. This great truth, which lies at the basis of all actions, muscular or psychic, is the keystone of the teaching of Aristotle, to whom the formation of habits was the basis of moral excellence. "In a word, habits of any kind are the result of actions of the same kind; and so what we have to do, is to give a certain character to these particular actions" (*Ethics*). Lift a seven months old baby to his feet—see him tumble on his nose. Do the same at twelve months—he walks. At two years he runs. The muscles and the nervous system have acquired the habit. One trial after another, one failure after another, has given him power. Put your finger in a baby's mouth, and he sucks away in blissful anticipation of a response to a mammalian habit millions of years old. And we can deliberately train parts of our body to perform complicated actions with unerring accuracy. Watch that musician playing a difficult piece. Batteries, commutators, multipliers, switches, wires innumerable control those nimble fingers, the machinery of which may be set in motion as automatically as in a pianola, the player all the time chatting as if he had nothing to do in controlling the apparatus—habit again, the gradual acquisition of power by long practice and at the expense of many mistakes. The same great law reaches through mental and moral states. "Character," which partakes of both, in Plutarch's words, is "long-standing habit."

Now the way of life that I preach is a habit to be acquired gradually by long and steady repetition. It is the practice of living for the day only, and for the day's work, *Life in day-tight compartments.* "Ah," I hear you say, "that is an easy matter, simple as Elisha's advice!" Not as I shall urge it, in words which fail to express the depth of my feelings as to its value. I started life in the best of all environments—in a parsonage, one of nine children. A man who has filled Chairs in four universities, has written a successful book, and has been asked to lecture at Yale is supposed popularly to have brains of a special quality. A few of my intimate friends really know the truth about me, as I know it! Mine, in good faith I say it, are of the most mediocre character. But what about those professorships, etc.? Just habit, a way of life, an outcome of the day's work, the vital importance of which I wish to impress upon you with all the force at my command.

Dr. Johnson remarked upon the trifling circumstances by which men's lives are influenced, "not by an ascendant planet, a predominating humour, but by the first book which they read, some early conversation which they have heard, or some accident which excited ardour and enthusiasm." This was my case in two particulars. I was diverted to the Trinity College School, but I found a man of the White of Selborne type, who knew nature, and who knew how to get boys interested in it.[1] The other happened in the summer of 1871, when I was attending the Montreal General Hospital. Much worried as to the future, partly about the final examination, partly as to what I should do afterwards, I picked up a volume of Carlyle, and on the page I opened there was the familiar sentence— *"Our main business is not to see what lies dimly at a distance, but to do what lies clearly at hand."* A commonplace sentiment enough, but it hit and stuck and helped, and was the starting-point of a habit that has enabled me to utilize to the full the single talent entrusted to me.

The workers in Christ's vineyard were hired by the day; only for this day are we to ask for our daily bread, and we are expressly bidden to take no thought for the morrow. To the modern world these commands have an Oriental savor, counsels of perfection akin to certain of the Beatitudes, stimuli to aspiration, not to action. I am prepared on the contrary to urge the literal acceptance of the advice. Change that hard saying "Sufficient unto the day is the evil thereof" into "the goodness thereof," since the chief worries of life arise from the foolish habit of looking before and after.

I stood on the bridge of one of the great liners, plowing the ocean at twenty-five knots. "She is alive," said my companion, "in every plate; a huge monster with brain and nerves, an immense stomach, a wonderful heart and lungs, and a splendid system of locomotion." Just at that moment a signal sounded, and all over the ship the watertight compartments were closed. "Our chief factor of safety," said the Captain. "In spite of the *Titanic*," I said. "Yes," he replied, "in spite of the *Titanic*." Now each one of you is a much more marvelous organization than the great liner, and bound on a longer voyage. What I urge is that you so learn to control the machinery as to live with "day-tight compartments" as the most certain way to ensure safety on the voyage. Get on the bridge, and see that at least the great bulkheads are in working order. Touch a button and hear,

[1] The Rev. W. A. Johnson, the founder of the school.

at every level of your life, the iron doors shutting out the Past—the dead yesterdays. Touch another and shut off, with a metal curtain, the Future—the unborn tomorrows. Then you are safe—safe for today! The petty annoyances, the real and fancied slights, the trivial mistakes, the disappointments, the sins, the sorrows, even the joys— bury them deep in the oblivion of each night. "Undress," as George Herbert says, "your soul at night," not by self-examination, but by shedding, as you do your garments, the daily sins whether of omission or of commission, and you will wake a free man, with a new life. To look back, except on rare occasions for stock-taking, is to risk the fate of Lot's wife. Many a man is handicapped in his course by a cursed combination of retro- and intro-spection, the mistakes of yesterday paralyzing the efforts of today, the worries of the past hugged to his destruction, and the worm Regret allowed to canker the very heart of his life. To die daily, after the manner of St. Paul, ensures the resurrection of a new man, who makes each day the epitome of a life.

The load of tomorrow, added to that of yesterday, carried today makes the strongest falter. Shut off the future as tightly as the past. No dreams, no visions, no delicious fantasies, no castles in the air, with which, as the old song so truly says, "hearts are broken, heads are turned." To youth, we are told, belongs the future, but the wretched tomorrow that so plagues some of us has no certainty, except through today. Who can tell what a day may bring forth? The future is today—there is no tomorrow! The day of a man's salvation is *now*—the life of the present, of today, lived earnestly, intently, without a forward-looking thought, is the only insurance for the future. Let the limit of your horizon be a twenty-four hour circle. . . . Look heavenward, if you wish, but never to the horizon—that way danger lies. Truth is not there, happiness is not there, certainty is not there, but the falsehoods, the frauds, the quackeries, the *ignes fatui* which have deceived each generation—all beckon from the horizon, and lure the men not content to look for the truth and happiness that tumble out at their feet. Once while at College climb a mountain-top, and get a general outlook of the land, and make it the occasion perhaps of that careful examination of yourself, that inquisition which Descartes urges every man to hold once in a lifetime—not oftener.

Waste of energy, mental distress, nervous worries dog the steps of a man who is anxious about the future. Shut close, then, the great fore and aft bulkheads, and prepare to cultivate the habit of a life of Day-Tight Compartments. Do not be discouraged—like every other habit, the acquisition takes time, and the way is one you must find for yourselves. I can only give general directions and encouragement, in the hope that while the green years are on your heads, you may have the courage to persist.

Now, for the day itself! What first? Be your own daysman! and sigh not with Job for any mysterious intermediary, but prepare to lay your own firm hand upon the helm. Get into touch with the finite, and grasp in full enjoyment that sense of capacity in a machine working smoothly. Join the whole creation of animate things in a deep, heartfelt joy that you are alive, that you see the sun, that you are in this glorious earth which nature has made so beautiful, and which is yours to conquer and to enjoy. Realize, in the words of Browning, that "There's a world of capability for joy spread round about us, meant for us, inviting us." What are the morning sensations? —for they control the day. Some of us are congenitally unhappy during the early hours; but the young man who feels on awakening that life is a burden or a bore has been neglecting his machine, driving it too hard, stoking the engines too much, or not cleaning out the ashes and clinkers. Or he has been too much with the Lady Nicotine, or fooling with Bacchus, or, worst of all, with the younger Aphrodite—all "messengers of strong prevailment in unhardened youth." To have a sweet outlook on life you must have a clean body. As I look on the clear-cut, alert, earnest features, and the lithe, active forms of our college men, I sometimes wonder whether or not Socrates and Plato would find the race improved. I am sure they would love to look on such a gathering as this. Make their ideal yours—the fair mind in the fair body. The one cannot be sweet and clean without the other, and you must realize, with Rabbi Ben Ezra, the great truth that flesh and soul are mutually helpful. . . . To keep the body fit is a help in keeping the mind pure, and the sensations of the first few hours of the day are the best test of its normal state. The clean tongue, the clear head, and the bright eye are birth-rights of each day. Just as the late Professor Marsh would diagnose an unknown animal from a single bone, so can the day be predicted from the first waking hour. The start is everything, as you well know, and to make a good start you must feel fit. . . . My own rule of life has been to cut out unsparingly any article of diet that had the bad taste to disagree with me, or to indicate in any way that it had abused the temporary hospitality of the lodging which I had provided. To drink, nowadays, but few students become addicted, but in every large body of men a few are to be found whose incapacity for the day results from the morning clogging of nocturnally flushed tissues. As moderation is very hard to reach, and as it has been abundantly shown that the best of mental and physical work may be done without alcohol in any form, the safest rule for the young man is that which I am sure most of you follow—abstinence. A bitter enemy to the bright eye and the clear brain of the early morning is tobacco. The other primal instinct is the heavy burden of the flesh which Nature puts on all of us to ensure a continuation of the species. To drive Plato's team taxes the energies of the best of us. One of the horses is a raging, untamed devil, who can only be brought into subjection by hard fighting and severe training. This much you all know as men: once the bit is between his teeth the black steed Passion will take the white horse Reason with you and the chariot rattling over the rocks to perdition.

With a fresh, sweet body you can start aright without those feelings of inertia that so often, as Goethe says, make the morning's lazy leisure usher in a useless day. Control of the mind as a working machine, the adaptation in it of habit, so that its action becomes almost as automatic as walking, is the end of education—and yet how rarely reached! It can be accomplished with deliberation and repose, never with hurry and worry. Realize how much time there is, how long the day is. Realize that you have sixteen waking hours, three or four of which at least should be devoted to making a silent conquest of your mental machinery. Concentration, by which is grown gradually the power to wrestle successfully with any subject, is the secret of successful study. No mind however dull can escape the brightness that comes from steady application. There is an old saying, "Youth enjoyeth not, for haste"; but worse than this, the failure to cultivate the power of peaceful concentration is the greatest single cause of mental breakdown. Plato pities the young man who started at such a pace that he never reached the goal. One of the saddest of life's tragedies is the wreckage of the career of the young collegian by hurry, hustle, bustle and tension—the human machine driven day and night, as no sensible fellow would use his motor. . . . Aristotle somewhere says that the student who wins out in the fight must be slow in his movements, with voice deep, and slow speech, and he will not be worried over trifles which make people speak in shrill tones and use rapid movements. Shut close in hour-tight compartments, with the mind directed intensely upon the subject in hand, you will acquire the capacity to do more and more, you will get into training; and once the mental habit is established, you are safe for life.

Concentration is an art of slow acquisition, but little by little the mind is accustomed to habits of slow eating and careful digestion, by which alone you escape the "mental dyspepsy" so graphically described by Lowell in the *Fable for Critics*. Do not worry your brains about that bugbear Efficiency, which, sought consciously and with effort, is just one of those elusive qualities very apt to be missed. The man's college output is never to be gauged at sight; all the world's coarse thumb and finger may fail to plumb his most effective work, the casting of the mental machinery of self-education, the true preparation for a field larger than the college campus. Four or five hours daily—it is not much to ask; but one day must tell another, one week certify another, one month bear witness to another of the same story, and you will acquire a habit by which the one-talent man will earn a high interest, and by which the ten-talent man may at least save his capital.

Steady work of this sort gives a man a sane outlook on the world. No corrective so valuable to the weariness, the fever and the fret that are so apt to wring the heart of the young. This is the talisman, as George Herbert says,

> The famous stone
> That turneth all to gold,

and with which, to the eternally recurring question, What is Life? you answer, I do not think—I act it; the only philosophy that brings you in contact with its real value and enables you to grasp its hidden meaning. Over the Slough of Despond, past Doubting Castle and Giant Despair, with this talisman you may reach the Delectable Mountains, and those Shepherds of the Mind—Knowledge, Experience, Watchful and Sincere. Some of you may think this to be a miserable Epicurean doctrine—no better than that so sweetly sung by Horace:—

> Happy the man—and happy he alone,
> He who can call to-day his own,

He who secure within can say,
To-morrow, do thy worst—for I have lived to-day.

I do not care what you think, I am simply giving you a philosophy of life that I have found helpful in my work, useful in my play. Walt Whitman, whose physician I was for some years, never spoke to me much of his poems, though occasionally he would make a quotation; but I remember late one summer afternoon as we sat in the window of his little house in Camden there passed a group of workmen whom he greeted in his usual friendly way. And then he said: "Ah, the glory of the day's work, whether with hand or brain! I have tried

To exalt the present and the real,
To teach the average man the glory of his daily work or trade."

In this way of life each one of you may learn to drive the straight furrow and so come to the true measure of a man.

With body and mind in training, what remains?

Do you remember that most touching of all incidents in Christ's ministry, when the anxious ruler Nicodemus came by night, worried lest the things that pertained to his everlasting peace were not a part of his busy and successful life? Christ's message to him is His message to the world—never more needed that at present: "Ye must be born of the spirit." You wish to be with the leaders—as Yale men it is your birth-right—know the great souls that make up the moral radium of the world. You must be born of their spirit, initiated into their fraternity, whether of the spiritually minded followers of the Nazarene or of that larger company, elect from every nation, seen by St. John.

Begin the day with Christ and His prayer—you need no other. As the soul is dyed by the thoughts, let no day pass without contact with the best literature of the world. Learn to know your Bible. In forming character and in shaping conduct, its touch has still its ancient power.

Fifteen or twenty minutes day by day will give you fellowship with the great minds of the race, and little by little as the years pass you extend your friendship with the immortal dead. They will give you faith in your own day. Listen while they speak to you of the fathers. But each age has its own spirit and ideas, just as it has its own manners and pleasures. But while change is the law, certain great ideas flow fresh through the ages, and control us effectually as in the days of Pericles. Mankind, it has been said, is always advancing, man is always the same. The love, hope, fear and faith that makes humanity, and the elemental passions of the human heart, remain unchanged, and the secret of inspiration in any literature is the capacity to touch the chord that vibrates in a sympathy that knows nor time nor place.

The quiet life in day-tight compartments will help you to bear your own and others' burdens with a light heart. Pay no heed to the Batrachians who sit croaking idly by the stream. Life is a straight, plain business, and the way is clear, blazed for you by generations of strong men, into whose labors you enter and whose ideals must be your inspiration. In my mind's eye I can see you twenty years hence —resolute-eyed, broad-headed, smooth-faced men who are in the world to make a success of life; but to whichever of the two great types you belong, whether controlled by emotion or by reason, you will need the leaven of their spirit, the only leaven potent enough to avert that only too common Nemesis to which the Psalmist refers: "He gave them their heart's desire, but sent leanness withal into their souls."

I quoted Dr. Johnson's remark about the trivial things that influence. Perhaps this slight word of mine may help some of you so to number your days that you may apply your hearts unto wisdom.

A GREAT LESSON FROM A
GREAT MAN

Stefan Zweig

Bury yourself utterly in what you are doing—let the word "perfunctory" be erased from your vocabulary. That is the essence of the message which a great writer brings us as the result of his observation of an even greater artist, Auguste Rodin. Here we see the young author, Zweig, eager for knowledge and success; and the great sculptor at the peak of his career, yet interested enough in the beginner to take him into his studio. And all unconscious that he is doing so, one gives the other an insight into his greatness which will last a lifetime.

Zweig's life was tragic, despite the success of such works as Marie
Antoinette *and* Mary, Queen *of Scotland, which were recognized as
masterpieces of biography. Born in Austria, he was driven from his homeland by the Nazi dictator and after a period of wandering, died in Brazil,
unable to adjust himself to new surroundings. Yet even at the end, bitterly
unhappy, he made use of that gift of concentration which Rodin had
taught him, to pour out works of fiction, biography, history and criticism.*

‹♫›

WHY did we choose this or that profession? Why did we decide to
settle in a particular town, in a particular house? What was the factor
that played the most essential role in shaping the ultimate course
of our lives? All of us ought at some time to spend a free moment
in reflecting upon what circumstance was of decisive importance
in determining the course of our lives. Almost always, I believe, it
was some trifling incident, of such insignificance that we later forgot all about it—a meeting with some individual, the reading of some
book, or a word let fall in conversation.

Thus I turn up this page in the book of memory, out of gratitude
to a great man and to show how, unwittingly and involuntarily, one
individual can help another.

I was about twenty-five at the time, and in the course of my university career, I had published poems and other literary pieces
without any real faith in my powers. Many people praised my
writings; many of them I liked myself. But deep down within me I
felt that they were not yet the best I could do; that my work lacked
an essential quality to give it the intensity it needed. I felt that all
that I wrote was merely a rehearsal for the real thing.

About this time I went to Paris, where I met writers and fellow-
students, and continued my studies and literary work. One evening
we were discussing art, at the house of Verhaeren, the famous Belgian
writer. An elderly painter was deploring the steady decline of the
plastic arts since the Renaissance; I, passionate and pugnacious, as
the young always are, vehemently opposed this view. Was there not
living, and in this very town, a sculptor like Rodin? And could one
not unhesitatingly rank him with the greatest artists of the past, with
Michelangelo, Donatello? Would not his "Penseur," his "Balzac,"
endure as long as the marble out of which he had fashioned them?
When my outburst was over, Verhaeren clapped me good-humoredly
on the back. "I am going to see Rodin in his studio tomorrow morning," he said. "If you like I'll take you along with me. Anyone who

admires a man as much as you do has a right to meet him."
I was almost thunderstruck with delight. Next morning we went to
Rodin's studio in the rue de Varennes—one of his eleven studios;
he never divulged in which of them he was working on a particular
day so that there was little chance of his being disturbed by casual
visitors. Verhaeren introduced me as a young enthusiast who was,
like Rodin himself, devoting himself to the arts. I glanced furtively
from time to time, while the two friends were chatting, at Rodin's
strong, hard, clayey peasant hands, which had fashioned so much
beauty. The whole time I felt as though I were an unwanted in-
truder; but as we took our leave, Rodin turned to me. "I imagine
you'd like to see one or two of my sculptures. I'm afraid I have hardly
anything here. But come and dine with me on Sunday at Meudon."
     Great men are nearly always the kindest; out of some instinctive
knowledge they encourage the very people who do not elbow themselves ahead. Rodin's country house was no larger, no more ostentatious than that of any Frenchman of the middle classes; a man
dedicated to a task in life remains simple and unpretentious. We
sat down at a small table to a homely meal, and it was Rodin's
very simplicity which gave me courage to speak without embarrassment. I forgot that the gray-haired man opposite me was probably
the most famous artist of the age. I was merely conscious of the
soft, warm, encouraging gaze of the eyes beneath the bushy brows
as I described to him the altarpiece by Michael Pacher in St. Wolf-
gang, which he had never seen and so ardently longed to see. When
I told him that Michael Pacher had worked at that one task for ten
years, from 1471 to 1481, in that out-of-the-way village near Salzburg,
he grew solemn. "Ten years on one piece of work," he said thoughtfully, "that's how one ought to work; that's the only way to live.
Then one would produce work of real value."
     After dinner he took me across to his studio, a primitive structure
with large windows. In addition to the big statues, there were hundreds of little plastic studies—an arm, a hand, sometimes only a
finger or a knuckle, and also a number of works that he had abandoned and left incomplete. On the tables lay piles of drawings and
sketches. Here, as in a museum, was assembled a whole lifetime of
restless seeking and labor, works merely begun and works completed,
a whole world in itself. And then suddenly there happened that
strange experience which was to be decisive for me for decades to
come. The whole thing began quite unexpectedly. On entering the

studio Rodin had put on his linen smock to protect his coat from plaster and clay and thereby seemed transformed from an elderly middle-class Frenchman into a workman. He paused before a pedestal still enveloped in wet cloths. "This is my latest work," he said, carefully removing the cloths and revealing a female torso brilliantly modeled in clay. "It's quite finished, I think." He took a step backwards, this heavily-built, broad-shouldered old man with the faded gray beard, to take a good look. "Yes, I think it's finished," he repeated. But after a moment of intense scrutiny he murmured, "Just there on the shoulder, the line is still too hard. *Excusez.*"

He picked up his scalpel. The wood passed lightly over the soft clay and gave the flesh a more delicate sheen. His strong hands were awakened to life, his eyes were kindled. "And there—and there." Again he made some improvement, again he changed something, stepped forward and then back, turned the pedestal, muttered to himself, strange, choking noises issuing from his throat; now his eye lighted up, now his eyebrows were knit in vexation. He kneaded small bits of clay, added them to the figure, scraped away. Without knowing it, without intending to, he had begun to work.

This went on for half an hour, an hour, an hour and a half. He never once addressed a word to me. He had completely forgotten my presence, was unaware of the stranger behind him whom he had invited to come. He did not know whether it was day or night, was oblivious of time and place. All that he saw was his work and, invisible behind it, the sublime, truer form that he wished to achieve. He was alone with his work, like God on the first day of the creation.

Nothing had ever so moved me in my young life as this realization that a man could so utterly, so completely forget time and place and the world. During that hour and a half I grasped the secret of all art and of all earthly achievement—concentration; the rallying of all one's forces for the accomplishment of one's task, large or small. The capacity to direct one's will, too often dissipated or scattered, upon the one thing that one truly desires.

I stood behind the great master, as silent and as motionless as the marble figures in that room, realizing what it was I had hitherto lacked—that fervor which enables a man to forget all else but the will to perfection. Only a man capable of losing himself utterly in his task, whether it be great or small, can really carry it out. There is—I realized it at that moment—no other magic formula.

At last he stepped back and once more surveyed the torso. His gaze was now different, no longer the seeking, tortured, unyielding gaze of before, the keen gaze of the hunter, but rather the contented yet exhausted gaze of one victorious after a bitter struggle. With a sigh of relief he threw down his scalpel, picked up the wet cloths, and wrapped them round the torso with the tender solicitude of a man placing a shawl round the shoulders of a beloved woman. Then he turned to go, once again the heavily-built old man.

At the last moment, just before he reached the door, he caught sight of me. Who was this? How had this young stranger got in here? Only now did he remember, and was visibly shocked at his own discourtesy. "Pardon, Monsieur, I had quite forgotten you. But you know . . ." He was about to go on. I was so moved that I took his hand and pressed it gratefully.

Perhaps he had an inkling of the fact that his complete forgetfulness of my presence had taught me the greatest lesson I could ever have learned, for he smiled affably and put his arm round my shoulder as he led me out of the studio in which I had learned more in one hour than in years at the university. For ever since then I have known how all human work must be done if it is to be good and worth while—with forgetfulness of self and of all ulterior motives, with complete concentration on the ultimate unattainable goal—perfection.

HOW TO FACE LIFE

Stephen S. Wise

Bury yourself in your work, says Stefan Zweig. But be sure, says Stephen S. Wise, that it is work worth doing, and that when it is done, it will give you honest pride of achievement. A famous rabbi, perhaps the greatest America has produced, he himself followed the path he here suggests. He was born in Hungary but came to New York, where he became head of the leading New York synagogue. He devoted much of his life to working for a Jewish homeland and at his death was a spiritual leader recognized by Americans of every creed.

༄

GIVE yourself to something great, enroll under the banner of a high cause, choose as your own some standard of self-sacrifice, attach yourself to a movement that makes not for your own gain but for the welfare of men, and you will have come upon a richly satisfying as well as engrossing adventure. Either your spirit will greatly and bravely, nobly and self-forgettingly adventure, or you will be in danger of yielding to the dominance of your appetites, you will be in peril of being overcome by your masterful passions. Dare to give every power of your life to the furtherance of a mighty cause. Let your spirit come under the dominance of a high and exalting enthusiasm. So will you gain the mastery over yourself, not as a matter of prudence, not as a matter of caution, not as a matter of timidity, not as a matter of duty.

Let something so high and noble come into your life that it shall be expulsive of everything low and mean. The men one honors most, the men one has reason to cherish most highly, are those into whose lives something so lofty and commanding has come as to have left no room for the mean and petty. Having given themselves to the furtherance of a high and exalted ideal, life leaves no place for the mean. The selfish and the unworthy retreats with the precipitancy of the coward before the imperiousness of the noble impulse, the divine aim.

HAVE YOU AN EDUCATED HEART?

———— *Gelett Burgess* ————

Without a sensitive awareness to the thoughts and feelings of others, no personality can be truly rounded, no life completely successful. The educated heart, to use Gelett Burgess's inspired phrase, practices a sort of golden rule of daily intercourse with others. In even the simplest of relationships it shows delicacy and tact. To do kindness is admirable, but to do it with style marks one as exceptional. Gelett Burgess was a writer who gained success by making people laugh quietly at their own foibles and those of the human race. Yet he had a way of piercing directly to the heart of problems of daily living. "Have you an educated heart?" is a question which, borne constantly in mind, will smooth existence for us and for those we know.

∽

LAST October I sent Crystabel a book. She acknowledged it, and promptly. But two months afterward she actually wrote me another letter, telling me what she thought of that book; and she proved, moreover, that she had read it. Now, I ask you, isn't that a strange and beautiful experience in this careless world? Crystabel had the educated heart. To such as possess the educated heart thanks are something like mortgages, to be paid in installments. Why, after five years Crystabel often refers to a gift that has pleased her. It is the motive for a gift she cares for, not its value; and hence her tactful, iterated gratefulness.

Everything can be done beautifully by the educated heart, from the lacing of a shoe so that it won't come loose to passing the salt before it is asked for. If you say only "Good morning," it can be done pleasingly. Observe how the polished actor says it, with that cheerful rising inflection. But the ordinary American growls it out with surly downward emphasis. Merely to speak distinctly is a great kindness, I consider. You never have to ask, "What did you say?" to the educated heart. On the other hand, very few people ever really listen with kindly attention. They are usually merely waiting for a chance to pounce upon you with their own narrative. Or if they do listen, is your story heard with real sympathy? Does the face really glow?

Consider the usual birthday gift or Christmas present. By universal practice it is carefully wrapped in a pretty paper and tied with ribbon. That package is symbolical of what all friendly acts should be—kindness performed with style. Then what is style in giving? Ah, the educated heart makes it a business to know what his friend really wants. One friend I have to whom I can't express a taste that isn't treasured up against need. I said once that I loved watercress, and lightly wished that I might have it for every meal. Never a meal had I at his table since, without finding watercress bought specially for me.

Do you think it's easy, this business of giving? Verily, giving is as much an art as portrait painting or the making of glass flowers. And imagination can surely be brought to bear. Are you sailing for Brazil? It isn't the basket of fine fruits that brings the tears to your eyes, nor the flowers with trailing yards of red ribbon—all that's mere kindness, ordinary everyday kindness. It's that little purse full of Brazilian currency, bills and small change all ready for you when you first trip ashore at Rio.

There was old Wentrose—he understood the Fourth Dimension of kindness, all right. Never a friend of his wife's did he puffingly put aboard a streetcar, but he'd tuck apologetically into her hand the nickel to save her rummaging in her bag. Real elegance, the gesture of inherent nobility, I call that.

Is it sufficient simply to offer your seat in a streetcar to a woman? The merely kind person does that. But he does it rather sheepishly. Isn't your graciousness more cultured if you give it up with a bow, with a smile of willingness? Besides the quarter you give the beggar, can't you give a few cents' worth of yourself too? The behavior of the educated heart becomes automatic: you set it in the direction of true kindness and courtesy and after a while it will function without deliberate thought. Such thoughtfulness, such consideration is *not* merely decorative. It is the very essence and evidence of sincerity. Without it all so-called kindness is merely titular and perfunctory.

Suppose I submit your name for membership in a club. Have I done you (or my club) any real service unless I also do my best to see that you are elected? And so if I go to every member of the committee, if I urge all my friends to endorse you, that is merely the completion of my regard for you. It is like salt—"It's what makes potatoes taste bad, if you don't put it on."

Must you dance with all the wallflowers, then? I don't go so far as that, although it would prove that you had imagination enough to put yourself in another's place. All I ask is that when you try to do a favor you do it to the full length of the rope. Don't send your telegram in just ten carefully selected words. Economize elsewhere, but add those few extra phrases that make the reader perceive that you cared more for him than you did for the expense.

No one with the educated heart ever approached a clergyman, or a celebrity, or a long-absent visitor with the shocking greeting: "You don't remember me, do you?" No, he gives his name first. No one with the educated heart ever said, "Now do come and see me, sometime!" The educated heart's way of putting it is apt to be, "How about coming next Wednesday?" And strongly I doubt if the educated heart is ever tardy at an appointment. It knows that if only two minutes late a person has brought just that much less of himself.

You call once or twice at the hospital. Do you ever call again? Not unless you have the educated heart. Yet the patient is still perhaps quite ill. One there was who used to bring a scrapbook every morning, pasted in with funny items from the day's news.

Truly nothing is so rare as the educated heart. And if you wonder why, just show a kodak group picture—a banquet or a class photograph. What does every one of us first look at, talk about? Ourself. And that's the reason why most hearts are so unlearned in kindness.

If you want to enlarge that mystic organ whence flows true human kindness, you must cultivate your imagination. You must learn to put yourself in another's place, think his thoughts. The educated heart, remember, does kindness *with style*.

WHY LAUGHTER HAS POWER

Bob Hope

Who has not seen Bob Hope's smiling face, who does not know his philosophy of laughter? It is not only an antidote to despair; in it there can be a spiritual quality which is in keeping with the values of religion itself. It was a philosophy learned in a difficult school, for small-time vaudeville, in which he began, was not notable for the elevation of its ideals. Perhaps it was an inner wholesomeness, which audiences sensed, which moved him so rapidly up the ladder to stardom. He has made millions of dollars and plowed back far more than the Biblical tithe into charity. And he has the deep satisfaction of knowing that the laughter he gives is health, contentment and part of the wise man's way of life.

✍

ONCE when I was in Shreveport, Louisiana, a minister offered me his pulpit for a sermon on "God and Hollywood."

Hastily I explained that in my business, success was measured by "yocks" versus "boffs." When that just confused him I said, "You know, yocks . . . little laughs . . . and boffs . . . great big ones. And if I got up there in your church I might still, unconsciously, be trying for those boffs."

We let the matter drop. But afterward, during a nightmare, I found myself in a pulpit and the laughs were rolling down the aisle shaking the dignified old rafters. I told a friend of this dream.

"And what would be so wrong about that?" he wanted to know. "Laughter has a spiritual value. An Englishman named John Donne had that pegged over four hundred years ago. He said, 'Religion is not a melancholy, the spirit of God is not a dampe.' "

He had a point. Certainly I knew that laughter has a constructive power. I have seen what a laugh can do. It can transform almost unbearable tears into something bearable, even hopeful.

Overseas in 1944 with USO Camp Shows Frances Langford and I saw it lift a whole ward at the service hospital in Pearl Harbor. We were working our way up a long aisle when a nurse touched my arm.

"That boy near the end in the very high bed. They pulled him out of a B-17. Herbert hasn't spoken a word for weeks. If there's anything you can do . . ."

As we got to that end of the ward I winked at Frances. "Okay, boys," I said. "Frances Langford is going to sing you a song . . . and Herbert," I pointed to the bed where we could just see a white face, bandages covering the eyes, "Herbert, this is for you."

Frances approached the bed slowly, beginning her song . . . "Embrace me, my sweet embraceable you." An unnatural stillness settled over the entire ward. One of those that doesn't feel right, too hushed and breathless. All you could hear was Frances' low plaintive song, "Embrace me, you irreplaceable you . . ." And then, just as she reached him, her voice broke off.

In two steps I was beside her looking at Herbert. Where his arms had been there were only short stumps.

For several seconds we all just stood there stunned. No one moved. But the part of the mind where habit and involuntary reaction holds sway provided me with a diversion.

A couple of guys laughed, bless 'em. On I rushed trying to build that chain of laughter while Frances regained her composure. But the miracle was Herbert. Herbert spoke, *for the first time in weeks.*

"It's all right, Miss Langford," he said. "Don't worry about it."

Laughter binds men together in a kind of secret free masonry.

Hear it sometime travel around a circle . . . then notice that, however large that circle may be, it is a closed one.

For a brief few hours in 1944 I met fifteen thousand Marines of the 21st Division at Pavuvu. They were on their way to the invasion of Peleliu. We were doing a routine series of camp shows on the Pacific Islands.

When an officer suggested the unscheduled stop he said, "We'll have to fly you over, a few at a time in small planes, and land you on a road. There's no airport. But it'll be worth it to them."

As we circled for our landing such a shout arose from fifteen thousand throats that we could actually *feel* it like a cushion of sound under our wings. We were from home! We were the promise of laughter . . . today. Tomorrow, and they knew it, they were staging a little show of their own and 40 per cent wouldn't come back.

We laughed and clowned as we landed. But looking at those faces I knew how Charles Lamb must have felt when he "jested that he might not weep."

Later back in the States, my wife and I at the dedication of Oak Knoll Hospital walked into a ward to be greeted with that same laughter. One of those explosions that happen between old friends.

Voices kept yelling, "Pavuvu! Pavuvu!" Dolores was a bewildered outsider. But I was in. It was the 21st Marines . . . or what was left of them.

Laughter can sometimes appeal beyond reason, prejudice and cynicism.

In a jungle I heard the jokes of padres lift G.I.'s spirits into wanting the fearlessness and gaiety of the men of God, where no amount of solemn approach would have inspired them.

And I have heard a minister devastate a profane agnostic with quiet wit.

It happened at a very swank club one night. After a pointless and slightly blasphemous story the comedian noticed that all eyes were suddenly fastened on the collar insignia of a big, silent man at the end of the table.

"F'r crissakes," blustered the story-teller. "Are you a chaplain?"

With a light smile and deliberate emphasis the chaplain replied, "Yes, for *Christ's* sake, I am."

Laughter can return a sense of proportion to a troubled mind, for it erases self-pity, self-justification, self-importance.

But perhaps the most important thing laughter can do is to bring back the will to live—and, when the time comes, give us the courage to go with good cheer.

I've seen the ones who aren't going to make it—American boys smiling their way right up to St. Peter's gate, and I've got a hunch they're holding a sure pass. Like one youngster who was stretched out on the ground getting a blood transfusion. "I see they're giving you the old raspberry, son," I said.

"It sure feels good," he laughed. "The guy who gave this must have been tax exempt or raised his own beef. It's strong stuff."

Before I had gotten twenty yards he had gone his way, smiling.

My young brother Sydney passed on five years ago and, for quite a while, he knew he was going. Someone with a very long face and a "religion of melancholy" had urged him to "prepare to meet his Maker" . . . to "petition Providence to provide for his poor little orphans."

It took the whole family and his five kids to convince him that "the spirit of God is not a dampe," here or hereafter, except for those who choose to have it so.

Every gay thing, every joyous or humorous or good thing that came to our attention we offered to my brother as proof of the infinite wisdom and kindness of God. When he went, he went smiling—and trusting. And we had done such a good job for him that we had healed ourselves of much of our grief.

A comedian can't take much credit either, because people insist they are funny. You become a habit—a laugh habit. Sometimes people laugh at me before I open my mouth—even when they can't see me. Mention the arrival of someone they've laughed at before and they relax. They drop their strain. They expect to laugh and so they do.

They depend, too, on the laughmaker to stay the same. They want new jokes but not too much change. I don't think they've ever forgiven Charlie Chaplin for abandoning his big shoes, cane and derby hat. When I go into a service hospital they expect me to louse up the joint. To go on being me. No sympathy. They want me to walk into a ward filled with guys harnessed to torturous contraptions and say, "Don't get up fellows."

When I come to a Christmas party if I notice the lone star atop a pathetic Christmas tree I'm supposed to say, "Don't tell me a Brigadier General is running this show too."

So I say it. And when people wonder how a guy can go on and on like that . . . well, the answer is that the results themselves keep you up. You can't possibly not do it. The power works both ways. You are sustained by *their* laughter.

Nor does the power belong exclusively to the professional funnyman. There is a kind of geniality that brings mirth, and confidence. Bing Crosby has that. If there are two kinds of people, people who lift and people who lean, Bing is a lifter. Geniality might be defined as strength to spare.

The power of laughter lies in its ability to lift the spirit. For laughter cannot exist with clipped wings. It cannot be dictated to. It must be spontaneous and free as the air you breathe. Thus it is a special property of free men in a free land who are able to laugh at anything . . . or anyone . . . especially themselves.

LOVE

Kahlil Gibran

There is power in laughter. There is even greater power in love. For without it all else—success, fame—is worthless. The poet and mystic, Kahlil Gibran, knew its value and knew the danger of too-ready acceptance. The ways of love, he cautioned in The Prophet, *"are hard and steep."*

∽

THEN said Almitra, Speak to us of Love.

And he raised his head and looked upon the people, and there fell a stillness upon them. And with a great voice he said:

When love beckons to you, follow him,

Though his ways are hard and steep.

And when his wings enfold you yield to him,

Though the sword hidden among his pinions may wound you.

And when he speaks to you believe in him,

Though his voice may shatter your dreams as the north wind lays waste the garden.

For even as love crowns you so shall he crucify you. Even as he is for your growth so is he for your pruning.

Even as he ascends to your heights and caresses your tenderest branches that quiver in the sun,

So shall he descend to your roots and shake them in their clinging to the earth.

Like sheaves of corn he gathers you unto himself.

He threshes you to make you naked.

He sifts you to free you from your husks.

He grinds you to whiteness.

He kneads you until you are pliant;

And then he assigns you to his sacred fire, that you may become sacred bread for God's sacred feast.

All these things shall love do unto you that you may know the secrets of your heart, and in that knowledge become a fragment of Life's heart.

But if in your fear you would seek only love's peace and love's pleasure,

Then it is better for you that you cover your nakedness and pass out of love's threshing-floor.

Into the seasonless world where you shall laugh, but not all of your laughter, and weep, but not all of your tears.

Love gives naught but itself and takes naught but from itself.

Love possesses not nor would it be possessed;

For love is sufficient unto love.

When you love you should not say, "God is in my heart," but rather, "I am in the heart of God."

And think not you can direct the course of love, for love, if it finds you worthy, directs your course.

Love has no other desire but to fulfil itself.

But if you love and must needs have desires, let these be your desires:

To melt and be like a running brook that sings its melody to the night.

To know the pain of too much tenderness.

To be wounded by your own understanding of love;

And to bleed willingly and joyfully.

To wake at dawn with a winged heart and give thanks for another day of loving;

To rest at the noon hour and meditate love's ecstacy;

To return home at eventide with gratitude;

And then to sleep with a prayer for the beloved in your heart and a song of praise upon your lips.

HAPPINESS

—————— *William Lyon Phelps* ——————

Lampson Professor of English Literature was his august title at Yale University. He was an authority on the beginnings of the English Romantic Movement. He wrote widely admired essays on the Russian novel. He was a teacher who attained the first rank in his profession. But to generations of Yale undergraduates he was simply "Billy" Phelps. They may have respected him for his erudition but they loved him for himself. In him there was a fellow-feeling for the most insignificant among them. In him there was a gaiety of spirit, a pure love of humankind which communicated itself to all of them. He was their friend and they knew it. He understood the art of happiness and communicated some of his knowledge to them. In this, perhaps his most popular essay, is the essence of what he knew and taught.

✍

No matter what may be one's nationality, sex, age, philosophy, or religion, everyone wishes either to become or to remain happy. Hence definitions of happiness are interesting. One of the best was given in my Senior year at college by President Timothy Dwight: "The happiest person is the person who thinks the most interesting thoughts."

This definition places happiness where it belongs—within and not without. The principle of happiness should be like the principle of virtue; it should not be dependent on things, but be a part of personality. Suppose you went to a member of a State Legislature, and offered him five hundred dollars to vote for a certain bill. Suppose he kicked you out of his office. Does that prove he is virtuous? No; it proves you can't buy him for five hundred. Suppose you went to the same man a month later and offered him a million dollars— that is, instead of making him a present, you make him and his family independent for life, for the best thing about having money is that if you have it, you don't have to think about it. Suppose, after listening to this offer, he should hesitate. That would mean he was already damned. He is not only not virtuous, he knows nothing about virtue. Why? Because his virtue is dependent not on any

32

interior standard, but on the size of the temptation. If the temptation is slight, he can resist; if alluring, his soul is in danger. Such
virtue is like being brave when there is no danger, generous when you
have nothing to give, cheerful when all is well, polite when you are
courteously treated.

Fortunately there are in every State Legislature some men who
have no price, who are never for sale, who look upon all bribes with
equal scorn—and these are the virtuous men. After the same order,
there are boys who are just as safe in Paris as in Binghamton; just as
safe at three o'clock in the morning as at three o'clock in the afternoon; just as safe with evil companions as with good companions.
Why? Because these boys do not allow place, time, and people to
determine their conduct, they attend to that matter themselves.
Their standards are within.

So far as it is possible—it is not always possible—happiness should
be like virtue. It should be kept or lost, not by exterior circumstances,
but by an inner standard of life. Yet some readers of this page will
lose their happiness before next Sunday, though I hope they recover
it. But why lose it, even for a season? There are people who carry
their happiness as a foolish woman carries a purse of money in her
hand while walking on a crowded thoroughfare. The first man who is
quick with his fingers, nimble with his feet, and untrammeled by
conscience, can and will take the purse away, and disappear with it.
He will have separated the woman and her money. Now if one's
happiness is like that, an exterior thing, dependent on an enemy's
volition, on a chance disaster, on an ill wind, on any one of a thousand accidents to which we are all exposed—then happiness can be
lost.

All of us have enemies. I regard myself as on the whole an amiable
person, and yet there are a considerable number of people who,
when they hear of my death, will feel relieved. I care as little about
that fact now as I shall then. I do not intend to let other people,
especially those who do not like me anyhow, determine whether I
shall have peace of mind or not. If some one reports to you a
malicious word that someone else has said of you, and in consequence
of that, you become unhappy, you have allowed another person to
hold the key of your heart, to settle whether you shall be happy or
not. I insist that you ought to determine that question for yourself.
Instead of being angry or distressed when people hate you, suppose
you regard it as amusing; for if you are honestly trying to do your

best, and incur hatred for your pains, there is about such a situation something funny. If you can appreciate the humor of it, you are free.

It is impossible for anyone to feel every moment exuberantly happy; to feel, on rising from bed every morning, like a young dog released from a chain. If you felt that way chronically, you would become an intolerable nuisance; you would get on everybody's nerves. But I am certain that with the correct philosophy, it is possible to have within one's personality sources of happiness that cannot permanently be destroyed. You will have days and nights of anguish, caused by ill-health, or worry, or losses, or the death of friends; but you will not remain in the Slough of Despond; you will rise above depression and disaster, because you will have within your mind the invincible happiness that comes from thinking interesting thoughts.

If the happiest person is the person who thinks the most interesting thoughts, then the mind is more important than either of those tremendous blessings, wealth and health. I never indulge in slighting remarks about money, because if I did, I should be a hypocrite. Money is a blessing; I should be glad to distribute a large sum to every one of my readers, of course reserving the usual commission. But money is not the chief factor in happiness. If it were, then everyone who had money would be happy and everyone without it would be unhappy; but there are so many wealthy people who are unhappy and so many poor people who are cheerful, that money, however important or desirable, is not the determining cause. It would be folly to speak slightingly of health. No one realizes what a blessing health is until one has lost it; then one has to devote time and energy and money to recovering it. Anyone who is careless of his health is a traitor; because one's usefulness, one's capacity to do good in the world, is usually seriously lessened by poor health. Yet even health is not the *sine qua non*. People without it think they would be perfectly happy if they were well. A man with a toothache imagines that everyone in the world without a toothache is happy— but it is not so. There are healthy people who are not happy; and there are invalids whose faces, eyes, and conversation reveal an inner source of happiness that enables them to triumph over bodily ills. They have overcome the world, the flesh, and the devil.

I should be sorry to lose what money I have, but unfortunate as it might be, such a loss would not permanently destroy my happiness. I should be sorry to be run over by an automobile, and lose my right leg; but such a loss would not permanently destroy my happiness.

Why not? Because my happiness is centered neither in my purse nor in my leg; but in my mind, my personality. The Irish dramatist, St. John Ervine, lost a leg in the war. I asked him which he would prefer, to have two sound and healthy legs again, and not be able to write novels and plays, or to be as he is now, with only one leg, but an accomplished man of letters? He did not hesitate. He said there was no comparison possible; he would far rather be a one-legged writer, than a two-legged something else. "And yet," he murmured thoughtfully, "I do miss that leg."

There is another important consideration. If the happiest person is the person who thinks the most interesting thoughts, *then we grow happier as we grow older.*

Of course I know that such a statement runs counter to the generally expressed opinion. The majority of novels and poems and the common gossip of society assume that youth is the golden time of life.

> Yet ah! that Spring should vanish with the rose!
> That youth's sweet-scented manuscript should close!
> The nightingale that in the branches sang
> Ah, whence and whither flown again, who knows?

When I was an undergraduate, a distinguished man addressed us, and he said emphatically, "Young gentlemen, make the most of these four years; for they are the happiest years you will ever know." The remark was given to us with that impressiveness that so often accompanies a falsehood. For it was a falsehood. My classmates and I have been out of college forty years; most of us are happier now than then.

I read many French novels, and I often see a woman of forty-five described as a "woman for whom life was over." Over at forty-five? and why? Because strange men do not stare at her. Doubtless it is sweet to be admired, doubtless flirtation is one of the normal pleasures of youth, doubtless it is agreeable to be regarded as a pretty animal; but is that all there is in life for a woman? One cannot penetrate below the surface of such a statement without finding an insult to personality.

No one should make a statement like "youth is the happiest time of life" without being prepared to accept its intellectual consequences. If it were really true that youth is the happiest time of life, nothing would be a more tragic spectacle than college boys and young maidens; for they would in their present state have attained the pinnacle, the climax of existence; before them lie fifty years of diminuendo, of decay, of accumulating loss, of descent into ever darkening days.

Some middle-aged silly women become romantically sad as they talk about what they are pleased to call their lost youth; I maintain that it is as absurd for a woman of fifty to mourn because she is no longer twenty as it would be for a woman of twenty to sob because she is no longer three. And indeed there are some idiots who declare that childhood is the happiest time of life. "Ah, that I were a child again!" Don't worry; you soon will be.

The belief that youth is the happiest time of life is founded on a fallacy—on a false definition of happiness. Many people think that to be free from physical pain and mental worry is perfection; knowing that as we grow older our physical pains and mental worries are apt to increase, they assume that youth is the happiest time of life. We are, of course, all animals; but we ought not to be merely animal. I suppose that in the case of animals, youth is the happiest time of life; a puppy is happier than an old rheumatic hound; a young jackass braying in the pasture is presumably happier than an old donkey laboriously drawing a cart; but these are merely animals, and lack man's greatest gift—the possibility of development.

Those who say that childhood is the happiest time are unconsciously postulating the animal definition; a child is happiest because he is healthy and has no worries; when he is cold, somebody covers him; when he is hungry, somebody feeds him; when he is sleepy, somebody puts him to bed. Yes, but when he is not sleepy somebody puts him to bed. There is the shadow on the sunny years; there is the fly in the ointment. Personally I had rather have a few worries and aches, and go to bed when I choose. A child is as dependent as a slave. If you would rather be a healthy, well-fed slave than an independent man, you will prefer childhood to maturity. A child is at the mercy of adults both physically and mentally. They are stronger than he and can force him to do what they wish; they are cleverer than he, and can invariably outwit him. Let me give an illustration of both.

When I was six years old, I was playing ball with a contemporary. It was my ball, my property; that is to say, father had given it to me. Well, I made a muff, the ball rolled into the street, and a bigger boy grabbed it. "Here," I shouted, "give me that back. That's my ball."

" 'Tain't yours now," said he, with a disagreeable grin, "I've got it."

"No, but it don't belong to you, it's mine!"

"It ain't yours any longer," he rejoined, and he was correct. It wasn't. He has got it still. I never saw it again. All I could do was to sit down and cry. Do I want to be a child again?

At about the same age, I was fortunate enough to own a silver three-cent piece. And in those days, one could really buy something for three cents. Not wishing to spend so large a sum at once, I decided to have it changed. I walked into a large grocery store, and asked the clerk to change my three-cent piece. He looked at my insignificant figure and said curtly, "We haven't any change in the store." I withdrew and stood on the sidewalk. A fat Irishman came along and glancing at me, inquired what was the matter.

"The matter, Sir, is that I have a three-cent piece and can't get it changed."

"Why don't you go into the store?"

"They have no change in the store, Sir."

"How do you know that?"

"They told me so, Sir."

"Sonny, you come along with me."

I put my tiny hand into the enormous paw of that Irishman, and we walked together into the store, and as luck would have it, we confronted exactly the same clerk who had informed me that there was no change. The Irishman said sharply, "This boy wants his three-cent piece changed."

To my absolute amazement, the clerk said civilly, "Why, certainly," opened a drawer, and gave me three coppers. It was one of the first great surprises of my life. Upon reflection, I perceived that if you had no influence, there was no change; the fact was variable, depending simply upon the individual's power to command influence. Today I have both change and influence, and do not care to be a child again.

Happiness is not altogether a matter of luck. It is dependent on certain conditions. One should prepare for happiness as an athlete prepares for a contest. Leave out the things that injure, cultivate the things that strengthen, and good results follow. It is important to grow old successfully, for everyone must either grow old or die; and although the pessimists tell us that life is not worth living, I observe that most individuals hang on as long as they can. It is sad to see so many men and women afraid of growing old. They are in bondage to fear. Many of them, when they find the first gray hair, are alarmed. Now one really ought not to be alarmed when one's hair turns gray; if it turned green or blue, then one ought to see a doctor. But when it turns gray, that simply means there is so much gray matter in the skull there is no longer room for it; it comes out and discolors the hair. Don't be ashamed of your gray hair; wear it proudly, like a flag. You are fortunate, in a world of so many vicissitudes, to have lived long enough to earn it.

There are some foolish people who say, "Well, I mean to grow old gracefully." It is impossible; it can't be done. Let us admit it, because it is true; old people are not graceful. Grace belongs to youth and is its chief charm. The poet Browning hints that youth has beauty and grace because youth would be intolerable without it. Young people are decorative; that is why we like them. They are slender, agile, fair and graceful, because nobody could stand them if they were otherwise. It would be horrible if boys and girls, knowing as little as they do, were also bald, gray-headed, fat, wrinkled, and double-chinned; then they would be unendurable. But Nature has so arranged matters that young people are physically attractive until they acquire some brains and sense, and are able to live by their wits; then they lose these superficial advantages. As responsibility grows, beauty and grace depart. The child sits on your knee, and reaches for your watch. You smile, and say, "Nice baby, can't have de watch!" But when he is thirty and reaches for your watch, you put him in jail. More is expected of us, more is demanded of us, as we grow older; nothing is more tragic therefore than a woman of mature years with the mind of a child. There is in civilized society no place for her.

But even if it were possible to grow old gracefully, it would be at best a form of resignation, a surrender; and a soldier of life should not take it lying down. Instead of growing old gracefully, suppose we grow old eagerly, grow old triumphantly. Is this possible? With the right mind and character, with the right attitude, with the right preparation, it is not only possible, it is probable. Joseph H. Choate was no deluded enthusiast; he was a hard-headed man of the world. When he was past seventy, in a public address in New York he maintained that the happiest time of life was between seventy and eighty years of age; "and I advise you all to hurry up and get there as soon as you can."

Let us examine another fallacy. It is said that as we grow older, we lose our illusions. Of course we do. I do not believe I have a single illusion left; if I have, I would gladly lose it today. For what happens when you lose an illusion? Every time you lose an illusion, you gain a new idea. Ideas are more interesting, hence pleasure-giving, than illusions. The world as it is, men and women as they are, are more worth knowing than fancy pictures created by ignorance and inexperience. We are told that youth is happy because youth looks on the world through rose-colored spectacles. But I have no desire to look at the world through rose-colored spectacles, and I can prove that you haven't. That repository of wisdom and experience, Robert Browning, at the age of seventy-seven, wrote:

> Friend, did you need an optic glass,
>   Which were your choice? A lens to drape
> In ruby, emerald, chrysopras,
>   Each object—or reveal its shape
> Clear outlined, past escape,
>
> The naked very thing?—so clear
>   That, when you had the chance to gaze,
> You found its inmost self appear
>   Through outer seeming—truth ablaze,
> Not falsehood's fancy-haze?

This can very easily be determined by our old friend in political economy, the law of supply and demand. Demand fixes the price; a thing in great demand is worth more than something for which the demand is feeble. Suppose you were going to Europe this summer, and stopped in at the optician's to buy a pair of powerful binoculars. Suppose he should suggest that instead of getting that, you took a kaleidoscope, where instead of looking at distant objects, you saw pretty rosettes, bright combinations of colored glass. "Do you think I am a child, to be amused with rose-colored toys?" "Ah, but distance lends enchantment to the view; when you see a ship five miles away, she is as beautiful as a swan. But if you look at her with binoculars, you see shreds and patches, washing hanging on the deck-lines, and other realities. Surely you don't want the truth." Surely you do. And the proof is that anyone can buy rose-colored glasses cheaply, but every time you increase the power of the lens, that is every time you bring reality nearer, the price goes up enormously. If then we are willing to pay cash to substitute truth for illusion, let us be done with saying that youth is happy because of illusion. As we grow older, our eyes become achromatic; rose-colors fall away, and we see life more nearly as it is, and find it more interesting.

It is also often said that as we grow older, we lose our enthusiasms. This need not be true; it is never true with right-minded individuals. There is a fallacy lurking in such a statement. The fallacy is this; we confound the loss of the object that aroused our enthusiasm with the loss of enthusiasm, a very different thing. Things that excite children often fail to arouse mature men and women—which is not a sign that maturity has lost sensitiveness to excitement; it may have lost interest in childish things. When I was a child, the happiest day in the year was the Fourth of July. It was not illusory happiness; it was real; it was authentic bliss. Its cause? On the Fourth of July my mother allowed me to rise at midnight, go out on the street and yell till daybreak. Think of it, I, who usually was forced to retire at eight, was out on a city street at three in the morning, shrieking and yelling! It was delirious joy. Now suppose you should tell me that tomorrow I may rise at midnight and yell till daybreak. I decline. Does that mean I have lost my happiness, or my enthusiasm? No; it means that I don't care to rise at midnight. During the daytime of the glorious Fourth, I used to shoot off firecrackers hour after hour, with undiminished zeal. Every now and then, I would see a very old man, about thirty-two, come along, and I would offer him an opportunity to share my delight. He always declined. "Poor fellow!" I reflected, "Life is over for him. He has lost his happiness." It never occurred to me that people over thirty had any fun. I supposed they had to go through the routine of life, but had no pleasure in it.

The fact that a girl of three is enchanted by the gift of a doll, and the same girl at seventeen insulted by it, does not mean that the girl at seventeen has lost either her happiness or her enthusiasm; but that the enthusiasm, formerly aroused by dolls, is now stimulated by something else.

If the happiest person is the person who thinks the most interesting thoughts, we are bound to grow happier as we advance in years, because our minds have more and more interesting thoughts.

A well-ordered life is like climbing a tower; the view halfway up is better than the view from the base, and it steadily becomes finer as the horizon expands.

Herein lies the real value of education. Advanced education may or may not make men and women more efficient; but it enriches personality, increases the wealth of the mind, and hence brings happiness. It is the finest insurance against old age, against the growth of physical disability, of the lack and loss of animal delights. No matter how many there may be in our family, no matter how many friends we may have, we are in a certain sense forced to lead a lonely life, because we have all the days of our existence to live with ourselves. How essential it is then, to acquire some intellectual or artistic tastes, in order to furnish the mind, to be able to live inside a mind with attractive and interesting pictures on the walls! It is better to be an interesting personality than to be an efficient machine. Many go to destruction by the alcoholic route because they cannot endure themselves; the moment they are left alone with their empty minds, they seek for stimulant, for something to make them forget the waste places. Others rush off to the motion-pictures, run anywhere, always seeking something to make them forget themselves.

Higher education, the cultivation of the mind, is more important for women than for men; because women are more often left alone. A large part of masculine activity is merely physical; men run around like dogs. But a woman, even in these emancipated days, is forced to be alone more than man. Now take the instance of a girl who has been brought up happily in a large family, with plenty of neighbours and friends, whose bright days pass in happy activities and recreations; she is married to a suburbanite in New Jersey. Every morning he takes the 7:37 train to New York, and does not return till the 6:48 in the evening. The young wife, rudely transplanted from a cheerful home, is placed in an empty house, in a town where she knows no one, and is alone all day. God help her if she has no mental interests, no ideas, no interesting thoughts!

I have no desire to underestimate the worth of physical comfort, or the charm of youth; but if happiness truly consisted in physical ease and freedom from care, then the happiest individual would not be either a man or a woman. It would be, I think, an American cow. American cows and American dogs are ladies and gentlemen of leisure; in Europe they hitch them up and make them draw loads. Take therefore an average day in the life of an American cow, and we shall see that it is not far from the commonly accepted ideal of human happiness. The cow rises in the morning and with one flick of her tail, her toilet is completed for the whole day. This is a distinct advantage over humanity. It takes the average woman (and it ought to) about three-quarters of an hour every single day to arrange her appearance. When Harriet Martineau was a child, she was appalled by the prospect of having to brush her teeth every day of her life. She lived to be ninety. The cow does not have to brush her teeth; the cow does not have to bob her hair; the cow does not have to select appropriate and expensive garments; or carry a compact; one flick, and she is ready. And when she is ready, breakfast is ready. She does not have to light the kitchen fire herself, or to mourn because the cook has left without notice. The grass is her cereal breakfast and the dew thereupon is the cream. After eating for an hour or so, she gazes meditatively into the middle distance querying first, whether that grass yonder is lusher and greener than this, and second, if it be so, whether peradventure it is worth the trouble to walk there and take it. Such an idea as that will occupy the mind of a cow for three hours. After grazing, without haste and without rest, she reaches by noon the edge of a stream. "Lo, here is water; what hinders me from descending and slaking my thirst?" She descends about waist deep into the cooling stream; and after external and internal refreshment, she walks with dignity to the shade of a spreading tree, and sits down calmly in the shadow. There and then she begins to chew the cud. Her upper jaw remains stationary, while the lower revolves in a kind of solemn rapture; there is on her placid features no pale cast of thought; the cow chewing the cud has very much the expression of a healthy American girl chewing gum. I never see one without thinking of the other. The eyes of a cow are so beautiful that Homer gave them to the Queen of Heaven, because he could not think of any other eyes so large, so lustrous, so liquid, and so untroubled. Cows are never perturbed by introspection or by worry. There are no agnostic cows; no Fundamentalist or Modernist cows; cows do not worry about the income tax or the League of Nations; a cow does not lie awake at night wondering if her son is going to the devil in some distant city. Cows have none of the thoughts that inflict upon humanity distress and torture. I have observed many cows, and there is in their beautiful eyes no perplexity; their serene faces betray no apprehension or alarm; they are never even bored. They have found some happy *via media* by which they escape from Schopenhauer's dilemma, who insisted that man had only the vain choice between the suffering of unsatisfied desire and the languor of ennui.

Well, since the daily life of an American cow is exactly the existence held up to us as ideal—physical comfort with no pains and no worries—who wouldn't be a cow? Very few human beings would be willing to change into cows, which must mean only one thing. Life, with all its sorrows, cares, perplexities, and heart-breaks, is more interesting than bovine placidity, hence more desirable. The more interesting it is, the happier it is. And the happiest person is the person who thinks the most interesting thoughts.

PART TWO

WITNESS TO THE TRUTH: SOCRATES

Edith Hamilton

In this second part of our section entitled "For a Way of Life," are glimpses of four men, among the greatest, whose lives offer guidance, each in its own way, for the attainment of a good and useful existence.

Socrates was the wisest man of ancient times and, next to Jesus himself, the one who has spoken in clearest tones of reason, goodness and decency to all the generations from his own day to the present. What was the quality which so endeared him to his contemporaries? What noble attributes in him did they feel so strongly, even while they sent him to his death? Her profound erudition and the dignity of her own life make Edith Hamilton as well prepared to answer these questions as anyone else now living. Her books The Greek Way *and* The Roman Way *have become classics in her own lifetime. As this is written, at the age of eighty-three, she remains avid for new knowledge, serene in her philosophy and still active in the writing of distinguished books. As we read the selection that follows we see Socrates as he saunters in the market place, as he discourses with his students, and as he calmly faces his accusers. And in "Socrates' Speech at the Trial," we hear him utter what he believes to be the ultimate truth that "no evil can happen to a good man, either in life or after death."*

SOCRATES never tried to put the truth he had found into words. He thought as Christ did that it was impossible to tell men what it was and then expect them to know it. He too had no ordered philosophy or theology and he too never wrote a word down. Like Christ he lived his truth and died for it. A life can be more lasting than systems of thought. Socrates has outlasted two millenniums.

He was a witness to all that is contained in the word goodness, to its reality and its power. It was said of a great English scientist, "He made it easy for people to believe in goodness." This Socrates did as few since the beginning of history. No one who knew him could doubt that, as he said, "Goodness has a most real and actual existence." He left the memory of a life which conquered through it, which was never defeated though he was imprisoned and put to death, and which has been kept in men's memories among the things that are eternal. During the four hundred years between his death and Christ's the Greek and the Roman world turned to him to learn how to live, and ever since men have seen through him the changelessness of the truth, the enduring verity of what he lived by. "That which existing among men is the form and likeness of God," Plato said.

He lived during the great age of Greece, in Athens of the fifth century B.C. No figure was more familiar there than his. He did not teach from some pulpit or teacher's desk, withdrawn from men in order to think great thoughts or to find God. The busy life of the city was his life. He knew everybody and everybody knew him. Wherever men met he was at home. In a sense he did not teach at all. He just talked spontaneously on anything that happened to come up as he walked the streets or went into a gymnasium or dined with a friend. He never thought, or at any rate he never spoke, about mankind or humanity or society or the public. What he was interested in was each individual he met. He felt an intense, overwhelming desire for the good of that particular person. Nothing could have been farther from him than the idea that for hundreds of years after his death people would turn to him for light. He never gave a thought to the future. He wanted good things for the Athenians whom he saw every day and whom he knew and loved and understood, and he wanted, so greatly, to open, at least a little bit, the eyes of that delightful young fellow who had just come up to him, or speak a word to that anxious father who was troubled about his son.

Athens was more and more hard pressed during his later life; she was at war and hardships were the order of the day but there was always time to stop and hear what Socrates was saying. He had a genius for conversation and the keen-witted Athenians were an eager audience. They were fighting, but they were thinking too, and ideas were very important. One of Plato's dialogues in which Socrates is the speaker begins: "Yesterday evening I got back from the army and I went straight to the gymnasium near the Archon's porch and found a number of people I knew. I was quite unexpected and they all greeted me and asked, 'However did you escape?' 'Well,' I replied, 'you see I am here.' 'It's reported that the battle went badly and many people we knew fell.' 'Not far from the truth,' I said.

'You were there?' 'Yes.' 'Well then, do sit down and tell us all about it.' So I sat down and gave them the news from the army. But when there had been enough of this I began to ask them how things were going on at home, especially how the pursuit of philosophy was prospering.

That is what Athens was like during the greater part of Socrates' life. The importance of "philosophy," the search for wisdom, for the truth, never lapsed or receded into the background, and he was happy and at home there. But later a change came over the city. The war with Sparta lasted twenty-seven years and ended in total defeat for the Athenians. It shook the moral and spiritual foundations of Athens and brought a great part of them crashing down. The old ideas of right and wrong seemed shown up as false or at least futile. The Spartan idea of what was good and desirable was quite unlike the Athenian, and the Spartans won the war. By every realistic standard they proved that what they thought was right and what the Athenians thought was wrong. The great historian of the war, Thucydides, says the whole point of view in Athens changed, the very meaning of words was altered, vices were praised, virtues despised. The reckless disregard of life was held to be fine and courageous; kindness and generosity were scorned as proofs of softness and weakness.

The lowest depth was reached when the city put Socrates to death. That was in 399, five years after the war ended, when he was seventy years old. The charge was "Impiety," that he had induced the young men of the city to give up believing in the state religion which was still Homer's jovial, amoral Olympians, impossible for any thinking person to take seriously. The indictment ran: "Socrates is an evil-doer and a corrupter of young men because he does not receive the gods the state receives, but introduces new divinities." In all the history of Athens we know of only four persons who were persecuted for their opinions and of the four, Socrates alone suffered the death penalty. But by that time Athens was ruined, overwhelmed by all that a crushing defeat brings to a proud people. The Athenians had lost their faith in everything they had stood for, their courage, too. They were a crushed, humiliated people, and they were afraid. They could not face the future; they could only look back, with an agony of regret for what they had lost. The passion for freedom, the instinct for reasonableness, which had marked them beyond all other qualities, were swept away in a wave of reaction. Socrates had new ideas;

the gods he believed in had not the slightest resemblance to the old, and only the old was dear at that moment of Athens' misery. The city which had been given to hospitality to men of all sorts and conditions of opinions, and which hundreds of years later, St. Paul reported, was desirous of nothing so much as to hear something new, condemned to death her best and greatest citizen because he taught a new religion. And for a moment Athens was satisfied that she had taken a step back to the familiar and the safe and away from the dark menace of the future.

As a teacher of religion Socrates was a very odd figure, an evangelist such as there has never been before or since. He lived in an evil day, but he never denounced any of the evils. He never thundered anathemas as the men of righteousness have had the habit of doing against the wickedness of their times. Nothing could appear less like Isaiah and Jeremiah and all the other passionate reformers through the ages than he does as we see him in Plato's pages, so gentle, urbane, and companionable, thinking only of winning men over, persuading them, convincing them, never denouncing or threatening them.

His temper of mind was all the other way. He did not look at people with stern disapproval; he liked them. Their ways did not irritate or anger him; they did often amuse him. He had a gay spirit; he saw the world with a humorous eye. "Bless me," he said, looking around in the market where all an Athenian wanted lay piled in glowing profusion, "what a lot of things there are a man can do without." In the brilliant society of Periclean Athens he was welcomed everywhere as the best of company. He had but to enter a gymnasium, that Athenian equivalent of a club, and eager young men gathered around him, greeting him as a boon companion, joking with him and making fun of him, with an undertone of loving delight in him. They really caught a glimpse of something lofty and beautiful in him never seen before.

He had a wonderful gift for making people feel at home with him. He did not seem to be trying to instruct them; he put forward no claim to know better than they did. He had a most disarming way of talking, a great taste for homely illustration and a great distaste for high-sounding talk, out of which, however, he got much amusement when anybody indulged in it. No one could be less pretentious. He seemed always to imply, "I know I may be quite wrong." And this was not merely his manner; he really had no fixed creed, no set of doctrines, which he felt he must make others believe. He had a profound conviction which ruled his life and which it was the effort of his life to communicate, but it did not present itself to him as a series of truths which it was imperative for all to accept. As a Greek his mind did not work that way. Greek religion was developed not by priests or prophets or saints, but by poets and artists and philosophers, all of them people who instinctively leave thought free. An Athenian's dearest right was to think for himself and he used it to the full.

So Socrates was only going along with his hearers when he declined to do their thinking for them. What he wanted was something much more difficult than that. Aristotle says happiness is activity of soul. It is a precise description of Socrates' way of making men happy. "God has sent me to attack this city," he told the Athenians, "as if it were a great horse sluggish from its size, which needs to be aroused by a gadfly. I think I am that gadfly. I will never cease from exhorting you: Are you not ashamed of caring so much for money and for reputation and for honour? Will you not think about wisdom and truth and what is good for your souls?" He would sting them into activity to see for themselves; he would not show them what they ought to see. His talks with them usually ended in some such fashion, as, "This may be true, but is also quite likely to be untrue, and therefore I would not have you too easily persuaded. Reflect well—and when you have found the truth, come and tell me."

No one less dogmatic ever lived. He spent his life in the search for the truth; it was all-important to him, but he did not leave behind him one hard and fast definition. He never stated, he only suggested—with a question mark. In his speech at his trial he spoke of "a divine agency which comes to me, a sign, a kind of a voice, which I was first conscious of as a child. It never commands me to do anything, but it does forbid me." That was all. He made no attempt to clarify or classify the experience; he knew he could not imprison within a formula the truth he saw. "To find the Maker and Father of all is hard," he said, "and having found him it is impossible to utter him."

But underneath this inconclusiveness was a clear purpose and a definite method. "The unexamined life is not worth living," he said. Each man must examine his own, look at himself, at what he is, in the light of the truth he could find if he sought for it. Socrates never offered to lead him to it. As he saw it, that would mean little.

Only what each man discovered for himself could be actually true to him. The truth he accepted at secondhand on the word of another remained always unreal to him. The one way to help men was to make them want to find. "Although my mind is far from wise," he said, "some of those who come to me make astonishing progress. They discover for themselves, not from me—and yet I am an instrument in the hands of God."

He was always the seeker, inquiring, not instructing, but his questions upset men's confidence in themselves and the comfortable conventions they lived by. "Laches, you are a soldier. Tell me, if you can, what is courage." "Indeed, Socrates, that is not difficult. He is courageous who does not run from the enemy, but stays at his post and fights." "Very good, Laches, but I see I did not express myself clearly. May not another man who fights by running from the enemy also be courageous?" "Why, Socrates, I do not understand." "Well, Laches, the Scythians fight by flying as well as by pursuing." "You are right, Socrates, but they are cavalry, not the heavy-armed Greek I was speaking of." "Yes, Laches, and I see I put my question badly. I meant to ask not only about the courage of heavy-armed soldiers, but of cavalry too, and not only those courageous in war, but in perils by sea and in disease and in poverty, and also those who have courage against their own desires as well as against fear and pain. What is that quality common to all these cases which we call courage?"

The first effect he had upon his hearers was usually perplexity and bewilderment, sometimes it was extreme distress. Alcibiades, most brilliant in that brilliant town, told the company at the dinner table in the *Symposium*, "I have heard Pericles and other great orators, but they never troubled me or made me angry at living a life no more worth living than a slave's life. But this man has often brought me to such a pass that I could hardly endure to go on as I was, neglecting what my soul needs. I have sometimes wished that he was dead."

That is how he could shake men's dispositions, although he himself would have said, It is not I. It is that they have found within themselves the light and in that clear shining they see the darkness they are living in and the meanness of their souls.

What he really was doing as he talked so easily and familiarly and humourously to the men of Athens, as he lived day by day so courteously and modestly and unobtrusively in his city that he loved, was establishing a new standard for the world. He believed with an unshakeable conviction that goodness and truth were the fundamental realities and that every human being had the capacity to attain to them. All men had within them a guide, a spark of the true light which could lead them to the full light of truth. This was Socrates' basic belief, in the words of the Gospel of John, "The true Light which lighteth every man that cometh into the world." His own mission he believed was to open blind eyes, to make men realize the darkness of their ignorance and evil and so to arouse in them a longing for the light; to induce them to seek until they caught a glimpse of the eternal truth and goodness "without variableness or shadow of turning" which underlay life's confusions and futilities. If once they could be shown them, could behold them in their beauty, they would inevitably, irresistibly, seek for a fuller and fuller sight. When men have attained to a perception of what Aristotle called "Excellence, much laboured for by the race of mortals," they do not let the vision go. Great thoughts endure. The false and the trivial pass away. And what is true of the race of men is true of the individual. Men are not able, it is not in them as human beings, if once they see the shining of the truth, to blot it out completely and forget it. We needs must love the highest when we see it. That is the great Socratic dogma.

Outside, in the wretched war-wracked city, all was in confusion, but everyone could create order in the one part of the world which was actually his own, his soul. The laws and the authority of the state might break down, but the laws of the life within, self-mastery, self-control, could not be touched by anything outside. And he who realized the divine order in himself made the great contribution toward bringing it into existence in the world. As St. Paul was to say four hundred years later, "The law of God after the inward man."

This was a new religion. Its centre was the soul. In that world of shaken moral values where people were saying, "Life is too short to find out if there are gods or not. Let us eat and drink, for tomorrow we die," Socrates came declaring that morality had an unshakeable foundation. The good, "that through whose presence the good are good," could be found by all. Morality was "of the nature of things"—human nature. "A good man in his dark strivings is somehow conscious of the right way." Goethe was truly Socratic when he said that. Each soul, Socrates believed, had the seed of divinity, the potentiality of finding the underlying reality, which in another aspect is God, and of realizing the moral order. Therefore, each was of supreme importance. "The things of men," he said, were what a man should be concerned about. Cicero understood him when he wrote, "He brought philosophy down from heaven into the cities and homes of men." He himself would altogether have agreed. Yes, he would have said, because those are the places of importance, the places where men dwell. Philosophy, which is the love of the truth, must come down and live with mankind, the only seekers and discoverers of it. Men have the highest destiny. They can know the truth.

It was the one concern of his life that they should find it. They were so made that only then, only when they had beheld the truth and their souls were penetrated by its goodness and its beauty, could they really live, fulfilling at last their own nature, in harmony with reality, with God. Centuries later St. Augustine said: "Thou hast made us for thyself and restless are our hearts until they rest in thee."

But it is not only or even chiefly through his faith in man and in God that he has lived for nearly two thousand five hundred years. It is because of what he himself was. He proved the truth of what he said by his life and even more by his death. He showed men what they could become, their own spiritual possibilities, and he showed them how they could meet "the mighty stranger, death." This great lesson was not obscured by later legends of marvels and miracles. No magical doings were ever related of Socrates.

Strongest of all was the overpowering impression made by the last days of his life. Throughout them he had as throughout his life a heart at leisure from itself. When he was arrested and taken to court he met his accusers in a spirit of kindly good will. He refused to save his life by promising to give up teaching, but he did so with complete courtesy.

When the sentence of death had been pronounced he ended his reply to it by comforting his judges for condemning him.

In his prison cell he was serene, sometimes humourous, always perfectly natural, just himself, sweetly thoughtful of the men who loved him and of what they were suffering for him, but showing no suffering on his own behalf. He was ready to meet death peacefully, entirely fearless. One who was there with him said to another who had been away from the city at the time: "I could not pity

him. He seemed to me beyond that. I thought of him as blessed.
I thought that he would be happy in the other world. What I felt
was a strange mixture of pleasure and pain."

In prison a devoted friend, Crito, came to him, begging him, "O
my beloved Socrates, let me entreat you to escape. Let us who can
well afford it, bribe your way out of prison. Oh, be persuaded." Socrates answered serenely, "No. That cannot be. No one may do wrong
intentionally. I will not break the law to save my life. I shall die,
but I shall die innocent of wrong. This, dear Crito, is what a voice
I seem to hear says to me and it prevents me from hearing any
other. Yet speak, if you have something to say." "Socrates, I have
nothing to say." "Then leave me, Crito, to fulfill the will of God
and to follow whither he leads."

When the time came for him to drink the hemlock he had a
kind word for the jailer who brought him the cup, and "quite
readily and cheerfully," the narrator tells us, "he drank off the
poison. In spite of my efforts my tears flowed fast. I wept, not
for him, but for myself. So all of us were cowards except Socrates.
He remained serene."

The talk that day in the prison had been of the immortal life
and Socrates had told his friends, "Our venture is a glorious one.
The soul with her own proper jewels which are justice and courage
and nobility and truth, in these arrayed she is ready to go on her
journey when her time comes." He broke off his discourse by ex-
claiming, "But I really must go and bathe so that the women may
not have the trouble of washing my body when I am dead." Crito
suddenly recalled from the delight of hearing him talk, to the stark
facts, cried out, "How shall we bury you?" "In any way you like,"
was the amused answer. "Only be sure that you get hold of me and
see that I do not run away." And turning to the others of the
gathering, "I cannot make this fellow realize that the dead body will
not be me. Don't let him talk about burying Socrates, for false
words infect the soul. Dear Crito, say only that you are burying my
body."

Some fifty years after his death Aristotle, who knew him well
through Plato, surely had him in mind when he wrote: "There is a
life which is higher than the measure of humanity. Men live it not
by virtue of their humanity, but by virtue of something in them
that is divine." Looking at Socrates, the Greek and Roman world

knew that that had been done. A human life had been lived divinely
and they took courage for their own lives.

His intensity of conviction is what we are left with. Men can
know what is true. And yet just before he died, in his last talk with
his friends, for a moment he faltered. He was face to face with
death. He was looking into the darkness not when he was enfeebled
by illness, not grown weak so that thought was impossible and the
eyes of the mind were closing along with those of the body to forget and drift away in sleep. His powers were strong, his intellect vig-
ourously alive. What was he to meet after he drank the poison?
Immortality or extinction? He had maintained earlier in the day
to those gathered around him, that he "had reason to be of good
cheer when he was about to die, and that after death he might hope
to obtain the greatest good in the other world," but as the argument went on, as he tried with all his powers to think through
whether the soul was in actual, factual, truth immortal, he felt
within himself a doubt. All that he had striven for, to see the clear
light of the truth, to arouse in others the longing to see it, to lift
men up to find the reality of the good, the reality of God, upon
which all that there is depends—was this to end in blank nothing-
ness? That was what he faced and the darkness rolled over him as it
did when Christ faced it upon the cross. But through the final
anguish of doubt the anchor of his whole life, the pure devotion
to the truth, held fast. His words are: "At this moment I know
that I have not the temper of a seeker after the truth. I am only a
partisan—who always cares nothing about the rights of a question,
but only to convince his hearers. The sole difference between such
a one and me at this moment is that he wants to convince his
hearers and I want to convince myself. Think how much I have
to gain if I can do this. If the soul is immortal, then it is well
for me to believe it. If there is nothing after death, then during the
short time still left me my wrong belief cannot lead me into any
harm. This is my state of mind as I begin the discussion. And I
would ask you to be thinking of the truth and not of Socrates.
Agree with me if I seem to you to be speaking the truth; if not,
oppose me with might and main that I may not in my desire deceive you as well as myself, and like the bee, leave my sting in
you before I die.—And now let us proceed."

So Socrates loved the truth and so he made it live. He brought it down into the homes and hearts of men because he showed it to them in himself, the spirit of truth manifest in the only way that can be, in the flesh.

SOCRATES' SPEECH AT THE TRIAL

Plato

TRANSLATED BY F. J. CHURCH

THE truth is this. I am more than seventy years old, and this is the first time I have ever come before a court of law. I have to defend myself, Athenians, against the charges of my accusers.

I have made many enemies and people say that I am "a wise man." For the bystanders always think that I am wise myself in any matter wherein I convict another man of ignorance. But, my friends, I believe that only God is really wise. And the young men follow me about, (and) try their hands at cross-examining other people, and I imagine they find a great abundance of men who think that they know a great deal when in fact they know little or nothing. And then the persons who are cross-examined get angry with me instead of with themselves and say that Socrates is an abominable fellow who corrupts young men.

Perhaps someone will say: "Are you not ashamed, Socrates, of following pursuits which are very likely now to cause your death?" I should answer him with justice, and say, "My friend, if you think that a man of any worth at all ought to reckon the hours of life and death when he acts, or that he ought to think of anything but whether he is acting rightly or wrongly, and as a good or a bad man would act, you are grievously mistaken." For this, Athenians, I believe to be the truth: wherever a man's post is, whether he has chosen it of his own will or whether he has been placed at it by his commander, there it is his duty to remain and face the danger, without thinking of death, or of any other thing except dishonor.

When the generals whom you chose to command me, Athenians, placed me at my post at Potidæa, and at Amphipolis, and at Delium, I remained where they placed me and ran the risk of death, like other men; and it would be very strange conduct on my part if I were to desert my post now from fear of death or of any other thing when God has commanded me, as I am persuaded that he has done, to spend my life in searching for wisdom, and in examining myself and others. For to fear death, my friends, is only to think ourselves wise without being wise: for it is to think that we know what we do not know. For anything that men can tell, death may be the greatest good that can happen to them; but they fear it as if they knew quite well that it is the greatest of evils.

If you were to say to me, "Socrates, this time we will let you go, but on this condition, that you cease from carrying on this search of yours, and from philosophy; if you are found following those pursuits again, you shall die": I say, if you offered to let me go on these terms, I should reply, "Athenians, I hold you in the highest regard and love, but I will obey God rather than you; and as long as I have breath and strength I will not cease from philosophy, and from exhorting you, and declaring the truth to every one of you whom I meet, saying, as I am wont, 'You are a citizen of Athens, a city which is very great and very famous for wisdom and power of mind. Are you not ashamed of caring so much for the making of money, and for reputation? Will you not think or care about wisdom, and truth, and the perfection of your soul?'" And therefore, Athenians, either acquit me, or do not acquit me; but be sure that I shall not alter my way of life; no, not if I have to die for it many times.

(He is found guilty, by 281 to 220 votes, and is condemned to death)

Perhaps, my friends, you think that I have been defeated because I was wanting in the arguments by which I could have persuaded you to acquit me. There are some things which neither I nor any other man may do in order to escape from death. There are many ways of avoiding death in every danger, if a man will not scruple to say and to do anything. But, my friends, I think that it is a much harder thing to escape from wickedness than from death; for wickedness is swifter than death. And now I, who am old and slow, have been overtaken by the slower pursuer; and my accusers, who are clever and swift, have been overtaken by the swifter pursuer, which is wickedness. And now I shall go hence, sentenced by you to death; and they will go hence, sentenced by truth to receive the penalty of wickedness and evil. Perhaps it was right for these things to be so; and I think that they are fairly measured.

If we reflect we shall see that we may well hope that death is a good. For the state of death is one of two things: either the dead man wholly ceases to be, and loses all sensation; or, according to the common belief, it is a change and a migration of the soul into another place. And if death is the absence of all sensation, and like the sleep of one whose slumbers are unbroken by any dreams, it will be a wonderful gain. If that is the nature of death, I for one count it a gain. For then it appears that eternity is nothing more than a single night.

But if death is a journey to another place, and the common belief be true, that there are all who have died, what good could be greater than this, my judges? What would you not give to converse with Orpheus and Hesiod and Homer? I am willing to die many times, if this be true.

And you, too, judges, must face death with a good courage, and believe this as a truth, that no evil can happen to a good man, either in life or after death.

PATTERN OF A LIFE: ROBERT E. LEE

—— Douglas Southall Freeman ——

When Douglas Southall Freeman chose the project to which he was to devote a major portion of his life he "gave himself to something great." His famous four-volume biography of the Southern hero, Robert E. Lee, is the biography not only of one man but of a whole short-lived nation. Freeman was a Southerner born and a Southerner all his life. At the age of twenty-nine, he became editor of one of the South's great newspapers, the Richmond News Leader, and held that position for over thirty years. During this period he wrote several delightful books about the South but his enduring claim to fame, for which he won the Pulitzer Prize, was the work from which we take the final chapter. In it, Freeman sums up the meaning of Lee's life, the essence of his philosophy. To most Americans, Lee's image is that of a gentle knight, without fear and without reproach. He was all of that, and yet as Freeman shows, his basic philosophy was one of honest simplicity. Do your duty, deal honestly, face problems as they come, and in the words of the Bible, "If any man will come after me, let him deny himself, and take up his cross, and follow me."

Out of such simple virtues, followed rigorously, there grew a life which became heroic in stature. It was based on qualities all of us can cultivate. But in the way Lee applied it, he was almost unique.

✍

BECAUSE he was calm when others were frenzied, loving when they hated, and silent when they spoke with bitter tongue, they shook their heads and said he was a superman or a mysterious man. Beneath that untroubled exterior, they said, deep storms must rage; his dignity, his reserve, and his few words concealed sombre thoughts, repressed ambitions, livid resentments. They were mistaken. Robert Lee was one of the small company of great men in whom there is no inconsistency to be explained, no enigma to be solved. What he seemed, he was—a wholly human gentleman, the essential elements of whose positive character were two and only two, simplicity and spirituality.

The first reference to Robert E. Lee in an extant letter is the significant statement of his father that "Robert was always good and will be confirmed in his happy turn of mind by his ever-watchful and affectionate mother. Does he strengthen his native tendency?"[1] Penned when the boy was ten, this language registered the impression the absent father had formed when Robert was not more than seven years of age. The stamp of character must, then, have been upon him from childhood. When he emerges dimly as a personality, in the later days of his cadetship at West Point, many of his essential qualities are apparent. Thereafter, from the time he appears clearly at Cockspur Island and at Fort Monroe, he exhibits every characteristic that later distinguished him. Subsequent change in his character was negligible and is simply the development of the man by challenging circumstance. Of this there can be no question. So consistent is the description of the young lieutenant of engineers, in the early 1830's, alike by those who became his foes and by those who remained his friends, that one need not fear the picture is touched up with the later remembrance of qualities the grizzled General displayed when he had endured the hard ordeal of the War between the States.

This early development of character, like everything else that relates to Lee as an individual, is easily understood. Despite the ill-health of the mother and her unhappiness during her pregnancy,

---

[1] Henry Lee to Charles Carter Lee, Feb. 9, 1817, *Henry Lee's Memoirs*, 65.

he had a strong and normal nervous system that was invigorated by a simple outdoor life. Although there is no evidence that Mrs. Ann Lee had any secret dread that her son would develop the recklessness of his father, there is abundant proof that, with tactful wisdom, she inculcated in him from childhood the principles of self-control. From earliest adolescence he had upon him the care of his mother. George Washington, the embodiment of character, was his hero, made real and personal in the environment of Alexandria. At West Point his ambition to excel in his class led Lee to subject himself willingly and with a whole heart to a discipline that confirmed every excellence he had acquired at home. Physically more developed than most of the cadets, he had from the outset a better appreciation of what the training of the academy was intended to accomplish. All his early assignments to engineering duty were of a sort to impose responsibility. These circumstances did not destroy his sunny exuberance of spirit, but they set his character so early and so definitely that it did not change with years or woes.

Whether it was at the Des Moines Rapids, or during his superintendency of West Point, or in the president's house at Washington College—wherever he was in full four decades when the burden of battle was not on him—an old acquaintance would have observed little difference in his daily outlook, his nature, or his manners. Only in four particulars was the man who went to that last vestry meeting at the Episcopal Church in Lexington unlike the lieutenant who bantered the "Beautiful Talcott" at Old Point in the moments he was not watching the contractors who might circumvent the government. His buoyant bearing had given place to a calmer cheerfulness, which might have been the case with any man who has bridged the chasm that divides the twenties of life from the sixties, even though no river of blood has flowed through the chasm. Again, the natural dignity of his person had settled into a more formal reserve, not because he had become less simple in heart or less approachable in manner, but because his conception of his duty to promote peace and national unity compelled him to put a wall between him and those who might have stirred unhappy memories and would certainly have kept open the old wounds of fratricidal war had he permitted them to talk of war. Even then it is quite likely that some of those who knew him after the war mistook their reverence for his reserve. He was changed, also, in that, after 1865, he put out of his heart the military career that long had fascinated him. All the misgivings he had felt before the war regarding the pursuit of arms were confirmed by five years at Lexington. He spoke his conviction, as always, when he told young Professor Humphreys that the great mistake of his life had been in pursuing the education of a soldier, and he was not jesting in his encomium to General Ewell on the delights of a civil life. It was not by chance that he failed to keep step with the superintendent of V.M.I. when the two walked together at the head of the column of cadets.

These things apart, any one who had worked with him on the wharf at Saint Louis would have felt at home in his office in Lexington and would have found him the same man in the habits of life, in the steady routine, and in the simplicity of spirit that were his very ego. He rose early and cheerfully and had his private devotions. If he was away from home, he would write his domestic letters before breakfast. At the meal hour he would appear promptly, with greetings to all and with gentle, bantering reproaches for his always tardy wife. Were his food the sumptuous fare of bountiful Arlington, he would enjoy and praise each dish, eating with heartiness; but when he sat down to the plain diet of the first hard days at Lexington he showed the same relish and made no complaint.

Family worship over, he would go to work immediately, neatly dressed and with the whitest of linens, but never ostentatiously apparelled. In his labor he was swift and diligent, prompt and accurate, always systematic and instinctively thrifty. His ambition was in his labor, whatever its nature. He did not covet praise. Blushing to receive it, he assumed that others would blush when he bestowed it, and he spared what he thought were their feelings, though no man was quicker to appreciate and, at the proper time, to acknowledge the achievement of others. Place and advancement never lured him, except as promotion held out the hope of larger opportunity and better provision for his family. Even then he was meticulous regarding the methods he would employ to further himself financially, and he would never capitalize his name or draw drafts on the good opinion of friends or public. Yet he had all his life the desire to excel at the task assigned him. That was the urge alike of conscience, of obligation, of his regard for detail, and of his devotion to thoroughness as the prime constituent of all labor. He never said so in plain words, but he desired everything that he did, whether it was to plan a battle or to greet a visitor, to be as nearly perfect as he could make it. No man was more critical of his own performance because none demanded more of himself. The engineer's impulse in him was most gratified if something was to be created or organized, but if it concerned another's happiness or had a place in the large design of worth-while things, he considered the smallest task proper to perform. Only the useless was irksome.

He endured interruption of his work without vexation. Rarely was he embarrassed in his dealings with men. He met every visitor, every fellow-worker, with a smile and a bow, no matter what the other's station in life. Always he seemed to keep others at a judicious distance and did not invite their confidences, but he sought as a gentleman to make every right-minded person comfortable in his presence. With a tact so delicate that others scarcely noticed it, when he was busy he kept conversation to the question at issue, and he sought to make his interviews brief; but even so, his consideration for the sensibilities of others cost him many a precious hour. Wrangles he avoided, and disagreeable persons he usually treated with a cold and freezing courtesy. Should his self-control be overborne by stupidity or ill-temper, his eyes would flash and his neck would redden. His rebuke would be swift and terse, and it might be two hours or more before he was completely master of himself. Whoever visited him meantime would perhaps find him irascible, though sure to make amends. Exacting of his subordinates, he still reconciled himself often to working with clumsy human tools. Resentments he never cherished. When he found men unworthy of his confidence, he made it his practice to see them as little as possible and to talk to them not at all. Silence was one of his strongest weapons. During the war he summarized his code when he wrote these words on a scrap of paper that nobody saw until after his death:

The forbearing use of power does not only form a touchstone, but the manner in which an individual enjoys certain advantages over others is a test of a true gentleman.

The power which the strong have over the weak, the employer over the employed, the educated over the unlettered, the experienced over the confiding, even the clever over the silly—the forbearing or inoffensive use of all this power or authority, or a total abstinence from it when the case admits it, will show the gentleman in a plain light. The gentleman does not needlessly and unnecessarily remind an offender of a wrong he may have committed against him. He can not only forgive, he can forget; and he strives for that nobleness of self and mildness of character which im-

part sufficient strength to let the past be but the past. A true man of
honor feels humbled himself when he cannot help humbling others.[2]

Lee sought to conclude his work by early afternoon, even if that
compelled him to set a late hour for the meal. When dinner was
done he was glad of a brief period of relaxation and sometimes of
a little sleep, usually upright in his chair. Then he sought his daily
exercise in a ride on his horse. He delighted to have a companion,
and if he had one, he talked of pleasant topics. Riding alone, which
he often did, he would close his mind to the difficulties of the day
and to the problems of the morrow and would soothe himself with
the discovered beauties of the countryside. Nothing of a physical
nature gave him the same thrill as a glowing sunset. Usually, on these
rides, he paid his calls on the sick and on strangers, as diligently as
if he had been the parson of the town. This he regarded as one of his
social duties, and he discharged it not only with willingness but
also with satisfaction. Whether his ride included social calls or
simply carried him to a given objective, he was always on the
alert for the children and he never passed them without a greeting,
and, usually, a chat.

His return home, like all his other movements, was according
to a precise schedule. Unless a sudden storm detained him, he
would be at his door promptly at dusk, and would soon be ready
for his light evening meal—"tea" as the family called it. The hours
then belonged to Mrs. Lee, to his children, and to his guests. He
would read to them or converse cheerfully until bedtime, which
was usually after ten o'clock. When he retired to his own room he
had his evening prayers and was soon asleep. His quarters at Lexington were always as neat as if he were still a cadet at West Point, but
the only suggestion of the soldier was the army pistol that hung in
its holster by the head of his bed. After Mrs. Lee's invalidism afflicted
her, he rarely went out to social affairs. Before that time he sometimes attended her to parties or to dinners, where he preferred the
company of women to that of men, and that of the daughters to
the mothers.' Always his address was dignified, but to the young girls
it was often bantering. Nothing delighted him more than gently
to tease some blushing young beauty. He had neither high wit nor
quick repartee, though occasionally he essayed a pun; but his smile,

[2] It is not known whether this and several other written notes in General
Lee's military valise were original with him or had been copied from some little-
known books that he had read.

his manners, and his quick understanding made him socially irresistible. His conversation, however, never turned to forbidden topics, nor was there in it anything suggestive or of *double entendre*. In all his letters, and there are several thousand of them, as in all his reported conversation, and there are countless anecdotes of him, no oath or vulgarism appears. He was clean-minded, though definitely and unfeignedly attracted to intelligent, handsome women.

Leaves and furloughs during his army service and vacations after the war found him ready to travel, not to distant lands but to the spas of Virginia or, better still, to the houses of congenial friends. Most of all did he relish a round of visits to his own kin, with whom he delighted to talk of the doings of their relatives. Chatter of this sort never bored him. Naturally sociable and devoted to his countless cousins, he sympathized with all their distresses and rejoiced in their little triumphs. Rarely was he too busy, when time allowed of his writing at all, to chronicle every wedding, every birth, every journey, every sickness, for the information of his family correspondents. At home, in his earlier periods of leisure, he shared in the sports of his sons, and to the end of his life he gave to each of his daughters a measure of courtly attention fitted to the temperament and age of each of them.

At intervals his habitual cheerfulness was marred by a sense of failure. This was most apt to overtake him when he was absent from home on long tours of military duty, for his simple nature made him dependent on his wife and children. Separated from them he often suffered loneliness and sometimes acute nostalgia. On occasion, and particularly during the difficult period when he was struggling to settle Mr. Custis' estate and to repair Arlington in 1857-59, this sense of frustration came upon him even at home. Then he would wonder why he did not advance more rapidly in the army and would puzzle himself to know how he could make adequate provision for his daughters, none of whom, in his heart of hearts, he wished to be married. These were the most unhappy times of his life, except perhaps those of his occasional illnesses. When sick, he would have few words even for his family, and was more than apt to lose his grip upon himself in dealing with others.

This was the pattern of his daily life. There is every reason to believe it was the mirror of his own soul. Those who look at him through the glamour of his victories or seek deep meaning in his silence will labor in vain to make him appear complicated. His language, his acts, and his personal life were simple for the unescapable reason that he was a simple gentleman.

Simple and spiritual—the two qualities which constitute the man cannot be separated. The strongest religious impulse in his life was that given him by his mother. After that, in youth, he probably came most under the indirect influence of Reverend William Meade, later bishop, the clergyman who did more than any one else to restore the Protestant Episcopal Church in Virginia from the ruin that had overtaken it during and after the American Revolution. Mr. Meade was rector in Alexandria for only eighteen months and then at a time when Robert was too young to heed his sermons; but he preached there often during Robert's youth and his spirit dominated the Episcopal Church in Virginia. He was a picturesque personality, one of the prophets of his generation. Holding to the beautiful forms of his faith, Mr. Meade breathed into its worship an evangelism as ardent as that of the younger American denominations. In his eyes, religion concerned itself equally with acts and with beliefs. No reformer was ever more uncompromising in his denunciation of cards or more unyielding in opposition to the old habit the barons of the Northern Neck had of staging races and of backing their horses with their dollars. None excoriated the stage with warnings more sulphurous than did Mr. Meade. Had he been sent to idolatrous Israel, he could not more solemnly have proclaimed the day of the vengeance of the Lord or have portrayed more darkly the fearsome punishment visited on the sinner for his hardness of heart. Yet he spoke "comfortably to Jerusalem." He gave the promise of forgiveness to the repentant, pictured glowingly to the faithful the bliss of a hard-won Heaven, and somehow planted in the hearts of the dominant class in that section of the Old Dominion a religion of simplicity, vigor, and sincerity.

It is a singular fact that young Robert Lee was not prompted by the exhortations of Mr. Meade or of like-minded clergymen to submit himself to confirmation. The reason cannot be surmised, unless it was that the theology of his youth had a vehemence and an emotionalism alien to his nature. He was content until he was past forty-five to hold to the code of a gentleman rather than to the formal creed of a church. The experiences of the Mexican War, the gentle piety of the Fitzhughs at Ravensworth, the example and death of Mrs. Custis, the simple faith of Mrs. Lee, and, more immediately, the purpose of his daughters to enter into the full fellowship of the church induced Lee in 1853 to renew his vows. After that time, first his sense of dependence on God for the uprearing of his boys during his long absences from home, and then the developing tragedy of the war, deepened every religious impulse of his soul.

And what did religion imply for him as he sent Pickett's men up Cemetery Ridge, as he rode to the McLean house, as he read of Military District No. 1, and as he looked down from the chapel platform at the scarred faces and patched garments of his students?

To answer that question is to employ the terms of a theology that now seems to some outworn and perhaps archaic. It was, however, the *credo* of a man who met the supreme tests of life in that he accepted fame without vanity and defeat without repining. To understand the faith of Robert E. Lee is to fill out the picture of him as a gentleman of simple soul. For him as for his grandfather, Charles Carter, religion blended with the code of *noblesse oblige* to which he had been reared. Together, these two forces resolved every problem of his life into right and wrong. The clear light of conscience and of social obligation left no zone of gray in his heart: everything was black or white. There cannot be said to have been a "secret" of his life, but this assuredly was the great, transparent truth, and this it was, primarily, that gave to his career its consistency and decision. Over his movements as a soldier he hesitated often, but over his acts as a man, never. There was but one question ever: What was his duty as a Christian and a gentleman? That he answered by the sure criterion of right and wrong, and, having answered, acted. Everywhere the two obligations went together; he never sought to expiate as a Christian for what he had failed to do as a gentleman, or to atone as a gentleman for what he had neglected as a Christian. He could not have conceived of a Christian who was not a gentleman.

Kindness was the first implication of religion in his mind—not the deliberate kindness of "good works" to pacify exacting Deity but the instinctive kindness of a heart that had been schooled to regard others. His was not a nature to waste time in the perplexities of self-analysis; but if those about him at headquarters had understood him better they might often have asked themselves whether, when he brought a refreshing drink to a dusty lieutenant who called with dispatches, he was discharging the social duty of a host or was giving a "cup of cold water" in his Master's name. His manner in either case would have been precisely the same.

Equally was his religion expressed in his unquestioning response to duty. In his clear creed, right was duty and must be discharged. "There is," he wrote down privately for his own guidance, "a true glory and a true honor: the glory of duty done—the honor of the integrity of principle." He probably never summed up this aspect of his religion more completely than in that self-revealing hour before he started to meet General Grant, when he answered all the appeals of his lieutenants with the simple statement: "The question is, is it right to surrender this army? If it is right, then I will take all the responsibility." It was a high creed—right at all times and at all costs —but daily self-discipline and a clear sense of justice made him able to adhere to it.

Humility was another major implication of his religion. So lofty was his conception of man's duty to his Maker and to his neighbors, so completely did his ambition extend, all unconsciously, into the realm of the spirit, that he was never satisfied with what he was. Those who stood with him on the red field of Appomattox thought that his composure was due to his belief that he had discharged his full duty, and in this they were partially correct; but he always felt, with a sincerity no man can challenge, that he had fallen immeasurably short of his ideal of a servant of God. "So humble was he as a Christian," wrote Mrs. Lee on the day of his death, "that he said not long ago to me he wished he felt sure of his acceptance. I said all who love and trust in the Savior need not fear. He did not reply, but a more upright and conscientious Christian never lived."

Born of this humility, this sense of unworthiness in the sight of God, was the submission to the Divine will that has so often been cited in these pages to explain his calmness in hours that would have wrecked the self-control of lesser men. There was nothing of blind fatalism in his faith. Resignation is scarcely the name for it. Believing that God was Infinite Wisdom and Eternal Love, he subjected himself to seeming ill-fortune in the confidence that God's will would work out for man's good. If it was a battle that had been won, to "Almighty God" he gave the glory; if it was a death that had brought grief to the family, he reminded his wife that their "Heavenly Father" knew better than they, and that there was eternal peace and sure reunion after life. Nothing of his serenity during the war or of his silent labor in defeat can be understood unless one realizes that he submitted himself in all things faithfully to the will of a Divinity which, in his simple faith, was directing wisely the fate of nations and the daily life of His children. This, and not the mere physical courage that defies danger, sustained him in battle; and this, at least equally with his sense of duty done, made him accept the results of the war without even a single gesture of complaint.

Of humility and submission was born a spirit of self-denial that prepared him for the hardships of the war and, still more, for the dark destitution that followed it. This self-denial was, in some sense, the spiritual counterpart of the social self-control his mother had inculcated in his boyhood days, and it grew in power throughout his life. He loved the luxury that wealth commanded. Had he been as rich as his Grandfather Carter, he would have lived in a style as hospitable. Fine horses and handsome clothes and lavish entertainments would have been his; Arlington would have been adorned, and his daughters would have enjoyed travel and the richest comfort. But Arlington was confiscated, its treasures were scattered, each stage of his sacrifice for the South brought him lower and lower in fortune until he was living in a borrowed tenant house and his wife was husbanding the scraps from a pair of trousers a farmer's wife had made for him. His own misfortunes typified the fate of the Confederacy and of its adherents. Through it all, his spirit of self-denial met every demand upon it, and even after he went to Washington College and had an income on which he could live easily, he continued to deny himself as an example to his people. Had his life been epitomized in one sentence of the Book he read so often, it would have been in the words, "If any man will come after me, let him deny himself, and take up his cross, and follow me." And if one, only one, of all the myriad incidents of his stirring life had to be selected to typify his message, as a man, to the young Americans who stood in hushed awe that rainy October morning as their parents wept at the passing of the Southern Arthur, who would hesitate in selecting that incident? It occurred in Northern Virginia, probably on his last visit there. A young mother brought her baby to him to be blessed. He took the infant in his arms and looked at it and then at her and slowly said, "Teach him he must deny himself."

That is all. There is no mystery in the coffin there in front of the windows that look to the sunrise.

PRESIDENT LINCOLN PARDONS A
SLEEPING SENTINEL

L. E. Chittenden

In all American history, there are only two men who have achieved a place equal to Lee's "in the hearts of their countrymen." One is Washington, and about Washington there remains an air of distance which, except for the apocryphal episode of the cherry tree, makes it difficult for moderns to understand and love him. The other is the gaunt and homely figure who was Lee's opponent and who brought him to defeat. With his awkward gait, his wry and unpredictable humor, his occasional flippancy, he seemed in some ways anything but an admirable figure. But this was not the essence of the man. There was in him a humanity which no ungainliness of body, no gaucherie could hide. He was compassionate. When the South lay prostrate, he planned to lift it up. When an obscure soldier was condemned to death, Lincoln would not have it. In the single episode which follows, we gain an insight into the meaning of the man's whole life. He saved a soldier as he would have saved all of humanity.

On a dark September morning in 1861, when I reached my office, I found waiting there a party of soldiers, none of whom I personally knew. They were greatly excited, all speaking at the same time, and consequently unintelligible. One of them wore the bars of a captain. I said to them pleasantly: "Boys, I cannot understand you. Pray let your captain say what you want and what I can do for you." They complied, and the captain put me in possession of the following facts.

They belonged to the Third Vermont Regiment, raised, with the exception of one company, on the eastern slope of the Green Mountains, and mustered into service while the battle of Bull Run was progressing. . . .

The story which I extracted from the boys was, in substance, this: William Scott, one of these mountain boys, just of age, had enlisted in Company K. Accustomed to his regular sound and healthy sleep, not yet inured to the life of the camp, he had volunteered to take the place of a sick comrade who had been detailed for picket duty, and had passed the night as a sentinel on guard. The next day he was himself detailed for the same duty and undertook its performance. But he found it impossible to keep awake for two nights in succession and had been found by the relief sound asleep on his post. For this offense he had been tried by a court-martial, found guilty, and sentenced to be shot within twenty-four hours after his trial and on the second morning after his offense was committed.

Scott's comrades had set about saving him in a characteristic way. They had called a meeting [and] appointed a committee with power to use all the resources of the regiment in his behalf. Strangers in Washington, the committee had resolved to call on me for advice because I was a Vermonter, and they had already marched from the camp to my office since daylight that morning.

The captain took all the blame from Scott upon himself. Scott's mother opposed his enlistment on the ground of his inexperience and had only consented on the captain's promise to look after him as if he were his own son. This he had wholly failed to do. He must have been asleep or stupid himself, he said, when he paid no attention to the boy's statement that he had fallen asleep during the day and feared he could not keep awake on the second night on picket. Instead of sending some one or going himself in Scott's place, as he should, he had let him go to his death. He alone was guilty—"if anyone ought to be shot, I am the fellow, and everybody at home would have the right to say so." "There must be some way to save him, Judge!" "He is as good a boy as there is in the army, and he ain't to blame. You will help us, now, won't you?" he said, almost with tears.

The other members of the committee had a definite if not a practicable plan. They insisted that Scott had not been tried and gave this account of the proceeding. He was asked what he had to say to the charge and said he would tell them just how it all happened. He had never been up all night that he remembered. He was "all beat out" by the night before and knew he should have a hard fight to keep awake; he thought of hiring one of the boys to go in his place, but they might think he was afraid to do his duty, and he decided to chance it. Twice he went to sleep and woke himself while he was marching, and then—he could not tell anything about it—all he knew was that he was sound asleep when the guard came. It was very wrong, he knew. He wanted to be a good soldier and do his duty. What else did he enlist for? They could shoot him, and perhaps they ought to, but he could not have tried harder; and if he was in the same place again, he could no more help going to sleep than he could fly.

One must have been made of sterner stuff than I was not to be touched by the earnest manner with which these men offered to devote even their farms to the aid of their comrade. The captain and the others had no words to express their emotions. I saw that the situation was surrounded by difficulties of which they knew nothing.

The more I reflected upon what I was to do, the more hopeless the case appeared. Thought was useless. I must act upon impulse, or I should not act at all.

"Come," I said, "there is only one man on earth who can save your comrade. Fortunately, he is the best man on the continent. We will go to President Lincoln."

I went swiftly out of the Treasury over to the White House and up the stairway to the little office where the President was writing. The boys followed in a procession. I did not give the thought any time to get a hold on me that I, an officer of the government, was committing an impropriety in thus rushing a matter upon the President's attention. The President was the first to speak.

"What is this?" he asked. "An expedition to kidnap somebody or to get another brigadier appointed or furlough to go home to vote? I cannot do it, gentlemen. Brigadiers are thicker than drum majors, and I couldn't get a furlough for myself if I asked it from the War Department."

There was hope in the tone in which he spoke. I went straight to my point. "Mr. President," I said, "these men want nothing for themselves. They are Green Mountain boys of the Third Vermont, who have come to stay as long as you need good soldiers. They don't want promotion until they earn it. But they do want something that you alone can give them—the life of a comrade."

"What has he done?" asked the President. "You Vermonters are not a bad lot, generally. Has he committed murder or mutiny, or what other felony?"

"Tell him," I whispered to the captain.

"I cannot! I cannot! I should stammer like a fool! You can do it better!"

"Captain," I said, pushing him forward, "Scott's life depends on you. You must tell the President the story. I only know it from hearsay."

He commenced like the man by the Sea of Galilee who had an impediment in his speech, but very soon the string of his tongue was loosened, and he spoke plain. He began to word-paint a picture with the hand of a master. As the words burst from his lips they stirred my own blood. He gave a graphic account of the whole story and ended by saying: "He is as brave a boy as there is in your army, sir. Scott is no coward. Our mountains breed no cowards. They are the homes of thirty thousand men who voted for Abraham Lincoln. They will not be able to see that the best thing to be done with William Scott will be to shoot him like a traitor and bury him like a dog! Oh, Mr. Lincoln, can you?"

"No, I can't!" exclaimed the President. It was one of the moments when his countenance became such a remarkable study. It had become very earnest as the captain rose with his subject; then it took on that melancholy expression which, later in his life, became so infinitely touching. I thought I could detect a mist in the deep cavities of his eyes. Then in a flash there was a total change. He smiled and finally broke into a hearty laugh as he asked me: "Do your Green Mountain boys fight as well as they talk? If they do, I don't wonder at the legends about Ethan Allen." Then his face softened as he said: "But what can I do? What do you expect me to do? As you know, I have not much influence with the departments."

"I have not thought the matter out," I said. "I feel a deep interest in saving young Scott's life. I think I knew the boy's father. It is useless to apply to General Smith. An application to Secretary Stanton would only be referred to General Smith. The only thing to be done was to apply to you. It seems to me that, if you would sign an order suspending Scott's execution until his friends can have his case examined, I might carry it to the War Department and so insure the delivery of the order to General Smith today, through the regular channels of the War Office."

"No! I do not think that course would be safe. You do not know these officers of the regular army. They are a law unto themselves. They sincerely think that it is a good policy occasionally to shoot a soldier. I can see it, where a soldier deserts or commits a crime, but I cannot in such a case as Scott's. They say that I am always interfering with the discipline of the army and being cruel to the soldiers. Well, I can't help it; so I shall have to go right on doing wrong. I do not think an honest, brave soldier, conscious of no crime but sleeping when he was weary, ought to be shot or hung. The country has better uses for him.

"Captain," continued the President, "your boy shall not be shot —that is, not tomorrow, nor until I know more about his case." To me he said: "I will have to attend to this matter myself. I have for some time intended to go up to the [camp]. I will do so today. I shall know then that there is no mistake in suspending the execution."

I remarked that he was undertaking a burden that we had no right to impose, that it was asking too much of the President in behalf of a private soldier.

"Scott's life is as valuable to him as that of any person in the land," he said. "You remember the remark of a Scotchman about the head of a nobleman who was decapitated. 'It was a small matter of the head, but it was valuable to him, poor fellow, for it was the only one he had.'"

Later in the day the President started in the direction of the camp. . . .

Within a day or two the newspapers reported that a soldier sentenced to be shot for sleeping on his post had been pardoned by the President and returned to his regiment.

It was a long time before Scott would speak of his interview with Mr. Lincoln. One night, when he had received a long letter from home, he opened his heart and told Evans the story.

Scott said: "The President was the kindest man I had ever seen; I knew him at once, by a Lincoln medal I had worn. I was scared at first, for I had never before talked with a great man. But Mr. Lincoln was so easy with me, so gentle, that I soon forgot my fright. He asked me all about the people at home, the neighbors, the farm, and where I went to school, and who my schoolmates were. Then he asked me about mother and how she looked, and I was glad I could take her photograph from my bosom and show it to him. He said how thankful I ought to be that my mother still lived and how, if he was in my place, he would try to make her a proud mother and never cause her a sorrow or a tear. I cannot remember it all, but every word was so kind.

He said nothing yet about that dreadful next morning. I thought it must be that he was so kindhearted that he didn't like to speak of it. But why did he say so much about my mother and my not causing her a sorrow or a tear when I knew that I must die the next morning. But I suppose that was something that would have to go unexplained, and so I determined to brace up and tell him that I did not feel a bit guilty and ask him wouldn't he fix it so that the firing party would not be from our regiment! That was going to be the hardest of all—to die by the hands of my comrades. Just as I was going to ask him this favor, he stood up, and he says to me, 'My boy, stand up here, and look me in the face.' I did as he bade me. 'My boy,' he said, 'you are not going to be shot tomorrow. I believe you when you tell me that you could not keep awake. I am going to trust you and send you back to your regiment. But I have been put to a good deal of trouble on your account. I have had to come up here from Washington when I have a great deal to do; and what I want to know is, how are you going to pay my bill?' There was a big lump in my throat; I could scarcely speak. I had expected to die, you see, and had kind of got used to thinking that way. To have it all changed in a minute! But I got it crowded down, and managed to say: 'I am grateful, Mr. Lincoln! I hope I am as grateful as ever a man can be to you for saving my life. But it comes upon me sudden and unexpected-like. I didn't lay out for it at all. But there is some way to pay you, and I will find it after a little. There is the bounty in the savings bank. I guess we could borrow some money on the mortgage of the farm.' There was my pay was something, and if he would wait until payday, I was sure the boys would help; so I thought we could make it up, if it wasn't more than five or six hundred dollars. 'But it is a great deal more than that,' he said. Then I said I didn't just see how, but I was sure I would find some way out—if I lived.

"Then Mr. Lincoln put his hands on my shoulders and looked into my face as if he was sorry and said: 'My boy, my bill is a very large one. Your friends cannot pay it, nor your bounty, nor the farm, nor all your comrades! There is only one man in all the world who can pay it, and his name is William Scott! If from this day William Scott does his duty, so that, if I was there when he comes to die, he can look me in the face as he does now, and say, "I have kept my promise, and I have done my duty as a soldier," then my debt will be paid. Will you make that promise and try to keep it?'

"I said I would make the promise and with God's help I would keep it. I could not say any more. I wanted to tell him how hard I would try to do all he wanted, but the words would not come; so I had to let it all go unsaid. He went away, out of my sight forever."

A MODERN MAN'S QUEST FOR THE HOLY GRAIL: ALBERT SCHWEITZER

Charles R. Joy

"I gave up my position as professor in the University of Strasbourg, my literary work, and my organ-playing, in order to go as a doctor to Equatorial Africa," wrote Albert Schweitzer in his book On the Edge of the Primeval Forest. *He had already achieved an outstanding position in all the fields he mentions. He was conceded to be one of the world authorities not only on the playing but also on the design and construction of the organ. He was considered to know more about the musical compositions of Bach than anyone else living. In the philosophy of religion, he was acknowledged a master. Yet he abandoned all these honors, all the easy, cultivated atmosphere of European civilization. He first spent years like any young medical student to learn the art and science of medicine. Then he chose one of the most savage and unhealthy regions on earth to practice his profession. For most people, who spend their lives in an atmosphere of materialism and self-seeking, the reason seems difficult to understand. It was simply Schweitzer's desire to help his fellow-men, and in particular those who shared least in the advantages of modern science and medicine. Recalling the parable of Dives and Lazarus, he said, "We sin against the poor man at our gate." And rather than take refuge in lofty utterances, he determined to do what he himself could to remedy the situation.*

Charles Joy is one of the foremost students of Schweitzer's life and work, the editor of a noteworthy anthology about him. His article is admirably titled. It could as well be called "A Saint in Our Day."

ॐ

THE poetry of Africa!

Before the window against a bright blue sky a palm tree rises. A light breeze blowing from the river rustles the fronds of it and brings a little soothing refreshment. Goats graze in the newly mown meadow, each of them with a white heron close beside it. It is a peaceful, silent Sunday afternoon. The weaver birds are quiet in the trees overhead, the monkeys have ceased to chatter.

The river below is a mirror. So unruffled is it that one can see in its placid glass not only the white birds and the blue birds that skim over the surface of the water, but also the ospreys that circle high in the air. Each bird is companioned by its bright image in the turbid stream. The huge mass of tree roots, which alone shows where the water meets the land, is covered with a tangle of vines gay with flowers. On the other side the forest rises, the primeval forest, deep, luxuriant, impenetrable, the great living trees mingling with the dead giants of the past. Far in the distance a low line of blue hills rises.

By the window a man sits writing letters to his friends. The small, neat handwriting, like copperplate in its delicacy, contrasts strangely with the size of the man himself. He is a big man, six feet tall; obviously a strong man also. He has a shock of brown hair, turning gray, and a bushy mustache. His deep-set eyes are blue and kindly. They twinkle with humor. A little fawn nudges him, asking to be petted, and the big hand drops its pen and gently strokes the animal.

He resumes his writing. He is describing with simple and touching sincerity a grace that has been given to him—strength to work. He pours out his heart in gratitude to the many friends in many lands who made it possible.

It all makes an idyllic picture—river and forest, birds and flowers and domestic animals, human strength and devotion and tenderness. Here is the poetry of Africa!

The prose of Africa!

Papyrus swamps, decaying villages round about, ragged Negroes inhabiting them, the unhealthiest climate on the face of the earth, tsetse flies bearing the germs of sleeping sickness, mosquitoes malignant with malaria, termites that destroy the work of man as quickly as the work is done, traveler ants leaving utter desolation in the wake of their marching columns, jiggers that burrow into the soles of unprotected feet, venomous snakes in the tall grass, deluded leopard-men, who wear leopards' claws on their hands and feet, or iron imitations of them, lurking in the forests to pounce on their human victims and sever the arteries of their throats. Disease, pain, distress everywhere!

The untiring activity, of which the big man with the graying hair is writing, has to do with very unpleasant things, for he is a doctor. He writes of patients stricken with dysentery, who dirty everything they sit or lie on, who have to be cared for by the white doctors and nurses, since the blacks will not do such disgusting work. He writes of men whose skin gradually changes from black to brown, whose fingers wear away, whose toes disappear. They are lepers. He describes his efforts to save a man who has been bored through by the tusks of an elephant, and another whose hand has been torn by the frightful teeth of a gorilla. He tells of the many thousands who die of sleeping sickness, which the natives call the "killing disease." He writes of the phagedenic ulcers which form on the lower legs of men, and he writes feelingly for he himself has suffered from them. He tells of the hideous pain caused by strangulated hernia, and the miraculous relief which an operation brings. He writes of the huge tumors of elephantiasis, of tuberculosis, the white man's scourge, which has now reached the black man, of little children lying in a state of malarial coma. With all these tragic ills he is concerned, he and a pitifully few companions in the only hospital for a radius of five hundred miles. This, to him, is the glorious activity of which he writes to his distant friends and supporters. This, to us, is the prose of Africa which underlies all the rhythm of its poetry.

Albert Schweitzer is seventy-two years old now. On the edge of this primeval forest, far from the hills and valleys of the Vosges, where a sheltered childhood was spent, far from the cultured circles of Europe where he moved about so easily during his early manhood, he has wrought a work of mercy, the meaning of which far surpasses the number of black lives he has saved, and the measure of devastating pain which he has assuaged. If, as his friends first thought, he has buried himself in the depths of the dark continent, then his is a living grave, lifted up, drawing all men unto it, seen by all the world.

On the banks of the Ogowe River, which flows into the Atlantic just north of the Congo, Dr. Schweitzer established his home. It stood on a small hill above Lambaréné, named Adende. A few kilometers away in the middle of the seventies of the nineteenth century, forty years before the appearance of Dr. Schweitzer, the young Trader Horn built his post at a place called Adolinanongo, to which the Schweitzer hospital was moved in 1925. If Trader Horn could return today he would find that the outward aspect of things had changed very little. "Crocodiles still sometimes sleep with wide-open jaws on sandbanks or on deadwood on the banks. Hippos still frequent the waters of Adolinanongo in the dry season. Pelicans still circle in the air. The islands and shores are still covered with bright green, impenetrable bush mirrored in the brown flood."[1]

From the veranda of the little bungalow the doctor looked out innumerable times over the river with its branches, its green islands, its native villages, over the dense forest to the dim blue hills. But from that same veranda the doctor likewise looked out on more distant scenes. He looked out over the black peoples of Africa. He looked out over the peoples of every race and color. He looked out over life in its farthest reaches, over the universe itself. The spiritual life of mankind became richer because this man sacrificed the rich cultural inheritance which was his, and defying all the conventions of his group he decided to minister to the neediest of earth's children in earth's most neglected and forgotten region. Now from Adolinanongo Albert Schweitzer still looks out over the people, for that is what this native place name means. And all over the world the people look up to him as a glowing exemplar of what religion can be in the life of man.

This selfless spirit has been able to work its miracle of healing on the bodies and the souls of men because the prose of the outer world was suffused with the essence of its poetry. Like Goethe, who has been for him one of life's most enduring influences, Schweitzer has lived in the closest communion with nature and with reality. But never has he been supremely contented in this contact. Even in the lovely Alsatian countryside, where he was born on January 14, 1875, he seldom knew a perfectly happy moment. He was troubled by the cruelty he saw, the sickness and pain he observed. He could not join the village boys in their bird hunts or their fishing expeditions. When the evening prayers were said, and his mother had kissed him good night, he added his own little prayer of childish faith: "Protect and bless all things that have breath: guard them from all evil, and let them sleep in peace." So began in tender, plastic years his concern for the humblest of all living things, a concern which has developed into the crowning principle of all his ethics—reverence, not simply for human life, but for all that lives everywhere, the gnat that flies into his reading lamp, the toad that falls into the posthole he is digging, the wayside primrose so thoughtlessly struck down,

[1] *My African Notebook*, p. 39.

the worm dying on the hard pavement. Who but Albert Schweitzer would have thought with searing anguish of all the living creatures whose lives were being forfeited, when the natives kindled fires in the forest to make clearings for their pathetic little banana plantations? Who but Albert Schweitzer would have prayed that the crazed hippopotamus, raging before his hospital, upsetting canoes in blind fury and killing the occupants in the water, might be led by some animal premonition to escape before he was shot? Yet this abiding conviction of the sacredness of all life everywhere, maintained in the face of ridicule, is a bit of the poetry of his soul lighting with its gentle, luminous radiance the dark recesses of man's inhumanity and nature's tragic cruelty.

In the midst of life's dull prose his mind went in search of beauty. The dark caverns of superstition and error and ignorance needed the light, and truth was the torch he bore. Even as a boy he had a daring mind, questioning like Jesus in the temple the hoary errors of the past. "Why," he asked, "did the wise men never return in later years to Jesus?" "Why were the shepherds of Bethlehem not among his disciples?" "If the wise men brought such rich and precious gifts to the manger of the child Jesus, why were his parents always so poor?" The crawling things that live beneath the stone of institutionalized falsehood hated the light of reason, and Albert Schweitzer's torch of truth was not a welcome one. When he dared to disagree with his distinguished theological teachers, and proved that Jesus had been mistaken in his eschatological expectations which he shared with the Jews of his age, there were many who were convinced that he was overturning the temple of religion and bringing it down to the dust. Jesus could not be wrong at any point, and remain the Jesus of their worship, they thought. They could not see that in making Jesus and Paul men of their own age, and not men of our age, Schweitzer had lifted them above the passing generations, and endowed their genuinely spiritual insight with enduring significance. For there was, as Schweitzer convincingly showed, a transient and a permanent element in the teaching of both. The transient was tied to their time, the permanent was freed for all time. Truth was poetry to Schweitzer, and the prose of organized Christianity needed the warm magic of its transforming and vitalizing touch. No one who seeks sincerely for truth needed to fear the outcome. That was his abiding faith.

Schweitzer speaks of the parable of Dives and Lazarus to explain the mission which so startled his friends. "We are Dives," he says, "for, through the advances of medical science, we now know a great deal about disease and pain, and have innumerable means of fighting them. . . . Out there in the colonies, however, sits wretched Lazarus, the colored folk, who suffers from illness and pain just as much as we do, nay, much more, and has absolutely no means of fighting them."[2]

Here, again, we have the great gulf yawning between poetry and prose, which Schweitzer has given his life to bridge. He could not endure the thought of suffering. He could not accept privileges for himself denied to others. The steaming broth on the parsonage table of his childhood became nauseous to him because the other village boys did not enjoy such nourishing food. Since the boys had no overcoat he would not wear one. He refused to wear leather shoes on weekdays, because all the others wore clogs. His mittens had no fingers because theirs had none. There in Günsbach, his boyhood home, the dominant motif of his life was clearly set down.

He could go on, it is true, to a distinguished career as a theologian, a philosopher, a musician, a teacher, but it was inevitable that in the end this must be given up, for there were always those who had no broth, no overcoat, no shoes. Out there beyond the horizon of his early vision was the beggar Lazarus, full of sores, lying at the gate, waiting for the crumbs to fall. Schweitzer could not long continue to be the rich man, clothed in purple and fine linen, faring sumptuously every day, even though the callous world tried to blind his eyes of pity by calling Dives the daring and brilliant critic of Kant, the pioneering New Testament scholar, the distinguished teacher and director of a theological faculty, the widely acclaimed organist and expert on organ construction, the sympathetic interpreter of the music of Bach. His cultured friends might call him all of these names, but his conscience used another term. He was still Dives, the rich man, clothed in purple and fine linen, dining sumptuously day by day! And out there was Lazarus!

Suddenly, the academic degrees earned with such exhausting intellectual toil, doctor of philosophy, doctor of theology, doctor of music, became vain baubles to him, and he knew that he must win another doctorate, that of medicine. The title meant nothing to him, but the title would take him out to Lazarus in Africa. So he became "the old doctor" to his black brothers, a man whose friends in

[2] *On the Edge of the Primeval Forest*, pp. 1 f.

Europe thought mad, whose friends in Africa thought a fool on earth, but not a fool in heaven.

To the prose of African degradation and deprivation Schweitzer brought the poetry of his gifted life, and in the blending of this prose and poetry found his happiness. When in 1927 he returned to Europe for a time, he had a feeling of pain that he had to tear himself loose from what had become to him a second home. "It seems to me incomprehensible," he wrote, "that I am leaving the natives for months. How fond of them one becomes, in spite of all the trouble they give one! How many beautiful traits of character we can discover in them, if we refuse to let the many and varied follies of the child of nature prevent us from looking for the man in him! How they disclose to us their real selves, if we have love and patience enough to understand them!"[3]

Music was one of the earliest passions of Schweitzer's life. Here was poetry in a new, enchanting form. There was a long line of organists in his family, so that the appearance of a talent for music was not surprising. He himself tells us that when he first heard the duet sung "In the mill by the stream" he had to hold on to the wall to keep himself from falling. "The charm of the two-part harmony of the song thrilled me all over, to my very marrow, and similarly the first time I heard brass instruments playing together I almost fainted from excess of pleasure."[4]

At five the boy was playing on the old square piano, and even before his legs were long enough to reach the pedals, he was at the organ. At nine he had already taken the place of the regular organist at a Günsbach service. The gifted young musician of Saint Stephen's in Mülhausen, Eugène Munch, introduced him to Bach, and the distinguished Parisian organist, Charles Marie Widor, took him as a private pupil. But the pupil quickly became himself a teacher, a master of the organ, a recitalist in universal demand, a writer in two languages on the life and work of Johann Sebastian Bach.

The poetry of his life flowered again in music, but this, too, had to be offered up on the altar of renunciation. It is true that he took with him to Africa a zinc lined piano, the gift of the Bach Society of Paris, but he fully expected to sacrifice his music in the medical service of Lazarus. Once more, however, he found that the poetry and prose of life made a new synthesis. In the quiet of the late

[3] *The Forest Hospital at Lambaréné*, p. 186.
[4] *Memoirs of Childhood and youth*, p. 24.

tropical evenings he kept up with his musical technique; in the long months of his internment during the First World War he was able to practise assiduously on a table and the floor. The full measure of the final sacrifice was not exacted. Music and medicine harmonized in the equatorial forest. The prose of his life was interfused with the poetry of it.

In Albert Schweitzer's writings about religion, civilization, ethics, and philosophy, certain *word-pairs* appear again and again. They are key words to the understanding of his thought. Among them are *rationalism* and *mysticism, pessimism* and *optimism, decay* and *restoration, world-* and *life-negation* and *world-* and *life-affirmation.* In them we hear again the treble and bass of his life, undertones of sadness and pain, overtones of confidence and joy, dissonance and consonance, out of which he is trying to build a divine symphony of sound and love.

Here, then, is Albert Schweitzer, the teacher, the thinker, the healer, the singer, the seeker. The world is becoming aware that his life and thought are destined to influence profoundly the spirit of our time. At once a Savonarola preaching doom and a St. Francis teaching and showing mercy, he can help this new world of ours, which stumbles blindly into the atomic age, to stop and ponder before it is too late. Over us hangs a fate that may turn our cities and our civilization into ashes. Schweitzer with his mystic reverence for love and light and life can save us from that fate. He can help us to spread balm on the wounds of the nations. He can give us beauty for ashes.

FORGIVENESS: A SERMON TO
AFRICAN NATIVES

Albert Schweitzer

Of the following sermon, Schweitzer writes:
"My sermon endeavors in a quite elementary way to be concerned with what the hearers have already themselves experienced, and with what they may experience if they have the will to let Jesus have power in their hearts.

"In order to be understood, I must diligently endeavor to speak as much as possible to the point. Thus, for example, I must not leave Peter's question to Jesus whether it is enough to forgive one's brother seven times, as a general proposition, but with examples from real life must show my natives what it may mean for one of them, as it did for Peter, to forgive seven times seven in one day."

ᔐ

Scarcely are you up in the morning and standing in front of your hut, when somebody whom all know to be a bad man comes and insults you. Because the Lord Jesus says that one ought to forgive, you keep silent instead of beginning a palaver.

Later on your neighbor's goat eats the bananas you were relying on for your dinner. Instead of starting a quarrel with the neighbor, you merely tell him that it was his goat, and that it would be the right thing if he would make it up to you in bananas. But when he contradicts you and maintains that the goat was not his, you quietly go off and reflect that God causes so many bananas to grow in your plantation that there is no need for you to begin a quarrel on this account.

A little later comes the man to whom you gave ten bunches of bananas in order that he might sell them for you at the market along with his own. He brings the money for only nine. You say, "That's too little." But he retorts, "You made a mistake in counting, and only gave me nine bunches." You are about to shout in his face that he is a liar. But then you can't help thinking about many lies, of which you alone know, for which God must forgive you, and you go quietly into your hut.

When you want to light your fire, you discover that somebody has carried off the wood that you fetched out of the forest yesterday, intending it to serve you for a week's cooking. Yet again you compel your heart to forgive, and refrain from making a search round all your neighbors' huts to see who can possibly have taken your wood so that you may bring an accusation against the thief before the headman.

In the afternoon, when you are about to go and work in your plantation, you discover that somebody has taken away your good bush-knife and left you in its place his old one, which has a jagged edge. You know who it is, for you recognize the bush-knife. But then you consider that you have forgiven four times and that you may want to forgive even a fifth time. Although it is a day on which you have experienced much unpleasantness, you feel as jolly as if it had been one of your happiest. Why? Because your heart is happy in having obeyed the will of the Lord Jesus.

In the evening you want to go out fishing. You put out your hand to take the torch which ought to be standing in the corner of your hut. But it isn't there. Then you are overcome by anger, and you think that you have forgiven enough for today, and that now you will lie in wait for the man who has gone fishing with your torch. But yet once more the Lord Jesus becomes master of your heart. You go down to the shore with a torch borrowed from a neighbor.

There you discover that your boat is missing. Another man has gone fishing in it. Angrily you hide behind a tree in order to wait for him who has done you this wrong, and when he comes back you mean to take all his fish away from him, and accuse him before the District Officer, so that he will have to pay you just compensation. But while you are waiting, your heart begins to speak. It keeps on repeating the saying of Jesus that God cannot forgive us our sins if we do not forgive each other. You have to wait so long that the Lord Jesus yet again gains the mastery over you. Instead of going for the other fellow with your fists, when at last in the grey of the morning he returns and tumbles down in a fright as you step out from behind the tree, you tell him that the Lord Jesus compels you to forgive him, and you let him go in peace. You don't even ask him to give up the fish, when he does not leave them to you of his own accord. But I believe he does give them to you from sheer amazement that you don't start a quarrel with him.

Now you go home, happy and proud that you have succeeded in making yourself forgive seven times. But if the Lord Jesus were to come into your village on that day, and you were to step in front of him and think he would praise you for it before all the people, then he would say to you, as to Peter, that seven times is not enough, but that you must forgive yet seven times, and yet again, and yet again, and yet many more times before God can forgive you your many sins. . . .

II. For the Struggle Against Odds

COURAGE

Ralph Waldo Emerson

In Edith Hamilton's portrait of Socrates, the Greek philosopher says, "Tell me, if you can, what is courage." And the simple Laches answers, "He is courageous who does not run from the enemy but stays at his post and fights." It takes only a few questions for Socrates to demolish such an unsophisticated reply and to ask, in broader terms, "What is that quality common to all those cases which we call courage?" For nearly twenty-five centuries, that question has intrigued and baffled mankind. John F. Kennedy, thirty-fifth President of the United States, wrote a book entitled Profiles in Courage _which discussed one aspect of the question. Years before him, another American, distinguished as a preacher, philosopher, poet and essayist, attempted to answer it in terms as large as those which Socrates suggested. Is courage physical bravery? Is it a much rarer quality of mind and spirit? Where is it found? How can it be cultivated? Why is it universally admired, in the huts of savages and in fashionable drawing rooms? Emerson himself knew whereof he spoke. Time and again he braved public opinion, attempting to shock men's minds into independent thought. On a matter of principle he resigned his ministry in the famous Second Church of Boston. Whom can we think of better qualified to write on "Courage," who more competent to explain its importance in the lives of men?_

I OBSERVE that there are three qualities which conspicuously attract the wonder and reverence of mankind:—

83

1. Disinterestedness.
2. Practical power.

3. The third excellence is courage, the perfect will, which no terrors can shake, which is attracted by frowns or threats or hostile armies, nay, needs these to awake and fan its reserved energies into a pure flame, and is never quite itself until the hazard is extreme; then it is serene and fertile, and all its powers play well. There is a Hercules, an Achilles, a Rustem, an Arthur or a Cid in the mythology of every nation; and in authentic history, a Leonides, a Scipio, a Cæsar, a Richard Cœur de Lion, a Cromwell, a Nelson, a Great Condé, a Bertrand du Guesclin, a Doge Dandolo, a Napoleon, a Massena, and Ney. 'Tis said courage is common, but the immense esteem in which it is held proves it to be rare. Animal resistance, the instinct of the male animal when cornered, is no doubt common; but the pure article, courage with eyes, courage with conduct, self-possession at the cannon's mouth, cheerfulness in lonely adherence to the right, is the endowment of elevated characters. I need not show how much it is esteemed, for the people give it the first rank. They forgive everything to it. What an ado we make through two thousand years about Thermopylæ and Salamis! What a memory of Poitiers and Crécy, and Bunker Hill, and Washington's endurance! And any man who puts his life in peril in a cause which is esteemed becomes the darling of all men.

Man begins life helpless. The babe is in paroxysms of fear the moment its nurse leaves it alone, and it comes so slowly to any power of self-protection that mothers say the salvation of the life and health of a young child is a perpetual miracle. The terrors of the child are quite reasonable, and add to his loveliness; for his utter ignorance and weakness, and his enchanting indignation on such a small basis of capital compel every by-stander to take his part. Every moment as long as he is awake he studies the use of his eyes, ears, hands, and feet, learning how to meet and avoid his dangers, and thus every hour loses one terror more. But this education stops too soon. A large majority of men being bred in families and beginning early to be occupied day by day with some routine of safe industry, never come to the rough experiences that make the Indian, the soldier, or the frontiersman self-subsistent and fearless.

But with this pacific education we have no readiness for bad times. I am much mistaken if every man who went to the army in the late war had not a lively curiosity to know how he should behave in action. Tender, amiable boys, who had never encountered any rougher play than a base-ball match or a fishing excursion, were suddenly drawn up to face a bayonet charge or capture a battery. Of course they must each go into that action with a certain despair. Each whispers to himself: "My exertions must be of small account to the result; only will the benignant Heaven save me from disgracing myself and my friends and my State. Die! O yes, I can well die; but I cannot afford to misbehave; and I do not know how I shall feel." So great a soldier as the old French Marshal Montluc acknowledges that he has often trembled with fear, and recovered courage when he had said a prayer for the occasion. Coleridge has preserved an anecdote of an officer in the British Navy who told him that when he, in his first boat expedition, a midshipman in his fourteenth year, accompanied Sir Alexander Ball, "as we were rowing up to the vessel we were to attack, amid a discharge of musketry, I was overpowered with fear, my knees shook and I was ready to faint away. Lieutenant Ball seeing me, placed himself close beside me, took hold of my hand and whispered, 'Courage, my dear boy! you will recover in a minute or so; I was just the same when I first went out in this way.' It was as if an angel spoke to me. From that moment I was as fearless and as forward as the oldest of the boat's crew. But I dare not think what would have become of me, if, at that moment, he had scoffed and exposed me."

Knowledge is the antidote to fear—Knowledge, Use, and Reason, with its higher aids. The child is as much in danger from a staircase, or the fire-grate, or a bath-tub, or a cat, as the soldier from a cannon or an ambush. Each surmounts the fear as fast as he precisely understands the peril and learns the means of resistance. Each is liable to panic, which is, exactly, the terror of ignorance surrendered to the imagination. Knowledge is the encourager, knowledge that takes fear out of the heart, knowledge and use, which is knowledge in practice. They can conquer who believe they can.

The sailor loses fear as fast as he acquires command of sails and spars and steam; the frontiersman, when he has a perfect rifle and has acquired a sure aim. The hunter is not alarmed by bears, catamounts, or wolves, nor the grazier by his bull, nor the dog-breeder by his bloodhound, nor an Arab by the simoon, nor a farmer by a fire in the woods. The forest on fire looks discouraging enough to a citizen: the farmer is skilful to fight it. The neighbors run together; with pine boughs they can mop out the flame, and by raking with the hoe a long but little trench, confine to a patch the fire which would easily spread over a hundred acres.

In short, courage consists in equality to the problem before us. The school-boy is daunted before his tutor by a question of arithmetic, because he does not yet command the simple steps of the solution which the boy beside him has mastered. These once seen, he is as cool as Archimedes, and cheerily proceeds a step farther. But we do not exhaust the subject in the slight analysis; we must not forget the variety of temperaments, each of which qualifies this power of resistance. It is observed that men with little imagination are less fearful; they wait till they feel pain, whilst others of more sensibility anticipate it, and suffer in the fear of the pang more acutely than in the pang. 'Tis certain that the threat is sometimes more formidable than the stroke, and 'tis possible that the beholders suffer more keenly than the victims.

Undoubtedly there is a temperamental courage, a warlike blood, which loves a fight, does not feel itself except in a quarrel, as one sees in wasps, or ants, or cocks, or cats. The like vein appears in certain races of men and in individuals of every race. In every school there are certain fighting boys; in every society, the contradicting men; in every town, bravoes and bullies, better or worse dressed, fancy-men, patrons of the cock-pit and the ring. Courage is temperamental, scientific, ideal. Swedenborg has left this record of his king: "Charles XII of Sweden did not know what that was which others called fear, nor what that spurious valor and daring that is excited by inebriating draughts, for he never tasted any liquid but pure water. Of him we may say that he led a life more remote from death, and in fact lived more, than any other man." Each has his own courage, as his own talent; but the courage of the tiger is one, and of the horse another. The dog that scorns to fight, will fight for his master. The llama that will carry a load if you caress him, will refuse food and die if he is scourged. The fury of onset is one, and of calm endurance another. There is a courage of the cabinet as well as a courage of the field; a courage of manners in private assemblies, and another in public assemblies; a courage which enables one man to speak masterly to a hostile company, whilst another man who can easily face a cannon's mouth dares not open his own.

There is a courage of a merchant in dealing with his trade, by which dangerous turns of affairs are met and prevailed over. Merchants recognize as much gallantry, well judged too, in the conduct of a wise and upright man of business in difficult times, as soldiers in a soldier.

There is a courage in the treatment of every art by a master in architecture, in sculpture, in painting, or in poetry, each cheering the mind of the spectator or receiver as by true strokes of genius, which yet nowise implies the presence of physical valor in the artist. This is the courage of genius, in every kind. A certain quantity of power belongs to a certain quantity of faculty. The beautiful voice at church goes sounding on, and covers up in its volume, as in a cloak, all the defects of the choir.

It gives the cutting edge to every profession. The judge puts his mind to the tangle of contradictions in the case, squarely accosts the question, and by not being afraid of it, by dealing with it as business which must be disposed of, he sees presently that common arithmetic and common methods apply to this affair. Perseverance strips it of all peculiarity, and ranges it on the same ground as other business. Morphy played a daring game in chess: the daring was only an illusion of the spectator, for the player sees his move to be well fortified and safe. . . .

Every creature has a courage of his constitution fit for his duties:— Archimedes, the courage of a geometer to stick to his diagram, heedless of the siege and sack of the city; and the Roman soldier his faculty to strike at Archimedes. Each is strong, relying on his own, and each is betrayed when he seeks in himself the courage of others.

Captain John Brown, the hero of Kansas, said to me in conversation, that "for a settler in a new country, one good, believing, strong-minded man is worth a hundred, nay, a thousand men without character; and that the right men will give a permanent direction to the fortunes of a state. As for the bullying drunkards of which armies are usually made up, he thought cholera, small-pox, and consumption as valuable recruits." He held the belief that courage and chastity are silent concerning themselves. He said, "As soon as I hear one of my men say, 'Ah, let me only get my eye on such a man, I'll bring him down,' I don't expect much aid in the fight from that talker. 'Tis the quiet, peaceable men, the men of principle, that make the best soldiers."

> 'Tis still observed those men most valiant are
> Who are most modest ere they came to war.

True courage is not ostentatious; men who wish to inspire terror seem thereby to confess themselves cowards. Why do they rely on it, but because they know how potent it is with themselves?

The true temper has genial influences. It makes a bond of union between enemies. As they confer, they understand each other swiftly; each respects the other. If opportunity allowed, they would prefer each other's society and desert their former companions. Enemies would become affectionate. Hector and Achilles, Richard and Saladin, Wellington and Soult, General Daumas and Abdel Kader, become aware that they are nearer and more alike than any other two, and, if their nation and circumstance did not keep them apart, would run into each other's arms.

The charm of the best courages is that they are inventions, inspirations, flashes of genius. The hero could not have done the feat at another hour, in a lower mood. Napoleon said well, "My hand is immediately connected with my head"; but the *sacred* courage is connected with the heart. The head is a half, a fraction, until it is enlarged and inspired by the moral sentiment. For it is not the means on which we draw, as health or wealth, practical skill or dexterous talent, or multitudes of followers, that count, but the aims only. The aim reacts back on the means. A great aim aggrandizes the means.

There is a persuasion in the soul of man that he is here for cause, that he was put down in this place by the Creator to do the work for which he inspires him, that thus he is an overmatch for all antagonists that could combine against him. There are ever appearing in the world men who, almost as soon as they are born, take a bee-line to the rack of the inquisitor, the axe of the tyrant. Look at Fox's *Lives of the Martyrs*, Sewel's *History of the Quakers*, Southey's *Book of the Church*, at the folios of the Brothers Bollandi, who collected the lives of twenty-five thousand martyrs, confessors, ascetics, and self-tormentors. There is much of fable, but a broad basis of fact. The tender skin does not shrink from bayonets, the timid woman is not scared by fagots; the rack is not frightful, nor the rope ignominious. The poor Puritan, Antony Parsons, at the stake, tied straw on his head when the fire approached him, and said, "This is God's hat." Sacred courage indicates that a man loves an idea better than all things in the world; that he is aiming neither at pelf or comfort, but will venture all to put in act the invisible thought in his mind.

He has not learned the lesson of life who does not every day surmount a fear. I do not wish to put myself or any man into a theatrical position, or urge him to ape the courage of his comrade. Have the courage not to adopt another's courage. There is scope and cause and resistance enough for us in our proper work and circumstance. And there is no creed of an honest man, be he Christian, Turk, or Gentoo, which does not equally preach it. If you have no faith in beneficent power above you, but see only an adamantine fate coiling its folds about nature and man, then reflect that the best use of fate is to teach us courage, if only because baseness cannot change the appointed event. If you accept your thoughts as inspirations from the Supreme Intelligence, obey them when they prescribe difficult duties, because they come only so long as they are used; or, if your skepticism reaches to the last verge, and you have no confidence in any foreign mind, then be brave, because there is one good opinion which must always be of consequence to you, namely, your own.

I am permitted to enrich my chapter by adding an anecdote of pure courage from real life, as narrated in a ballad by a lady to whom all the particulars of the fact are exactly known.

GEORGE NIDIVER

Men have done brave deeds,
    And bards have sung them well:
I of good George Nidiver
    Now the tale will tell.

In Californian mountains
    A hunter bold was he:
Keen his eye and sure his aim
    As any you should see.

A little Indian boy
    Followed him everywhere,
Eager to share the hunter's joy,
    The hunter's meal to share.

And when the bird or deer
    Fell by the hunter's skill,
The boy was always near
    To help with right good-will.

One day as through the cleft
    Between two mountains steep,

Shut in both right and left,
   Their questing way they keep,

They see two grizzly bears
   With hunger fierce and fell
Rush at them unawares
   Right down the narrow dell.

The boy turned round with screams,
   And ran with terror wild;
One of the pair of savage beasts
   Pursued the shrieking child.

The hunter raised his gun,—
   He knew *one* charge was all,—
And through the boy's pursuing foe
   He sent his only ball.

The other on George Nidiver
   Came on with dreadful pace:
The hunter stood unarmed,
   And met him face to face.

I say *unarmed* he stood.
   Against those frightful paws
The rifle butt, or club of wood,
   Could stand no more than straws.

George Nidiver stood still
   And looked him in the face;
The wild beast stopped amazed,
   Then came with slackening pace.

Still firm the hunter stood,
   Although his heart beat high;
Again the creature stopped,
   And gazed with wondering eye.

The hunter met his gaze,
   Nor yet an inch gave way;
The bear turned slowly round,
   And slowly moved away.

What thoughts were in his mind
It would be hard to spell:
What thoughts were in George Nidiver
I rather guess than tell.

But sure that rifle's aim,
Swift choice of generous part,
Showed in its passing gleam
The depths of a brave heart.

THE CONQUEST OF FEAR

Basil King

*There is, as Shakespeare says, a tide in the affairs of men which, taken
at the flood, leads on to fortune. But there is another and darker tide
which carries them down to the depths. That is the tide which must be
met with the fullest measure of courage unless it is to destroy us. Where
is such courage to be found? With all our might we strive but it is not
enough; we cannot find it without ouside aid because it does not exist
within us.*

*Basil King faced such a situation. In a strange land, sick in body and
mind, he felt that there was no solution to his problem. And then, after
thirty years, out of the distant past, a fragment from his childhood religious
training gave him the answer. Here he tells us about the seed which took
so long to germinate and which finally brought him assistance. Such assistance, he says, if it does not reside within you, is surely present in the
Universe of which we are all a part. In the words of the Bible, "Fear
not," for life is organized to do you good.*

WHEN I say that during most of my conscious life I have been a prey
to fears I take it for granted that I am expressing the case of the
majority of people. I cannot remember the time when a dread of
one kind or another was not in the air. In childhood it was the fear
of going to bed, of that mysterious time when regular life was still
going on downstairs, while I was buried alive under sheets and
blankets. Later it was the fear of school, the first contact of the
tender little soul with life's crudeness. Later still there was the experience which all of us know of waking in the morning with a feel-

ing of dismay at what we have to do on getting up; the obvious duties in which perhaps we have grown stale; the things we have neglected; those in which we have made mistakes; those as to which we have willfully done wrong; those which weary or bore or annoy or discourage us. Sometimes there are more serious things still: bereavements, or frightfully adverse conditions, or hardships we never expected brought on us by someone else.

Look at the people you run up against in the course of a few hours. Everyone is living or working in fear. The mother is afraid for her children. The father is afraid for his business. The clerk is afraid for his job. The worker is afraid of his boss or his competitor. There is hardly a man who is not afraid that some other man will do him a bad turn. There is hardly a woman who is not afraid that things she craves may be denied her, or that what she loves may be snatched away. There is not a home or an office or a factory or a school or a church in which some hang-dog apprehension is not eating at the hearts of the men, women, and children who go in and out. I am ready to guess that all the miseries wrought by sin and sickness put together would not equal those we bring on ourselves by the means which perhaps we do least to counteract. We are not sick all the time; we are not sinning all the time; but all the time all of us—or practically all of us—are afraid of someone or something. If, therefore, one has the feeblest contribution to make to the defeat of such a foe it becomes difficult to withhold it.

In my own case the reaction against fear was from the beginning more or less instinctive. With the first exercise of the reasoning faculty I tried to argue against the emotion. I remember that as a little boy I was afraid of a certain dog that barked at me when I went to a certain house to which I was sent perhaps two or three times a week. The house had a driveway, and from the minute of passing the entrance my knees trembled under me. But even then, I recall, it seemed to me that this terror was an incongruous thing in life, that it had no rightful place there, and that, if the world was what my elders told me it was, there must be in it a law of peace and harmony which as yet I hadn't arrived at. I cannot say that when the dog barked this reasoning did more than nerve me to drag my quaking limbs up to the doorstep, whence my enemy, a Skye terrier, invariably took flight.

During a somewhat stormy childhood and boyhood, in which there was a good deal of emotional stress, I never got beyond this

FOR THE STRUGGLE AGAINST ODDS

point. Specific troubles were not few, and by the time I reached early manhood a habit of looking for them had been established. "What's it going to be now?" became a formula of anticipation before every new event. New events presented themselves most frequently as menaces. Hopes rarely loomed up without accompanying probabilities of disappointment. One adopted the plan of "expecting disappointment" as a means of cheating the "jinx." I am not painting my early life as any darker than most lives. It was, I fancy, as bright as the average life of youth.

It strikes me as strange, on looking back, that so little attempt was made to combat fear by religion. In fact, as far as I know, little attempt was made to combat fear in any way. One's attention was not called to it otherwise than as a wholly inevitable state. You were born subject to fear as you were born subject to death, and that was an end of it. In my fight against fear, in as far as I made one, God was for many years of no help to me, or of no help of which I was aware.

At the same time it was to a small detail in my religious training —or to be more exact in the explanation of the Bible given me as a boy—that I harked back when it became plain to me that either I must conquer fear or fear must conquer me. Having fallen into my mind like a seed, it lay for well on to thirty years with no sign of germination, till that "need," of which I shall have more to say presently, called it into life.

Let me state in a few words how the need made itself pressing.

It was, as life goes, a tolerably dark hour. I was on the borderland between young manhood and early middle age. For some years I had been losing my sight, on top of which came troubles with the thyroid gland. For reasons which I need not go into I was spending an autumn at Versailles in France, unoccupied and alone.

If you know Versailles you know that it combines all that civilization has to offer of beauty, magnificence, and mournfulness. A day's visit from Paris will give you an inkling of this, but only an inkling. To get it all you must live there, to be interpenetrated by its glory of decay. It is always the autumn of the spirit at Versailles, even in summer, even in spring; but in the autumn of the year the autumnal emotion of the soul is poignant beyond expression.

Amid these surroundings a man ill, lonely, threatened with blindness, can easily feel what I may call the spiritual challenge of the ages. He must either be strong and rule; or he must be weak and go down. He must get the dominion over circumstance, or circumstance must get the dominion over him. To be merely knocked about by fate and submit to it, even in the case of seemingly inevitable physical infirmity, began to strike me as unworthy of a man.

It is one thing, however, to feel the impulse to get up and do something, and another to see what you can get up and do. For a time the specter of fear had me in its power. The physical facts couldn't be denied, and beyond the physical facts I could discern nothing.

It was then that my mind went back all of a sudden to the kernel planted so many years before, in my island home, in the Gulf of St. Lawrence. Had it not been for the few words spoken then I should not, as far as I can see, now have such mastery over self as I have since attained—not very much—but I should not be writing these lines.

My boyhood was placed in the times when Darwin's *Origin of Species* and *Descent of Man* had thrown the scientific and religious worlds into convulsion. The struggle between the old ideas and the new calls for no more than a reference here; but the teacher to whom I owe most was one who, while valuing the old, saw only an enrichment in the new, explaining the Bible in that spirit. So it happened that he spoke one day of the extraordinary ingenuity of the life-principle, which somehow came to the earth, in adapting itself to perpetually new conditions.

Nothing defeated it. For millions of years it was threatened by climatic changes, by the lack of food, by the ferocity of fellow-creatures. Heat, cold, flood, drought, earthquake, and volcanic eruption were forever against it. Struggling from stage to stage upward from the slime a new danger was always to it a new incentive to finding a new resource.

Whatever the Fount of Being from which the life-principle first came into the waters of our earth there is no question but that with it came a conquest-principle as well. Had it been possible to exterminate the life-principle it would never have gone further than the age which saw the extinction of the great reptiles. The great reptiles went, but the life-principle stayed on, with the ability to assume, within our limited observation, all the forms between the bacillus and the elephant, while as to what lies beyond our observation the possibilities are infinite.

Long before it works up to man we see this amazing force stemming an uncountable number of attacks, and meeting ruinous conditions with daring contrivances. For one kind of danger it develops a shell, for another a sting, for another a poison, for another a protective coloration. To breathe in the sea it puts forth gills, and makes lungs for itself when stranded on the land. To resist, to survive, to win through, is the end to which the life-principle sets itself with such singleness of aim as to unfold a wealth of potentiality astounding to us in looking backward.

This was the idea which came back to me that autumn at Versailles, and from which in the course of time I drew my conclusions.

Briefly, those conclusions were to the effect that as individuals we need difficulties to overcome, and that fear is a stimulus to overcoming them. Otherwise expressed, fear loses much of its fearfulness when we see it as the summons to putting forth new energies.

Man was born into fear in that he was born into a world of which most of the energies were set against him. He was a lone thing fighting his own battle. A man could count on no one but himself.

Perhaps this conviction that a man's strength lay in standing single-handed against circumstance was the first small discovery I made in my own fight with fear. Looking back on the developments which had brought man into the world I saw a marvelous power of getting round difficulties when you couldn't cut through them. Just as a river which cannot flow over a rock can glide about its feet and turn it into a picturesque promontory, so I recognized in myself an inborn human faculty for "sidestepping" that which blocked my way, when I couldn't break it down.

I left Versailles with just that much to the good—a perception that the ages had bequeathed me a store of abilities which I was allowing to lie latent. Moving into Paris, to more cheerful surroundings, I took up again the writing of the book I had abandoned more than a year previously. After long seclusion I began to see a few people, finding them responsive and welcoming. My object in stating these unimportant details is merely to show that in proportion as I ceased to show fear the life-principle hastened to my aid. Little by little I came to the belief that the world about me was a system of co-operative friendliness, and that it was my part to use it in that way.

To use it in that way was not easy. I was so accustomed to the thought of Nature as a complex of self-seeking cruelties, the strong preying on the weak, and the weak defenseless, that the mere idea of its containing a ruling co-operative principle seemed at times far-fetched. To the common opinion of the day, my own included, the conception of a universe that would come to a man's aid the minute a man came to his own was too much like a fairy tale. It may indeed be a fairy tale. All I know is that in my own case it is the way in which it seems to have worked. I think I have caught a glimpse of a constructive use for that which I had previously thought of as only destructive and terrible.

This is what I mean. The life-principle having, through unknown millions of years, developed the conquest-principle by meeting difficulties and overcoming them, the difficulties had a value. To man, especially, the menace of Nature, the ferocity of the beast, and the enmity of his fellow-man furnished the incentive to his upward climb. Had all been easy he would have stayed where he was. He would never have called mental powers to his physical aid, nor appealed to spiritual faculties when the mental fell short of his requirements. Spurred on by a necessity which grew more urgent in proportion as the life-principle widened its scope, the conquest-principle became an impulse which would brook no denying. Man grew by it; but the fact remains that he would not have grown had there been nothing for him to struggle with.

To me it seems basic to the getting rid of fear to know that our trials, of whatever nature, are not motiveless. In our present stage of development we could hardly do without them. So often looking like mere ugly excrescences on life they are in reality the branches by which we catch on and climb. They are not obstacles to happiness for the reason that the only satisfying happiness we are equal to as yet is that of wrestling with the difficult and overcoming it. Every call of duty has its place in this ideal, every irksome job, every wearisome responsibility. Whatever summons us to conflict summons us to life, and life, as we learn from a glance at the past, never shirks the challenge.

It never shirks the challenge, and, what is more, it never fails to find the expedient by which the new demand is to be satisfied. To the conquest of fear that plank must be foundational. As far as we can learn there never was an emergency yet which the life-principle was not equipped to meet. When all existing methods had been used up it invented new ones; when seemingly at the end of its new resources it was only beginning to go on again.

The deduction I make is this, that a law which was operative on such a scale before man had come into the world at all must be still more effective now that we can help to carry it out.

The individual is thus at liberty to say: "The force which never failed before is not likely to fail in my case. The fertility of resource which circumvented every kind of obstacle to make me what I am— a vertebrate, breathing, walking, thinking entity, capable of some creative expression of my own—will probably not fall short now that I have immediate use for it. That life-principle is my principle. It is the seed from which I spring. It is my blood, my breath, my brain. I cannot cut myself off from it; it cannot cut itself off from me. Having formed the mastodon to meet one set of needs and the butterfly to meet another, it will form something to meet mine, even if something altogether new. The new—or what seems new to me—is apparently the medium in which it is most at home. It repeats itself never—not in two rosebuds, not in two snowflakes. Who am I that I should be overlooked by it, or miss being made the expression of its infinite energies?"

WHEN HANNAH VAR EIGHT YAR OLD

—— *Katherine Peabody Girling* ——

We turn from the general to the particular, from studies of what courage is and how fear can be checked to actual examples of courage in action. The first of these is short but it is calculated to stir us to admiration and pity—the more so as the little girl who showed such bravery had little idea of her own "wonderful" quality. Hannah in later life was a housemaid. She did not have the education nor, in all probability, the intelligence to lift her above that station. Yet in one quality at least, in her indomitable will to fight through against almost insuperable odds, she ranked with the great ones of the earth.

 formula

"WERE you a little girl, Hannah, when you came to America?" I asked.

"No," she replied, letting her sewing fall in her lap as her grave eyes sought mine slowly, "I var a big girl eight yar old."

"Eight years old? How big you must have been! Can you tell me about it? Why you came?"

The recent accounts of people driven to America by tragedy, or drawn by a larger hope of finding a life to live in addition to earning a living, had colored my thoughts for days. Have all immigrants—the will-less, leaden people who pass in droves through our railway stations; the patient, indifferent toilers by the roadside; the maids who cook and mend for us; this girl who sits sewing with me today—a memory and a vision? Is each of them in some degree a Mary Antin? So I closed the magazine and asked her.—"A big girl eight yar old," she said.

"Oh, well," Hannah explained, "in Old Country if you are eight yar old and comes younger child'n in familie, you are old woman; you gotta be, or who shall help de moder?"

"Yes? Did your father and mother bring you?" I continued, probing for the story.

"No—fader and moder var daid. My h'aunt, my fader's broder's wife, se came for us. It cost her twenty-eight dollar, but se do it."

"But surely you can't go to Sweden and return for twenty-eight dollars!"

"Seventeen yar ago, yes, but of course you must to take your own providings. It don't require much." Hannah's shoulders drew together expressively. "Madam knows se is apt to miss her appetite at sea!"

"But too well." I shrugged sympathetically. Then we both laughed.

"I can to tell you how it is I came on Ahmericah, but—" Hannah waited for words to express her warning— "it will make you a sharp sadness."

"Please."

"I don't know if I can tell it to you good, but I tell it so good as I can. My fader he var Swedish fisherman vat h'own his boat and go away by weeks and weeks, and sometimes comes strong wedder and he can't make it to get home quick." Hannah hesitated, and then in lowered tones of soft apology added, "My moder se var a ver' pretty woman. Var three child'n more as me—Olga var six yar old, and Hilda four, and Jens—well, Jens var just a baby, suppose yar and half. We live in a little house close on by de sea. It is yust a little house, but it can to have a shed with a floor of stone. The door of de shed is broken so it is like a window mitout glass.

"The house is close on by a big dock where in somer time comes big excursion steamer mit—suppose hundert tourist people who climb on de mountain up de road. My moder se sell dem hot coffee, also bread and cheese, but dat is not de reason why we live in de little so lonesome house. It is de big dock is de reason. My fader he can to come home from late fishings mitout needing dat he sall walk on de roads. In Sweden in winter de roads swallow snow till it makes dangersome to you to walk because hides holes to step in. We live dere all somer, but in late autumn my fader he say, 'What about de winter?'

"My moder se say, 'I don't know, but anyway ve try it vonce.'

"Den my fader he go away in his boat and my moder se get bad cold and comes sickness on her, and ven se couldn't to keep care on us by reason se is too weak, se lay on de cot in de kitchen room and vatch on me dat I sall learn to keep care on de child'n."

"But what did you live on? How did you keep warm?"

"Oh—is plenty fuel, and ve make hot stew of dried meat mit rice and raisins.

"One day my moder se say me, 'Hannah,' se say, 'you bain a big girl; I must to tell you sometings. You fader is very late, it seems, and winter comes now. I cannot to wait much more. It is soon I got to go. You mustn't take a fear of me if I come all white like de snow and don't talk mit you any more. De little child'n dey will take a fear and cry. I cannot to bring a fear on my little child'n.'

"So se tell me what I sall do—I sall close bot' her eyes up and tie her hands togeder and lock de shed door."

"The shed door!"

"Ya."

Hannah had resumed her sewing. Her thread fairly snapped as stitch fell by even stitch with monotonous rhythm. In quiet, uneventful tone she continued:—

"So one night pretty soon se make dat I sall bring her best nightgown and help her mit to put it on. Den se kiss de little child'n in deir sleepings and se sit on a stool by de fire and say I sall put Jens in her arms. Se try to rock back and fort' and se sing on him a little hymn. But se is too weak, and I must to take him. Den se put on me a shawl and tie it behind under my arms, and se lean heavy on me, and we go out into de shed. My moder se do her bare feet on de stone floor. Se have yust but her nightgown on, but it is her best one mit crocheted lace at de neck and wrists. Se tell me I sall put de ironing board across two chair seats, but it is too heavy and se sall try to help me, but comes coughing on her and se must to hold on by de shed door. Se look out across de road and de mountain all mit snow white and mit moonlight cold. And blood is on her lips, but se wipe it away mit a snow bunch. Well, anyway, we do de ironing board across de chair seats and I spread a white sheet and put a head cushion and my moder lie down and I cover her mit a more other sheet over.

" 'Oh, moder," I say, 'let me make some warm covering on you.'

" 'No,' se say, so soft dat I listen mit my ear, 'I must to come here while I yet have de stren'th, but I want to go quick away, and in de cold I go more quick. Oh, Hannah!' se say, 'my big daughter! You are so comfortable to me!'

"So I hold my moder's hand. Pretty soon it comes cold. I klapp it mit mine, but it comes more cold. I crumple it up and breathe my hot breath in it, but it comes not warm any more. So mit my fader's Sunday handkerchief I bind her eyes like if you play Blindman mit de child'n, and mit an apron string I tie her hands together. Den I go back and make my hands warm in de kitchen room and I take de comb down off de string, and I go back to my mother and make her hair in two braids like as I did all when se was sick. My moder se haf very strong hair; it is down by her knees on and so yellow—so yellow as a copper teakettle! It could do haf been red, but it yust are not. Den I lock de shed door and crawl in bed mit de child'n to make me warm.

"Next day I tell de child'n dat moder is gone away. Dey cry some, but pretty soon dey shut up. Anyway, it is so long se haf lain on de cot in de kitchen room dat dey don't haf to miss her.

"So I keep care on de child'n and play mit dem, and some days go by. Comes stronger wedder mit storms of sleet and snow, and de wind sob and cry. Comes nobody on. At night when de child'n are sleeping I unlock de shed door and go to see if it makes all right mit my moder. Sometimes it is by the moonlight I see on her, but more often it is by a candle glimmer."

Hannah broke the subdued tone of her narrative to add in a lower, more confiding note, "It is mit me now dat when I see a candle on light I haf a sharp sadness.

"Pretty soon de wedder is more better, and comes a man trompling troo de snow to tell my moder dat her husband can't come home yust yet—he is drowned in de sea. When he see how it is mit my moder and mit me and de little child'n, de water stands in his eyes—ya. And he go on, troo de snow, tree, four miles nearer on de city to de big castle where live de lady vat h'own all de land and se come in sleigh mit four horsen and big robes of fur and yingling bells. Se see on my moder and se go quick away, but so soon as it can, se come again and se do on my moder a white robe, heavy mit lace, most beautiful! And white stockings of silk and white slippers broidered mit pearlen. Se leaf my moder's hair, as I fix it, in two braids, but se put a wreath of flowers, white and green, yust like de real ones. Is few real flowers in Sweden in winter. Anyway, dese var like de flowers a girl vat gets married should to wear. Den my lady se send her sleigh dat all de people should come and see on de so brave woman vat couldn't to bring a fear on her little child'n. And de people dey make admiration on my moder. Dey sey it is de prettiest dey ever see it, and dey make pity dat se couldn't to see it herself." She paused and breathed deeply. "I wish se could have to seen dose slippers!"

"And did no one tell you that you were a wonderful little girl?"

"Oh, vell—I var eight yar old."

"But what became of you all?"

"My lady took us home in her sleigh mit—I want to stay mit my moder, but se say I sall come to keep care on de child'n dat dey don't cry. And dey don't cry—dey laugh mit de yingling bells. De need was on me strong, but I don't cry before my lady. Se var great dame vat go in de court mit de queen. Se sent men and dey do my moder in a coffin and carry her to a little chapel house in cemetaire and in de spring ven de snow is gone dey bury her. My lady se put a white stone mit my moder's name and some poetry—I can't to say it good in English, but it says, 'The stren'th in the heart of her poor is the hope of Sweden.' "

"And then did your aunt come?"

"Ya; my lady se wrote on my fader's broder vat var in Ahmericah. Se say we can to stay mit her, but my oncle he send his wife, and we come back mit her on Ahmericah, und dat is all how I came to be here."

From THE DIARY OF A YOUNG GIRL

Anne Frank

There was another girl, older than Hannah, who faced adversity of another sort in a way which has won for her the admiration of the entire

*world. She was Anne Frank, who, still in her early teens, was forced with
her family to go into hiding from the Nazi invaders of Holland. In their
hideaway, for endless months they attempted as best they could to make
some sort of existence for themselves. And there, with almost miraculous
literary ability for one so young, she confided her thoughts, her loves,
her despairs—and above all her courageous acceptance of her situation—
to a diary which accidentally escaped the notice of her oppressors and
later was published in many languages. In the end, she was discovered
by the Nazis and sent to a concentration camp, where she died. But the
diary she left behind speaks for her in clear and living tones. Why has
it been so universally successful? Why did a play made from it draw
capacity audiences in America, in England, and even in Germany? The
answer lies in the fact that it speaks for all the oppressed who, whatever
the prisons they are forced to occupy, refuse to be spiritually undone.
From the diary we take a single entry, but no more than this is needed
to express the deepening of understanding of this young girl whose words,
in the end, spoke louder than those of all the dictators.*

ॐ

Tuesday, 7 March, 1944

DEAR KITTY,

If I think now of my life in 1942, it all seems so unreal. It was
quite a different Anne who enjoyed that heavenly existence from
the Anne who has grown wise within these walls. Yes, it was a
heavenly life. Boy friends at every turn, about twenty friends and
acquaintances of my own age, the darling of nearly all the teachers,
spoiled from top to toe by Mummy and Daddy, lots of sweets,
enough pocket money, what more could one want?

You will certainly wonder by what means I got around all these
people. Peter's word "attractiveness" is not altogether true. All the
teachers were entertained by my cute answers, my amusing remarks,
my smiling face, and my questioning looks. That is all I was—a terrible flirt, coquettish and amusing. I had one or two advantages, which
kept me rather in favor. I was industrious, honest, and frank. I would
never have dreamed of cribbing from anyone else. I shared my sweets
generously, and I wasn't conceited.

Wouldn't I have become rather forward with so much admiration?
It was a good thing that in the midst of, at the height of, all this
gaiety, I suddenly had to face reality, and it took me at least a year
to get used to the fact that there was no more admiration forth-
coming.

How did I appear at school? The one who thought of new jokes and pranks, always "king of the castle," never in a bad mood, never a crybaby. No wonder everyone liked to cycle with me, and I got their attentions.

Now I look back at that Anne as an amusing, but very superficial girl, who has nothing to do with the Anne of today. Peter said quite rightly about me: "If ever I saw you, you were always surrounded by two or more boys and a whole troupe of girls. You were always laughing and always the center of everything!"

What is left of this girl? Oh, don't worry, I haven't forgotten how to laugh or to answer back readily. I'm just as good, if not better, at criticizing people, and I can still flirt if . . . I wish. That's not it though, I'd like that sort of life again for an evening, a few days, or even a week; the life which seems so carefree and gay. But at the end of that week, I should be dead beat and would be only too thankful to listen to anyone who began to talk about something sensible. I don't want followers, but friends, admirers who fall not for a flattering smile but for what one does and for one's character.

I know quite well that the circle around me would be much smaller. But what does that matter, as long as one still keeps a few sincere friends?

Yet I wasn't entirely happy in 1942 in spite of everything; I often felt deserted, but because I was on the go the whole day long, I didn't think about it and enjoyed myself as much as I could. Consciously or unconsciously, I tried to drive away the emptiness I felt with jokes and pranks. Now I think seriously about life and what I have to do. One period of my life is over forever. The carefree schooldays are gone, never to return.

I don't even long for them any more; I have outgrown them, I can't just only enjoy myself as my serious side is always there.

I look upon my life up till the New Year, as it were, through a powerful magnifying glass. The sunny life at home, then coming here in 1942, the sudden change, the quarrels, the bickerings. I couldn't understand it, I was taken by surprise, and the only way I could keep up some bearing was by being impertinent.

The first half of 1943: my fits of crying, the loneliness, how I slowly began to see all my faults and shortcomings, which are so great and which seemed much greater then. During the day I deliberately talked about anything and everything that was farthest from my thoughts, tried to draw Pim to me; but couldn't. Alone I had to face the difficult task of changing myself, to stop the everlasting re-proaches, which were so oppressive and which reduced me to such terrible despondency.

Things improved slightly in the second half of the year, I became a young woman and was treated more like a grownup. I started to think, and write stories, and came to the conclusion that the others no longer had the right to throw me about like an india-rubber ball. I wanted to change in accordance with my own desires. But *one* thing that struck me even more was when I realized that even Daddy would never become my confidant over everything. I didn't want to trust anyone but myself any more.

At the beginning of the New Year: the second great change, my dream. . . . And with it I discovered my longing, not for a girl friend, but for a boy friend. I also discovered my inward happiness and my defensive armor of superficiality and gaiety. In due time I quieted down and discovered my boundless desire for all that is beautiful and good.

And in the evening, when I lie in bed and end my prayers with the words, "I thank you, God, for all that is good and dear and beau-tiful," I am filled with joy. Then I think about "the good" of going into hiding, of my health and with my whole being of the "dearness" of Peter, of that which is still embryonic and impressionable and which we neither of us dare to name or touch, of that which will come sometime; love, the future, happiness and of "the beauty" which exists in the world; the world, nature, beauty and all, all that is ex-quisite and fine.

I don't think then of all the misery, but of the beauty that still remains. This is one of the things that Mummy and I are so entirely different about. Her counsel when one feels melancholy is: "Think of all the misery in the world and be thankful that you are not sharing in it!" My advice is: "Go outside, to the fields, enjoy nature and the sunshine, go out and try to recapture happiness in yourself and in God. Think of all the beauty that's still left in and around you and be happy!"

I don't see how Mummy's idea can be right, because then how are you supposed to behave if you go through the misery yourself? Then you are lost. On the contrary, I've found that there is always some beauty left in—nature, sunshine, freedom, in yourself; these can all help you. Look at these things, then you find yourself again, and God, and then you regain your balance.

And whoever is happy will make others happy too. He who has courage and faith will never perish in misery!

Yours,

ANNE

THE FELLOWSHIP OF THOSE WHO
BEAR THE MARK OF PAIN

—————— *Albert Schweitzer* ——————

As introduction to an article by one of the bravest of modern Americans, Thomas A. Dooley, we offer a short selection from the works of the man who most inspired him. We have already read something about Dr. Schweitzer and his philosophy of life. Here he tells us who are the members of the fellowship of pain. And his short discussion is followed by Dooley's inspired picture of how he, in some measure, helped the ignorant natives of Laos to help themselves.

There are in Dooley's story two messages. First we see the people of the country, surrounded by filth and disease, preyed on by witch doctors as ignorant and superstitious as themselves, yet facing life's difficulties as best they can, trying to overcome their handicaps, eager to learn, for "no one really wants to be miserable." The second message is never stated by Dr. Tom Dooley but it is implicit in everything he has ever done or written. Here is a man who, like Dr. Schweitzer, gave up all the good things which were his almost for the asking, to bury himself in a savage wilderness. In the end, as we now know, he was to die of a cancer which was caused by a fall on one of the difficult trails he was forced to travel.

Tom Dooley and Albert Schweitzer are brothers in the Fellowship of Helpers of those who are members of the Fellowship of Pain. They are blessed men—their lives are a testament of courage.

ᢒ

WHO are the members of this fellowship? Those who have learned by experience what physical pain and bodily anguish mean, belong together all the world over; they are united by a secret bond. One and all they know the horrors of suffering to which man can be exposed, and one and all they know the longing to be free from pain.

He who has been delivered from pain must not think he is now free again, and at liberty to take life up just as it was before, entirely forgetful of the past. He is now a "man whose eyes are open" with regard to pain and anguish, and he must help to overcome those two enemies (so far as human power can control them) and to bring to others the deliverance which he has himself enjoyed. The man who, with a doctor's help, has been pulled through a severe illness, must aid in providing a helper such as he had himself, for those who otherwise could not have one. He who has been saved by an operation from death or torturing pain, must do his part to make it possible for the kindly anaesthetic and the helpful knife to begin their work, where death and torturing pain still rule unhindered. The mother who owes it to medical aid that her child still belongs to her, and not to the cold earth, must help, so that the poor mother who has never seen a doctor may be spared what she has been spared. Where a man's death agony might have been terrible, but could fortunately be made tolerable by a doctor's skill, those who stood around his deathbed must help, that others, too, may enjoy that same consolation when they lose their dear ones. Such is the fellowship of those who bear the mark of pain.

THE FELLOWSHIP OF PAIN

Thomas A. Dooley

EACH morning I walked into the hospital compound with the feeling that I was travelling backward in time to a disease-ridden world that had ceased to exist long before I was born.

Ironically, I was always reminded of what the profs had told us in medical school: "We can now look upon leprosy, gentlemen, as a disease belonging to the Biblical era. . . . These yaws, dysentaries, and worm infestations you will probably never encounter in civilian practice. . . . We may say that the terrors of diphtheria, typhoid, smallpox vanished with the advent of modern vaccine therapy. . . ."

Ah, yes! But here they are—with others even more terrible—crowded into my own "waiting room"—the commonplace problems of any average day. True, this is Asia in the 20th Century. But not the 20th Century that western man knows!

Our patients were numerous. Ignorance and superstition were prevalent. Traumatic injuries, often neglected or mistreated, made surgery a 'round the clock nightmare. Usually the symptoms were of the kind which are apparent to the naked eye. There were pregnant mothers, frequently tuberculars, carrying small children foul with smallpox or covered with sores. There were doddering oldsters with yaws, or swollen spleens, or wasting with leprosy. Then there were always the pathetic kids with skinny arms and legs, pinched faces, and enormous bellies.

We were often dealing with critical health problems born of colossal ignorance. These people have become so inured to disease, which is simply a part of their existence, that they speak of *kia tamada*, "normal fever." Malaria, for example, is a normal fever. You just live with it until, eventually, the spleen and liver are greatly enlarged and as hot as stones left out in the noonday sun.

They have lived on the edge of starvation for so long (despite the availability of natural nourishment) that their bodies have lost the capacity to store vitamins, fats, proteins. Only a few days illness can throw the system into negative balance.

We pumped them full of vitamins, and passed out huge quantities of that heaven-sent MPF provided by Meals for Millions. I was often tempted to start hygiene classes, such as we held so successfully in Vang Vieng. But in Nam Tha there wasn't time. Sometimes it seemed that every other case I saw at sick-call required some kind of surgery, and my schedule grew top-heavy.

So we did the best we could. Sick-call itself became the classroom, and each case served as a lesson. Naturally a garrulous Irishman, I talked incessantly, but as simply as possible, for hours on end. Chai and Si, Maggie and Old Joe, the nurses and the coolies would jabber away in the various dialects. Thus, we tried to make the crowd in the yard understand why this woman or child was suffering, and how the suffering could have been avoided.

The people listened with wide-eyed attention. They were eager to learn. I could see in their faces what I am convinced is universal truth: No one really *wants* to be sick and miserable. Even the most "backward" people, given half a chance, will follow simple rules in order to be healthier and stronger.

So I think our sick-call "lectures" really did some good. Of course, the multi-lingual bedlam made those hours that much harder on our frazzled nerves. Fortunately, none of us had ever expected them to be easy. . . .

Harriet was not her real name. The boys had a habit of Anglicizing unpronounceable Lao names, and of bestowing entirely new names when that was difficult or impossible. This pathetic young mother, about twenty years old, was a Kha, a people who once were slaves and now comprise the Lao servant class—the humblest "hewers of wood and drawers of water." So they called her Harriet.

She came to us on a litter, delirious. . . . She needed many weeks of emergency treatment and pre-operative care. After that came a series of operations extending over many months.

When Denny left in March Harriet seemed more like a human being. She was still in bed, suffering considerable pain and discomfort. . . . But she was on the mend when we placed Paul in the ward across from her.

Paul was a terminal cancer case. . . . We could do no more than excise the tumors, and give him sedatives. He would improve some, then, in a few weeks, the malignant process would light up again with even greater fury.

Harriet and Paul required much more nursing care than we were able to give them. But we could do just so much and no more. However, out of the pain and suffering of these two miserable strangers, a beautiful and compassionate relationship was born. When the sedation wore off, Paul would moan and writhe in agony. Harriet would struggle out of bed and come to fix Paul's pillows, and comfort and feed him.

Then Paul would have his "good days." He would insist upon taking care of Harriet. Once, when he felt particularly strong, he was missing from the ward. The Lao nurse found him down at the river's edge laboriously washing out some of Harriet's soiled garments.

At last, Harriet was well enough to be discharged. She went to work as a laundress in the village. But she was unable to pay anything for all the care she had received. So, remembering that pride is strong even among the lowly Kha, we accepted her offer to work in the hospital as part-time cleaning woman and attendant. There she spent most of her evenings. Paul, who now needed constant care, became her special charge.

I was in the distant mountain village of Ban Phu Van when death brought a merciful end to Paul's suffering. The Lao nurses told me later that Harriet was at his bedside to the very end. They were as deeply moved as I was by the devotion of these two people. We had been privileged to glimpse the true nobility of what Albert Schweitzer calls "The Fellowship of Those Who Bear the Mark of Pain." . . .

As the months passed, there was an occasional evening when sickness and death seemed to take a respite, although never for long. Then I liked to wander around the town of Nam Tha, greeting friends and neighbors, and nursing in my heart a secret joy. We were Americans, our skins were white, our speech and manners and habits were different. But we weren't strangers or curiosities any more. We "belonged."

At the base of the big triangle which was the "town square" (or the Main Drag, as the boys called it), we hung a huge sheet, 180 square feet overall, between the trees. This served as our movie screen. Directly behind it, the projector was on the front porch of our house, and the amplifiers placed on a tree stump. Thus, on an average evening, as many as 1,000 people, squatting on both sides of the screen, could enjoy the movies. . . .

When the show starts, I stroll leisurely down the Main Drag. I pass the Police Headquarters, home of our bodyguards, and greet the weary, mud-caked cops lounging on the porch after a hard day of jungle patrol. I stop before the Buddhist temple, a magnificent pagoda covered with gilt and porcelain, and admire the two angels, exquisitely carved from jade, that flank the steps. Beyond the Buddhist temple is the abode and shop of Mrs. Phouma-Sassady, weaver, seamstress, merchant of sorts, and our benefactor and friend. . . .

Mrs. Sassady has another distinction, which Denny Shepard discovered the day we arrived in Nam Tha. She owns the only Singer Sewing Machine in town—an ancient, pedal-operated model, but capable of wonders. Denny brought Mrs. Sassady bolts of linen from our stores, and she hemmed and sewed them for surgical drapes. She has been sewing for us ever since, mending our clothes, and making new garments patterned on the old. She refuses to accept payment. But, knowing that even Americans must "save face," she does accept an occasional chocolate bar. Bless you, Mrs. Sassady! . . .

On the Saturday before Easter, we were busy with sick-call when two tall, rugged characters, obviously Americans, appeared at the hospital and saluted us with a hearty Hello. They introduced themselves as Pastor H. Carl Currie, a slim, balding man of about forty, and Pastor R. C. Hall, a smiling, crew-cut chap in his early thirties. They were both missionaries, of the Seventh Day Adventist Church. Pastor Hall said that when they landed at the airstrip some native had simply picked up their baggage and brought them to us. Where else would a couple of white men be going in Nam Tha?

We found two empty boxes and asked them to sit by while we finished with sick-call. Then we took them over to our house and started a conversation that continued far into that night. With only a break for sleep, chow, chores, and our prayers, we continued talking well into the Easter day.

The Adventists have a fine medical center in Bangkok, and several medical missions in Northern Thailand. Pastor Currie, one of the keenest and most devoted men I've ever met, told me they were exploring the possibilities of setting up a mission in Laos. He kept plying me with questions, and I told him all I knew about conditions in the central and northern parts of the country. . . .

The more I saw of Pastors Currie and Hall, the more I was convinced that they could perform a wonderful service for Laos, and I encouraged them to try it. . . .

The supplies were still holding out, though I did write to Pfizer for some refills. They sent me all the more I needed. Meals for Millions sent me some more protein powder. Here this powder was referred to as "Ya mi henh." The vitamins, being a solution, were called "Ya mi henh nam" while the powder did not get the word "nam" added to it. "Ya" means medicine. "Mi" is "to have." "Henh" means "great strength."

The people of this country live on the edge of starvation. They seem to have no storage element for vitamins, fats or proteins. Only a few days of illness throws them into negative balance. Beriberi, a vitamin B-1 deficiency, was our most frequent complaint. Vitamin deficiencies were also the cause of much of our eye problems. Deca-Vi-Sol was given to nearly every patient who came to our sick call. Meals for Millions was given to all who seemed to need "strength." This included the naked, shining, pot-bellied children, the pregnant tubercular women, and the oldsters plagued with yaws, malaria or other sicknesses.

I tried to get the parents to bring the children to me as soon as they became sick or developed a fever. But they did not understand this. As I have explained, they considered many fevers as "normal" and it was almost impossible to convince them that there was no such thing as *kia tamada*. By the time we would get the child he would be plunged into beriberi, if not something even more serious. The basic fight in Laos is ignorance, not disease.

In Vang Vieng we had formal classes in the village school three times a week. We taught the rudiments of hygiene and sanitation. In Nam Tha, as the lines were longer and surgery more time-consuming, we could not have these formal classes. But we held sick-call in such a way that each case we discussed became a class. All the waiting line would be huddled on the porch. When a child would be placed before us with this or that malady, we would instruct the mother on the care or prevention of such a sickness. All of the crowd sitting before the open doors on the porch would listen attentively to what we would say. They were eager to learn. They do not wish to be miserable. . . .

Every week Chinese came down from the Yunnan and Canton. They were really political refugees. . . . The refugees I remember with the most tenderness is an old couple who came all the way from Canton. We took care of them, gave them blankets, medicines, and "*Ya mi henh.*" The Governor gave them a small hut not too far from his. Weeks later this old Chinese came to our house and gave me a gift. As I was a mandarin, for my size 11-C feet he had made a pair of black cloth Chinese shoes about size seven.

A very rich Chinese once came down from Muong Sing, on the Burma border. He brought his attractive fifteen-year-old daughter who was cursed with a huge harelip. We repaired her and after her discharge from the ward, they disappeared into the underbelly of China. The Chao Khuong claims that he was a Red Chinese Army Officer. All we know is that he was very co-operative and most appreciative of what the Americans had done for his daughter. We transformed her from a somewhat hideous little girl to a very acceptable one. I think it will be more difficult for him to hate us now. . . .

Our surgery was just about as busy as any operating room of comparable size in the States. We once had a young man who had been hacking bamboo from the jungle to be used in building his home.

His large machete-like knife hit a green bamboo and skewered off it, slicing deeply into his ankle. He severed most of his Achilles' tendon, with only a little bleeding. He was brought to us, and we were able to approximate the tendon ends and the sheath, and cast him in an extended position. Many months later we saw him, and he had regained nearly complete control of his leg. . . .

Just a few days later we had had a mail delivery from America and I had received one of the most touching letters I believe ever written. It was from a woman who said that she was "dying" from bone cancer but "no one tells me so." She said that the excruciating deep agony in her leg and arm bones was a great cross for her to endure. But she said that she was glad she had pain because she wanted to offer it to God in order to gain grace for "people like you boys." To me it was the power of her prayers that gave us sufficient talent, time and medicines to effect a cure for a little lad with shattered bones.

We repaired a lot of harelips. It is not any more common in Laos than anywhere else, but the problem is that the word spread around the mountains that the white medical team could cure this congenital defect. . . .

Chai once told me that he had been in the market place and heard a child describing an operation. This child was born with a hideous harelip. He was thirteen before the white doctor came to his village. The parents brought him to us immediately, and we scheduled him for surgery. The operation had good results and the only remains of the huge defect was a small line scar. With much ado he was telling his companions of the procedure. "The white witch doctor, the tall one who talks so fast, told his assistants to pick me up. The two assistant witch doctors put me on that long table that they have over in their hospital hut. Then one of the assistants put some sort of charm over my face that looked like a piece of cloth. Then they dripped some horrible sweet smelling magical liquid on my nose. I almost vomited but was soon transported somewhere else, like in a dream. I don't remember anything, but later I woke up in another one of their huts. My family was around, and they had a small piece of metal for me to look in. I saw my face like I can see it re-flected in the clear river. The white doctor had pulled my upper lip shut and sewed it up like my mother stitches her sarong. Mother says that she watched them through the window and that I bled all over the place. They collected it in pieces of material and put it all in buckets on the floor. My face was no longer my old face, but a new face just as you see it now. Strange, these white men."

We had no electricity, therefore no X-ray was available. Fractured arms and legs were set by the touch alone. Plenty of plaster and buckets of prayers, and these fractures healed adequately. . . .

The physical layout of our living in Nam Tha was better than Vang Vieng. But it had to be because the circumstances in which we lived were ten times worse. Nam Tha was a village in medieval times. It was a constant task to keep our house in "livable condition." We had constantly to repaint, rescrub and rebuild. One afternoon a whole lower side of the wall fell out. These walls are made from woven bamboo, then a mixture like wattle is made from cow dung, rice straw, betel juice, lime, and some other ingredients known only to God and the natives. This paste is then spread on each side of the bamboo. The overall effect is sort of a smelly adobe.

Many say that the Lao are a lazy people. From my experience of living like a Lao, in a hut like his own, I am of the opinion that this is not true. Let me mention a few things a man must do. He must forge the iron, and make and repair his plow, carving the shaft and yoke himself. He must constantly rebuild a new harrow and blade. He must repair his house, weave new walls, cut thatch for the roof, repair the tools of the kitchen. He must keep his cart, feed his oxen, make rope and fiber. He must make hemp and weave the nets, then fish for his meals. He must build his loom so his wife and daughter can weave. But first he must grow, gin, mill and dye the cotton. He must care for the sick buffalo, cultivate his fields, practice his religion, and raise chickens, ducks, and grow a garden. This man is not lazy.

He may be ignorant, but a merely well-informed man is the most useless bore on God's earth. The Lao man has culture, and expert knowledge in a specific direction; narrow to be sure, but nevertheless, deep. . . .

One of the few visitors we ever had in Nam Tha was a woman. Her name was Marion Dix, a lecturer and photographer from Hollywood. She had heard of our work and had done documentary films on Operation Brotherhood, on Viet Nam, and other parts of Southeast Asia. She wrote and asked if she could come to our place. Months later when she received the answer in the affirmative, it took her only a few weeks to arrive in Nam Tha.

Most people were fearful of visiting Dooley. Many fluttering females would never have thought of boondogging it into Nam Tha. Many American men would take no chance on being so close to the Chinese border, with a chance of becoming marooned. But plucky Marion Dix left her chromeplated Hollywood and, in slacks and a halter, arrived at the airstrip with a hundred pounds of cameras. She stayed with us over a week. I told Marion that we thought she was a great gal. To come all the way to Nam Tha was risky enough, but to come during the monsoon season was doubly dangerous. We apologized for her being forced to live in a houseful of men. She answered, "Why, this is what every woman dreams of!" She said that while cooking our dinner, so you see 'twas good to have a woman around the house. . . .

We were always being thrown from one extreme to the other. We would behave for a few minutes like stateside Americans and this was fun. Then suddenly some horror would make us again painfully aware of the rim of hell upon which we were balanced. . . .

Four Thai Dam men arrived in Nam Tha in near exhaustion. They had two stout bamboo poles on their shoulders between them and hanging from this was a roughly made litter. On top was a thin mattress and nearly hidden beneath cotton blankets was a headful of hair and the haggard gaunt face of a young boy. His friends and his brother had carried this boy down from a village several days away. They managed to get this crude-looking stretcher across the mountains and through the valley. They set the pitiful load before the hospital and we went out to examine the child. The first thing we noticed was how horribly infested he was with lice. He had head lice in his hair and scabies over all of his body. As we pulled the cloth blankets off of him, we saw a horrible sight. This boy looked like a man recently released from Dachau. His whole body was contorted with pain and frozen in this twisted position. He had a deep muscle infection of the left leg and had had this for a long time. Because he lay on his mat of a bed and never moved, all the rest of his body wasted away, atrophied. His left leg, the good leg, was no bigger around in the thigh than my wrist is. His knee was swollen and infected and the thigh and calf muscles looked like the meat on frog legs. He had several huge bed sores on his spine and back. He was so filthy that even as he lay there the ever-present flies started to crawl over his face, around his lips and into his eyes and ears. His brother kept constantly brushing these hideous creatures off him.

We agreed to keep the boy, Nai, in the hospital but the first thing we demanded was that he go down to the river and be thoroughly scrubbed up. Reed Carnrick Pharmaceutical House in New Jersey had sent us a shampoo called Kwell which kills body lice immediately. They also sent some ointment which, upon one application, will clear up a severe case of scabies. After a thorough washing with soap for the first time in his life, we finally admitted him into the ward.

The next morning my boys constructed an orthopedic bed. This consisted of a stout bed with teakwood posts around it and a frame overhead. From this frame a trapeze bar was hung. The antibiotics along with surgical incision and drainage cleared up the infection in a few days. The fight was now physiotherapy. Nai had many months of exercise ahead of him. We taught him how to do various exercises which would help to restore his muscle strength. His heel tendons were almost frozen in a position which made his toe point straight out, and he could not flex his foot upwards. His younger brother stayed at the hospital and cared for him. This youngster learned how to do all of the exercises and spent most of his day passively moving his brother's arms and legs. He also kept urging Nai to do it himself, actively. I believe it would behoove divorce-ridden America to learn of the devotion to family that exists amongst the primitive people.

Months later on a cane that his brother had made for him, Nai could stand at the side of his bed. Soon he walked around the bed though clutching at the wooden frame. Later he could get across the ward, and one day he called to me. He had walked across the compound and stood before us at the main building as proud as any boy in the world could be. And we were proud of him too. Nai had conquered his disease and with his own guts he overcame his muscle atrophy. A few weeks later the boy who had come to us near death returned to his village. He held his head high, walked straight and well, and was dressed in American khakis wearing blooming good health.

The force of kindness and love exhibited by my boys and by his brother redeemed Nai from ugliness and tragedy. The greatest bond among nations is faith in this force. An Asian brother and some American helpers, both taking care of a stricken lad, taught him how to walk again. Kindness is close to God and disarms man the quickest. You will never find this boy nor his brothers fighting against an American. They will remember us, with love.

AND NOW TO LIVE AGAIN

—————— Betsey Barton ——————

What of the people who have been injured in war or accident? What
of those born with disabilities which prevent them from leading normal
lives? How are they to face their handicaps and find the courage to go on?
Those who have gone through such disasters and have developed a
new philosophy of life can speak of such questions with a knowledge no
uninjured person can have. Betsey Barton is such a person. At the age
of sixteen she had great beauty, high intelligence and all the advantages
which her famous father, Bruce Barton, was able to give her. Then
came an automobile accident in which her back was broken. For months
she lay in hospital beds, while every weapon of medical science was
brought to bear on her case. The situation was hopeless and she remained permanently paralyzed. Even when the pain began to lessen and
she was able to use a wheelchair, her will to live was almost dead. And
then slowly, with infinite agony of spirit, she returned to life, to find, in
her own words, that "wisdom and vision are granted to few, and the
few who gain these do so . . . in the degree that they suffer."
Betsey Barton has lived a satisfying life—not the life she would have
lived if she had not been injured, but a life made up in part of service
to those in similar plight. Here is her own practical guide for the disabled
and for the family and friends who love them.

THERE are, it seems to me, two tragic facts in human existence: We
do not appreciate what we have until we lose it. And we only advance
through suffering.

A man must indeed lose his life to find it—to appreciate what he
has lost more fully. And we are awakened and sensitized to the
beauty and preciousness of life, to the mysterious and implacable
rules by which it was planned for us by a guiding spirit, only through
suffering.

I would have denied both these facts not so long ago. I would have
said that one man can learn by another's experience. I would have
said that suffering did not lead to anything but despair and death.
My circle of suffering has completed its full turn, however. And I
see now that the reason the advance of the human race seems so pain-

fully slow, the reason it seems to be of so little use to study history, is because we cannot learn by example: we must learn by direct experience.

Each generation must go through the same struggles and pitfalls as the one before. No generation can blame another. We can only wait our turn at the helm of the world-ship and pass on our inadequate charts to the quicker eyes and hands of those who follow. Wisdom and vision are granted to few, and the few that gain these do so, I have come to believe, in the degree that they are sensitive, in the degree that they suffer.

It is for this reason that the salvaging of the life of one who has been badly hurt is so important. Here is the raw stuff of wisdom and of vision. Too often it is allowed to dwindle into bitterness and failure because of ignorance. Yet if the salvage work is successful, it is like assisting at a birth, a rebirth.

The growth must be guided by skilled workers and good advice, by understanding, and by love. And when the job is completed, the person who was denied, the person who lost and fell behind in the race with the others, will, like the tortoise, come out ahead. For he will have grown in vision. He will know the value of what he has lost and of what he has dared to regain. And, through his new and wiser eyes, he will see that although he lost one life, he has won a new life that in many delicate and tender ways is a far better one.

Had I read this years ago when first I lost the use of my legs I would have thrown down the book in disgust. I was not ready then for any such philosophical phrases. There seemed to be no existing compensation for a boy who has lost a leg, for a child who is born a spastic, for the man who has tuberculosis, or for a girl who cannot move her hand. Yet it has been pressed in upon me that the power which created us, provided for this, too: for faith in the face of despair, for courage in the face of loss, and for tenderness in the face of hopelessness. We are never, we cannot be, left alone. We are taken care of, if we allow ourselves to be, and the law of compensation is a fact. He who loses his life, can find it, in the fullest and most complete sense of the word "find."

If you have a son, or a husband, or a friend, who has suddenly joined the ranks of the invalid, you are privileged. Through them you can watch this process of rebirth take place. You can assist it, or hinder it; you can gain insight into your own education. Just as the study of the insane helps us to understand our own behavior more clearly, because we see ourselves and our behavior dramatized and distorted, so will the study of and participation in the re-education of a person who has been suddenly hurt, help you to understand yourself. For here, in exaggerated and visible form, is bared the fretwork of human character in the making under pressure. Hidden resources will be tapped. People who seemed weak before may suddenly appear strong. The heroic, stubborn will to survive raises its impressive head. And some who long for death will not die because of this instinct, which is stronger than ourselves, and that pulls us through sickness and shock long after our conscious striving has ceased.

The dread effects of disaster and disease are a constant in all of human life. The agony my parents suffered over my accidents was sharper than my own. I know this now. For the spirit that created us steps in again here and at first the shock is so great it anesthetizes. We who recently suffered the blow of disaster do not feel it or understand its consequences. We are saved from apprehension by the force of the thing that struck us down, but those who stand beside us are not so preserved. They can assess the strength of the blow and look ahead to its consequences, and they suffer more for us than we do ourselves because there is nothing they can do at first to alleviate our hurt.

When I look back I see my parents waiting helplessly in the anterooms of hospitals time and again while I was wheeled by them on a stretcher, a still, white, unconscious figure, going up into the mysteries of dreaded places to remain for long hours while the doctors did necessary things to me in the name of healing. Those times were not hard for me. I was carefully taken care of, preserved from pain. But the suffering of my parents while they waited for the elevator doors to open and for the long stretcher to emerge was very great. They knew what the operations entailed. They knew what was at stake.

The things that were done for me, endlessly—they come back now. They come tumbling through the years that have gone and buried them over. I remember a little yellow canary my father bought that he placed in the hospital window, to help while the hours away. The canary was a stout fellow and he sat there in the only shaft of sunlight that struck the room through the canyon of the tall buildings outside. He stood on his perch and shouted his heart out for me. And I did not notice.

Someone thought to give me some pet fish. Exotic and tiny they were, silver and vermilion with wide fan tails. They swam beside the bed there in their high, complicated tank. They swam and ate and mated and died. They flirted with me and invited me to look. And I did not notice.

All the things. The special pillows that were bought. The ideas for meals to tempt my shrunken appetite. The books and friends and things arranged. All these come tumbling back now. I had not thought of them for years. But I accepted them all, I think, and sighed and turned away.

How can we be gentle enough to these, the fallen? How can we start to win them back to some belief? How can we, while they lie or sit or stand in our homes, so different? So much the same; so still and weak.

I try to remember how it was with me, so I can tell you now. But nothing comes except time. Time, and days passing. And time again and days passing. Time in which the wounds healed, and the muscles once more held me when I tried to sit up. And time passing once more before the deep scars in the mind began to knit and draw together, before the bitterness receded and the negative, detached feeling lifted. For before I could get well, I had to be taught to care again.

And love here must have a greater love for the hurt one than that of the immediate attachment. It must be wise, it must look ahead. For here is a beaten thing. Something in it has died. And we do not want to suffocate it with too much offered it yet, as the small, tender plant is killed by the noonday sun. Yet we must try to reach out again and again, as they did with me so long ago, try to reach out and create appetites where there is no appetite for anything. Create the appetite for doing a little more, for wanting a little more strength, a little more activity. Create it and then feed it. And never give food that is too strong meat for the weak-tea capacity, but create the hunger, and give it food in accord with the smallness of its need.

Disaster doesn't prepare us. Or if it would prepare, we do not heed the warnings. The soldier in battle sees his comrades fall and is still convinced that he will be safe, until the constant fire and the long time without adequate food and sleep wears his resistance to the ragged edge, and he begins to suspect that every shell has his name written on it. Our friends are hit by a drunken driver, or their child is struck by infantile paralysis—but these things do not happen to us. We are safe, somehow caught in the miraculous fallacy of the human race, the assurance that we are guarded, that it is all right to cross the street carelessly where many have been killed because we are secure, we have a lucky star.

When disaster comes, then, depriving us of an arm, or a leg, or twisting the muscles into uselessness, the reaction must be hard.

The swift plunge from one life to another, the exchange of one costume for another in the dressing-room of Time—this was too quick. It cannot help but fill the victim with dismay, especially if he was used to a normal healthy life before. I do not know for those born into a different, abnormal body. I can only look, as you can, and enter into their lives through the penetrating key of imagination. But I know this: the swift exchange of a once normal body for an impaired, abnormal one is very hard.

The memories are there, you see. The memories of laughter and of running in the wind, of climbing hill-tops, of walking through the dim and smoky afternoon of a New England fall. Of scrunching to the waves' edge upon the beach's stretch—memories of ease, of light, swift motion, of speed, of grace, of perfect co-ordination. And the memories cannot be denied at first. They crowd and cluster in each cell of earth and air, of fire and water, that compose the body shell. They crowd and cluster and jostle and mock. They are loud, these memories, blatant.

The memories have their use, however. They can be used as a bridge into the new life. There need be nothing wasted or lost in all of our experience. There is an economy within the body-mind that can be valuable, that can be turned into coin of the realm—if we run into the right economist. The memories can act as the bridge to recovery in this way:

The nurse takes the withered leg of the child who has just had infantile in her hand and puts it through the motions of bending and straightening. She says to the child as she does it: "Remember how it was when you could do this for yourself. Use those memories in the muscles there. Remember that."

Dr. Earl Carlson, who was born a spastic and who has overcome his disease to a great extent, adds evidence on this. In his book he writes of a young baseball player who had been ill with sleeping sickness. He came to Carlson for help and stood inertly upon the lawn of his house, unable to think straight, unable to move. Someone picked up a baseball and shouted and threw the ball straight at the young man. And, suddenly, his right arm shot out and caught the ball and his body swung into the graceful, easy pose of the pitcher as he sped the ball back to the man who had thrown it, then he stood still, once more inert. But the memories were there and they responded.

We are trained in the business of life as animals are trained: by the whip and the sugar. As we advance into life we learn to avoid those things which give us pain and center ourselves around those which give us pleasure. Pain is the great teacher. We rarely let pleasure teach us; we prefer to learn by pain.

Prolonged pain can destroy our morale; it can reduce us to the level of beasts. And the pressure of painful circumstance does not necessarily make men of character rise where there were none before. If a man would find strength and courage in himself, he does not have to go out and lose a foot, or an arm, or undergo war shock. Nor does the wounded man necessarily become a saint through his painful readjustment to a new life. He can and has become a total failure, a professional charity case.

There are those rare few who readjust immediately to their new life, who assess what has happened to them, and accepting it, forge ahead. Such a one is Major Seversky, who lost a leg in the last war. He writes:

Increasingly despair receded. What remained was a great challenge to everything that was strongest in my character. Somehow the loss of a leg made the life ahead of me more exciting than ever. It added dimensions of satisfaction to the things I was determined to do . . . things which were ordinary, routine and commonplace for other people would now be haloed with excitement and thrill for me by reason of my handicap.

The extreme pressures working on all of us today will probably mold us into extremes. We will become either heroes or cowards. There may be little in between. There is a certain amount of predestination in us; we must carry some of the seeds of what will happen to us within us at the time of birth. And since most of us take no conscious charge of our character development, but let it run or ravel as it will, we will react as badly or as well to our re-education as the seeds within our characters enable us.

Every autobiography or biography is the record of someone who succeeded in the face of disability, in the face of handicap. Poverty, greed, pride, vanity, shyness, selfishness—are these not handicaps? If a man succeeds in becoming whole, he succeeds in spite of these as much as we succeed in spite of any physical hurt. Our lives are what we make them.

As we advance along the road we find that the freedom we are obtaining comes at a high price. And throughout the paying we find the symbiotic thread, the double requirement for our new life: the help of ourselves by ourselves and the help of ourselves by others.

In winning our way to this freedom, the first of these must always be the most important. The love and help of others can only strengthen our courage to help ourselves. And when the shock of disaster is over and we are ready to start life again, we will find that what we make of the remaining fragments of ourselves is up to us alone. And in this firing of the raw materials of our broken selves into some sort of tolerable whole, we will get exactly what we have had the courage and the persistence to earn. We will win what we have the courage to fashion as the crucible for our minds and hearts, the crucible in which we still must have our being.

The first part of the freedom we are winning and have won must be the freedom from fear. We had many new fears thrust upon us by the disaster and we discovered many more within us as we took up the tools to start along the way. All the little things—the gaining of strength and health, the meeting of social situations, the small victories over facing children, over fatigue, over the awkwardnesses in our living skill—lead us gently, as we are successful, out of fear into faith. Each time we win our fight over some small thing, each time do we add that much strength to our faith. The treatment of the mind and body and heart as a whole, their nourishment, aid in overcoming the fears and adding to our faith. We must have works in order to have faith in anything, at first. We begin to be healed because we have found something that works, that adds to our healing. And we lose our fear as we begin to believe in the tools of our reeducation, tested by experience and found to hold true.

The new fears which rushed in on us, and which continue to come and go as we progress along this road, are met each day by our accumulating weight of faith, faith that we *can do*, faith that there is a way to independence which we can make endless use of now that we have been shown how, faith that we are not finished, faith in ourselves.

Fear is the great bogey of mankind. It is doubtful that any of us except the most wise and saintly are ever free of it altogether. And fear in those of us who have fallen in some way, who are crushed by disaster, must be an even stronger thing. But if our own effort and the guidance of those who are wise in re-education continue hand in hand, then we can not help accumulating a well of faith from which we can draw until we are able, finally, to meet any new fears completely by ourselves.

When I was exercising in front of my teacher one day I stood on my head for the first time. It thrilled me, and I tumbled down and laughed up at him. "I'm beginning to believe I can do anything with my body," I said.

"That's a sign that you can," he answered me.

"Is this faith?" I asked, curiously.

"Yes," he said. "And the more sure you are that you *can* do, the quicker it will come."

The faith I gained at first was so small, so dependent on the works of my re-education, that I earned the vision of what I could become slowly and over long weeks of work. I came to believe that my faith was a frail thing, demanding a great deal of sweat and tears, and giving in return no stunning rewards of merit.

I was working, as we all must work, in hope, in blind faith, in the dark. No signs that my faith was justified had yet shown themselves, and this was to be true for many months. But as the faith within me grew with the success of my effort, I found the fears within me presented by new situations, or by nightmare visions, to be growing less. I had some little measure of strength now with which to fight them down.

This then, perhaps, is the first signpost along the road of re-education, the first little sign that we are getting well: when we begin to be released, to a degree, from the terrors of both the known and the unknown that have persistently dogged us.

The second move toward freedom must be the beginning of freedom from self. We were plunged into ourselves by the force of the disaster. For many weeks, while we were whirled by fever and pain and sleepless nights and seeing our families again for the first time in awkward situations, we spent much time shrunk within ourselves, rallying all our forces to overcome the rising, spreading, suffocating sense of this new self which we inhabited. We could not look outside the pale and shaken walls within which we lived. We retreated from feeling, from reaching out to others, because we had been hurt and were afraid that in our reaching out now we would be hurt again.

Somewhere, in the early days of my recovery, I wrote: "As I look back now, I see that my dead legs were, in their way, bad enough. But worse than that, a death crept up through my body until it took my heart. The death of the legs had been accident, but this was a deliberated death, a cultivated one; I retreated from feeling. I shut it off. I asked myself not to feel because feeling hurt too much."

We must step out, away, forward, leaving what we thought the greatest pain we knew for a new unknown pain, which may be twice as great. Advance comes at great price, but not to advance exacts a greater price; it ends in death.

As we reach out of ourselves in our new faith and self-giving, we find freedom and release growing stronger. The walls of our self-made prison slide back and expose the widening and growing vision. And the road is traveled more quickly when we work with others like ourselves, for here indeed is our chance to give of ourselves, to expand out of the tight ego in helping others, to learn from their experiences and to add all that we can from ours to smooth and make easier their way.

The third landmark in freedom's road must come finally in the growing freedom from the fear of want. When we are able at last to undertake our job training and to go out and find work, the road to freedom seems almost complete.

We have overcome our major fears; we are learning to be free of the paralyzing self-consciousness and self-centeredness which all inward conflicts demanding the total regimentation of all our forces must bring. We are allowing ourselves to feel, perhaps to love, and to be loved in return. We have, as far as possible, helped others like ourselves to learn to walk or to find some confidence in themselves. And now we have a job.

Re-education seems complete. Freedom from fear, from self, from want. There remains yet another freedom to be obtained, however, before the road is done: freedom of spirit, freedom within.

And this is the most important freedom of all.

From THE STORY OF MY LIFE

Helen Keller

There was another woman whose handicap seemed in the beginning to be even more nearly insurmountable than that of Betsey Barton. As everyone knows, Helen Keller, at the age of nineteen months, suffered an attack of scarlet fever which left her totally blind and deaf. Barely past infancy, she had no way of entering the normal world, nor of appreciating its richness and beauty. Yet this was the child who later learned to speak, who graduated from Radcliffe, who wrote books and poems and words of comfort to the afflicted and who, later in life, was honored with a degree from a great English university. She herself was unable to hear the deafening applause as she took this degree. The growth of her mind and soul is an example of courage in adversity which all the world has come to admire. Indeed, as this is written a play about her and her teacher Anne Sullivan, The Miracle Worker, is playing to packed houses on Broadway. Here is her own description of her first stumbling steps toward achievement.

✍

THE most important day I remember in all my life is the one on which my teacher, Anne Mansfield Sullivan, came to me. I am filled with wonder when I consider the immeasurable contrast between the two lives which it connects. It was the third of March, 1887, three months before I was seven years old.

On the afternoon of that eventful day, I stood on the porch, dumb, expectant. I guessed vaguely from my mother's signs and from the hurrying to and fro in the house that something unusual was about to happen, so I went to the door and waited on the steps. The afternoon sun penetrated the mass of honeysuckle that covered the porch, and fell on my upturned face. My fingers lingered almost unconsciously on the familiar leaves and blossoms which had just come forth to greet the sweet southern spring. I did not know what the future held of marvel or surprise for me. Anger and bitterness had preyed upon me continually for weeks and a deep languor had succeeded this passionate struggle.

"Light! give me light!" was the wordless cry of my soul, and the light of love shone on me in that very hour. I felt approaching foot-

125

steps. I stretched out my hand as I supposed to my mother. Someone took it, and I was caught up and held close in the arms of her who had come to reveal all things to me, and, more than all things else, to love me.

The morning after my teacher came she led me into her room and gave me a doll. The little blind children at the Perkins Institution had sent it and Laura Bridgman had dressed it; but I did not know this until afterward. When I had played with it a little while, Miss Sullivan slowly spelled into my hand the word "d-o-l-l." I was at once interested in this finger play and tried to imitate it. When I finally succeeded in making the letters correctly I was flushed with childish pleasure and pride. Running downstairs to my mother I held up my hand and made the letters for doll. I did not know that I was spelling a word or even that words existed; I was simply making my fingers go in monkey-like imitation. In the days that followed I learned to spell in this uncomprehending way a great many words, among them *pin*, *hat, cup,* and a few verbs like *sit, stand* and *walk.* But my teacher had been with me several weeks before I understood that everything has a name.

One day, while I was playing with my new doll, Miss Sullivan put my big rag doll into my lap also, spelled "d-o-l-l" and tried to make me understand that "d-o-l-l" applied to both. Earlier in the day we had a tussle over the words "m-u-g" and "w-a-t-e-r." Miss Sullivan had tried to impress it upon me that "m-u-g" is *mug* and that "w-a-t-e-r" is *water,* but I persisted in confounding the two. In despair she had dropped the subject for the time, only to renew it at the first opportunity. I became impatient at her repeated attempts and, seizing the new doll, I dashed it upon the floor. I was keenly delighted when I felt the fragments of the broken doll at my feet. Neither sorrow nor regret followed my passionate outburst. I had not loved the doll. In the still, dark world in which I lived there was no strong sentiment or tenderness. I felt my teacher sweep the fragments to one side of the hearth, and I had a sense of satisfaction that the cause of my discomfort was removed. She brought me my hat, and I knew I was going out into the warm sunshine. This thought, if a wordless sensation may be called a thought, made me hop and skip with pleasure.

We walked down the path to the well-house, attracted by the fragrance of the honeysuckle with which it was covered. Someone was drawing water and my teacher placed my hand under the spout. As the cool stream gushed over one hand she spelled into the other the word *water*, first slowly then rapidly. I stood still, my whole attention fixed upon the motions of her fingers. Suddenly I felt a misty consciousness as of something forgotten—a thrill of returning thought; and somehow the mystery of language was revealed to me. I knew then that "w-a-t-e-r" meant the wonderful cool something that was flowing over my hand. That living word awakened my soul, gave it light, hope, joy, set it free! There were barriers still, it is true, but barriers that could in time be swept away.

I left the well-house eager to learn. Everything had a name, and each name gave birth to a new thought. As we returned to the house every object which I touched seemed to quiver with life. That was because I saw everything with the strange, new sight that had come to me. On entering the door I remembered the doll I had broken. I felt my way to the hearth and picked up the pieces. I tried vainly to put them together. Then my eyes filled with tears; for I realized what I had done, and for the first time I felt repentance and sorrow.

I learned a great many new words that day. I do not remember what they all were; but I do know that *mother, father, sister, teacher* were among them—words that were to make the world blossom for me, "like Aaron's rod, with flowers." It would have been difficult to find a happier child than I was as I lay in my crib at the close of that eventful day and lived over the joys it had brought me, and for the first time longed for a new day to come.

I had now the key to all language, and I was eager to learn to use it. Children who hear acquire language without any particular effort; the words that fall from others' lips they catch on the wing, as it were, delightedly, while the little deaf child must trap them by a slow and often painful process. But whatever the process, the result is wonderful. Gradually from naming an object we advance step by step until we have traversed the vast distance between our first stammered syllable and the sweep of thought in a line of Shakespeare.

At first, when my teacher told me about a new thing I asked very few questions. My ideas were vague, and my vocabulary was inadequate; but as my knowledge of things grew, and I learned more and more words, my field of inquiry broadened, and I would return again and again to the same subject, eager for further information. Sometimes a new word revived an image that some earlier experience had engraved on my brain.

I remember the morning that I first asked the meaning of the word, "love." This was before I knew many words. I had found a few early violets in the garden and brought them to my teacher. She tried to kiss me; but at that time I did not like to have anyone kiss me except my mother. Miss Sullivan put her arm gently round me and spelled into my hand, "I love Helen."

"What is love?" I asked.

She drew me closer to her and said, "It is here," pointing to my heart, whose beats I was conscious of for the first time. Her words puzzled me very much because I did not then understand anything unless I touched it.

I smelt the violets in her hand and asked, half in words, half in signs, a question which meant, "Is love the sweetness of flowers?"

"No," said my teacher.

Again I thought. The warm sun was shining on us.

"Is this not love?" I asked, pointing in the direction from which the heat came, "Is this not love?"

It seemed to me that there could be nothing more beautiful than the sun, whose warmth makes all things grow. But Miss Sullivan shook her head, and I was greatly puzzled and disappointed. I thought it strange that my teacher could not show me love.

A day or two afterward I was stringing beads of different sizes in symmetrical groups—two large beads, three small ones, and so on. I had made many mistakes, and Miss Sullivan had pointed them out again and again with gentle patience. Finally I noticed a very obvious error in the sequence and for an instant I concentrated my attention on the lesson and tried to think how I should have arranged the beads. Miss Sullivan touched my forehead and spelled with decided emphasis, "Think."

In a flash I knew that the word was the name of the process that was going on in my head. This was my first conscious perception of an abstract idea.

For a long time I was still—I was not thinking of the beads in my lap, but trying to find a meaning for "love" in the light of this new idea. The sun had been under a cloud all day, and there had been brief showers; but suddenly the sun broke forth in all its southern splendor.

Again I asked my teacher, "Is this not love?"

"Love is something like the clouds that were in the sky before the sun came out," she replied. Then in simpler words than these, which at that time I could not have understood, she explained: "You cannot touch the clouds, you know, but you feel the rain and know how glad the flowers and the thirsty earth are to have it after a hot day. You cannot touch love either; but you feel the sweetness that it pours into everything. Without love you would not be happy or want to play."

The beautiful truth burst upon my mind—I felt that there were invisible lines stretched between my spirit and the spirits of others.

From the beginning of my education Miss Sullivan made it a practice to speak to me as she would speak to any hearing child; the only difference was that she spelled the sentences into my hand instead of speaking them. If I did not know the words and idioms necessary to express my thoughts she supplied them, even suggesting conversation when I was unable to keep up my end of the dialogue.

The next important step in my education was learning to read.

As soon as I could spell a few words my teacher gave me slips of cardboard on which were printed words in raised letters. I quickly learned that each printed word stood for an object, an act, or a quality. I had a frame in which I could arrange the words in little sentences; but before I ever put sentences in the frame I used to make them in objects. I found the slips of paper which represented, for example, "doll," "is," "on," "bed" and placed each name on its object; then I put my doll on the bed with the words *is, on, bed* arranged beside the doll, thus making a sentence of the words, and at the same time carrying out the idea of the sentence with the things themselves.

One day, Miss Sullivan tells me, I pinned the word *girl* on my pinafore and stood in the wardrobe. On the shelf I arranged the words, *is, in, wardrobe*. Nothing delighted me so much as this game. My teacher and I played it for hours at a time. Often everything in the room was arranged in object sentences.

From the printed slip it was but a step to the printed book. I took my *Reader for Beginners* and hunted for the words I knew; when I found them my joy was like that of a game of hide-and-seek. Thus I began to read. Even when I studied most earnestly it seemed more like play than work. Everything Miss Sullivan taught me she illustrated by a beautiful story or a poem. Whenever anything delighted or interested me she talked it over with me just as if she were a little girl herself. What many children think of with dread, as a painful plodding through grammar, hard sums and harder definitions, is today one of my most precious memories.

I cannot explain the peculiar sympathy Miss Sullivan had with my pleasures and desires. Perhaps it was the result of long association with the blind. Added to this she had a wonderful faculty for description. She went quickly over uninteresting details, and never nagged me with questions to see if I remembered the day-before-yesterday's lesson. She introduced dry technicalities of science little by little, making every subject so real that I could not help remembering what she taught.

We read and studied out of doors, preferring the sunlit woods to the house. All my early lessons have in them the breath of the woods—the fine, resinous odor of pine needles, blended with the perfume of wild grapes. Seated in the gracious shade of a wild tulip tree, I learned to think that everything has a lesson and a suggestion. "The loveliness of things taught me all their use." Indeed, everything that could hum, or buzz, or sing, or bloom, had a part in my education—noisy-throated frogs, katydids and crickets held in my hand until, forgetting their embarrassment, they trilled their reedy note, little downy chickens and wildflowers, the dogwood blossoms, meadow-violets and budding fruit trees. I felt the bursting cottonbolls and fingered their soft fiber and fuzzy seeds; I felt the low soughing of the wind through the cornstalks, the silky rustling of the long leaves, and the indignant snort of my pony, as we caught him in the pasture and put the bit in his mouth—ah me! how well I remember the spicy, clovery smell of his breath!

Arithmetic seems to have been the only study I did not like. From the first I was not interested in the science of numbers. Miss Sullivan tried to teach me to count by stringing beads in groups, and by arranging kindergarten straws I learned to add and subtract. I never had patience to arrange more than five or six groups at a time. When I had accomplished this my conscience was at rest for the day, and I went out quickly to find my playmates.

In this same leisurely manner I studied zoology and botany.

Once a gentleman, whose name I have forgotten, sent me a collection of fossils—tiny mollusk shells beautifully marked, and bits of sandstone with the print of birds' claws, and a lovely fern in bas-relief. These were the keys which unlocked the treasures of the antediluvian world for me. With trembling fingers I listened to Miss Sullivan's descriptions of the terrible beasts, with uncouth, unpronounceable names, which once went tramping through the primeval forests, tearing down the branches of gigantic trees for food, and died in the dismal swamps of an unknown age. For a long time these strange creatures haunted my dreams, and this gloomy period formed a somber background to the joyous Now, filled with sunshine and roses and echoing with the gentle beat of my pony's hoof.

Another time a beautiful shell was given me, and with a child's surprise and delight I learned how a tiny mollusk had built the lustrous coil for his dwelling place, and how on still nights, when there is no breeze stirring the waves, the Nautilus sails on the blue waters of the Indian Ocean in his "ship of pearl." After I had learned a great many interesting things about the life and habits of the children of the sea—how in the midst of dashing waves the little polyps build the beautiful coral isles of the Pacific, and the foraminifera have made the chalk-hills of many a land—my teacher read me "The Chambered Nautilus," and showed me that the shell-building process of the mollusks is symbolical of the development of the mind. Just as the wonder-working mantle of the Nautilus changes the material it absorbs from the water and makes it a part of itself, so the bits of knowledge one gathers undergo a similar change and become pearls of thought.

Once there were eleven tadpoles in a glass globe set in a window full of plants. I remember the eagerness with which I made discoveries about them. It was great fun to plunge my hand into the bowl and feel the tadpoles frisk about, and to let them slip and slide between my fingers. One day a more ambitious fellow leaped beyond the edge of the bowl and fell on the floor, where I found him to all appearance more dead than alive. The only sign of life was a slight wriggling of his tail. But no sooner had he returned to his element than he darted to the bottom, swimming round and round in joyous activity. He had made his leap, he had seen the great world, and was content to stay in his pretty glass house under the big fuchsia tree until he attained the dignity of froghood. Then he went to live in the leafy pool at the end of the garden, where he made the summer nights musical with his quaint love-song.

Thus I learned from life itself. At the beginning I was only a little mass of possibilities. It was my teacher who unfolded and developed them. When she came, everything about me breathed of love and joy and was full of meaning. She has never since let pass an opportunity to point out the beauty that is in everything, nor has she ceased trying in thought and action and example to make my life sweet and useful.

My teacher is so near to me that I scarcely think of myself apart from her. How much of my delight in all beautiful things is innate, and how much is due to her influence, I can never tell. I feel that her being is inseparable from my own, and that the footsteps of my life are in hers. All the best of me belongs to her—there is not a talent, or an aspiration or a joy in me that has not been awakened by her loving touch.

It was in the spring of 1890 that I learned to speak. The impulse to utter audible sounds had always been strong within me. I used to make noises, keeping one hand on my throat while the other hand felt the movements of my lips. I was pleased with anything that made a noise and liked to feel the cat purr and the dog bark. I also liked to keep my hand on a singer's throat, or on a piano when it was being played. Before I lost my sight and hearing, I was fast learning to talk, but after my illnesss it was found that I had ceased to speak because I could not hear. I used to sit in my mother's lap all day long and keep my hands on her face because it amused me to feel the motions of her lips; and I moved my lips, too, although I had forgotten what talking was. My friends say that I laughed and cried naturally, and for awhile I made many sounds and word-elements, not because they were a means of communication, but because the need of exercising my vocal organs was imperative. There was, however, one word the meaning of which I still remembered, *water*. I pronounced it "wa-wa." Even this became less and less intelligible until the time when Miss Sullivan began to teach me. I stopped using it only after I had learned to spell the word on my fingers.

In 1890 Mrs. Lamson, who had been one of Laura Bridgman's teachers, and who had just returned from a visit to Norway and Sweden, came to see me, and told me of Ragnhild Kaata, a deaf and blind girl in Norway who had actually been taught to speak. Mrs. Lamson had scarcely finished telling me about this girl's success before I was on fire with eagerness. I resolved that I, too, would learn to speak. I would not rest satisfied until my teacher took me, for advice and assistance, to Miss Sarah Fuller, principal of the Horace Mann School. This lovely, sweet-natured lady offered to teach me herself, and we began the twenty-sixth of March, 1890.

Miss Fuller's method was this: she passed my hand lightly over her face, and let me feel the position of her tongue and lips when she made a sound. I was eager to imitate every motion and in an hour had learned six elements of speech: M, P, A, S, T, I. Miss Fuller gave me eleven lessons in all. I shall never forget the surprise and delight I felt when I uttered my first connected sentence, "It is warm." True they were broken and stammering syllables but they were human speech. My soul, conscious of new strength, came out of bondage, and was reaching through those broken symbols of speech to all knowledge and all faith.

No deaf child who has earnestly tried to speak the words which he has never heard—to come out of the prison of silence, where no tone of love, no song of bird, no strain of music ever pierces the stillness—can forget the thrill of surprise, the joy of discovery which came over him when he uttered his first word. Only such a one can appreciate the eagerness with which I talked to my toys, to stones, trees, birds and dumb animals, or the delight I felt when at my call Mildred ran to me or my dogs obeyed my commands. It is an unspeakable boon to me to be able to speak in winged words that need no interpretation. As I talked, happy thoughts fluttered up out of my words that might perhaps have struggled in vain to escape my fingers.

But for Miss Sullivan's genius, untiring perseverance and devotion, I could not have progressed as far as I have toward natural speech. In the first place, I labored night and day before I could be understood even by my most intimate friends; in the second place, I needed Miss Sullivan's assistance constantly in my efforts to articulate each sound clearly and to combine all sounds in a thousand ways. Even now she calls my attention every day to mispronounced words.

All teachers of the deaf know what this means, and only they can at all appreciate the peculiar difficulties with which I had to contend. In reading my teacher's lips I was wholly dependent on my fingers; I had to use the sense of touch in catching the vibrations of the throat, the movements of the mouth and the expression of the face; and often this sense was at fault. In such cases I was forced to repeat the words or sentences, sometimes for hours, until I felt the proper ring in my own voice. My work was practice, practice,

practice. Discouragement and weariness cast me down frequently; but the next moment the thought that I should soon be at home and show my loved ones what I had accomplished, spurred me on, and I eagerly looked forward to their pleasure in my achievement.

"My little sister will understand me now," was a thought stronger than all obstacles. I used to repeat ecstatically, "I am not dumb now." I could not be despondent while I anticipated the delight of talking to my mother and reading her responses from her lips.

When I had made speech my own, I could not wait to go home. At last the happiest of happy moments arrived. I had made my homeward journey, talking constantly to Miss Sullivan, not for the sake of talking, but determined to improve to the last minute. Almost before I knew it, the train stopped at the Tuscumbia station, and there on the platform stood the whole family. My eyes fill with tears now as I think how my mother pressed me close to her, speechless and trembling with delight, taking in every syllable that I spoke, while little Mildred seized my free hand and kissed it and danced, and my father expressed his pride and affection in a big silence. It was as if Isaiah's prophecy had been fulfilled in me, "The mountains and the hills shall break forth before you into singing, and all the trees of the field shall clap their hands!"

THE TRIAL OF JOAN OF ARC

— From the Orléans Manuscript —

Most of us would say that courage in the face of certain death is the greatest courage of all. Certainly the world has given its fullest meed of admiration to those who, even at the very moment of death, have refused to bow before enemy man or enemy nature. Excepting only one other, the martyrdom of Joan of Arc is the most famous in the history of man. Who does not know the story of this Maid of Orléans, of her leadership of an army of France, of her capture by her enemies, of her trial by Frenchmen under the domination of the English, of her recantation and later affirmation of her beliefs, and of her final death at the stake? Here are brief excerpts from the verbatim day-by-day report of her trial and execution. Through the centuries comes an overpowering feeling of high drama—the cautious men-at-law, the frail and human, yet in the end indomitable, heroine, the inevitable tragedy, and the crowds speaking the universal hatred of oppression, "And many, both noble and peasant, murmured greatly against the English."

∽

The Public Admonition

THE same day Jeanne was brought before the judges in this trial. The bishop, in their presence, admonished her that she should follow the advice and admonitions which had been given to her by Maître Jean de Châtillon, doctor in theology, for the salvation both of her soul and her body, and if she were unwilling so to do, she would fall into grave danger both of body and soul.

And then the judges begged de Châtillon to proceed charitably to the said admonitions.

To which de Châtillon answered that he would gladly do so.

Firstly, he pointed out to her that all loyal Christians are obliged to believe and hold the articles of the Faith.

And he showed her the form and manner thereof, as she had previously been shown.

He then asked her whether she was willing to correct herself and amend her faults in accordance with the deliberation.

To which she answered: Read your book,

That is to say, the schedule which the bishop was holding.

And then I will answer you. I wait upon God my Creator in all. I love Him with all my heart.

Questioned as to whether she desires to answer to this general admonition,

She answered: I trust in my judge, that is the King of Heaven and earth.

She was then told: Formerly you said that your deeds were seen and cross-examined, as is contained in the schedule.

She answered that she gives the same answer now.

When it was explained to her what the Church Militant meant, and [she was] admonished to believe and hold the article *Unam Sanctam Ecclesiam*, etc., and to submit to the Church Militant,

She answered: I believe in the Church on earth; but for my deeds and words, as I have previously said, I refer the whole matter to God, Who caused me to do what I have done.

She said also that she submits to God her Creator, Who caused her to do what she did; and refers it to Him in His own Person.

Asked if she means that she has no judge on earth, and our Holy Father the Pope is not her judge,

She replied: I will tell you nothing else. I have a good Master, Our Lord, in Whom I trust for everything, and not in any other.

She was told that if she did not wish to believe in the Church and in the article *Ecclesiam Sanctam Catholicam*, she would be a heretic to uphold [her views], and that she would be punished by other judges who would sentence her to be burned.

She answered: I will tell you nothing else. And [even] if I saw the fire, I should tell you what I have told you, and nothing else.

The Threat of Torture

On the Wednesday, IXth of May, in the great dungeon of the castle of Rouen,

The monitions and exhortations being done,[1]

Jeanne replied to the judges and assessors: Truly, if you were to tear me limb from limb and make my soul leave my body, I would not say to you anything else. [And if you force me to do so], then afterwards I shall say that you made me say so by force.

She said also that on Holy Cross Day she received comfort from Saint Gabriel. And that her voices had told her that it was Saint Gabriel.

She said further that she had asked them whether she ought to submit to the Church, since the churchmen were pressing her strongly to do so, and they told her that if she wished Our Lord to help her, she should wait on Our Lord for all her deeds.

She said that she well knew that Our Lord was always master of her deeds; and that the Enemy never had power over them.

Furthermore she said that she had asked Saint Michael and her other voices if she would be burned; and that the voices had told her that she must wait on Our Lord and He would help her.

Concerning the sign of the crown which she said had been given to the Archbishop of Rheims, being asked whether she wished him to be consulted about it,

[1] Jeanne was shown the instruments of torture and was told that if she did not answer truthfully she would be put to the torture, in order to procure the salvation of her soul. Many years afterwards, the Master Executioner said: "On this occasion she answered with such prudence that all present marvelled. I retired without doing anything."

She answered: Have him come here, that I may hear him speak; then I shall answer you. He would not dare to tell you the contrary of what I have said to you.

The Charitable Admonition

After the Articles had been read to Jeanne, together with the Opinion of the University of Paris, she was admonished by the said doctor that she should carefully consider her words and deeds, especially with reference to the final Article; speaking to her as follows:

Jeanne, my very dear friend, it is now time, at the end of your trial, to think carefully of what you have said and done. . . . I do admonish, beg and exhort you, by the pity that you feel for the Passion of Our Saviour your Creator, and the desire you must have for the salvation of your soul and body, to correct and amend your faults and return into the way of truth, obeying and submitting yourself to the judgment and decision of the Church. And in so doing you will save your soul, and deliver, as I hope, your body from death. But if you do contrary, and persist [in your evil courses], be assured that your soul will be damned, and I fear also the destruction of your body. From which may God preserve you. Amen.

After Jeanne had been thus admonished, and had heard all the exhortations, she answered in the manner following:

As for my words and deeds, I refer to what I said at my trial, and I will maintain them.

Questioned by the said Maître Pierre [Maurice] if she believes that she is not bound to submit her words and deeds to the Church Militant or to any other than God,

She answered: I will maintain what I have always said at my trial. And if I were to be condemned and saw the fire lit and the wood prepared and the executioner who was to burn me ready to cast me into the fire, still in the fire would I not say anything other than I have said. And I will maintain what I have said until death.

After this, the judges asked the promoter of the trial and Jeanne herself if either of them wished to say anything further, to which they both answered no.

Then the bishop proceeded to the conclusion of the trial, according to a schedule which he held in his hands, of which the tenor follows.

We, the judges competent in this trial, declare and have declared Ourselves so to be, as much as is required, and declare this trial ended. And We do assign to-morrow to hear Our verdict in this matter, and to proceed further in accordance with law and equity.

The Abjuration

[At a solemn assembly publicly held in the cemetery of Saint Ouen at Rouen, before the lord Bishop of Beauvais and the Vice-Inquisitor . . . the preacher said to Jeanne: "Here are my lords the judges, who have time and again summoned and required you to submit your words and deeds to our Mother Holy Church, inasmuch as it seems to the learned clerks that there are many things contained in these words and deeds which it is not good either to say or to uphold."

To which Jeanne replied: "I will answer you." As to submission to the Church she said, "I have already told you that concerning all that I have done I appeal, after God, to our Holy Father the Pope. Everything that I have done, I have done at God's command." . . . And she was told that this did not suffice, for it was not possible to send to the Holy Father, being so far away, and that the Ordinaries were each one judge in his own diocese, and that therefore she must submit to our Mother Holy Church. She was thus admonished three times.

And when the Sentence was partly read, she said that she was willing to hold all that the judges and the Church desired, and to be obedient to them.

Then, in the presence of the afore-named persons and a great multitude of people, she recanted and made her abjuration in the manner following.]

Here follows the abjuration of Jeanne the Pucelle, made the XXIIIIth of May, in the year MIIIIXXXI

I Jeanne, called the Pucelle, a miserable sinner, after I recognized the snare of error in which I was held; and now that I have, by God's grace, returned to our Mother Holy Church; in order that it may be apparent that not feignedly but with good heart and will I have returned to her; I do confess that I have grievously sinned, in falsely pretending that I have had revelations from God and His Angels, Saint Catherine and Saint Margaret, etc.

And all my words and deeds which are contrary to the Church, I do revoke; and I desire to live in unity with the Church, nevermore departing therefrom.

In witness whereof my sign manual,

signed JHENNE+

The Reading of the Sentence

Here follows the Definitive Sentence, pronounced by the Bishop of Beauvais, after the abjuration and the [signing of the] schedule, beginning:

IN THE NAME OF THE LORD, AMEN

All pastors of the Church who would faithfully lead God's people, must carefully and diligently watch lest the devil, through his subtle arts, seduces and deceives the flock of Jesus Christ, to do which he labours ceaselessly. Wherefore there is need of great diligence to resist his false and sinful wiles.

Since you, Jeanne, commonly called the Pucelle, have been found guilty of many errors in the Faith of Jesus Christ, for which you have been called to judgment, and concerning which you have been heard; and since all the points and articles of your trial, your confessions, answers and assertions have been examined by Us, and the whole trial has been seen and deliberated upon by the masters and doctors of the Faculty of Theology in Paris, as well as by a number of prelates and doctors in law, both canon and civil, who are in this town of Rouen, by whom you have been charitably admonished with long appeals for your change of heart.

Notwithstanding these warnings and remonstrances, and after the abjuration made to you, you have rashly and wantonly fallen into sin.

Wherefore, that you may make salutary penance, We have condemned you, and do now condemn you by this Definitive Sentence to perpetual imprisonment, with the bread of sorrow and the water of affliction, that you may weep for your sins, and nevermore commit them. Saving Our grace and moderation, if hereafter you shall deserve them.

Visit of the Judges to the Prison

The following Monday, the twenty-eighth day of May, the judges went to the prison. . . .

Questioned whether since last Thursday she had heard the voices of Saint Catherine and Saint Margaret,

She answered yes.

And that they told her that God had sent her word by them that she had put herself in great danger of perdition in that she had consented to make the abjuration and renunciation in order to save her life; and that she was damned for doing so.

And she said that, before Thursday, her voices had told her what she ought to do, and that she had done it.

She said also that her voices had told her that, when she was on the platform, she should answer the preacher boldly. And she said that the preacher was a false preacher, for he said that she had done many things which she had never done.

She said further that in saying that God had not sent her she had damned herself, for truly God had sent her. And since Thursday her voices had told her that she had done great wrong to God in confessing that what she had done was not well done.

And after this, before all the clerks who were present in the chapel, the confessions and assertions which she had made the day before were read; after which, their opinions were asked as to what should be done, and they were all of the opinion and stated that she ought to be considered a heretic, and should be left to secular justice, with a request that they should treat her more kindly than she had deserved.

[*At seven the next morning Jeanne was visited in her cell by the two Dominicans, Ladvenu and Toutmouillé, who came to prepare her for death. The former heard her in confession, and (most inconsistently in the case of a judgment for relapse) Cauchon permitted her to receive Holy Communion.*

It is impossible to understand what Cauchon meant when he gave this permission; the reception of the Sacrament by a relapsed person, necessarily unabsolved, is not consonant with the fact that communion demands the prerequisite of absolution. If she were absolved, she could no longer be in lapse.

The Host was brought to her cell, as Massieu said, "irreverently, without stole and lights, at which Brother Martin, who had confessed her, was ill-content, and so a stole and lights were sent for, and thus Brother Martin administered It to her." It is on record that Jeanne said to her confessor, "Where shall I be to-night?" to which he replied, "Have you no faith in Our Lord?" "Yes, God helping me, today I shall be with Him in Paradise."]

The Definitive Sentence

IN THE NAME OF THE LORD, AMEN

We Pierre, by Divine pity, humble Bishop of Beauvais, and We, Brother Jean le Maître, deputy of the Inquisitor of the Faith, judges competent in this matter,

Since you, Jeanne, called the Pucelle, have been found by Us relapsed into divers errors and crimes of schism, idolatry, invocation of devils, and various other wickednesses.

And since for these reasons by just judgment We have found you so to be,

Nevertheless, since the Church never closes her arms to those who would return to her, We did believe that, with full understanding and unfeigned faith, you had left all the errors which you had renounced, vowing, swearing and publicly promising that never again would you fall into such errors, nor into any other heresies, but would live in Catholic unity and communion with our Church and our Holy Father the Pope, as is stated in a schedule signed by your own hand.

None the less time and again you have relapsed, as a dog that returns to its vomit, as We do state with great sorrow.

Wherefore We declare that you have again incurred the Sentence of excommunication which you formerly incurred, and are again fallen into your previous errors, for which reasons We now declare you to be a heretic.

And by this Sentence, seated upon Our tribunal of justice, as it is herein written, We do cast you forth and reject you from the communion of the Church as an infected limb, and hand you over to secular justice, praying the same to treat you with kindness and humanity in respect of your life and of your limbs.

The Execution

After the Sentence was read, the bishop, the Inquisitor, and many of the judges went away, leaving Jeanne upon the scaffold.

Then the Bailli of Rouen, an Englishman, who was there, without any legal formality and without reading any Sentence against her, ordered that she should be taken to the place where she was to be burned.

When Jeanne heard this order given, she began to weep and lament in such a way that all the people present were themselves moved to tears.

The said Bailli immediately ordered that the fire should be lighted, which was done.

And she was there burned and martyred tragically, an act of unparalleled cruelty.

And many, both noble and peasant, murmured greatly against the English.

LAST MARCH

——— *Robert Falcon Scott* ———

There is another famous chapter in the story of courage which is hardly less moving than that of Joan. Robert Falcon Scott, a captain in the British Navy, was fascinated by the Antarctic and hoped to be the first to reach the South Pole. In an ill-fated expedition, in 1911, he started on a dash which was to end in death for the picked men who were the participants. Ironically, Scott discovered on this trip that the Norwegian Amundsen had beaten him to the goal. And now, on his return, he found traveling conditions more and more difficult. The story of the journey—in which every member of his party exhibited unexampled courage and heroism—is contained in Scott's last diary, which was later found beside his body. It is impossible to read the account, with all its seemingly prosaic details, without thrilling to the bravery of Oates, who wandered off to die rather than encumber his comrades, and of Scott himself, whose last selfless words were, "For God's sake look after our people."

ဢ

Sunday, *February* 18.—R. 32. Temp. −55°. At Shambles Camp. We gave ourselves 5 hours' sleep at the lower glacier depot after the horrible night, and came on at about 3 today to this camp, coming fairly easily over the divide. Here with plenty of horsemeat we have had a fine supper, to be followed by others such, and so continue a more plentiful era if we can keep good marches up. New life seems to come with greater food almost immediately, but I am anxious about the Barrier surfaces.

Monday, February 20.—R. 34. Lunch Temp. −13°; Supper Temp. −15°. Same terrible surface; four hours' hard plodding in morning brought us to our Desolation Camp, where we had the four-day blizzard. We looked for more pony meat, but found none. After lunch we took to ski with some improvement of comfort. Total mileage for day 7—the ski tracks pretty plain and easily followed this afternoon. We have left another cairn behind. Terribly slow progress, but we hope for better things as we clear the land. There is a tendency to cloud over in the S.E. tonight, which may turn to our advantage. At present our sledge and ski leave deeply plowed tracks which can be seen winding for miles behind. It is distressing, but as usual trials are forgotten when we camp, and good food is our lot. Pray God we get better traveling as we are not so fit as we were, and the season is advancing apace.

Tuesday, February 21.—R. 35. Lunch Temp. +9½°; Supper Temp. —11°. Gloomy and overcast when we started; a good deal warmer. The marching almost as bad as yesterday. Heavy toiling all day, inspiring gloomiest thoughts at times. Rays of comfort when we picked up tracks and cairns. . . . We never won a march of 8½ miles with greater difficulty, but we can't go on like this. We are drawing away from the land and perhaps may get better things in a day or two. I devoutly hope so.

Wednesday, February 22.—R. 36. Supper Temp. —2°. There is little doubt we are in for a rotten critical time going home, and the lateness of the season may make it really serious. . . . The wind is dying down tonight and the sky clearing in the south, which is hopeful. Meanwhile it is satisfactory to note that such untoward events fail to damp the spirit of the party. Tonight we had a pony hoosh so excellent and filling that one feels really strong and vigorous again.

Thursday, February 23.—R. 37. Lunch Temp. —9.8°; Supper Temp. —12°. Started in sunshine, wind almost dropped. . . . Covered 8.2 miles in 7 hours, showing we can do 10 or 12 on this surface. Things are again looking up, as we are on the regular line of cairns, with no gaps right home, I hope.

Friday, February 24.—Lunch. Beautiful day—too beautiful—an hour after starting loose ice crystals spoiling surface. Saw depot and reached it middle forenoon. Found store in order except shortage oil—shall have to be *very* saving with fuel—otherwise have ten full days' provision from tonight and shall have less than 70 miles to go. . . . Poor Wilson has a fearful attack snow-blindness consequent on yesterday's efforts. Wish we had more fuel.

Night camp R. 38. Temp. —17°. A little despondent again. We

had a really terrible surface this afternon and only covered 4 miles. We are on the track just beyond a lunch cairn. It really will be a bad business if we are to have this pulling all through. I don't know what to think, but the rapid closing of the season is ominous. It is great luck having the horsemeat to add to our ration. Tonight we have had a real fine "hoosh." It is a race between the season and hard conditions and our fitness and good food.

Saturday, February 25.—Lunch Temp. —12°. Managed just 6 miles this morning. Started somewhat despondent; not relieved when pulling seemed to show no improvement. Bit by bit surface grew better, less sastrugi, more glide, slight following wind for a time. Then we began to travel a little faster. But the pulling is still *very* hard; undulations disappearing but inequalities remain.

Twenty-six Camp walls about 2 miles ahead, all tracks in sight— Evans' track very conspicuous. This is something in favor, but the pulling is tiring us, though we are getting into better ski drawing again. Bowers hasn't quite the trick and is a little hurt at my criticisms, but I never doubted his heart. Very much easier—write diary at lunch—excellent meal—now one pannikin very strong tea—four biscuits and butter.

Hope for better things this afternoon, but no improvement apparent. Oh! for a little wind—E. Evans evidently had plenty.

R. 39. Temp. —20°. Better march in afternoon. Day yields 11.4 miles—the first double figure of steady dragging for a long time, but it meant and will mean hard work if we can't get a wind to help us. Evans evidently had a strong wind here, S.E. I should think. The temperature goes very low at night now when the sky is clear as at present. As a matter of fact this is wonderfully fine weather—the only drawback the spoiling of the surface and absence of wind. We see all tracks very plain, but the pony-walls have evidently been badly drifted up. Some kind people had substituted a cairn at last camp 27. The old cairns do not seem to have suffered much.

Sunday, February 26.—Lunch Temp. —17°. Sky overcast at start, but able see tracks and cairn distinct at long distance. Did a little better, 6½ miles to date. Bowers and Wilson now in front. Find great relief pulling behind with no necessity to keep attention on track. Very cold nights now and cold feet starting march, as day footgear doesn't dry at all. We are doing well on our food, but we ought to have yet more. I hope the next depot, now only 50 miles, will find us with enough surplus to open out. The fuel shortage still an anxiety.

R. 40. Temp. —21°. Nine hours' solid marching has given us 11½ miles. Only 43 miles from the next depot. Wonderfully fine weather, but cold, very cold. Nothing dries and we get our feet cold too often. We want more food yet and especially more fat. Fuel is woefully short. . . .

Monday, February 27.—Desperately cold last night: —33° when we got up, with —37° minimum. Some suffering from cold feet, but all got good rest. We *must* open out on food soon. But we have done 7 miles this morning and hope for some 5 this afternoon. Overcast sky and good surface till now, when sun shows again. It is good to be marching the cairns up, but there is still much to be anxious about. We talk of little but food, except after meals. Land disappearing in satisfactory manner. Pray God we have no further setbacks. We are naturally always discussing possibility of meeting dogs, where and when, &c. It is a critical position. We may find ourselves in safety at next depot, but there is a horrid element of doubt.

Camp R. 41. Temp. —32°. Still fine clear weather but very cold— absolutely calm tonight. We have got off an excellent march for these days (12.2) and are much earlier than usual in our bags. 31 miles to depot, 3 days' fuel at a pinch, and 6 days' food. Things begin to look a little better; we can open out a little on food from tomorrow night, I think. . . .

Tuesday, February 28.—Lunch. Thermometer went below —40° last night; it was desperately cold for us, but we had a fair night. I decided to slightly increase food; the effect is undoubtedly good. Started marching in —32° with a slight northwesterly breeze— blighting. Many cold feet this morning; long time over foot gear, but we are earlier. Shall camp earlier and get the chance of a good night, if not the reality. Things must be critical till we reach the depot, and the more I think of matters, the more I anticipate their remaining so after that event. . . .

Wednesday, February 29.—Lunch. Cold night. Minimum Temp. —37.5°; —30° with northwest wind, force 4, when we got up. Frightfully cold starting; luckily Bowers and Oates in their last new finnesko; keeping my old ones for present. Expected awful march and for first hour got it. Then things improved and we camped after 5½ hours marching close to lunch camp—22½. Next camp is our depot and it is exactly 13 miles. It ought not to take more than

1½ days; we pray for another fine one. The oil will just about spin out in that event, and we arrive 3 clear days' food in hand. The increase of ration has had an enormously beneficial result. Mountains now looking small. Wind still very light from west—cannot understand this wind.

Thursday, March 1.—Lunch. Very cold last night—minimum —41.5°. Cold start to march, too, as usual now. Got away at 8 and have marched within sight of depot; flag something under 3 miles away. We did 11½ yesterday and marched 6 this morning. Heavy dragging yesterday and *very* heavy this morning. Apart from sledging considerations the weather is wonderful. Cloudless days and nights and the wind trifling. Worse luck, the light airs come from the north and keep us horribly cold. For this lunch hour the exception has come. There is a bright and comparatively warm sun. All our gear is out drying.

Friday, March 2.—Lunch. Misfortunes rarely come singly. We marched to the [Middle Barrier] depot fairly easily yesterday afternoon, and since that have suffered three distinct blows which have placed us in a bad position. First we found a shortage of oil; with most rigid economy it can scarce carry us to the next depot on this surface [71 miles away]. Second, Titus Oates disclosed his feet, the toes showing very bad indeed, evidently bitten by the late temperatures. The third blow came in the night, when the wind, which we had hailed with some joy, brought dark overcast weather. It fell below —40° in the night, and this morning it took 1½ hours to get our foot gear on, but we got away before eight. We lost cairn and tracks together and made as steady as we could N. by W., but have seen nothing. Worse was to come—the surface is simply awful. In spite of strong wind and full sail we have only done 5½ miles. We are in a *very* queer street since there is no doubt we cannot do the extra marches and feel the cold horribly.

Saturday, March 3.—Lunch. We picked up the track again yesterday, finding ourselves to the eastward. Did close on 10 miles and things looked a trifle better; but this morning the outlook is blacker than ever. Started well and with good breeze; for an hour made good headway; then the surface grew awful beyond words. The wind drew forward; every circumstance was against us. After 4½ hours things so bad that we camped, having covered 4½ miles. . . . God help us, we can't keep up this pulling, that is certain. Amongst ourselves we are unendingly cheerful, but what each man feels in his heart

I can only guess. Putting on foot gear in the morning is getting slower and slower, therefore every day more dangerous.

Sunday, March 4.—Lunch. Things looking *very* black indeed. As usual we forgot our trouble last night, got into our bags, slept splendidly on good hoosh, woke and had another, and started marching. Sun shining brightly, tracks clear, but surface covered with sandy frost-rime. All the morning we had to pull with all our strength, and in 4½ hours we covered 3½ miles. Last night it was overcast and thick, surface bad; this morning sun shining and surface as bad as ever. One has little to hope for except perhaps strong dry wind—an unlikely contingency at this time of year. Under the immediate surface crystals is a hard sastrugi surface, which must have been excellent for pulling a week or two ago. We are about 42 miles from the next depot and have a week's food, but only about 3 to 4 days' fuel—we are as economical of the latter as one can possibly be, and we cannot afford to save food and pull as we are pulling. We are in a very tight place indeed, but none of us despondent yet, or at least we preserve every semblance of good cheer, but one's heart sinks as the sledge stops dead at some sastrugi behind which the surface sand lies thickly heaped. For the moment the temperature is on the —20°—an improvement which makes us much more comfortable, but a colder snap is bound to come again soon. I fear that Oates at least will weather such an event very poorly. Providence to our aid! We can expect little from man now except the possibility of extra food at the next depot. It will be real bad if we get there and find the same shortage of oil. Shall we get there? Such a short distance it would have appeared to us on the summit! I don't know what I should do if Wilson and Bowers weren't so determinedly cheerful over things.

Monday, March 5.—Lunch. Regret to say going from bad to worse. We got a slant of wind yesterday afternoon, and going on 5 hours we converted our wretched morning run of 3½ miles into something over 9. We went to bed on a cup of cocoa and pemmican solid with the chill off. (R. 47.) The result is telling on all, but mainly on Oates, whose feet are in a wretched condition. One swelled up tremendously last night and he is very lame this morning. We started march on tea and pemmican as last night—we pretend to prefer the pemmican this way. Marched for 5 hours this morning over a slightly better surface covered with high moundy sastrugi. Sledge capsized twice; we pulled on foot, covering about 5½ miles.

We are two pony marches and 4 miles about from our depot. Our fuel dreadfully low and the poor Soldier nearly done. It is pathetic enough because we can do nothing for him; more hot food might do a little, but only a little, I fear. We none of us expected these terribly low temperatures, and of the rest of us Wilson is feeling them most; mainly, I fear, from his self-sacrificing devotion in doctoring Oates' feet. We cannot help each other, each has enough to do to take care of himself. We get cold on the march when the trudging is heavy, and the wind pierces our warm garments. The others, all of them, are unendingly cheerful when in the tent. We mean to see the game through with a proper spirit, but it's tough work to be pulling harder than we ever pulled in our lives for long hours, and to feel that the progress is so slow. One can only say "God help us!" and plod on our weary way, cold and very miserable, though outwardly cheerful. We talk of all sorts of subjects in the tent, not much of food now, since we decided to take the risk of running a full ration. We simply couldn't go hungry at this time.

Tuesday, March 6.—Lunch. We did a little better with help of wind yesterday afternoon, finishing 9½ miles for the day, and 27 miles from depot. But this morning things have been awful. It was warm in the night and for the first time during the journey I overslept myself by more than an hour; then we were slow with foot gear; then, pulling with all our might (for our lives) we could scarcely advance at rate of a mile an hour; then it grew thick and three times we had to get out of harness to search for tracks. The result is something less than 3½ miles for the forenoon. The sun is shining now and the wind gone. Poor Oates is unable to pull, sits on the sledge when we are track-searching—he is wonderfully plucky, as his feet must be giving him great pain. He makes no complaint, but his spirits only come up in spurts now, and he grows more silent in the tent. We are making a spirit lamp to try and replace the primus when our oil is exhausted. It will be a very poor substitute and we've not got much spirit. If we could have kept up our 9-mile days we might have got within reasonable distance of the depot before running out, but nothing but a strong wind and good surface can help us now, and though we had quite a good breeze this morning, the sledge came as heavy as lead. If we were all fit I should have hopes of getting through, but the poor Soldier has become a terrible hindrance, though he does his utmost and suffers much I fear.

Wednesday, March 7.—A little worse I fear. One of Oates' feet *very* bad this morning; he is wonderfully brave. We still talk of what we will do together at home.

We hope against hope that the dogs have been to Mt. Hooper; then we might pull through. If there is a shortage of oil again we can have little hope. One feels that for poor Oates the crisis is near, but none of us are improving, though we are wonderfully fit considering the really excessive work we are doing. We are only kept going by good food. No wind this morning till a chill northerly air came ahead. Sun bright and cairns showing up well. I should like to keep the track to the end.

Thursday, March 8.—Lunch. Worse and worse in morning; poor Oates' left foot can never last out, and time over foot gear something awful. Have to wait in night foot gear for nearly an hour before I start changing and then am generally first to be ready. Wilson's feet giving trouble now, but this mainly because he gives so much help to others. We did 4½ miles this morning and are now 8½ miles from the depot—a ridiculously small distance to feel in difficulties, yet on this surface we know we cannot equal half our old marches, and that for that effort we expend nearly double the energy. The great question is, What shall we find at the depot? If the dogs have visited it we may get along a good distance, but if there is another short allowance of fuel, God help us indeed. We are in a very bad way, I fear, in any case.

Saturday, March 10.—Things steadily downhill. Oates' foot worse. He has rare pluck and must know that he can never get through. He asked Wilson if he had a chance this morning, and of course Bill had to say he didn't know. In point of fact he has none. Apart from him, if he went under now, I doubt whether we could get through. With great care we might have a dog's chance, but no more. The weather conditions are awful, and our gear gets steadily more icy and difficult to manage. At the same time of course poor Titus is the greatest handicap. He keeps us waiting in the morning until we have partly lost the warming effect of our good breakfast, when the only wise policy is to be up and away at once; again at lunch. Poor chap! it is too pathetic to watch him: one cannot but try to cheer him up.

Yesterday we marched up the depot, Mt. Hooper. Cold comfort. Shortage on our allowance all round. I don't know that anyone is to blame. . . .

This morning it was calm when we breakfasted, but the wind

came from the W.N.W. as we broke camp. It rapidly grew in strength. After traveling for half an hour I saw that none of us could go on facing such conditions. We were forced to camp and are spending the rest of the day in a comfortless blizzard camp, wind quite foul.

Sunday, March 11.—Titus Oates is very near the end, one feels. What we or he will do, God only knows. We discussed the matter after breakfast; he is a brave fine fellow and understands the situation, but he practically asked for advice. Nothing could be said but to urge him to march as long as he could. One satisfactory result to the discussion; I practically ordered Wilson to hand over the means of ending our troubles to us, so that any one of us may know how to do so. Wilson had no choice between doing so and our ransacking the medicine case. We have 30 opium tabloids apiece and he is left with a tube of morphine. So far the tragical side of our story. [R. 53.]

The sky completely overcast when we started this morning. We could see nothing, lost the tracks, and doubtless have been swaying a good deal since—3.1 miles for the forenoon—terribly heavy dragging—expected it. Know that 6 miles is about the limit of our endurance now, if we get no help from wind or surfaces. We have 7 days' food and should be about 55 miles from One Ton Camp tonight, 6 × 7 = 42, leaving us 13 miles short of our distance, even if things get no worse. Meanwhile the season rapidly advances.

Monday, March 12.—We did 6.9 miles yesterday, under our necessary average. Things are left much the same, Oates not pulling much, and now with hands as well as feet pretty well useless. We did 4 miles this morning in 4 hours 20 min.—we may hope for 3 this afternoon, 7 × 6 = 42. We shall be 47 miles from the depot. I doubt if we can possibly do it. The surface remains awful, the cold intense, and our physical condition running down. God help us! Not a breath of favorable wind for more than a week, and apparently liable to head winds at any moment.

Wednesday, March 14.—No doubt about the going downhill, but everything going wrong for us. Yesterday we woke to a strong northerly wind with temp. —37°. Couldn't face it, so remained in camp [R. 54] till 2, then did 5½ miles. Wanted to march later, but party feeling the cold badly as the breeze (N.) never took off entirely, and as the sun sank the temp. fell. Long time getting supper in dark. [R. 55.]

This morning started with southerly breeze, set sail and passed another cairn at good speed; half-way, however, the wind shifted to W. by S. or W.S.W., blew through our wind clothes and into our mits. Poor Wilson horribly cold, could [not] get off ski for some time. Bowers and I practically made camp, and when we got into the tent at last we were all deadly cold. Then temp. now midday down —43° and the wind strong. We *must* go on, but now the making of every camp must be more difficult and dangerous. It must be near the end, but a pretty merciful end. Poor Oates got it again in the foot. I shudder to think what it will be like tomorrow. It is only with greatest pains rest of us keep off frostbites. No idea there could be temperatures like this at this time of year with such winds. Truly awful outside the tent. Must fight it out to the last biscuit, but can't reduce rations.

Friday, March 16 or Saturday 17.—Lost track of dates, but think the last correct. Tragedy all along the line. At lunch, the day before yesterday, poor Titus Oates said he couldn't go on; he proposed we should leave him in his sleeping-bag. That we could not do, and we induced him to come on, on the afternoon march. In spite of its awful nature for him he struggled on and we made a few miles. At night he was worse and we knew the end had come.

Should this be found I want these facts recorded. Oates' last thoughts were of his Mother, but immediately before he took pride in thinking that his regiment would be pleased with the bold way in which he met his death. We can testify to his bravery. He has borne intense suffering for weeks without complaint, and to the very last was able and willing to discuss outside subjects. He did not—would not—give up hope till the very end. He was a brave soul. This was the end. He slept through the night before last, hoping not to wake; but he woke in the morning—yesterday. It was blowing a blizzard. He said, "I am just going outside and may be some time." He went out into the blizzard and we have not seen him since.

I take this opportunity of saying that we have stuck to our sick companions to the last. In case of Edgar Evans, when absolutely out of food and he lay insensible, the safety of the remainder seemed to demand his abandonment, but Providence mercifully removed him at this critical moment. He died a natural death, and we did not leave him till two hours after his death. We knew that poor Oates was walking to his death, but though we tried to dissuade him, we knew it was the act of a brave man and an English gentleman. We all hope to meet the end with a similar spirit, and assuredly the end is not far.

I can only write at lunch and then only occasionally. The cold is intense, −40° at midday. My companions are unendingly cheerful, but we are all on the verge of serious frostbites, and though we constantly talk of fetching through I don't think any one of us believes it in his heart.

We are cold on the march now, and at all times except meals. Yesterday we had to lay up for a blizzard and today we move dreadfully slowly. We are at No 14 pony camp, only two pony marches from One Ton Depot. We leave here our theodolite, a camera, and Oates' sleeping-bags. Diaries, &c., and geological specimens carried at Wilson's special request, will be found with us or on our sledge.

Sunday, March 18.—Today, lunch, we are 21 miles from the depot. Ill fortune presses, but better may come. We have had more wind and drift from ahead yesterday; had to stop marching; wind N.W., force 4, temp. −35°. No human being could face it, and we are worn out *nearly.*

My right foot has gone, nearly all the toes—two days ago I was proud possessor of best feet. These are the steps of my downfall. Like an ass I mixed a small spoonful of curry powder with my melted pemmican—it gave me violent indigestion. I lay awake and in pain all night; woke and felt done on the march; foot went and I didn't know it. A very small measure of neglect and have a foot which is not pleasant to contemplate. Bowers takes first place in condition, but there is not much to choose after all. The others are still confident of getting through—or pretend to be—I don't know! We have the last *half* fill of oil in our primus and a very small quantity of spirit—this alone between us and thirst. The wind is fair for the moment, and that is perhaps a fact to help. The mileage would have seemed ridiculously small on our outward journey.

Monday, March 19.—Lunch. We camped with difficulty last night, and were dreadfully cold till after our supper of cold pemmican and biscuit and a half a pannikin of cocoa cooked over the spirit. Then, contrary to expectation, we got warm and all slept well. Today we started in the usual dragging manner. Sledge dreadfully heavy. We are 15½ miles from the depot and ought to get there in three days. What progress! We have two days' food but barely a day's fuel. All our feet are getting bad—Wilson's best, my right foot worst, left all right. There is no chance to nurse one's feet till we can get hot food into us. Amputation is the least I can hope for now, but will the trouble spread? That is the serious question. The weather doesn't give us a chance—the wind from N. to N.W. and −40° temp. today.

Wednesday, March 21.—Got within 11 miles of depot Monday night;[1] had to lay up all yesterday in severe blizzard. Today forlorn hope, Wilson and Bowers going to depot for fuel.

Thursday, March 22 *and* 23.—Blizzard bad as ever—Wilson and Bowers unable to start—tomorrow last chance—no fuel and only one or two of food left—must be near the end. Have decided it shall be natural—we shall march for the depot with or without our effects and die in our tracks.

Thursday, March 29.—Since the 21st we have had a continuous gale from W.S.W. and S.W. We had fuel to make two cups of tea apiece and bare food for two days on the 20th. Every day we have been ready to start for our depot 11 *miles* away, but outside the door of the tent it remains a scene of whirling drift. I do not think we can hope for any better things now. We shall stick it out to the end, but we are getting weaker, of course, and the end cannot be far.

It seems a pity, but I do not think I can write more.

R. SCOTT

Last entry.
For God's sake look after our people.

[1] The 6oth camp from the Pole.

III. For the Lengthening Shadows

LIFE

Georg Brandes

Life is a stairway with many treacherous steps. For some, as Georg Brandes relates, the pitfall lies beneath the twentieth step, for others beneath the sixty-third. No one knows where the step fatal to him will be, but for all the destiny is inescapable. What then are we to do about it? Accept the fact, says Brandes, and in our own workshop accomplish what we can from day to day. Thus we will have no time and no desire to foresee what lies in store.

Georg Brandes was perhaps the foremost critic of his day. He was born and educated in Copenhagen, traveled extensively on the Continent, and lectured in Russia, England and America. So great was his influence that reputations were made and broken on his word. At seventy he looked back on his life's adventure and wrote the fanciful essay that follows. Like the worker he writes about, his life had been so full that he had had little time to count the steps.

THERE is a tower that all must climb. At most, a hundred stairs lead up it. The tower is hollow, and if once a man has reached the top, he falls down through it and is crushed. But hardly anybody falls down from so high up. It is the fate of each individual that if he reaches a certain appointed stair whose number he does not know beforehand, the stair gives way under his feet, reveals itself as the covering to a pitfall, and he disappears. Only he does not know whether the stair is the twentieth or the sixty-third, or what its number is; but that one of these stairs will give way under him, this he surely knows.

At first to ascend is easy, but slow. The ascent itself causes not the slightest difficulty, and at each stair the view through the peep-holes in the tower gives pleasure enough. Everything is so new. The eyes dwell with a lingering interest on what is near as well as what is far away. And there is so much still in prospect. By degrees, the ascent causes more difficulty; the eyes grow more indifferent to the view, which always looks the same; and at the same time it seems as if there is hardly any lingering on each single stair, but as though one mounted more swiftly than before and took several stairs at a time; which, however, cannot be.

As often as, once a year, a man mounts a stair, his fellow-travelers wish him joy of not yet having disappeared. Each time that he has ten stairs behind him and begins on a new landing, the congratulations are warmer; and each time the ever more paradoxical hope that his journey may long continue is more cordially expressed. The man concerned is generally deeply moved, and forgets both how little satisfaction he has behind him and what adversity is still in store.

So life passes for the majority of so-called normal people who remain spiritually in the same place.

But there is also a pit shaft into which those who desire to dig themselves galleries under the earth may descend, and likewise those whose desire is set on exploring the galleries others in the course of the centuries have dug. From year to year these continually go deeper down, to where metals and minerals lie hid. They make themselves familiar with the subterranean world, find their way among the labyrinthine galleries, direct or understand or take part in the work down there, and in this forget how the years are passing.

This is their life who in the deep-delving labor of thought and inquiry forget the events of the day, and who, busied in their quiet avocation, survive the losses and sorrows the years bring and the joy the years steal away. When death draws near, they, like Archimedes in his day, make petition: "Do not disturb my circles!"

There is also a wide field that stretches out endlessly before the eye, like all those kingdoms of the world the Tempter showed the Savior from a mountain; and some there are, those that eternally thirst after life and are covetous for conquest, for whom life is this: to take care that they gain ever more ground, attain an ever wider range of vision, a fuller experience, a greater mastery over men and things. Warlike expeditions tempt them, and power is their delight; their constant wish is to secure themselves ever more in men's minds and women's hearts. Insatiate they are, incalculable, strong. They use the years so that the years do not weary them. They keep all youth's characteristics—its love of danger, love of life, love of conflict, vigor and freshness of will; and however old they grow, they die young. As the salmon against the stream, so their instincts go against the stream of the years.

But there is also a workshop—a workshop in which the laborer is so at ease that, all his life long, he works and thrives there every day, and so is not aware that he is ageing. For surely there are certain things that are done best in the freshest years of youth; those for which knowledge and experience are but little needed, but where to begin well is the only thing that counts. Yet there are many other things that he does best who knows most and has seen most. In this workshop into which life may be transformed it is good to be and comfortable to journey, because the beginner realizes that it depends on himself whether he becomes master and because the master knows that no talk is more stupid than talk of the discontinuance of the mastership after a certain set number of years. He tells himself that there is not an experience, however painful it may be, not an observation so insignificant nor an investigation so sweeping, not a joy nor a sorrow, not a defeat and not a victory, not a dream, a conjecture, a fancy, a human whim, but may in one way or another benefit his work. And therefore the work must of necessity be richer the older he grows. He fears no danger from his own nature; he relies on his instincts, entrusts himself to them with a quiet mind, certain that they will lead him aright, since they are his own, and certain that he will be able to make use in his workshop of all to which they lead. So his days pass without hope of a happiness that may fail to come and without fear of any evil that might lurk in his own being, or of the loss of its powers.

If his workshop be not big, it is big enough for him; big enough for him to be able in it to give figures shape and thoughts expression. Busy as he is, he has no time to glance across at the hour-glass in the corner in which the sand is always running. But when kindly thoughts are sent him, he is aware of it as though a loving hand had turned the hour-glass and so delayed its running out.

A RECIPE

Stephen S. Wise

There is one simple solution to the problem of growing old, and that is to stay young in heart and mind. Nor is this as impossible as might at first appear. There are some people we all have met, whose hair is gray and faces are wrinkled, but who retain the gaiety and freshness of their juniors. They do it, says Rabbi Wise, by listening to the three sublime voices of God—truth, duty and love. Just as these ideals do not age, so do those who believe in them retain their youth. We must hold to those things which, because they are universal in value, will still be fresh and new when our years are many.

WOULD you avoid growing old? Do you will even to seem not to grow old? Then have a vision of life and amid a multiplicity of things have and hold, cherish and pursue an ideal. To the man of ideals, to the man who in other words lives, age comes not. Age cannot touch nor wither nor blast the life pervaded and smitten through by ideals. Would you grow old, or rather would you not grow old, then live, and live by the stars. Such are the lives of the unaging. In order not to grow old, I say again, grow on in faith and hopefulness, in vision and serviceableness. Being without these things, some men cannot grow old, they are old. Unhappily for them, they were born old, as other men, whatever be the number of their years, die young. Having these things, age cannot ravage the spirit.

Such men and women are age-proof, their heads may be silver white, their frames bowed, their limbs palsied, but age they know not—the men I have in mind, such men as that great physician who, after sixty years and more of unwearied and unrivaled service, is still an impassioned pleader for the right of the child, of the merest, puniest babe. Who will dare say that he is aged, who at fourscore and more spends himself utterly in the service of the least of these? I am thinking of yet another friend of fourscore and more, whose life is nobly dedicated to the furtherance of amity between faith and faith, who serves all men as brothers, who proves that he is a Christian by the love he bears the Jew. And I am thinking of yet another man who likewise has lived for fourscore years, perhaps the foremost educator of our generation, a publicist of matchless felicity in utterance and conduct alike, a man who at eighty and more steps into the arena with all the power and eagerness of youth in order to take up arms on behalf of another great though much wronged servant of the nation.

It was once said of Theodore Parker that he gave himself un-reservedly and with abandon to whatever truth, duty, love, the three sublime voices of God—the real trinity in our souls—commanded. Truth, duty, love! Have you tried these things? Have you dared to live by them and for them, by and for any one of them? Does not this word bear out what was recently said by a great American physician about a noble social worker—that individual, who has no object in life, who simply works day by day, with the idea that he is making a dollar and is going to use the dollar for his own comfort, cannot have a very peaceful mind. But if one has an object in life, to attain certain things which will be helpful to others, and whose day is filled with that sort of work, that individual deserves—and other things being equal—will have an old age.

Truth, duty, love—obey their command and when you do you shall find age a fiction and life alone a reality. What if old age be without teeth and eyes if it be not without hope and faith and fadeless memories!

> To suffer and endure,
> To keep the spirit pure—
> The fortress and abode of holy Truth—
>   To serve eternal things
>   Whate'er the issue brings
> This is not broken Age, but ageless Youth.

If then life be centered on self, old age may rest in the certitude of disappointment and disillusion. But if self be centered on life, then may come what Morley described, touching Edmund Burke, as "an unrebellious temper and hopes undimmed for mankind."

Twofold must be the hope of man—for a future for self and for the future for all. And when the soul is so freighted with hopes, then shall it be said of a man as it was said of the great poet: "He was one of those on the lookout for every new idea and for every old idea with a new application, which may tend to meet the growing requirements of society; one of those who are like men standing on a watch-tower to whom others apply and say, not 'What of the night?' but 'What of the morning and of the coming day?' "

My one word of counsel is—let life not be centered on self, for to live for self is to invite cruel disaster in old age. The saddest, in truth the most tragic, lives I know are those of old men and women who have nothing to live for because they have lived for self and self alone—and self is nothing. Their lives are piteously empty. For the restlessness and excitement of youth may hide this truth, but age, like death, is a revealer. And there are many types of selfishness. I speak of two which must suffice. There are those who live for self—for selfissimus, giving not the utmost for the highest but for the nighest—self, self, self, self's pleasure and profit and power and vantage and fame. These are the most crude and obvious types of the selfful, who shall pay the penalty of their folly and their moral disease.

But, though it be said to your dismay, there are other types of selfishness, though less obvious—the selfishness of those who project self into and magnify self in family relationship. For there are those who simply extend the horizon of self enough to include other forms of self, one's own, one's nearest, one's flesh and blood. And here, too, disillusion is bound to come and ought to come, for one's own cannot and ought not to fill one's life forever. One might well excuse our mothers and fathers for giving their thought and attention to their own, for these were many and life was hard and life's struggle oft-times bitter. But for the fewest is such excuse valid now—if ever it was valid—especially seeing that we concentrate upon the giving to others of things rather than upon helping others to their highest and best. In truth, people concentrate upon self, upon their own interests and wishes, and these things pass and little or nothing is left in life save self. Live for yourself, and you live two years in one; live in the life of others, and you divide your years with another.

Is not all this a paraphrase of what Emerson has said better than any other? He who loves is in no condition old. Not lives and lives for self, not loves self and self alone, but he who loves! Emerson, building better perhaps than he knew, has voiced the deepest truth of the soul. Love cannot die and love will not let die nor yet grow old. And yet as a final word, and more needed than all else, I would say that there is only one way to grow old, and that too is the only way not to grow old. That way is to know, to love, to serve.

> Grow old along with me!
> The Best is yet to be,

The last of life for which the first was made;
Our times are in His hand
Who saith, "A whole I planned,"
Youth shows but half: Trust God: see all nor be afraid.

ON STAYING YOUNG

——— *Maurice Maeterlinck* ———

The ideas and ideals of youth will keep you young. Maurice Maeter-linck, believing at sixty-three that death was nigh, failed to comprehend this idea. He was a Belgian poet and dramatist whose writing had achieved world renown. Such successful plays as Pelléas and Mélisande *and* The Bluebird *were concerned primarily with problems of the soul. Now this great man found his own soul "depressed and uneasy." It took the example of an untutored farmer to bring back his zest for life. The farmer had learned a lesson which Maeterlinck, with all his worldly success, had not understood.*

৵

AT the age of sixty, I confess I thought myself approaching death. My mind seemed to have lost its alertness, its interest in new ideas and its capacity for work; I felt—or imagined that I felt—disturbing physical indications of the body's last weariness. It was as if a veil had dropped between my eyes and all the color and beauty of the world.

Today I am seventy-eight. And the harmony I now feel between body and mind would have seemed a miracle to me when I was sixty. I know it is nothing of the sort. I know it is as simple as this: that if the mind is young, the body is young.

I did not learn that myself; someone taught it to me. It is to him, perhaps first of all, that I owe my life today.

I met him at that time I have spoken of, when I was depressed and weary mentally and physically. One morning I went for a walk along a country path I had not explored before. I saw a farmhouse across the fields, so pleasant-looking a place that it held out an irresistible invitation for the passer-by. A boy of nine or ten ran out as I approached, and presently we were sitting talking together on a wooden bench beneath an old apple tree.

Soon, above the boy's sprightly chatter, I became aware of another voice, coming from the cottage. It was a woman's voice, querulous in tone. I looked at the boy, and he smiled broadly. "That's Mother," said he. "She's arguing with Grandad."

"Why?" I asked.

"Oh, because he wants to go to town to see the new fire engine, and she doesn't want him to. She says he'll lose his way or be run over or something, and she says it's silly anyhow." He gave an excited little hop. "But I want to go too, and Grandad'll take me, you watch!"

At that moment, scorning further argument, Grandad himself came out, stepping stoutly through the cottage doorway. He was a very old man, yes, but with lively blue eyes and a frisky manner about him. He nodded to me pleasantly, and I told him I had stopped to rest awhile, if he did not mind.

"As long as you want!" he said. "It is a nice place to sit, isn't it? A good view, don't you think? I'd like to stay and point out some of the interesting things around here to you, but the boy and I are off for town, and we'll miss the old bus at the corner if we don't hurry." On an impulse I asked if I might walk to the corner with them. "Come along!" he said; and off we started.

I glanced back as we turned into the path and saw the boy's mother standing in the cottage door. There was an expression of melancholy foreboding on her face and she shook her head disapprovingly. It occurred to me that I had seen that same sort of expression somewhere else a very short time before, and then the sudden realization startled me—yes, in the mirror that very morning, and the face was my own.

"Poor woman!" the old man said, as if he knew my thoughts. "She thinks I should tuck my scarf around me, sit in the sun like an old donkey and never stir. If I heeded her, I believe I'd be dead in a year!"

When we parted, he asked me to come back soon for another visit. And I did, not once but many times, for I felt that I had found not only a friend but a counselor—and a physician. He lived in a small farming section of the country, the "town" he visited occasionally was not much more than a village; he had never had the money to travel farther. But to him this small sphere was as wide as the world, because he knew it so well. He paused to talk with its people and inquire about their affairs; he crossed their lives with his. If he noticed that a shopkeeper in the village had decked out his store with a new fitting, he paused to compliment him on it; if he had an idea that he thought might benefit that man's business, or, say, help a housewife in her labors, or make her garden prettier to see, he gave it for what it was worth.

Of friendship he was spendthrift.

And so it was impossible to think of him as an old man. He was young. He had been a young man all his life. He had never permitted the years to wither his mind, and therefore in great part they had spared his body.

His one secret was his unconquerable interest in life. His second was as simple. On excursions to town or merely on walks along neighboring roads, his usual companion was the little boy. He never lost touch with childhood.

It was to this, indeed, that I think the Biblical patriarchs owed their long, sound years. In that pastoral life the family remained a unit, closely knit, no matter to what size it grew. There were always children around the elders. Children through whose eyes they might see again the wonder and beauty of the world, through whose questions they might find once more their own far childhood. For myself, after my meeting with my old young friend, I took stock and swept the shelves. I realized that I must unburden myself of the precautions of old habit, the poisons of resignation and fear. Previously I had cringed before the prospect of a journey, thinking myself too old to venture from my safe warm corner in the sun. I had resisted the friendly advances of younger people, fancying that I could be only a trial to them. I had shuddered at facing unfamiliar things—people, scenes, ideas.

Now, in my new determination and with that old man before me as a model, I welcomed all these, knowing that only by welcoming them could I live. I tried to touch life with all my senses, as the blind man illuminates his mind by the blessed touch of his fingers on the raised letters.

For the belief in life, not fear of it, is the very essence of youth. Today as we listen to the roar of history, it may seem hard, impossible at times, to hold to one's belief. It can be reaffirmed and renewed, I think, by things so close at hand that we scarcely see them at all; the changing fields and trees, the colors of first dawn and last evening light, the child that plays next door.

I remember a strange and lovely story a friend once told me. She and her husband had bought a beautiful villa in the South of France, and they wished to share their pleasure in it with their closest and dearest friends. They invited several to spend the first week end with them in the new house. They intended the guest of honor to be my friend's mother, a woman of eighty and some years, and they addressed a most special invitation to her. Despite her years, they knew, the journey would not be too much for her.

The old lady refused their invitation, but in her refusal I think can be read the reason why at her venerable age she was still alive and youthful and loved. For she said in her response that some time before a friend had given her a certain rare Oriental plant that, every four years, bloomed into an indescribably beautiful flower. The little bud of this flower was now swelling almost visibly before her eyes as she watched it every day. She could be with her daughter and son-in-law again, but perhaps never again could she see the bud burst and flower; and if in leaving it she missed the spectacle of that rare blooming, she would have missed one of the precious beauties of life; that beauty she could not sacrifice.

I think that in the old lady's eyes, as they watched the bud burst, there must have been something of that same gleam of youth eternal that I saw in the eyes of my old farmer friend.

ACCEPTANCE

Alice Hegan Rice

With some sooner and with others later, the limbs will fail and the mind fail to comprehend. Let us then begin "to prepare for old age while still young," says Alice Hegan Rice. Mrs. Rice was the author of Mrs. Wiggs of the Cabbage Patch *and other novels which have delighted millions; but she was also widely known for the distilled wisdom in her books of advice and inspiration. One of them,* Happiness Road, *remains highly successful to the present, and it is from this book that the following counsel of acceptance and adjustment has been taken.*

I know the night is near at hand,
The mists lie low on hill and bay,

The autumn sheaves are dewless, dry;
But I have had the day.

Yes, I have had, dear Lord, the day:
When at Thy call I have the night,
Brief be the twilight as I pass
From light to dark, from dark to light.

S. WEIR MITCHELL

THE most difficult lesson we have to learn is the final one, the dread of old age being only second to the dread of death. Yet the spirit of acceptance and co-operation with the laws of nature should come with the years and bring a peace and beauty that belongs to autumn. The end of a great symphony is not filled with confusion and rebellion; instead, it is a triumphant consummation of what has preceded it.

Paradoxical as it sounds, one must begin to prepare for old age while still young. Unless we early acquire the habits of self-reliance, of appreciation for our minor blessings, and of finding constant opportunities for service, there is little chance of developing those traits when we are old. Some cynic said that "old age is but a caricature of our youth," an observation which is all too often true.

Nothing is more futile than a frantic clinging to life beyond its natural span. We may laugh at the Irishman who wished he knew where he was going to die so he could never go near the place, but it is the attitude of many of us. Increased years seldom bring more physical vigor, personal enjoyment, or opportunities for service. We have had our chance at life, and for good or ill must abide by what we have made of it. Youth does not bewail the loss of the toys of childhood, neither should maturity bemoan the withdrawal of youthful pastimes. The frantic clinging to a past decade, whether it be girlish effervescence in a woman of sixty, or boyish capers in an elderly swain, can but result in absurdity. When one has glimpsed the more permanent realities he exposes his shallowness in being absorbed in trivialities.

It is useless to minimize the discomfort of old age; failing strength, curtailment of activities, the loss of beloved contemporaries test the courage of the bravest. But there is much we can do to prepare ourselves if we begin in time.

Much has been written about the temptations of youth, but too little has been said about the temptations of age. Captious criticism, intolerance of changing customs, susceptibility to unintentional slights, sentimental clinging to the past, complaints of physical infirmities, all contribute to the unhappiness of advancing years. Scott Fitzgerald, that incorrigible spokesman of youth, said that "the worst thing about old age was its vulnerability."

As human beings we can not expect to evade our share of tragedy, illness, and sorrow. It is the price we pay for living, and neither hopeless stoicism nor bitter fatalism suffice to sustain us in the struggle.

Only when we feel that through all our vicissitudes some unfathomable purpose runs, and that by meeting life nobly and courageously we can co-operate in the fulfillment of that purpose, do we find peace.

Philosophy assures us there are compensations in growing old, if we have but the wit to find them. No longer must we strive to make our personalities felt, comparison with the achievement of others is no longer necessary. For better or for worse, we are what we are. Freed from many of the duties and conventions that once hampered us, we can now afford to indulge our tastes, cultivate our hobbies and live our own lives. We have more time to read, write and think; more opportunity to observe and evaluate; and, if we are lucky, more leisure to enjoy "the beautiful foolishness" of things. The human drama begins to show form and meaning, the heterogenous events of the past to fall into pattern and evolve a plot. White is not so white, nor black so black as we thought. Subtleties and nuances are more discernible, and we are free to exercise "a heart at leisure with itself to soothe and sympathize."

Could we but cultivate a kindly tolerance toward the foibles of others, a sympathy and understanding with youth, and a serene faith in an ultimate good, we would free age of its worst terrors.

When our life's work is ended and our long journey nearing its close, we should be able to catch the light of a new dawn beyond the horizon, and to travel fearlessly, even happily, toward it.

Some one has beautifully said: "The kiss of God is upon him whose last sigh issues from smiling lips," but in order to smile at the end of the journey, one must have acquired the habit all along the way.

ON GROWING OLDER

Arthur Christopher Benson

It is a far cry from the little town of Shelbyville, Kentucky, where Alice Hegan Rice was born, to Magdalene College at Cambridge University, where Arthur Christopher Benson was a fellow and lecturer. She was the product of a simple Midwestern background. He was one of the intellectual leaders of England. Benson was a well-known biographer, a student of the works of Pater and Rossetti, an authority on the reign of Queen Victoria. Yet the wisdom he had gained from his background of culture was startlingly similar to that of Mrs. Rice. To each period of life its own blessings, said Benson. He could watch the athletic young men rowing on the river without a pang. With the advancing years, all his values and standards had changed. He was well content with what he had.

సౌ

THE sun flares red behind leafless elms and battlemented towers as I come in from a lonely walk beside the river; above the chimney-tops hangs a thin veil of drifting smoke, blue in the golden light. The games in the Common are just coming to an end; a stream of long-coated spectators sets towards the town, mingled with the parti-colored, muddied figures of the players. I have been strolling half the afternoon along the river bank, watching the boats passing up and down; hearing the shrill cries of coxes, the measured plash of oars, the rhythmical rattle of rowlocks, inter-mingled at intervals with the harsh grinding of the chain-ferries. Five-and-twenty years ago I was rowing here myself in one of these boats, and I do not wish to renew the experience. I cannot conceive why and in what moment of feeble good-nature or misapplied patriotism I ever consented to lend a hand. I was not a good oar, and did not become a better one; I had no illusions about my performance, and any momentary complacency was generally sternly dispelled by the harsh criticism of the coach on the bank, when we rested for a moment to receive our meed of praise or blame. But though I have no sort of wish to repeat the process, to renew the slavery which I found frankly and consistently in-tolerable, I find myself looking on at the cheerful scene with an amusement in which mingles a shadow of pain, because I feel that I have parted with something, a certain buoyancy and elasticity of body, and perhaps spirit, of which I was not conscious at the time, but which I now realize that I must have possessed. It is with an admiration mingled with envy that I see these youthful, shapely figures, bare-necked and bare-kneed, swinging rhythmically past. I watch a brisk crew lift a boat out of the water by a boat-house; half of them duck underneath to get hold of the other side, and they march up the grating gravel in a solemn procession. I see a pair of cheerful young men, released from tubbing, execute a wild and inconsequent dance upon the water's edge; I see a solemn conference of deep import between a stroke and a coach. I see a neat, clean-limbed young man go airily up to a well-earned tea, without, I hope, a care or an anxiety in his mind, expecting and intending to spend an agreeable evening. "Oh, Jones of Trinity, oh, Smith of Queen's," I think to myself, "*tua si bona nôris!* Make the best of the good time, my boy, before you go off to the office, or the fourth-form room, or the country parish! Live virtuously, make honest friends, read the good old books, lay up a store of kindly recollections, of firelit rooms in venerable courts, of pleasant talks, of innocent festivities. Very fresh is the brisk morning air, very fragrant is the newly lighted bird's-eye, very lively is the clink of knives and forks, very keen is the savor of the roast beef that floats up to the dark rafters of the College Hall. But the days are short and the terms are few; and do not forget to be a sensible as well as a good-humored young man!"

What then, if any, are the gains that make up for the lack of youthful prowess? They are, I can contentedly say, many and great. In the first place, there is the loss of a quality which is productive of an extraordinary amount of pain among the young, the quality of self-consciousness. How often was one's peace of mind ruined by *gaucherie*, by shyness, by the painful consciousness of having nothing to say, and the still more painful consciousness of having said the wrong thing in the wrong way! Of course, it was all immensely exaggerated. If one went into chapel, for instance, with a straw hat, which one had forgotten to remove, over a surplice, one had the feeling for several days that it was written in letters of fire on every wall. I was myself an ardent conversationalist in early years, and, with the charming omniscience of youth, fancied that my opinion was far better worth having than the opinions of Dons encrusted with pedantry and prejudice. But if I found myself in the society of these petrified persons, by the time that I had composed a suitable remark, the slender opening had already closed, and my contribution was either not uttered at all, or hopelessly belated in its appearance. Or some deep generalization drawn from the dark backward of my vast experience would be produced, and either ruthlessly ignored or contemptuously corrected by some unsympathetic elder of unyielding voice and formed opinions. And then there was the crushing sense, at the conclusion of one of these interviews, of having been put down as a tiresome and heavy young man. I fully believed in my own liveliness and sprightliness, but it seemed an impossible task to persuade my elders that these qualities were there. A good-natured, elderly friend used at times to rally me upon my shyness, and say that it all came from thinking too much about myself. It was as useless as if one told a man with a toothache that it was mere self-absorption that made him suffer. For I have no doubt that the disease of self-consciousness is incident to intelligent youth. Marie Bashkirtseff, in the terrible self-revealing journals which she wrote, describes a visit that she paid to someone who had expressed an interest in her and a desire to see her. She says that as she passed the threshold of the room she breathed a prayer, "O God, make me worth seeing!" How often used one to desire to make an impression, to make oneself felt and appreciated!

Well, all that uneasy craving has left me. I no longer have any particular desire for or expectation of being impressive. One likes, of course, to feel brisk and lively; but whereas in the old days I used to enter a circle with the intention of endeavoring to be felt, of giving pleasure and interest, I now go in the humble hope of receiving either. The result is that, having got rid to a great extent of this pompous and self-regarding attitude of mind, I not only find myself more at ease, but I also find other people infinitely more interesting. Instead of laying one's frigate alongside of another craft with the intention of conducting a boarding expedition, one pays a genial visit by means of the long-boat with all the circumstance of courtesy and amiability. Instead of desiring to make conquests, I am glad enough to be tolerated. I dare, too, to say what I think, not alert for any symptoms of contradiction, but fully aware that my own point of view is but one of many, and quite prepared to revise it. In the old days I demanded agreement; I am now amused by divergence. In the old days I desired to convince; I am now only too thankful to be convinced of error and ignorance. I now no longer shrink from saying that I know nothing of a subject; in old days I used to make a pretense of omniscience, and had to submit irritably to being tamely unmasked. It seems to me that I must have been an unpleasant young man enough, but I humbly hope that I was not so disagreeable as might appear.

Another privilege of advancing years is the decreasing tyranny of convention. I used to desire to do the right thing, to know the right people, to play the right games. I did not reflect whether it was worth the sacrifice of personal interest; it was all-important to be in the swim. Very gradually I discovered that other people troubled their heads very little about what one did; that the right people were often the most tiresome and the most conventional, and that the only games which were worth playing were the games which one enjoyed. I used to undergo miseries in staying at uncongenial houses, in accepting shooting invitations when I could not shoot, in going to dances because the people whom I knew were going. Of course one has plenty of disagreeable duties to perform in any case; but I discovered gradually that to adopt the principle of doing disagreeable things which were supposed to be amusing and agreeable was to misunderstand the whole situation. Now, if I am asked to stay at a tiresome house, I refuse, I decline invitations to garden parties and public dinners and dances, because I know that they will bore me; and as to games, I never play them if I can help, because I find that they do not entertain me. Of course there are occasions when one is wanted to fill a gap, and then it is the duty of a Christian and a gentleman to conform, and to do it with a good grace. Again, I am not at the mercy of small prejudices, as I used to be. As a young man, if I disliked the cut of a person's whiskers or the fashion of his clothes, if I considered his manner to be abrupt or unpleasing, if I was not interested in his subjects, I set him down as an impossible person, and made no further attempt to form acquaintance.

Now I know that these are superficial things, and that a kind heart and an interesting personality are not inconsistent with boots of a grotesque shape and even with mutton-chop whiskers. In fact, I think that small oddities and differences have grown to have a distinct value, and form a pleasing variety. If a person's manner is unattractive, I often find that it is nothing more than a shyness or an awkwardness which disappears the moment that familiarity is established. My standard is, in fact, lower, and I am more tolerant. I am not, I confess, wholly tolerant, but my intolerance is reserved for qualities and not for externals. I still fly swiftly from long-winded, pompous, and contemptuous persons; but if their company is unavoidable, I have at least learned to hold my tongue. The other day I was at a country-house where an old and extremely tiresome General laid down the law on the subject of the Mutiny, where he had fought as a youthful subaltern. I was pretty sure that he was making the most grotesque misstatements, but I was not in a position to contradict them. Next the General was a courteous, weary old gentleman, who sat with his finger-tips pressed together, smiling and nodding at intervals. Half an hour later we were lighting our candles. The General strode fiercely up to bed, leaving a company of yawning and dispirited men behind. The old gentleman came up to me and, as he took a light, said with an inclination of his head in the direction of the parting figure, "The poor General is a good deal misinformed. I didn't choose to say anything, but I know something about the subject, because I was private secretary to the Secretary for War."

REFLECTIONS ON MY
EIGHTIETH BIRTHDAY

——————— *Bertrand Russell* ———————

Bertrand Russell is a philosopher, writer and scholar of world renown. His has been a life of great achievement and great controversy. The grandson of an earl, he was born into one of Great Britain's most aristocratic families. He became a fellow of Trinity College, Cambridge, but was dismissed in 1918 because of his pacifist viewpoint. With Alfred North Whitehead, he was the author of the monumental Principia Mathematica, *which is recognized as one of the great classics on the subject. In 1940, when he was appointed to the faculty of the College of the City of New York, he became the center of a controversy which resulted in the cancellation of the appointment. Yet in 1950 he won the Nobel Prize in literature. He himself speaks of "bitter lessons . . . learned by tragic experience." Out of his life, Russell says, has come "something that I feel to be victory."*

✌

MY work is near its end, and the time has come when I can survey it as a whole. How far have I succeeeded, and how far have I failed? From an early age I thought of myself as dedicated to great and arduous tasks. Sixty-one years ago, walking alone in the Tiergarten through melting snow under the coldly glittering March sun, I determined to write two series of books: one abstract, growing gradually more concrete; the other concrete, growing gradually more abstract. They were to be crowned by a synthesis, combining pure theory with a practical social philosophy. Except for the final synthesis, which still eludes me, I have written these books. They have been acclaimed and praised, and the thoughts of many men and women have been affected by them. To this extent I have succeeded.

But as against this must be set two kinds of failure, one outward, one inward.

To begin with the outward failure: Communists, Fascists, and Nazis have successively challenged all that I thought good, and in defeating them much of what their opponents have sought to preserve is being lost. Freedom has come to be thought weakness, and tolerance has been compelled to wear the garb of treachery. Old ideals are judged irrelevant, and no doctrine free from harshness commands respect.

The inner failure, though of little moment to the world, has made my mental life a perpetual battle. I set out with a more or less religious belief in a Platonic eternal world, in which mathematics shone with a beauty like that of the last Cantos of the *Paradiso.* I came to the conclusion that the eternal world is trivial, and that mathematics is only the art of saying the same thing in different words. I set out with a belief that love, free and courageous, could conquer the world without fighting. I ended by supporting a bitter and terrible war. In these respects there was failure.

But beneath all this load of failure I am still conscious of something that I feel to be victory. I may have conceived theoretical truth wrongly, but I was not wrong in thinking that there is such a thing, and that it deserves our allegiance. I may have thought the road to a world of free and happy human beings shorter than it is proving to be, but I was not wrong in thinking that such a world is possible, and that it is worth while to live with a view to bringing it nearer. I have lived in the pursuit of a vision, both personal and social. Personal: to care for what is noble, for what is beautiful, for what is gentle; to allow moments of insight to give wisdom at more mundane times. Social: to see in imagination the society that is to be created, where individuals grow freely, and where hate and greed and envy die because there is nothing to nourish them. These things I believe, and the world, for all its horrors, has left me unshaken.

YANKEE FROM OLYMPUS
OLIVER WENDELL HOLMES

—— *Catherine Drinker Bowen* ——

What is more beautiful and more inspiring than a serene and honored old age? To feel that one is a burden to none, to have the young appealing for advice and to feel the continuing stir of intellectual curiosity, to be able even at ninety to read the greatest books and think the greatest thoughts is a fate which all of us might envy. Rarely has it been achieved so completely as by the grand old man about whom the following selection is written. His was one of the most distinguished New England families. His grandfather, for whom he was named, had been a great physician and a great literary figure. As a young man, the grandson was wounded three times in the Civil War. He became an attorney and wrote The Common Law, *which greatly influenced the development of jurisprudence in the United States. Then as Professor of Law at Harvard and as Justice of the Supreme Court of the United States, he became nationally revered. Known as the "great dissenter" because of his willingness to defend minority causes, he made a permanent contribution to our national heritage. But the time came, even while he remained vigorously able to dissent from his brethren on the Court, when he felt he must*

*step down. He was then ninety years old. Catherine Drinker Bowen
here tells the moving story of his final years. Mrs. Bowen has achieved
an outstanding position in American literature. She has written a number of perceptive and successful biographies, of which* Yankee from
Olympus *is one. She is a gifted amateur musician and her inspirational
essays have been widely read.*

✍

WHEN Court opened for the autumn term, Chief Justice Taft
looked at his brethren with an anxious eye. Old age, it seemed, had
in no way modified Holmes's wrong-headedness; he still read the
Fourteenth Amendment the way Brandeis read it, and he was
almost a fanatic on the subject of free speech.

By all the laws of nature, Holmes should retire. As the New
Year approached, newspapermen came round with the usual question. Taft read Holmes's reply and was not comforted. "I shall not
resign or retire," Holmes had said stoutly, "until the Almighty Himself requests it."

But the Almighty saw fit to request—and suddenly—a quite
different retirement. On Holmes's eighty-ninth birthday, March
8, 1930, Taft himself died, aged seventy-three.

The President appointed Hughes Chief Justice. Coming back
to Court after fourteen years, Hughes watched Justice Holmes
a trifle apprehensively. Was a man of eighty-nine capable of a
full day's work in this most exacting job? Lately, Holmes's legs
had become very weak. On that first day, Hughes noted how Brandeis
helped him to his seat.

The first lawyer stood up. Holmes took out his notebook, unlocked
it, slipped the key in his pocket and began to write. The Chief
Justice smiled; he had forgotten this old trick of Holmes's. At the
lunch hour he asked to see the notebook. . . . Holmes had not
missed a detail. It was a perfect synopsis.

But after lunch when the Justices were in their places and the
lawyer had talked for ten minutes, Holmes put his fingers to his
forehead and went off to sleep. Hughes reached out cautiously,
poked him in the leg. Later that afternoon, McReynolds interrupted a lawyer who was young and obviously inexperienced.
Holmes took his hand from his forehead and leaned forward. "I
wouldn't answer that question if I were you," he said clearly to
the young man, and went back to sleep.

In May, Holmes got ready a dissent that would sum up what he had tried to say so often concerning the rights of the states to make their own economic experiments. This was a tax case— the third in rapid succession where a man's heirs balked at paying a transfer tax on bonds moved across the state line. In all three cases McReynolds, speaking for the Court, said it was a violation of the Fourteenth Amendment for a man to be taxed in two states on transferred securities, and in all three cases Holmes dissented.

Preparing his dissent in the last case—*Baldwin v. Missouri*— Holmes talked about it to his secretary. Of course it was disagreeable for a bond owner to be taxed in two places at once, and he would say so in Court. But why did men make such an infernal fuss over these things? With taxes a man buys civilization—by no means a bad bargain.

If Missouri wanted to levy this particular kind of tax, Holmes saw nothing in the Constitution to prevent it. In nullifying these state taxes the Court, it seemed to him, acted on their own economic theories—and then called upon the Constitution as a sanction. Holmes had already stated his views briefly in the first two cases. But there was more to say and he intended to say it:—

"I have not yet adequately expressed," he began on that day of May 26, "the more than anxiety that I feel at the ever increasing scope given to the Fourteenth Amendment in cutting down what I believe to be the constitutional rights of the States. As the decisions now stand, I see hardly any limit but the sky to the invalidating of those rights if they happen to strike a majority of this Court as for any reason undesirable. . . ."

No limit but the sky. The phrase caught the nation's ear. The *New Republic* said no graver words had been spoken on the Supreme Court since Justice Curtis read his dissent in the Dred Scott case. The Baltimore *Sun* said Holmes had given an "inside spanking" to a Court that was far too concerned with property rights. The Chicago *Daily News*, the New York *World*, the Milwaukee *Journal*, applauded this judicial prod in the ribs of a property-conscious Bench. Holmes's picture was printed, showing him walking to work on his eighty-ninth birthday. "Alert Justice Holmes," the caption read.

Holmes saw it. *Alert*—that was how he felt himself; it was good to know he was not deceived. The phrase was more reassuring somehow than any compliment to his intellectual powers or that "legal acumen" the papers loved to talk about. . . . Standing before the hall mirror on a fine afternoon late in May, Holmes looked at his reflection. His light gray suit fitted him nicely, the Legion button looked well on it too. He put on his gray fedora with the wide black band and stepped back. . . . This was a better effect than that portrait his secretaries had commissioned last summer for the Law School. Charles Hopkinson had painted it—full length in judicial robes, crowned with white hair and mustache. "That isn't me," Holmes had said when it was finished, "but it's a damn good thing for people to think it is."

Holmes's ninetieth birthday—March 8, 1931—fell on a Sunday. The newspapers greeted him warmly. "He is one of us, and few people can say that of such a man. He is part of all our past. It is hard to think of a future that he will not share."

Sitting in his library, Holmes read his birthday messages. From England came notice that he had been made a member of the Honorable Society of Lincoln's Inn—the first time the Benchers had elected anyone outside the British Empire. The *Harvard Law Review* for that month was dedicated to him. The Lord High Chancellor and the Attorney-General of Great Britain had written in it; so had Pollock, Chief Justice Hughes, and Roscoe Pound. Frankfurter came down from Harvard, in his hand a new book entitled *Mr. Justice Holmes*, filled with articles about him by such men as Cardozo, John Dewey, Professor Wigmore, Walter Lippmann, Judge Learned Hand. Frankfurter himself had an article in it. Holmes turned the pages slowly as Frankfurter, beaming with pleasure, stood before him.

Holmes looked up, trying to joke it all away, but could not, and wept a little instead at the tone of affection that lay so plainly beneath these public greetings. . . . Strange not to hear Fanny's voice, breaking in. "*Wendell! Your hair needs cutting.* . . . *Wendell, did you know the New York* Journal *thinks you are 'the laboring man's hope'?*" . . . So many to praise—but none, not one, to cut through with the sharp familiar voice that alone dares bring a man back to earth, back to the battle where he belongs while his powers endure. . . . "*Wendell—I see by the* Transcript *that if you keep on you may be almost as famous as your father, some day.*"

That Sunday evening there was a microphone on Holmes's

desk. At half-past ten, the President of the Bar Association and Dean Clark of the Yale Law School would speak from New York, Chief Justice Hughes from Washington. Holmes was to answer them briefly. The day before, the Associated Press had said the Justice would probably not use all his five minutes; he didn't like speeches and publicity. "But let everyone listen; this man is one of the few who make literature out of law."

Up in Cambridge, five hundred people gathered in Langdell Hall. There were speeches about Holmes, and reminiscences, until at last the room was silent, all faces turned to the microphone. The familiar voice came through, speaking slowly—a little tired but clear and articulate, rhythmic as always:—

In this symposium my part is only to sit in silence. To express one's feelings as the end draws near is too intimate a task.

But I may mention one thought that comes to me as a listener-in. The riders in a race do not stop short when they reach the goal. There is a little finishing canter before coming to a standstill. There is time to hear the kind voices of friends and to say to one's self: "The work is done." But just as one says that, the answer comes: "The race is over, but the work never is done while the power to work remains." The canter that brings you to a standstill need not be only coming to rest. It cannot be while you still live. For to live is to function. That is all there is in living.

And so I end with a line from a Latin poet who uttered the message more than fifteen hundred years ago:—

"Death plucks my ear and says, Live—I am coming."

Next day—Monday—the nation noted with pride that Justice Holmes was at his place on the Bench and delivered a majority opinion. All that spring he did not miss a day. To watch him was a miracle. "Justice Holmes," the papers said, "makes of old age a pleasure, something to look forward to."

But the people near him, the household, knew that his strength was very limited now—that he tired quickly and could no longer work at night. Next autumn, after the summer at Beverly, a great change was noticeable. Holmes was bent nearly double. In the afternoons after Court, Brandeis came round to go driving with him. They walked down the steps and across the pavement to the car, Brandeis on one side, Buckley on the other. "Straighten up there, Judge!" Buckley would say imploringly. "You don't want to walk all bowed over like that." Together the two men tried to pull him straight. "It's not so easy as you think," Holmes said.

On the morning of January 11, 1932, Holmes had a majority opinion to deliver—a case under the Prohibition Act: *James Dunn v. the United States*. In the robing room, Arthur Thomas, the tall, gray-haired Negro who had been Holmes's messenger for so long, helped him on with the heavy silk gown. The Justices entered the Courtroom, climbed the dais. Brandeis was not in Court that day. Chief Justice Hughes, holding tightly to Holmes's arm, felt him lean heavily, stagger a little.

When his time came Holmes leaned forward, picked up the papers in *Dunn v. the United States*. Spectators noticed how well he looked; the cheeks were pink against the white hair and mustache. But when he began to read, Holmes's voice faltered, thickened. He shook his head impatiently and went on. But what he said was barely audible beyond the front row of benches.

At the noon recess, Holmes left the Courtroom with the other Justices, ate his box lunch and returned to the Bench. When Court rose at four-thirty, he got his hat and coat, walked over to the Clerk's desk. "I won't be down tomorrow," he said.

That night, Holmes wrote his resignation to the President . . . *The time has come and I bow to the inevitable. I have nothing but kindness to remember from you and from my brethren. My last word should be one of grateful thanks.*

It was Brandeis who missed him most. Next day at noon the Justices wrote to Holmes and sent the note around by messenger. Holmes sent back his reply:—

My Dear Brethren:

You must let me call you so once more. Your more than kind, your generous, letter, touches me to the bottom of my heart. The long and intimate association with men who so command my respect and admiration could not but fix my affection as well. For such little time as may be left for me I shall treasure it as adding gold to the sunset.

Affectionately yours,
Oliver Wendell Holmes

Holmes's resignation left a solid conservative majority on the Bench. At such a time this was more than a misfortune, it was a disaster. The choice was in Hoover's hands—and in January, 1932, three years of depression had wiped out the nation's confidence in its President's ability to do anything right, let alone choose a liberal justice. The Senate had turned down Hoover's last appointee to the Court—Judge Parker of North Carolina; with protest they had accepted Hughes as Chief Justice.

What if Hoover put in Calvin Coolidge? His name was on the list. Or John W. Davis, or Rugg of Massachusetts? Republican insurgents like Senator Norris, Democratic Senators from Arkansas, Montana, Texas, issued statements that were half praise for the departed, half angry warning for the future. Holmes, of course, was a Republican. The actual party affiliations of the new Justice wouldn't matter; the history of the Supreme Court proved that. What mattered desperately was whether Hoover's appointee was going to vote down every reform Congress put through. In this worst financial panic of history, the nation turned to the government for relief, asked control over prices, credit, commerce. The demand, carrying more power and more desperation than any such popular demand before, bore almost the aspect of revolution.

The nation, in short, asked protection against a system that had let disaster come upon it. Newspapers ran angry editorials:—

Government is at stake! The resignation of that noble old justice, Holmes, destroys a liberal majority of one. Let the U. S. Senate put Hoover's choice of that liberal majority of one under a microscope—and fight to the last ditch for a new justice having the views—if not the legal acumen—of an Oliver Wendell Holmes!

Holmes read the reports, heard all over the nation the alarums sound—and was not afraid. Ninety years of living does not encourage a man to panic. People talked of revolution. An ugly word, a terrible word. Holmes had heard it before. Seventy years ago he had seen the country come through a revolution—they called it a Civil War. He had prophesied that not internal disputes but competition from new races would test whether our government "could hang together and could fight." He still believed it. There were plenty of things wrong with the United States Government and while free speech endured there would be, fortunately, plenty of people to stand up and shout about it. But Holmes believed the United States Government was strong and would endure. He had said so more than once.

As for his own immediate successor on the Court, he hoped it would be Cardozo. Not only was Cardozo's legal philosophy close to his own; the man's sensitiveness of perception, his generosity of view, were extraordinary. But it was not Holmes's business to make known his choice. He was out of it. He had resigned, retired.

Silence, resignation. To sit in one's library in the morning and read eulogies of oneself, receive admiring visitors. . . . Was there any praise, were there any crowns in heaven or earth to take the place of the work a man loved and had relinquished? In all his life, Holmes had never been without a job. At night the papers on his desk, the Year Book with the marker at the page—these had been for him the bridge between night and morning. The very act of waking each day had been exciting, with the battle waiting. *"Bugler, blow the charge! I am ready. . . ."*
And now the bugler blew his charge no more. The battle was over, the challenger was still. Holmes felt tired, exhausted. When he tried to write his friends about his resignation, it was hard even to hold the pen.

Anxiously the household watched him. For the past ten years Dr. Adams, the family physician, had said the Judge would die if he stopped work. Holmes, indeed, had said it himself. Now the prophecy seemed in danger of fulfillment.

But it was not fulfilled. For Holmes, fate had not reserved this particular defeat—to die of heartbreak because he was no longer useful. Three years of life remained, and they were not to be unhappy years. Once more Holmes rallied, once more his spirit reasserted itself.

It was to Pollock he gave testimony. It was "wonderful and incredible to have no duties"; he could not have believed how much he would like it. There was so much to learn! His secretary read aloud by the hour while Holmes played solitaire or sat listening. Often he seemed to doze, but if the secretary stopped reading, Holmes sat forward instantly. "What?" he would say. "What, Sonny?" And he would begin instantly to discuss the book. Just before they went to Beverly Farms, Holmes wrote to Pollock that he must surely be getting cultivated—his secretary calculated they had read 4,500,000 words! Spengler and John Dewey, Salter and Belloc and McDougall and C. E. Broad— "sweetened," Holmes said, by rereading all of Sherlock Holmes. He couldn't agree with Parrington and Beard that the American

Constitution represented a triumph of the money power over democratic individualism. Belittling arguments always have a force of their own. "But you and I," Holmes added to Pollock, "believe that high-mindedness is not impossible to man."

Frankfurter came, one day, with the manuscript of a book about Brandeis, a companion volume to the one he had got out about Holmes. Would the Judge write an introduction? Very gladly, Holmes said. He had known Brandeis—how long? Why, it was half a century! Ever since the '70s when Brandeis emerged from the Law School to be Sam Warren's partner on State Street. . . . "In moments of discouragement that we all pass through," Holmes wrote, "Brandeis always has had the happy word that lifts one's heart. It came from knowledge, experience, courage and the high way in which he has always taken life. Whenever he left my house I was likely to say to my wife, 'There goes a really good man.' "

Beverly that summer was beautiful. Fanny's rose garden bloomed riotously and his own patch of wild flowers seemed lovelier than ever. Old friends came out from Boston, bringing their grandchildren. Holmes enjoyed these young people. There was a singular and striking beauty now to Holmes's face, a quality almost luminous. Sitting on the porch he discussed life with Betsy Warder, aged sixteen. "I won't refrain from talking about anything because you're too young," Holmes told her, "if you won't because I'm too old."

In the fall when he returned to Washington, Frankfurter sent down a new secretary as usual. It would do the young men good, he said, to be with Holmes even if he was no longer on the Court. Holmes protested, but he was very glad to have a man in the house to talk to. The secretary, arriving in October, watched the Judge with amazement, particularly at breakfast. Why, the old man attacked his breakfast like a cavalry officer in the field! Porridge—a heaping plateful with thick cream, lots of sugar. Fruit, broiled fish, muffins, marmalade, coffee. After breakfast the Judge announced he was going to loaf all day. "Ninety-two has outlived duty," he said with what seemed a vast satisfaction. Half an hour later he was calling for the secretary to read to him. "Let's have a little self-improvement, Sonny."

Beyond all other traits, this perpetual thirst to learn surprised both young and old. Franklin D. Roosevelt, a few days after his inauguration in 1933, came round to call. He found Holmes in his library, reading Plato. The question rose irresistibly. "Why do you read Plato, Mr. Justice?"

"To improve my mind, Mr. President," Holmes replied.

It was true. *The rule of joy and the law of duty seem to me all one.* Years ago, Holmes had said it, and time had not disproved it. To the beholder there was something enormously reassuring in this spectacle of a man so old and so wise, who still desired to learn.

The morning the President called, Frankfurter was there, and Harold Laski. Three days earlier—March 5—Roosevelt had closed the banks, laid an embargo on gold and called a special session of Congress for March ninth. March ninth was tomorrow. Tomorrow the President, standing before Congress, would present his plan for the national emergency.

Rising when his visit was ended, Roosevelt paused at the door, turned earnestly to Holmes and addressed him as the greatest living American. "You have lived through half our country's history; you have seen its great men. This is a dark hour. Justice Holmes, what is your advice to me?"

Holmes looked at him. "You are in a war, Mr. President," he said. "I was in a war, too. And in a war there is only one rule: *Form your battalions and fight.*"

The seasons rolled by. . . . Spring and summer. . . Beverly, with Fanny's delphinium still blue and tall by the gate. Washington again, with the Justices coming round to call. Brandeis and Cardozo, Stone with a new etching for Holmes to pass upon. Frankfurter, bounding up the long stairs to the library, his arms full of new books, talk bubbling on his tongue. More than ever, the country was impatient with the Supreme Court. The papers were full of it; except for Stone, Brandeis, and Cardozo the Court didn't have an idea which way the world was turning.

Roosevelt's National Recovery Act was under bitterest attack. Obviously, the Court was going to vote it out of existence. They did. Reporters rang the bell at I Street. "There is nothing to howl about," Holmes told them. "There have always been changes in the interpretation laid on the Constitution, and there always will be."

One day—it was the twenty-third of February, 1935—Holmes

came down the steps in the early afternoon with his secretary and got in the car to go for a drive. It was a bitter day, windy, with a threat of snow. Next morning Holmes had a cold. "You shouldn't have let him go out," Mary Donnellan told the secretary. "Mrs Holmes wouldn't have let him, on such a day." The household gathered round reproachfully. "Why don't you call the doctor, Mr. Rowe? Mrs. Holmes would have called the doctor."

The Judge went to bed, sneezing, and the sneeze turned to a cough, to something worse. Holmes was ninety-three, and he had pneumonia. By the first of March, the city knew that he was mortally ill.

Holmes knew it too, and was not dismayed. "Why should I fear death?" he had remarked to his secretary a few weeks earlier. "I have seen him often. When he comes he will seem like an old friend." Holmes had loved life. . . . "If the good Lord should tell me I had only five minutes to live, I would say to Him, 'All right, Lord, but I'm sorry you can't make it ten.'" He had loved life and he had believed in it. . . . "*If I were dying my last words would be: Have faith and pursue the unknown end.*"

Now he was dying—and he said nothing half so dramatic. He lay quietly, joking with the nurses. What was the use of all this trouble—coaxing an old man to eat, giving him stimulants? Life was—what had he called it, in that speech at Harvard? "Life is action and passion." People said death was a rest from labors. It wasn't a rest—it was an obliteration, a passing of bone into dust, of one set of chemicals into another set of chemicals. And that was right too. Very right and proper.

He had had his share. Six years ago, half of life had died, with Fanny. But even half of life had been good. *To have done what lay in you to do, to say that you have lived, and be ready for the end* . . . Oliver Wendell Holmes waited quietly in his bed.

March 2, 3, 4 . . . Across the street in an office building, newspapers held the death watch. Was the Justice going to live until his ninety-fourth birthday? Photographers hung round the front door, taking pictures of Chief Justice Hughes, of Brandeis and Mrs. Roosevelt. Taxi drivers, cruising by, called out to the policeman stationed at the door. "How is he? How is the Judge?"

In his long white iron bed, Holmes breathed heavily now, his eyes closed. In the next room, the doctors consulted and beyond that in the secretary's study a group of men sat. Mark Howe and

Tom Corcoran and Rowe. Frankfurter, John Palfrey, Edward Jackson Holmes, down from Boston.

On the fifth of March, late in the afternoon, newspapermen saw an ambulance stop outside the door. An oxygen tent was carried in. Holmes, opening his eyes, watched the huge, unwieldy contraption wheeled to the bed, saw them lift the tent above his face.

People were kind; they went to enormous trouble to give an old man a few more breaths. . . . His father hadn't died this way, boxed under a tent with a glass window. His father had died sitting in the library at home. The book had fallen from his hand. . . . How red the sky had been, above the Charles River! . . . *What is it for me, Wendell-King's Chapel? Very well, that is all I want to know.*

Very well . . . very well. . . . *It is well.* . . . There was something his mother used to read to him and Ned and Amelia, on Sundays, from the Bible. . . . "And they asked, 'Is it well with thee? Is it well with the child?' And she answered, '*It is well.*'". . . . .

At two in the morning the doctors knew the end was near. They took the oxygen tubes away. Holmes lay with his eyes closed, breathing quietly. Outside, in the March garden, wet branches creaked and from the alley came the sound of wheels. As the doctors watched, Holmes died, taking his departure so quietly it was hard to tell when he was gone.

Mark Howe, the signs of grief plain on his face, went downstairs, opened the front door. From across the street a dozen newsmen rushed at him, notebooks in hand. They listened, then raced for the telephone. Justice Oliver Wendell Holmes was dead.

The funeral was held at All Souls Church—the old, white-pillared building that stands at the head of Sixteenth and Harvard Streets. A wet wind blew across the square. People stood on the curb, watching the Justices at the church steps. The bell tolled. . . . That was Brandeis, they said, going up the steps; the Justices were to be pallbearers. Those six men waiting beside them had been Holmes's secretaries. The service wouldn't be long. Afterward the army would carry the Judge to Arlington.

"*And Moses chose from among the people able men, such as feared God, men of truth, hating unjust gains, and set them over the people to judge them at all seasons. . . .*"

The minister's voice was slow. . . . Outside, mounted policemen turned traffic away from the church. . . . "At the grave of a hero—"

the minister was reading from Holmes's own words now—"at the grave of a hero we end, not with sorrow at the inevitable loss, but with the contagion of his courage; and with a kind of desperate joy we go back to the fight."

The President and Justices waited beside Holmes's grave. The procession came in sight, winding down the hill past Lee's house. Soldiers lifted the coffin, covered with the American flag, bore it across wet turf. Eight infantrymen raised their rifles and fired . . . a volley for each wound. . . .

Ball's Bluff . . . Antietam . . . Fredericksburg.

A soldier, standing a little apart, raised his bugle and blew taps.

OLIVER WENDELL HOLMES
CAPTAIN AND BREVET COLONEL
20th Massachusetts Volunteer Infantry, Civil War
JUSTICE SUPREME COURT OF THE UNITED STATES
March 1841   *March 1935*

From the floor of Congress, from the White House, from the Inns of Court in London, scholars and statesmen gave tribute, and for a few days the people mourned. But Holmes's real fame was to come slowly; the growth of his influence was to be as measured, as deep and sure, as the forces that had shaped him. Time, events, history itself, would prove his dissents. One by one they became law . . . *Hammer v. Dagenhart.* Child labor can be regulated by Congress. . . . *Lochner v. New York.* The liberty of the citizen to do as he pleases does not mean he can force other men to work twelve hours a day. . . . *Coppage v. Kansas.* . . . *Truax v. Corrigan,* and in Massachusetts, *Vegelahn v. Guntner* and *Plant v. Woods.* "I think the strike a lawful instrument in the universal struggle for life."

Free speech, like truth itself, cannot be achieved by statute. But the Bill of Rights was still worth fighting for. *Abrams v. the United States . . . Gitlow v. the People of New York . . . United States v. Rosika Schwimmer . . .* "Free thought—not free thought for those who agree with us but freedom for the thought that we hate."

There was indeed a great contagion in this courage—a courage not born with Holmes but handed down with all the accumulated force, the deep spiritual persuasion, of the generations behind him. Abiel Holmes and Abiel's father, Captain David. Great-grandmother

Hewet, teaching herself to read Virgil in a log cabin. Sally Wendell and Sally's father the Judge. Abiel's eldest son, small and light-minded but as fierce, when his heart was roused, as any patriot of them all . . . "Ay, tear her tattered ensign down!" . . . "I am too much in earnest for either humility or vanity, but I do entreat those who hold the keys of life and death to listen. . . ."

Men called the doctor's son the Great Dissenter. The title was misleading. *To want something fiercely and want it all the time—* this is not dissent but affirmation. The things Holmes wanted were great things, never to be realized. How can man realize the infinite? *Have faith and pursue the unknown end.*

"Whether a man accepts from Fortune her spade and will look downward and dig, or from Aspiration her axe and cord, and will scale the ice, the one and only success which it is his to command is to bring to his work a mighty heart."

A PIONEER MOTHER

Hamlin Garland

For our final selection on the Lengthening Shadows, we offer a portrait of a woman with little education and no wealth, who lived in obscurity and who would have died unremembered had not her writer son preserved her memory in a book. The meaning of her life lies in her devotion to duty, in her love for her children, in her unselfish helpfulness to her neighbors. Hamlin Garland's works, such as A Son of the Middle Border *and* Main-Travelled Roads, *described the heroism of the pioneers during the last century. From personal experience he knew the harshness of the life he portrayed. His story of his mother has significance for all who come in contact with old people. "Fill their rooms with sunshine," says Garland, "let them share in your success."*

❧

SHE was neither witty, nor learned in books, nor wise in the ways of the world, but I contend that her life was noble. There was something in her unconscious heroism which transcends wisdom and the deeds of those who dwell in the rose-golden light of romance. Now that her life is rounded into the silence whence it came, its significance appears.

To me she was never young, for I am her son, and as I first remember her she was a large, handsome, smiling woman—deft and powerful of movement, sweet and cheery of smile and voice. She played the violin then, and I recall how she used to lull me to sleep at night with simple tunes like "Money Musk" and "Dan Tucker." She sang, too, and I remember her clear soprano rising out of the singing of the Sunday congregation at the schoolhouse with thrilling sweetness and charm. Her hair was dark, her eyes brown, her skin fair and her lips rested in lines of laughter.

My father's return from the war brought solace and happiness, but increased her labors, for he set to work with new zeal to widen his acres of plow-land.

I have the sweetest recollections of my mother's desire to make us happy each Christmas-time, and to this end she planned jokes for herself and little surprises for us. We were desperately poor in those days, for my father was breaking the tough sod of the natural meadows and grubbing away trees from the hillside, "opening a farm," as he called it, and there was hardly enough extra money to fill three stockings with presents. So it came about that mother's stocking often held more rags and potatoes than silks or silverware. But she always laughed and we considered it all very good fun then. Its pathos makes my heart ache now.

I don't know what her feelings were about these constant removals to the border, but I suspect now that each new migration was a greater hardship than those which preceded it. With the blindness of youth and the spirit of seeking which I inherited I saw no tear on my mother's face. I inferred that she, too, was eager and exalted at the thought of "going West." I now see that she must have suffered each time the bitter pangs of doubt and unrest which strike through the woman's heart when called upon to leave her snug, safe fire for a ruder cabin in strange lands.

Our new house was a small one with but three rooms below and two above, but it had a little lean-to which served as a summer kitchen. It was a bare home, with no touch of grace other than that given by my mother's cheery presence. Her own room was small and crowded, but as she never found time to occupy it save to sleep I hope it did not trouble her as it does me now as I look back to it.

Each year, as our tilled acres grew, churning and washing and cooking became harder, until at last it was borne in upon my boyish mind that my mother was condemned to never-remitting labor. She was up in the morning before the light, cooking breakfast for us all, and she seldom went to bed before my father. She was not always well and yet the work had to be done. We all worked in those days, even my little sister ran on errands; and perhaps this was the reason why we did not realize more fully the grinding weight of drudgery which fell on this pioneer's wife.

Churning and milking we boys did for her, and the old up and down churn was a dreaded beast to us as it was to all the boys of the countryside; and yet I knew mother ought not to do such work, and I went to the dasher regularly but with a wry face. Father was not niggardly of labor-saving implements, and a clothes-wringer and washer and a barrel churn came along and they helped a little, but work never "lets up" on a farm. There are always three meals to get and the dishes to wash, and each day is like another so far as duties are concerned. Sunday brings little rest for house-wives even in winter.

But into those monotonous days some pleasure came. The neighbors dropped in of a summer evening, and each Sunday we drove away to church. In winter we attended all the "lyceums" and church "sociables," and took part in occasional "surprise parties." In all these neighborhood jollities my mother had a generous hand. Her coming always added to the fun. "Here comes Mrs. Garland!" someone would say, and every face shone brighter because of her smile.

At last a great change came to us all. My parents and sister and brother journeyed westward into South Dakota and settled in the little town of Ordway, on a treeless plain, while I turned eastward, intent on further education.

I mention this going especially because, when it became certain that my people were leaving never to return, the neighbors thronged about the house one August day to say good-by, and with appropriate speeches presented mother with some silver and glassware. These were the first nice dishes she had ever owned and she was too deeply touched to speak a word of thanks. But the givers did not take so much virtue to themselves. Some of them were women who had known the touch of my mother's hand in sickness and travail. Others had seen her close the eyes of their dead—for she had come to be a mother to everyone who suffered. Those who brought the richest gifts considered them a poor return for her own unstinting helpfulness.

I did not see her again for nearly four years, and my heart contracted with a sudden pain at sight of her. She was growing old. Her hair was gray, and as she spoke, her voice was weak and tremulous. She was again on the farm and working as of old—like one on a treadmill. My father, too, was old. He had not prospered. A drought had swept over the fair valley and men on all sides were dropping away into despair.

Old as she was, and suffering constantly from pain in her feet and ankles, she was still mother to everyone who suffered. Even while I was there she got up on two demands in the middle of the night and rode away across the plain in answer to some suffering woman's call for help. She knew death intimately. She had closed the eyes of many a world-weary wife or suffering child, and more than once a poor outcast woman of the town, sick and alone, felt the pitying touch of her lips.

I saw with greater clearness than ever before the lack of beauty in her life. She had a few new things, but they were all cheap and poor. She now had one silk dress—which her son had sent her. All else was calico. But worse than all was the bleak, burning, windswept plain—treeless, scorched, and silent save for the song of the prairie lark. I felt the monotony of her surroundings with greater keenness than ever before.

Our parting at this time was the most painful moment of my life. I had my work to do in Boston. I could earn nothing out on the plain, so I must go, but I promised it would not be for long. In my heart I determined that the remainder of her life should be freer from care and fuller of joy. I resolved to make a home for her in some more hospitable land, but the cling of her arms to my neck remained with me many days.

I have a purpose in this frank disclosure of my mother's life. It is not from any self-complacency, God knows, for I did so little and it came so late—I write in the hope of making some other work-weary mother happy. There is nothing more appealing to me than neglected age. To see an old father or mother sitting in loneliness and poverty dreaming of an absent son who never comes, of a daughter who never writes, is to me more moving than Hamlet or Othello. If we are false to those who gave us birth we are false indeed.

Most of us in America are the children of working people, and the toil-worn hands of our parents should be heaped to overflowing with whatever good things success brings to us. They bent to the plow and the washboard when we were helpless. They clothed us when clothing was bought with blood, and we should be glad to return this warmth, this protection, an hundredfold. Fill their rooms with sunshine and the odor of flowers—you sons and daughters of the pioneers of America. Gather them around you, let them share in your success, and when someone looks askance at them, stand beside them and say: "These gray old heads, these gnarled limbs, sheltered me in days when I was weak and life was stern."

Then will the debt be lessened—for in such coin alone can the wistful hearts be paid.

IV. For a Time of Sorrow

THE FOLLY OF MOURNING

—— From the Gospel of Buddha ——

It is not the purpose of this book to draw on the writings of the world's great religions. Yet this short fable of a woman mourning the death of her only son, taken from the scriptures of Buddhism, is so homely in its message and has such universal application after a lapse of twenty-five centuries that we use it as the opening selection in this section, "For a Time of Sorrow."

AND Kisā Gotamī had an only son, and he died. In her grief she carried the dead child to all her neighbors, asking them for medicine, and the people said: "She has lost her senses. The boy is dead."

At length Kisā Gotamī met a man who replied to her request: "I cannot give thee medicine for thy child, but I know a physician who can."

And the girl said: "Pray tell me, sir; who is it?" And the man replied: "Go to Sakyamuni, the Buddha."

Kisā Gotamī repaired to the Buddha and cried: "Lord and Master, give me the medicine that will cure my boy."

The Buddha answered: "I want a handful of mustard-seed." And when the girl in her joy promised to procure it, the Buddha added: "The mustard-seed must be taken from a house where no one has lost a child, husband, parent, or friend."

Poor Kisā Gotamī now went from house to house, and the people pitied her and said: "Here is mustard-seed; take it!" But when she asked, "Did a son or daughter, a father or mother, die in your family?" they answered her: "Alas! the living are few, but the dead are many. Do not remind us of our deepest grief." And there was no house but some beloved one had died in it.

Kisā Gotamī became weary and hopeless, and sat down at the wayside, watching the lights of the city, as they flickered up and were extinguished again. At last the darkness of the night reigned everywhere. And she considered the fate of men, that their lives flicker up and are extinguished. And she thought to herself: "How selfish am I in my grief! Death is common to all; yet in this valley of desolation there is a path that leads him to immortality who has surrendered all selfishness."

Putting away the selfishness of her affection for her child, Kisā Gotamī had the dead body buried in the forest. Returning to the Buddha, she took refuge in him and found comfort in the Dharma, which is a balm that will soothe all the pains of our troubled hearts.

The Buddha said:

"The life of mortals in this world is troubled and brief and combined with pain. For there is not any means by which those that have been born can avoid dying; after reaching old age there is death; of such a nature are living beings.

"As ripe fruits are early in danger of falling, so mortals when born are always in danger of death.

"As all earthen vessels made by the potter end in being broken, so is the life of mortals.

"Both young and adult, both those who are fools and those who are wise, all fall into the power of death; all are subject to death.

"Of those who, overcome by death, depart from life, a father cannot save his son, nor kinsmen their relations.

"Mark! while relatives are looking on and lamenting deeply, one by one mortals are carried off, like an ox that is led to the slaughter.

"So the world is afflicted with death and decay, therefore the wise do not grieve, knowing the terms of the world.

"In whatever manner people think a thing will come to pass, it is often different when it happens, and great is the disappointment; see, such are the terms of the world.

"Not from weeping nor from grieving will any one obtain peace of mind; on the contrary, his pain will be the greater and his body will suffer. He will make himself sick and pale, yet the dead are not saved by his lamentation.

"People pass away, and their fate after death will be according to their deeds.

"If a man live a hundred years, or even more, he will at last be separated from the company of his relatives, and leave the life of this world.

"He who seeks peace should draw out the arrow of lamentation, and complaint, and grief.

"He who has drawn out the arrow and has become composed will obtain peace of mind; he who has overcome all sorrow will become free from sorrow, and be blessed."

TO PROVE HOW MUCH YOU LOVE

Princess Ileana

"Put not your trust in princes" is a proverb which does not apply to the beautiful and compassionate Princess Ileana of Rumania. Even when her family were the rulers of that country she had a deep and abiding interest in the nation's poor. Forced by the Communists to retire to her country home, she founded a hospital which she named in honor of her mother Queen Marie, and without adequate supplies or assistance ministered as best she could to the neighboring peasants. Years later, when she had come to America, she told the story in her book, Hospital of the Queen's Heart, *from which the following selection is taken. In it she tells how out of a young bride's sorrow was distilled an experience so great that she was able to say, "I never knew that there was such happiness in the world."*

∽

A YOUNG man, married for only three months, came to us with a long history of stomach trouble, suddenly grown worse. After examination we felt sure it was cancer. When we opened him we found cancer indeed, and so far advanced that Puscariu knew further intervention was useless. We closed him up without doing anything.

The patient's mother and young wife sat in the waiting room during the operation, and once again it was my heavyhearted duty to be the bearer of bad tidings. So I went to them. They rose anxiously as I came in. They were peasants; the girl had graduated from the University of Bucharest and had taught school for a year or two before she married and came to a village near Bran to live.

I greeted them, said briefly that the patient was still under anesthetic, and we sat down together. I wondered a little frantically how to begin, and then I began in the middle, for I could think of no preliminaries.

"Look," I said earnestly to the girl, my hands nervously tightened into fists in the lap of my white apron. "You do love your husband, don't you?"

She nodded, her eyes fixed on mine.

"And you've been happy together? Your marriage is a good one?"

Her eyes lit up instantly. "Oh, yes, Domnitza," she said quickly. "We are very happy."

"Well, my dear," I went on, "you will have a chance to prove how much you love him. You are going to have to love him as you never did before, and in a much harder way."

She sat very still, her eyes still on my face.

"The operation on your husband has not been successful. In fact, it was hardly an operation at all. Your husband has cancer, so badly that we cannot do anything for him."

"Is he going to die?" she interrupted in a small, steady voice, agony in her eyes.

"Yes." I made no qualifications. She had asked a straight, courageous question, worthy of a straightforward answer. "But you can do something wonderful for him before he does.

"He need never know the truth. If you love him enough you can make him believe that all is well with him, that the operation was a success, and he will get well. He is not going to live very long, and these last months of his life are in your hands. You can make them whatever you choose—gloriously happy or full of misery.

"Today we did our best for him in the operating room. It amounted to just exactly nothing. Everything, now, is up to you."

She heard me through, her eyes serious and comprehending. Tears trickled down her face as I ceased speaking.

"I understand, Domnitza," she said. "Thank you very much. I will know the things to do."

The mother leaned back against the wall while her daughter-in-law and I talked. In peasant fashion, she had covered her mouth with her hands, and now she stood up, glanced at the icon, and crossed herself.

"If this is the will of God," she said, "the Lord giveth and the Lord taketh away. We will make his last days happy."

None of us lied to the young man; we said nothing either way, but he took for granted that the operation had been a successful one. Every day during his convalescence his wife came to visit him. She brought him flowers and little nonsensical gifts, and their laughter sounded through the ward as they opened them together. Everyone shared their fun. There seemed to be no shadow upon them. She played her role admirably.

But when she left the ward after carefree, loving farewells, I was always waiting for her in the passage. She used to lay her head against my shoulder and sob silently in my arms. I did not try to speak comfort to her for there were no words to be said, but she knew that I understood her ordeal, and that I loved her.

We duly discharged her husband, and they went home together. He lived for six months. Soon after he died, his wife went to Bucharest to resume her teaching, but first she came to Bran to tell me the outcome of her tragic, loving guile.

"We had all the happiness of a long married life rolled into those months," she said. "Because every hour might be his last one, I tried to make each one as perfect as I could. It wasn't hard, for really it all consisted of little things—not hours or days, but moments. You can always take care of the moments! And then I discovered that I was doing it for myself, for my own pleasure and satisfaction. I cannot tell you how our happiness grew, Domnitza —and our love, so fast and so deep—in so short a while. Perhaps because there was no time for silly little quarrels, or my wanting my own way, or wasting precious time in foolish things that don't matter.

"I never knew that there was such happiness in the world. I'm certain that I would never have found it otherwise—only through the loss that I knew was going to come.

"Domnitza—"she leaned toward me earnestly—"why do we need to be on the edge of the grave to learn this? Just you think— how wonderful if he and I could have had the joy for many years that we had for a few months! But would we, if he hadn't been so ill, and you hadn't taught me to put him before myself?"

I was silent, for I was thinking, Who knows?

She answered her own question. "I think it is a question of knowing that such a marriage is possible, and then working at it—taking the trouble and the pains to make it turn out."

IN MY DARKEST HOUR — HOPE

Helen Hayes

The name of Helen Hayes is part of the enduring record of the American theater. She made her first stage appearance when she was six, and before she was twenty had starred in such plays as Pollyanna, Penrod *and* Dear Brutus. *Later such dramas as* What Every Woman Knows *and* Victoria Regina *lifted her to the summit of stardom. In 1918 she married Charles MacArthur, a noted American playwright. It would seem that such a life would be filled with happiness, but a great sorrow came to her when her daughter Mary died of polio in 1949. In the following selection, she tells how this sorrow affected her and how through an unusual encounter she was rescued from the numbness of despair.*

ᵔ

ON each New Year's Eve the mail brings me a gift that is done up in ordinary brown paper, yet is precious beyond price. It is from Mr. and Mrs. Isaac Frantz, Brooklyn. To understand the value of this gift you must know something about the Frantzes.

They came into my life in 1949, just after my daughter, Mary, had died of polio and I was being tortured by the unanswerable question—Why? Mary had been so lovely and talented, so young and free from sin. Why had this happened to her? I could only feel that her death had been a cruel, senseless thing.

This was a self-destroying mood, for an artist needs the belief that life holds some beauty and meaning. I could not create beauty or meaning on the stage if there was none within me. So to save myself I began to search for God. I read St. Thomas Aquinas, explored the life and works of Gandhi, read the Bible. But the search failed. My daughter was dead! That brutal fact overwhelmed me, blinded my heart.

All during this time I accepted no professional or social engagements and saw only my family and most intimate friends. But, in this self-imposed isolation, I became aware that a Mr. Isaac Frantz was telephoning almost every day, trying to get through to me. My husband finally talked to him and reported: "He has just lost a little boy with polio and he seems to think it would help his wife if she could see you."

"Oh, Charles—no! I have no strength to give her. I have barely enough for myself. I simply can't do it."

"Of course, darling. That's what I told him."

But Isaac Frantz kept telephoning and we finally agreed to let him bring his wife to our home.

I steeled myself for the ordeal.

When they arrived in their Sunday best, they were ill at ease, but they had a quiet dignity that surmounted their painful self-conscious-ness. Coming face to face with us was obviously something that demanded all their courage. Charles and I tried to put them at ease.

Now I discovered the truth about their visit. It had been the husband's idea entirely and he had arranged it without his wife's knowledge. But he was so sure that a meeting would bring some comfort to his wife that he forced himself to ask it. As for his wife, she was appalled when she heard of the completed arrangements, but knowing how difficult it had been for her husband, and how important to him, she consented to come. Each was doing this for the other—in the moment of great need.

The Frantzes owned a tiny stationery store and obviously had to struggle for the necessities of life. Charles and I had never known anything but success, fame, luxury. And yet the four of us suddenly had one thing to share, the tragic loss of our children.

Mrs. Frantz soon began talking about her son in a most natural manner, and, before I quite knew what was happening, I had plunged into a series of stories about Mary. Then a glance at Charles's surprised face made me realize that I was actually mentioning her name for the first time since her death. I had taken her memory out of hiding, and I felt better for it.

Then Mrs. Frantz told us of her plans to adopt an orphan from Israel, and for a moment I was shocked.

"You are thinking I am letting him take my little boy's place?" she asked gently, guessing my thoughts. "No one could ever do that. But in my heart there is still love and maybe wisdom, too. Should

I let these dry up and go to waste?"

"I—I don't know, Mrs. Frantz," I said.

"No, my dear, we cannot die because our children die. I should not love less because the one I loved is gone—but more should I love because my heart knows the suffering of others."

While she talked I thought about my child. Mary had been a big and wonderful part of my life. Even though that part had ended, I was a better human being for having had Mary, for having hoped and dreamed and worked for her. Tragic that it should have ended, but how much better than if it had never existed.

These were the things that Mrs. Frantz was saying, in her own way. These were the things that I now understood. Then I thought how ironic it was that I hadn't wanted Mrs. Frantz to come because I feared she would draw upon my feeble strength. It was I who drew upon hers!

When they finally rose to leave, I realized why my search for God had been fruitless—I had looked in the wrong places. He was not to be found between the covers of a book, but in the human heart.

LETTER TO MRS. BIXBY

Abraham Lincoln

DEAR MADAM:—

I have been shown in the files of the War Department a statement of the Adjutant-General of Massachusetts that you are the mother of five sons who have died gloriously on the field of battle. I feel how weak and fruitless must be any words of mine which should attempt to beguile you from the grief of a loss so overwhelming. But I cannot refrain from tendering to you the consolation that may be found in the thanks of the Republic they died to save. I pray that our Heavenly Father may assuage the anguish of your bereavement, and leave you only the cherished memory of the loved and lost, and the solemn pride that must be yours to have laid so costly a sacrifice upon the altar of freedom.

Yours, very sincerely and respectfully.

A. LINCOLN

To Mrs. Bixby, Boston, Mass.

A WORD FROM FRANCES

Frances Gunther

In a classic and beautiful story of sorrow and love, Death Be Not
Proud, *a world-famous reporter, John Gunther, has told of the death
of his son Johnny from cancer. A master journalist, the author of such
books as* Inside Europe *and* Inside Asia, *he described the unavailing
efforts to save his son. The book stirred a chord of sympathy and fellowship in the hearts of many thousands who had suffered like bereavement.
Not the least inspiring part of the book was a testament from the boy's
mother, Frances Gunther, herself a skillful writer. We reprint this
selection below. Through love Frances Gunther has attained peace.*

✧

DEATH always brings one suddenly face to face with life. Nothing,
not even the birth of one's child, brings one so close to life as his
death.

Johnny lay dying of a brain tumor for fifteen months. He was in
his seventeenth year. I never kissed him good night without wondering whether I should see him alive in the morning. I greeted him
each morning as though he were newly born to me, a re-gift of God.
Each day he lived was a blessed day of grace.

The impending death of one's child raises many questions in one's
mind and heart and soul. It raises all the infinite questions, each answer ending in another question. What is the meaning of life? What
are the relations between things: life and death? the individual and
the family? the family and society? marriage and divorce? the individual and the state? medicine and research? science and politics and
religion? man, men, and God?

All these questions came up in one way or another, and Johnny
and I talked about them, in one way or another, as he was dying for
fifteen months. He wasn't just dying, of course. He was living and
dying and being reborn all at the same time each day. How we loved
each day. "It's been another wonderful day, Mother!" he'd say, as I
knelt to kiss him good night.

There are many complex and erudite answers to all these questions,
which men have thought about for many thousands of years, and

about which they have written many thousands of books.

Yet at the end of them all, when one has put away all the books, and all the words, when one is alone with oneself, when one is alone with God, what is left in one's heart? Just this:

I wish we had loved Johnny more.

Since Johnny's death, we have received many letters from many kind friends from all parts of the world, each expressing his condolence in his own way. But through most of them has run a single theme: sympathy with us in facing a mysterious stroke of God's will that seemed inexplicable, unjustifiable and yet, being God's will, must also be part of some great plan beyond our mortal ken, perhaps sparing him or us greater pain or loss.

Actually, in the experience of losing one's child in death, I have found that other factors were involved.

I did not for one thing feel that God had personally singled out either him or us for any special act, either of animosity or generosity. In a way I did not feel that God was personally involved at all. I have all my life had a spontaneous, instinctive sense of the reality of God, in faith, beyond ordinary belief. I have always prayed to God and talked things over with Him, in church and out of church, when perplexed, or very sad, or also very happy. During Johnny's long illness, I prayed continually to God, naturally. God was always there. He sat beside us during the doctors' consultations, as we waited the long vigils outside the operating room, as we rejoiced in the miracle of a brief recovery, as we agonized when hope ebbed away, and the doctors confessed there was no longer anything they could do. They were helpless, and we were helpless, and in His way, God, standing by us in our hour of need, God in His infinite wisdom and mercy and loving kindness, God in all His omnipotence, was helpless too.

Life is a myriad series of mutations, chemical, physical, spiritual. The same infinitely intricate, yet profoundly simple, law of life that produced Johnny—his rare and precious soul, his sweetness, his gaiety, his gallantry, his courage: for it was only after his death, from his brief simple diaries, written as directly as he wrote out his beloved chemical experiments, that we learned he had known all along how grave was his illness, and that even as we had gaily pretended with him that all was well and he was completely recovering, he was pretending with us, and bearing our burden with the spirit, the élan, of a singing soldier or a laughing saint—that law of life which out of infinite mutation had produced Johnny, that law still mutating, destroyed him. God Himself, no less than us, is part of that law. Johnny was an extraordinarily lovable and alive human being. There seemed to be no evil, only an illuminating good, in him. Everybody who knew him, his friends and teachers at Lincoln, Riverdale, and Deerfield, our neighbors in the country at Madison, felt the warmth of his goodness and its great vitality in him. Yet a single cell, mutating experimentally, killed him. But the law of mutation, in its various forms, is the law of the universe. It is impersonal, inevitable. Grief cannot be concerned with it. At least, mine could not.

My grief, I find, is not desolation or rebellion at universal law or deity. I find grief to be much simpler and sadder. Contemplating the Eternal Deity and His Universal Laws leaves me grave but dry-eyed. But a sunny fast wind along the Sound, good sailing weather, a new light boat, will shake me to tears: how Johnny would have loved this boat, this wind, this sunny day!

All the things he loved tear at my heart because he is no longer here on earth to enjoy them. All the things he loved! An open fire with a broiling steak, a pancake tossed in the air, fresh nectarines, black-red cherries—the science columns in the papers and magazines, the fascinating new technical developments—the Berkshire music festival coming in over the air, as we lay in the moonlight on our wide open beach, listening—how he loved all these! For like many children of our contemporary renaissance, he was many-sided, with many loves. Chemistry and math were his particular passion, but as a younger child at school, he had painted gay spirited pictures of sailing boats and circuses, had sculpted some lovable figures, two bears dancing, a cellist playing, and had played some musical instruments himself, piano, violin, and his beloved recorder. He collected stamps, of course, and also rocks; he really loved and knew his rocks, classified them, also cut and polished them in his workshop, and dug lovely bits of garnet from the Connecticut hillsides.

But the thing closest to his heart was his Chem Lab which he cherished passionately. It grew and expanded in town and country. He wanted to try experiments that had not been done before. He liked to consider abstract principles of the sciences, searched intuitively for unifying theories.

He had many worthy ambitions which he did not live long enough to achieve. But he did achieve one: graduation with his class at Deerfield. Despite the long illness that kept him out of school a year and a half, he insisted on being tutored in the hospital and at home, taking his class exams, and the college board exams for Harvard, and then returning to Deerfield for commencement week. The boys cheered him as he walked down the aisle to receive his diploma, his head bandaged but held high, his young face pale, his dark blue eyes shining with the joy of achievement. A fortnight later, he died.

What is the grief that tears me now?

No fear of death or any hereafter. During our last summer at Madison, I would write in my diary when I couldn't sleep.

Look Death in the face. To look Death in the face, and not be afraid. To be friendly to Death as to Life. Death as a part of Life, like Birth. Not the final part. I have no sense of finality about Death. Only the final scene in a single act of a play that goes on forever. Look Death in the face: it's a friendly face, a kindly face, sad, reluctant, knowing it is not welcome but having to play its part when its cue is called, perhaps trying to say, "Come, it won't be too bad, don't be afraid, I understand how you feel, but come—there may be other miracles!" No fear of Death, no fight against Death, no enmity toward Death, friendship with Death as with Life. That is—Death for myself, but not for Johnny, God, not yet. He's too young to miss all the other parts of Life, all the other lovely living parts of Life. All the wonderful, miraculous things to do, to feel, to see, to hear, to touch, to smell, to taste, to experience, to enjoy. What a joy Life is. Why does no one talk of the joy of Life? shout, sing, write of the joy of Life? Looking for books to read with Johnny, and all of them, sad, bitter, full of fear, hate, death, destruction, damnation, or at best resignation. No great books of enjoyment, no sense of great utter simple delight pleasure fun sport joy of Life.

All the things Johnny enjoyed at home and at school, with his friends, with me. All the simple things, the eating, drinking, sleeping, waking up. We cooked, we experimented with variations on pancakes, stews, steaks. We gardened, we fished, we sailed. We danced, sang, played. We repaired things, electric wires, garden tools, chopped wood, made fires. We equipped the Chem Lab Workshop, in the made-over old boathouse, with wonderful gadgets, and tried out experiments, both simple and fantastic.

All the books we read. All the lovely old children's books, and boys' books, and then the older ones. We read Shaw aloud—how G.B.S. would have enjoyed hearing the delighted laughter of the boys reading parts in *Man and Superman* in the kitchen while I washed up the supper dishes!—and Plato's *Republic* in Richards' *Basic English*, and Russell, and St. Exupéry. On Sundays, we would have church at home: we'd sit outdoors on the beach and read from The Bible of the World, the Old Testament and the New, the Prophets and Jesus, also Buddha, Confucius, and Mahomet. Also Spinoza, Einstein, Whitehead, Jeans, Schroedinger, and Maugham.

We talked about everything, sense and nonsense. We talked about the news and history, especially American history, and its many varied strains; about the roots of his own great double heritage, German and Hebrew; about empires past and present, India's non-violent fight for freedom, and about reconciliation between Arabs and Jews in Palestine. We talked about Freud and the Oedipus complex, and behavior patterns in people and societies, getting down to local brass tacks. And we also played nonsense games, stunts, and card tricks.

We sailed, and got becalmed, and got tossed out to sea, and had to be rescued. And we planned sailing trips.

All the things we planned! College, and work, and love and marriage, and a good life in a good society.

We always discussed things a little ahead. In a way I was experimenting with Johnny as he dreamed of doing with his elements, as artists do with their natural materials. I was trying to create of him a newer kind of human being: an aware person, without fear, and with love: a sound individual, adequate to life anywhere on earth, and loving life everywhere and always. We would talk about all this as our experiment together.

He did his part in making our experiment a success. Missing him now, I am haunted by my own shortcomings, how often I failed him. I think every parent must have a sense of failure, even of sin, merely in remaining alive after the death of a child. One feels that it is not right to live when one's child has died, that one should somehow have found the way to give one's life to save his life. Failing there, one's failures during his too brief life seem all the harder to bear and forgive. How often I wish I had not sent him away to school when he was still so young that he wanted to remain at home in his own room, with his own things and his own parents. How I wish we had maintained the marriage that created the home he loved so much. How I wish we had been able before he died to fulfill his last heart's desires: the talk with Professor Einstein, the visit to Harvard Yard, the dance with his friend Mary.

These desires seem so simple. How wonderful they would have been to him. All the wonderful things in life are so simple that one is not aware of their wonder until they are beyond touch. Never have I felt the wonder and beauty and joy of life so keenly as now in my grief that Johnny is not here to enjoy them.

Today, when I see parents impatient or tired or bored with their children, I wish I could say to them, But they are alive, think of the wonder of that! They may be a care and a burden, but think, they are alive! You can touch them—what a miracle! You don't have to hold back sudden tears when you see just a headline about the Yale-Harvard game because you know your boy will never see the Yale-Harvard game, never see the house in Paris he was born in, never bring home his girl, and you will not hand down your jewels to his bride and will have no grandchildren to play with and spoil. Your sons and daughters are alive. Think of that—not dead but alive! Exult and sing.

All parents who have lost a child will feel what I mean. Others, luckily, cannot. But I hope they will embrace them with a little added rapture and a keener awareness of joy.

I wish we had loved Johnny more when he was alive. Of course we loved Johnny very much. Johnny knew that. Everybody knew it. Loving Johnny more. What does it mean? What can it mean, now?

Parents all over the earth who lost sons in the war have felt this kind of question, and sought an answer. To me, it means loving life more, being more aware of life, of one's fellow human beings, of the earth.

It means obliterating, in a curious but real way, the ideas of evil and hate and the enemy, and transmuting them, with the alchemy of suffering, into ideas of clarity and charity.

It means caring more and more about other people, at home and abroad, all over the earth. It means caring more about God.

I hope we can love Johnny more and more till we too die, and leave behind us, as he did, the love of love, the love of life.

HOW HANDLE TRAGEDY?

———— *Harry Emerson Fosdick* ————

Harry Emerson Fosdick is considered our greatest preacher by many Americans. Keenly aware of both practical and spiritual values, he is best known for his pastorate at the Riverside Church in New York and for his many successful books. He himself would no doubt say that one of his greatest satisfactions in life has been helping the thousands of troubled people who have come to him for advice. Out of this experience with actual cases, he has written, at the age of eighty-three, a book entitled Dear Mr. Brown, *from which "How Handle Tragedy?" is taken. Ted Brown is a fictional character, but, says Dr. Fosdick, "I have corresponded with men and women like him for many years, and have spent countless hours in personal conference with them."*

It is fitting that in dealing with that most profound of subjects, immortality, we should use a statement from a minister of Dr. Fosdick's eminent standing and great experience with troubled humanity. Most people believe that in immortality are bound up our most sacred aspirations. Does it not seem inconceivable, they ask, that all the meaning and purpose of a human being's life shall be snuffed out incontinently by the physical happening of death? It is not so, says Dr. Fosdick in this message of consolation and inspiration. "My Dear Ted," to whom he addresses this letter, could be any one of us in time of sorrow.

✍

MY DEAR TED:

There must be something in telepathy. All this last week I have had you on my mind, hoping that everything was going well with you and tempted to write or phone you to find out, and now your letter comes, telling me of the tragedy that has befallen your home —the sudden and utterly unexpected death of your mother. I never felt closer to you than now. Reading your letter I have relived that day when, a student in the theological seminary, I received a letter from my father saying that my mother was very ill with pneumonia, that I was not to worry but that he thought I ought to know. I didn't wait. I took the next train home, but my mother had died before I arrived. So, to use Ezekiel's figure, I have sat where you sit, and my warm sympathy goes out to you and to your father.

You say that you have waited a week before writing me, so that the first emotional shock might subside and you might gain some perspective around your experience. I am deeply impressed by what you write me now, the twofold gist of which seems to be that for the first time in your life the question of immortality has become of burning importance to you and, second, that the actual experience of personal tragedy seems to add a quite new dimension to life. You have had your normal difficulties, you write, the ordinary perplexities and troubles, but now for the first time a poignant grief has struck home to your heart, and you can see that what you do with it is of vital significance. You are certainly right about that. Nowhere more than in dealing with personal tragedy are Aldous Huxley's words true: "Experience is not what happens to a man. It is what a man does with what happens to him."

What a strange paradox our life is! We dread tragedy, we deplore and abhor it, and yet there is nothing on earth which we admire more than a character that handles it triumphantly. One scene I wish I could have witnessed—the convocation at the University of Glasgow when Helen Keller was given an honorary doctorate. There she stood, one of the most pitiably handicapped and yet one of the most radiant and useful personalities of her generation, while the award was given, the national anthem was sung, and her companion spelled into her hand the story of what was going on. Later, through the lips of her companion she made a brief response, thanking them for "a deed of generosity from the masters of knowledge and light to those who live under the covert of denial." These were her closing words: "Darkness and silence need not bar the progress of the immortal spirit." Then, says the Scottish reporter, "there was thunderous applause, which only she could not hear." It is a mysterious paradox that while we deplore Helen Keller's calamity, we admire beyond the power of words to express the spirit with which she has handled it. So one woman, hopelessly crippled in an accident, said to her family: "I'll show you how to take trouble. How you take it is the only thing about it that's important."

I often think of this with reference to the best-loved character in American history. He was a young lawyer in Springfield, Illinois, who ran for the legislature and was defeated. Then he tried business and failed, and spent many years paying the debts of a worthless partner. He fell passionately in love with a girl of his choice, who loved him in return, and then she died. He was elected to Congress in 1846 and served one term, but was defeated when he ran for re-election. Next, he tried to get an appointment to the United States Land Office and failed. Then, as a candidate for the United States Senate he was defeated, and in 1856 as a candidate for the vice-presidential nomination he was beaten again. And when at last he become President, he faced the Civil War which he would have given his life to prevent. But in Washington today there is a Memorial to him which I can never enter without having to force back the tears. Moreover, much as we deplore the hardships and troubles which

Lincoln suffered, we know that his quality of character never could have come from ease, comfort, and pleasantness alone. He did not simply endure his tragedies; he built character out of them. You are right, Ted, trouble and grief can add a new dimension to life. No hardship, no hardihood; no fight, no fortitude; no suffering, no sympathy; no pain, no patience. We may not like that kind of world, but that is the kind of world we live in.

> When was it Dante learned that he was Dante,
> Endowed by God with gifts of deathless song?
> Not till his lusts were slain, his comforts scanty,
> Himself an exile and his haters strong.

Nothing that I can write can adequately express how warmly my heart goes out to you. The death of one's mother is the end of an era—especially when the mother is as lovely as yours. You are having your first experience of real tragedy and sorrow, but in my similar experience one thing that helped me most was the conviction that I could handle my sorrow in such a way that my mother would be proud of me. It may seem at first a strange thing to say, but it is important: don't waste sorrow, it is too precious. Recall the Bible's similes for trouble. It is a "refiner's fire"; it can separate the gold in us from the alloy. It is "tribulation," that is "threshing"—it can separate the grain in us from the chaff. It is "chastening"—it can discipline, correct, purify. Don't misunderstand me. I'm not singing a hymn of praise to trouble. We all alike dread it, but it is inevitably here to be dealt with one way or another. An old adage says, "The same fire that melts the butter hardens the egg." Some people end in defeat and collapse or, as Mark Twain described them, scoffing "at the pitiful world, and the useless universe, and the violent, contemptible human race," and deriding "the whole paltry scheme." Others—thank God!—can say with Paul, "We triumph even in our troubles."

Undoubtedly a major factor in Paul's ability to triumph in his troubles was his faith in life's abiding meaning and purposefulness, reaching beyond death into life eternal. You say in your letter that you have never been especially interested in immortality so far as your own continued existence after death was concerned, but that now what happens after death looms large in your thought because of your love for your mother. Ted, that puts you in the great tradition. As one of Hugh Walpole's characters says, "There is a sniff of immortality about our love for one another." Many people seem to think that we believers in immortality are victims of self-importance, and that we want to live on because we egotistically cannot endure facing our own extinction. They do not know the great tradition of faith in immortality. One never understands *that* until one sees that love, not egotism, has been the major fountainhead of all high faith in life eternal. I can say, as well as you, that I never have discerned in myself any clamarous desire to go on beyond death, as though I thought the universe demanded my individual continuance. But when love, that great discoverer of values, comes, I cannot be so nonchalant. I may say that I do not mind what happens to me, but when a well-loved soul, nobly worth the loving, dies, I may not say, "I do not mind what happens to *you*." At that point one's whole philosophy of life's meaning is involved. Faith in immortality at its best has sprung from the love of admirable persons, and the recognition that nothing in this universe is so marvelous and so priceless. So George H. Palmer, when he was professor of philosophy at Harvard, put it: "The most consummately beautiful thing in the universe is the rightly fashioned life of a good person." Unless creation is senseless and purposeless it cannot snuff out like a guttering candle the fairest thing it has created.

Read Plato's *Phaedo*—the grandest pre-Christian argument for immortality. Let L. P. Jacks point out the gist of it: "All through that wonderful dialogue Plato keeps us thinking, not about ourselves and what is going to happen to us, but about Socrates and what is going to happen to that wise and admirable man. And gradually he works up to the point that, when Socrates takes the hemlock and passes away before our eyes, the thought that he is done for, that so great and beautiful a light is gone out forever, becomes incredible." That is the great tradition of faith in life eternal. So in Christianity Easter morning represents no egoistic self-importance on the part of the first disciples—far from it! It represents devoted love for a soul so revered that they were sure death ought not, must not, could not, did not have dominion over him.

As I read your letter I recalled a noble Christian woman, her early years rich in service, her last years courageous in endurance. As her body was carried to the grave, her husband summed up in a single sentence his conviction about the deathless value of such a person: "God must not let anything happen to her." That, I take it, is what you are feeling about your mother.

In my own thinking another consideration has also been very important. Some people seem to think it noble to declare that life after death does not concern them, that what matters is to live usefully so that they leave the world a better place for those who come after them. But that position forgets a crucial fact: *This planet is not permanent.* Once it was uninhabitable and sometime it will be uninhabitable again. If, therefore, death is the final end of personality, that is not just an individual matter. That means that all our forefathers are extinct, that we will all be extinct, that all our children's children born on earth will be extinct, and that at last everything will be as though nothing had ever been at all. That means that nothing will last except the endless, meaningless, futile process of not lasting. Without immortality it is not simply true of individuals that, as another put it, life is "a blind, brief flicker between two oblivions"; in the long run that is also true of the whole human race. I cannot believe it. And if that same futile process is afoot on other planets also, that only makes it worse. As Canon Streeter exclaimed, "What shall we say of the Power behind the universe, if it treats the individuality of heroic souls like oyster shells at a banquet, whisked from the table to make room for the next course?" A good question!—especially in view of the fact that some day on this planet there will be no next course.

This means that I have faith in the reasonableness and purposefulness of creation and its Creator. Everything worth while in life, one way or another, depends on confidence in the trustworthiness of creation. We could not carry on agriculture without faith in the reliability of the recurring seasons. All science is built on faith in the dependability of universal laws. In the background of every significant human activity is the discovery of something in the cosmos that we can rely on, depend on, have faith in, and the more we know about the universe the more we find factors here that answer our trust so that we can act on the basis of their dependability. How can we stop short of carrying such faith up into the spiritual world? Can we not trust the Creator to fulfill the promises and possibilities he has put within our souls?

Let me illustrate what I am trying to say. The developing eye of the embryo in the mother's womb is a marvelous thing. No light has ever fallen there in the unbroken darkness, but the eye is developing. No scenes are there for it to look upon, but the eye is in preparation for a world invisible and as yet unvisited. Moreover, we can trust nature. That developing eye is a dependable prophecy. There is a world where light reigns and beauty waits. In a dependable universe the developing eye itself is prediction of a reality that waits for the eye to come. So is man's spiritual life predictive. It presages more than earthly life can fulfill, and it will find more. Paul said it when, quoting Isaiah, he described the world prepared for God's loyal servants as "What no eye has ever seen, what no ear has ever heard, and what never entered the mind of man." Ted, I am convinced of that. Man's intellectual and spiritual life on earth is not a circle, rounded and complete, but a parabola that runs out into infinity. To suppose that any conceivable God creates such personality only to destroy it, and in the end on an uninhabitable planet is content with the destruction of all personalities, is to me incredible.

Of course there are endless problems, questions, difficulties, concerning immortality where the mystery is too deep for our plummets. You say that when you try to imagine your mother without the familiar body with which you long have identified her, she "disappears into invisibility and becomes unreal." I cannot help you picture what life after death is like, for I do not know. Nobody does. That is God's responsibility, not ours. But perhaps it may help a little to call your attention to the fact that you yourself are invisible now. You are a self-conscious personality, with powers of mind, volition, emotion, but no one ever saw consciousness, or a self, or an idea, a purpose, a love. You are absolutely invisible—I can see your body but not you. You never saw a thought, a hope, a desire, a devotion, an affection, or anything else that makes you the intellectual, purposive, emotional being that you are. Never say, I am a body and have a soul. The fact is the opposite of that: you are a soul and have a body. They say that if all the liquids were eliminated from our physique, and all the atoms collapsed into solid matter, a human body would be no larger than a pinhead. You are not *that*. They say that if all the chemicals in a human body were sold at market prices, they would bring no more than ninety-eight cents. Such is the body of any great scientist, artist, philanthropist. Such was the body of Jesus. But he himself was not that. Don't let your mother "disappear into invisibility." Your mother always was invisible; never in all your life did you see *her*—her self, her thoughts, loves, loyalties. Out of the unseen we came, in the unseen we live, to the unseen we go.

This fact does at least one thing for me: it shifts the mystery from our survival after death to our arrival in the first place. Take any character you most admire, and is not his arrival so great a marvel that you feel his survival is inevitable, if creation is not utterly senseless, aimless, meaningless? I knew a man once in the full tide of an important medical career, on whom disease fell and who was eighteen months adying. Here is what one friend said about him, and remember that this is one scientific man of medicine talking about another:

Those who were fortunate in seeing him during those eighteen months when he and death sat face to face—who dreaded their first visits and came out gladly inspired with a new faith in the nobility and courage to which rare men can attain—these know that the ugliness and cruelty of death were defeated. Death had no triumph, and he died as he had lived, with the simple faith of a trustful child, and the superb gallantry of a great soul.

Well, which do you think is the more marvelous, the arrival of such a soul, invisible even when embodied, or his survival, victorious over death?

In the thinking of many people the greatest obstacle to faith in immortality is the way in which they emphasize the dependence of the mind on the body. The brain, the nervous system, the glands, were here first, they say, and only as these physical structures developed did intellect, volition, character, emerge. So, they argue, when the body decays these spiritual emergents, which came from the body and are dependent on it, must disappear. But this argument forgets one of the most significant and recurrent facts in nature: that endless things start by being dependent, like an unhatched eaglet in an egg, only to achieve independence. That process seems to me clearly to be going on in the relationship of mind and body. To be sure, there are obvious areas where the mind is dependent on the body, but there are wide areas where the body is dependent on the mind, where, for example, medical science recognizes that ills of the body can be caused and cured by the mind.

The idea that the spiritual personality is altogether and inescapably dependent on the activity of physical cells seems to me to break down in one psychological area after another, such as memory, hypnotism, telepathy, extrasensory perception, etc., but most of all when we are dealing with great creative souls. Can the genius of Shakespeare, Beethoven, Einstein, be explained as due simply to a superior quality of physical brain cells? Did your mother love you simply with a nervous system? No! Mind, the self, personality, is real; it emerges from any physical dependence into a world of its own; it is essentially unlike anything physical, and what Bertrand Russell says about man seems to me incredible: "his origin, his growth, his hopes and fears, his loves and beliefs are but the outcome of accidental collocations of atoms." So, *that* is the explanation of Christ's character and of all the intellectual and spiritual grandeur and beauty we have known—only the outcome of accidental collocations of matter! The Athanasian Creed is easier to believe than that.

Don't take this as a preacher's special pleading. Dr. J. A. Hadfield, one of the most distinguished psychologists of my generation, in an essay on *The Mind and the Brain* argues on a scientific basis "that in the course of evolution the mind shows an ever-increasing tendency to free itself from physical control and, breaking loose from its bonds, to assert its independence and live a life undetermined except by the laws of its own nature."

Imagine two unborn babes in a mother's womb, conversing about the prospect that lies ahead of them. Says one: "Leaving this womb can mean nothing but death. We are absolutely dependent on this matrix which sustains and feeds us." Says the other: "But nature has been developing us for nine months. Nature is not utterly irrational. She is preparing us for something." Answers the unbelieving babe: "Describe, if you can, the kind of world you think we are going to be born into. What is it like?" That, of course, would completely stump the believing babe. "I can't describe it," he replies. "I have no idea what it is like. But I am sure that nature never would do what she has been doing all these months with no meaning or purpose in the process." To which the unbelieving babe answers with scorn: "That is blind faith." But the believing babe was right. Dependence, issuing in independence, is one of the most familiar events in nature.

I sometimes wonder what the space age is going to do to some people's faith in life eternal. For that faith means that God cares for us, one by one, and imagination finds that difficult to picture. We are so small and the universe is so immense. You mention this difficulty in your letter, and I can sympathetically understand it. But knowledge at its best is not extensive only, but intensive, not telescopic alone but microscopic also. Once a bassoon player came to Toscanini just before a rehearsal and in despair reported that his

instrument had suffered an accident, so that it could not play E-flat.
Toscanini bowed his face in his hands for a few moments, and then
lifted it again. "That's all right," he said. "The note, E-flat, does not
appear in your music today." Real knowledge is thus detailed, particular, intensive, not extensive only. So Jesus conceived God's knowledge of, and care for, us: "It is not the will of your Father in heaven
that a single one of these little ones should be lost." Despite all the
problems, I believe in that kind of God and, as I close this letter,
feeling for you a sympathy which I cannot adequately express, I
commend to you Emerson's confident affirmation:

> What is excellent,
> As God lives, is permanent;
> Hearts are dust, hearts' loves remain;
> Hearts' love will meet again.

AFFECTIONATELY YOURS,

PEACE AT EVENTIDE

Helen Keller

*We have read in a previous section how Helen Keller made her first
attempts to break out of the dark cell to which her disabilities had
consigned her. We know of the triumphant progress of her career, of
the honors and achievements that have been hers. Yet despite all these
successes, Helen Keller has necessarily remained a person apart. Better
than those who were normal, she knew the meaning of the poet's words,
"None but the lonely heart can know my sorrow." She had suffered,
but like Dr. Fosdick, she saw a way out. "Peace at Eventide" is a moving
testament of faith.*

ᔐ

WE bereaved are not alone. We belong to the largest company in
all the world—the company of those who have known suffering.
When it seems that our sorrow is too great to be borne, let us think
of the great family of the heavy-hearted into which our grief has
given us entrance, and inevitably, we shall feel about us their arms,
their sympathy, their understanding.

Vainly the tortured soul gropes in darkness for a Reason. Bereavement has come; life is lonely and bitter, and almost too terrible to be endured. Abraham Lincoln, when his little son died in his arms, said: "The Almighty has His own purposes."

"Those who struggle can never learn to float; they must relinquish themselves utterly to the mercy of the water, relax every muscle, be trustful of the element to which they give themselves." Thus said a teacher of swimming to his pupils. It is so with Eternal Love. In times of trouble if we resist and beat against the waves of misfortune we sink and are swallowed up in darkness unutterable. But if we trust, and if we relinquish our own will, and yield to the Divine will, then we find that we are afloat on a buoyant sea of peace and under us are the everlasting arms.

On chill autumn days we wander along the highroads and byways, or through the God-painted forests. We return at last, cold and weary, to our own home, and find warmth and comfort before a blazing fire on our own hearth. So in life, we wander until we are cold and weary, and at last find warmth and rest before the peacefully glowing flame of Eternity, for: Death is the hearthstone of life.

It is not so wretched to suffer loss as not to be capable of enduring it.

It is necessary for the endurableness of life that we should believe that the uncertainty, the darkness in which we are struggling, shall one day be illumined by the light of solution; and even now we possess signs and traces of the knowledge which shall come when we see that Light face to face.

The grave cannot be the habitation of one whom we have loved.

In our excess of grief and bitterness, we feel that the hand of God is against us. We look round the happy circle of our friends and it seems to us that we are the only ones bereaved; the only ones to whom has come this terrible emptiness, this dark void of loneliness. When this thought overwhelms us, it is well to remember that we are not alone in our sorrow, that

> There is no flock, however watched and tended,
>   But one dead lamb is there.
> There is no fireside, howsoe'er defended,
>   But has one vacant chair.

In the first dark hours of our grief there is no comfort in all the world for us. The anxious efforts of our friends to console us seem an intrusion. "Leave us alone," we cry in our hearts; "leave us alone with our sorrow. That is the only precious thing left to us." But when our friends depart how quickly we change, how we creep to the side of some trusted loved one and reach out wistful hands for affection and understanding. Life is like that. Bereaved though we are, we are not ghosts, but living, breathing human beings, vibrant and eager for contact with our kind. And that is as it should be. God has taken away the beloved and left us here for some purpose. There is work to be done and people to be loved and helped. No normal human being can live with shadows.

"Our friend and we were invited abroad on a party of pleasure, which is to last for ever. His chair was ready first, and he has gone before us. We could not all conveniently start together; and why should you and I be grieved at this, since we are soon to follow, and know where to find him." Benjamin Franklin wrote these words concerning death, and they seem to me very beautiful.

Our beloved ones have not "gone to a far country," it is only the veil of sense that separates them from us, and even that veil grows thin when our thoughts reach out to them.

"There's so little I can say." This is often said in apology by friends. If they but knew that any words—the most beautiful—are an intrusion at such a time, and that the truest sympathy comes with the warm close handclasp.

Is there not comfort for us in the thought that our departed dear ones have entered a broader field of usefulness than was possible for them here on earth?

Life without faith is uneasy, timorous, and wholly spent in running away from misfortunes which are in the nature of things inescapable.

My friend has long since gone into the Light; but his presence, loved and familiar, walks noiselessly by my side, his guiding hand in mine.

There is a Christmas story of a bereaved mother whose tears fell so long, they dimmed the candle of joy her little one held in his hand. Let us resolve that our grief shall not cast a shadow upon the happiness of our loved ones.

Sometimes it is well not to think. The mind mills over and over again its eternal problems of Why and When and Where. "Why" am I made thus to suffer? "When" shall I see my dear one again? "Where" is he, now that he is lost to me? It is well to remember at such a time with Cardinal Newman: "It is thy very energy of thought which keeps thee from thy God." Cease thinking, questioning, wondering; relax on the bosom of faith, and faith will not betray you.

It is because our loved ones are in the Sun, and we in the shadow, that we do not see each other.

All the aeons and aeons of time before we were born, before the spirit awoke to its present consciousness—where were we then? All the aeons and aeons of time after we are dead, after the spirit has sunk again to sleep from its present consciousness, where then shall we be? Vain questions; vain wondering. But if the spirit is eternal, we have no more reason to dread the future of the spirit than to shudder at its past. Rather, it is better to consider this, our life, merely as "a gleam of time between two Eternities," and to believe that most of the truth, most of the beauty, most of the real splendor and fulfillment lies rather in those eternities than in the here-and-now.

There is beauty in Benjamin Franklin's self-written epitaph. Here it is:

"The body of Benjamin Franklin, Printer (like the cover of an old book, its contents torn out and stripped of its lettering and gilding), lies here, food for worms. Yet the work itself shall not be lost, for it will (as he believes) appear once more in a new and more beautiful Edition, corrected and amended by the Author."

They tell me that a flash of lightning reveals everything within the range of vision clearly for an instant. Death is the penetrating flash that illumines the spirit-world which material existence veils from us in our happier hours.

Surely we would not weep if some beloved friend had the good fortune to move from a humble and uncomfortable house to a mansion into which the sunlight streamed, and whose grounds were a never-ending maze of beauty and wonder and delight. We would say that that was a fortunate friend, and, a bit wistfully, we would look forward to the time when we too might leave the burden of our daily tasks and join him in his house of beauty and light.

I am blind and have never seen a rainbow, but I have been told of its beauty. I know that its beauty is always broken and incomplete. Never does it stretch across the heavens in full perfection. So it is with all things as we know them here below. Life itself is as imperfect and broken for every one of us as the span of a rainbow. Not until we have taken the step from life into Eternity, shall we understand the meaning of Browning's words: "On the earth, the broken arc; in heaven, a perfect round."

Remember that in the Country where your loved ones have gone, the things that were impossible here become glorious realities.

As the fruit is the essence of the tree, so sympathy is the essence distilled from pain.

In the presence of suffering and death we cry in the bitterness of our hearts, "Why cannot we cast it out?" Listen, ye that mourn, and ye shall hear the wonderful answer from Matthew xvii. 20: "Because of your unbelief: for verily I say unto you, if ye have faith as a grain of mustard seed, ye shall say unto this mountain, Remove hence to yonder place; and it shall remove; and nothing shall be impossible unto you."

This from Plutarch: "Diogenes, the cynic, when, a little before death, he fell into a slumber, and his physician rousing him out of it asking whether anything ailed him, answered: 'Nothing, sir; only one brother anticipates another: Sleep before Death.'" It is well to look upon Death in this friendly, everyday way. Sleep we welcome every night, knowing from experience that there is nothing to fear. Then why should we fear the coming of our other Brother—Death?

A father, who had lost a beloved child, could not bear the companionship of his fellowmen, and turned to wood and field for solace accompanied only by his dog. His friends attempted to dissuade him from this course, but they were wrong. Gradually healing came to his spirit, breathed to him in silent understanding of trees, of grass, of sky, of his faithful canine friend. Thus we are taught that each of us who are in pain and sorrow must seek consolation after his own manner, and seeking, shall find it.

Death cannot separate those who truly love. Each lives in the other's mind and speech.

> It lies around us like a cloud,
> A world we do not see;
> Yet the sweet closing of an eye,
> May bring us there to be.

Harriet Beecher Stowe, author of *Uncle Tom's Cabin*, had a beautiful faith in the after-life. She wrote the above lines and believed them. A sweet sincerity, a child-like belief, rings in every word.

Earth-life cannot appease the soul's hunger. It is Death that flings wide the portals of eternal life. Released by death, the soul sheds its drab covering to don the radiant robe of immortality.

Never should the evening of life, any more than the evening of a single day, be thought of with fear. For evening is a time for homecoming, and of peace. We should say, as Tagore said: "The evening sky to me is like a window, and a lighted lamp, and a waiting behind it." "A lighted lamp and a waiting behind it"—there is a comforting, a beautiful certainty and serenity in those words.

There are moments when the veil between us and the spiritual world lifts, and we behold our Heavenly home in sudden light. The open door, the smiling faces of our dear ones, birds twittering in the trees, the sweet keen smell of grass and flowers, the sound of happy voices—all yield their delight once more.

"Bon voyage," call those who stay behind, to their friends who are departing for foreign lands. Cheerfully they face the separation as the water widens between them and those they love. Why can it not be just so when those whom we love have gone upon that last long voyage of death? The answer will be: "Because this is a parting for all eternity. There is no returning from the country to which these dear lost ones have turned their faces." Only those who have faith know the truth: "for those who live with God there is no last meeting."

I believe in the goodness of life, in the recreative power of the spirit, in the ennobling possibilities of suffering.

It is an encouraging thought that however difficult life may be, we are not living it alone, that above and beneath and around us are the resources of the Eternal Spirit.

"Drawing near her death, she sent most pious thoughts as harbingers to heaven; and her soul saw a glimpse of happiness through the chinks of her sickness-broken body." So said Thomas Fuller in his *Life of Monica*. Is it not selfish and cruel to want to keep with us those who suffer? For, after all, their worn bodies are but as prison cells, through which they see wistfully and longingly, as did Monica, "a glimpse of happiness."

It is a day bright with sunshine. Then, from somewhere, unexpected, comes a veil of mist and then another, until the face of the sun is hid from us, and all is dark before our eyes. Yet we never doubt for a moment the sun is still there. Some poet has said that Life itself is "A wisp of fog between us and the sun." I think that is true; I think that we—that the spirit-part of us—is eternal, that the Sun of true love and happiness is eternal, and that life, with its hurry, its bustle, its materialism, comes between us and the Sun, like a wisp of fog, a veiling cloud.

Death is not the end. "In our embers is something that doth live that nature yet remembers."

"From the voiceless lips of the unreplying dead there comes no word, but in the night of Death, Hope sees a star and listening love can hear the rustling of a wing." Thus spoke Robert G. Ingersoll, the agnostic, at his brother's grave.

A brave faith is the only bridge over which the feet of our loved ones may cross to us.

Robbed of joy, of courage, of the very desire to live, the newly-bereaved frequently avoids companionship, feeling himself so limp with misery and so empty of vitality that he is ill suited for human contacts. And yet no one is so bereaved, so miserable, that he cannot find someone else to succor, someone who needs friendship, understanding, and courage more than he. The unselfish effort to bring cheer to others will be the beginning of a happier life for ourselves.

Death comes to those we love, and it seems impossible that, in the face of our dark grief, the sun should shine, birds should sing, men and women should go on laughing and living and treading all the multitudinous sunny paths of normal life. But, before grief came upon us, we lived and laughed while others sorrowed, and, hard as it is to believe, we shall live and laugh again. For that is the way of life.

We think too much of the darkness of night and too little of the stars that shine in it. So with Death; we think too much of its blackness, and too little of the bright star of Immortality which robs it of its terrors.

Often the thoughts of great men run parallel. Robert Louis Stevenson says: "To believe in immortality is one thing, but it is first needful to believe in life." And Henry van Dyke says: "There is only one way to get ready for immortality, and that is to love this life, and live it as bravely and faithfully and cheerfully as we can." We should not mourn for those who have lived nobly, but should look upon their having thus lived as the most splendid and beautiful Preparation for the Life into which they have now entered.

Life is everlasting, and the living spirit moves always upward toward the road to perfection. Life on earth is only one phase of the universal life. Then why are we terrified by Death which is only a milepost on the journey toward perfect and eternal life?

"And God shall wipe away all tears from their eyes; and there shall be no more death, neither sorrow, nor crying, neither shall there be any more pain, for the former things are passed away." In Revelation xxi:4 come these words, and to the lonely and bereft they are as cool rain falling on parched flowers.

They are wise who perceive that Spirit is stronger than Material force—thought rules the world. Confronted by the seeming fact of material death we can learn to see that the surviving spirit is stronger than the force that has taken from us the body of our loved one. As long as our dear one lives in our thought he is not dead.

Rebellion, anguish, doubt; the unceasing questioning as to why this sorrow had to come, and what the future holds of reunion and joy and love! If only we would remember that "whatsoever there is to know, that shall we know some day," how soothed and happy we should be. Those who have gone before already know, and are waiting behind the veil of Eternity to whisper to us, when we join them, the beautiful secret of Life and Death.

The spiritual world enfolds in its ample bosom all the visible world. Our earth-home is merely a perceptible point. Here we play with shadows; there we live the reality.

Often when the heart is torn with sorrow, spiritually we wander like a traveler lost in a deep wood. We grow frightened, lose all sense of direction, batter ourselves against trees and rocks in our attempt to find a path. All the while there is a path—the path of Faith—that leads straight out of the dense tangle of our difficulties into the open road we are seeking.

Let us not weep for those who have gone away when their lives were at full bloom and beauty. Who are we that we should mourn them and wish them back? Life at its every stage is good, but who shall say whether those who die in the splendor of their prime are not fortunate to have known no abatement, no dulling of the flame by ash, no slow fading of life's perfect flower.

Doubt not that thy dear one lives immortally in Paradise, with bright angels for companions, and high tasks for accomplishment.

The World of Spirit is a real world full of sunshine and friendly inhabitants, not a mystical fantasy.

It is necessary to pass through deep waters to reach the Shore of Fulfillment.

The brave thought that comes to you after days of grieving may be News from Heaven.

In the Valley of the Shadow God's Love still lights the way. Though my eyes be blind with tears, I clasp God's guiding Hand, knowing that He is Lord of the night as of the day.

I conceive Heaven as a vast society where everyone serves some purpose of good.

It gladdens me to think that in the spiritual world we whose tasks on earth have been small and slow shall compass a hundredfold our range of accomplishment.

O wondrous alchemy of pain, transmuting loss into golden harvests of good!

Heaven is not the sordid world we know. It is a happy and benignant realm where kindness reigns, and selfishness is not, and angels move softly, dropping as they go the golden fruit of knowledge for all to share, and love is lived, and God is very near.

If your faith burns strong and bright, others will light their candle at it.

The more we dwell on the happy state of our dear departed ones, the closer we shall be to them.

Spring and autumn, seedtime and harvest, rain and sun, winter's cold and summer's heat—everything changes. Observing the transience of all things, why should we dwell on the ultimateness of death? Why should we not face life and death alike, unafraid?

The more you try to realize your nobler self on earth, the closer you will be to your loved one who breathes the large and charitable air of Heaven.

The soul goes forth into God's Fullness of Life, freed at last from the trammels of curtailing circumstance.

For three things I thank God every day of my life: thanks that he has vouchsafed me knowledge of His Works; deep thanks that He has set in my darkness the lamp of faith; deep, deepest thanks that I have another life to look forward to—a life joyous with light and flowers and heavenly song.

V. The Gifts of Nature and Art

TRAVEL IN CONCORD

Henry David Thoreau

America's greatest nature writer was Henry David Thoreau, the New England philosopher. He preached that "the mass of men lead lives of quiet desperation" because they devoted themselves to unimportant things; and that their salvation lay in divorcing themselves from non-essentials to come "to a hard bottom . . . which we call reality."

From July 4, 1845 to September 6, 1847 he lived in the utmost simplicity in a small house he had built with his own hands. Walden, his masterpiece, the story of this adventure, is more, however, than a celebration of the simple life. It is also a paean of love and appreciation of nature. In all Thoreau's books, there is a quality of understanding, of "oneness" with the trees, the sky, the water, even the snowflakes. That feeling is especially strong in Travels in Concord, from which the following brief selection is taken. The reader cannot fail to get a feeling of aliveness, almost of humanness in animate nature from Thoreau's writing.

I THINK that no experience which I have today comes up to, or is comparable with the experiences of my boyhood. And not only this is true, but as far back as I can remember I have unconsciously referred to the experiences of a previous state of existence, "For life is a forgetting," etc. Formerly, methought, nature developed as I developed, and grew up with me. My life was ecstasy. In youth, before I lost any of my senses, I can remember that I was all alive,

223

and inhabited my body with inexpressible satisfaction; both its weariness and its refreshment were sweet to me. This earth was the most glorious instrument, and I was audience to its strains. To have such sweet impressions made on us, such ecstasies begotten of the breezes! I can remember how I was astonished. I said to myself—I said to others—"There comes into my mind such an indescribable, infinite, all-absorbing, divine, heavenly pleasure, a sense of elevation and expansion, and [I] have had nought to do with it. I perceive that I am dealt with by superior powers. This is a pleasure, a joy, an existence which I have not procured myself. I speak as a witness on the stand, and tell what I have perceived." The morning and the evening were sweet to me, and I led a life aloof from society of men. I wondered if a mortal had ever known what I knew. I looked in books for some recognition of a kindred experience, but strange to say, I found none. Indeed, I was slow to discover that other men had had this experience. . . .

A man asked me the other night whether such and such persons were not as happy as anybody; being conscious, as I perceived, of much unhappiness himself and not aspiring to much more than an animal content. "Why!" said I, speaking to his condition, "the stones are happy, Concord River is happy, and I am happy too. When I took up a fragment of a Walnut shell this morning, I saw by its very grain and composition, its form and color, etc., that it was made for happiness. The most brutish and inanimate objects that are made suggest an everlasting and thorough satisfaction; they are the homes of content. Wood, earth, mold, etc., exist for joy. Do you think that Concord River would have continued to flow these millions of years by Clamshell Hill and round Hunt's Island, if it had not been happy —if it had been miserable in its channel, tired of existence, and cursing its Maker and the hour that it sprang?"

This afternoon, being on Fair Haven Hill, I heard the sound of a saw, and soon after from the Cliff saw two men sawing down a noble pine beneath, about forty rods off. I resolved to watch it till it fell, the last of a dozen or more which were left when the forest was cut and for fifteen years have waved in solitary majesty over the sproutland. I saw them like beavers or insects gnawing at the trunk of this noble tree, the diminutive manikins with their cross-cut saw which could scarcely span it. It towered up a hundred feet, as I afterward found by measurement, one of the tallest, probably, in the township and straight as an arrow, but slanting a little toward the hillside, its top seen against the frozen river and the hills of Conantum. I watch closely to see when it begins to move. Now the sawers stop, and with an ax open it a little on the side toward which it leans, that it may break the faster. And now their saw goes again. Now surely it is going; it is inclined one-quarter of the quadrant, and breathless, I expect its crashing fall. But no, I was mistaken; it has not moved an inch; it stands at the same angle as at first. It is fifteen minutes yet to its fall. Still its branches wave in the wind, as if it were destined to stand for a century, and the wind soughs through its needles as of yore; it is still a forest tree, the most majestic tree that waves over Musketaquid. The silvery sheen of the sunlight is reflected from its needles; it still affords an inaccessible crotch for the squirrel's nest; not a lichen has forsaken its mast-like stem, its raking mast—the hill is the hulk. Now, now's the moment! The manikins at its base are fleeing from their crime. They have dropped the guilty saw and ax. How slowly and majestically it starts! as if it were only swayed by a summer breeze, and would return without a sigh to its location in the air. And now it fans the hillside with its fall; and it lies down to its bed in the valley, from which it is never to rise, as softly as a feather, folding its green mantle about it like a warrior, as if, tired of standing, it embraced the earth with silent joy, returning its elements to the dust again.

I went down and measured it. It was about four feet in diameter where it was sawed, about one hundred feet long. Before I had reached it the axmen had already half divested it of its branches. Its gracefully spreading top was a perfect wreck on the hillside, as if it had been made of glass; and the tender cones of one year's growth upon its summit appealed in vain and too late to the mercy of the chopper. Already he has measured it with his ax, and marked off the mill-logs it will make. And the space it occupied in upper air is vacant for the next two centuries. It is lumber. He has laid waste the air. When the fish hawk in the spring revisits the banks of the Musketaquid, he will circle in vain to find his accustomed perch, and the hen-hawk will mourn for the pines lofty enough to protect her brood. A plant which it has taken two centuries to perfect, rising by slow stages into the heavens, has this afternoon ceased to exist. Its sapling top had expanded to this January thaw as the forerunner of summers to come. Why does not the village bell sound a knell? I hear no knell tolled. I see no procession of mourners in the streets, or the woodland aisles. The squirrel has leaped to another tree; the hawk has circled farther off, and has now settled upon a new eyrie; but the woodman is preparing [to] lay his ax at the root of that also.

The thin snow now driving from the north and lodging on my coat consists of those beautiful star crystals, not cottony and chubby spokes, as on the 13th December, but thin and partly transparent crystals. How full of the creative genius is the air in which these are generated! I should hardly admire more if real stars fell and lodged on my coat. Nature is full of genius, full of the divinity; so that not a snowflake escapes its fashioning hand.

A divinity must have stirred within them before the crystals did thus shoot and set. Wheels of the storm-chariots. The same law that shapes the earth-star shapes the snow-star. As surely as the petals of a flower are fixed, each of these countless snow-stars comes whirling to earth, pronouncing thus, with emphasis, the number six, Order, kóomos.

On the Saskatchewan, when no man of science is there to behold, still down they come, and not the less fulfill their destiny, perchance melt at once on the Indian's face. What a world we live in! where myriads of these little disks, so beautiful to the most prying eye, are whirled down on every traveler's coat, the observant and the unobservant, and on the restless squirrel's fur, and on the far-stretching fields and forests, the wooded dells, and the mountaintops. Far far away from the haunts of man, they roll down some little slope, fall over and come to their bearings, and melt or lose their beauty in the mass, ready anon to swell some little rill with their contribution, and so at last, the universal ocean from which they came. There they lie, like the wreck of chariot wheels after a battle in the skies. Meanwhile the meadow mouse shoves them aside in his gallery, the schoolboy casts them in his snowball, or the woodman's sled glides smoothly over them, these glorious spangles, the sweeping of heaven's floor. And they all sing, melting as they sing of the mysteries of the number six—six, six, six, He takes up the water of the sea in his hand, leaving the salt; He disperses it in mist through the skies; He re-collects and sprinkles it like grain in six-rayed snowy stars over the earth, there to lie till He dissolves its bonds again.

Very little evidence of God or men did I see just then, and life not as rich and inviting an enterprise as it should be, when my attention was caught by a snowflake on my coat sleeve. It was one of those perfect, crystalline, star-shaped ones, six-rayed, like a flat wheel with six spokes, only the spokes were perfect little pine trees in shape, arranged around a central spangle. This little object, which, with many of its fellows, rested unmelting on my coat, so perfect and beautiful, reminded me that Nature had not lost her pristine vigor yet, and why should man lose heart? . . . I may say that the Maker of the world exhausts his skill with each snowflake and dewdrop that he sends down. We think that the one mechanically coheres, and that the other simply flows together and falls, but in truth they are the produce of *enthusiasm*, the children of an ecstasy, finished with the artist's utmost skill.

PEACE IN THE HEART

Archibald Rutledge

The feelings of a Thoreau are of an intensity which betokens genius. But nature can also be appreciated in a simpler, more ordinary but equally satisfying way, the way of Archibald Rutledge. Rutledge is the author of a number of widely read books, of which Peace in the Heart *is one. A man of wealth and consequence in his own community, Rutledge would no doubt have preferred to describe himself as merely a country gentleman. Certainly the greatest satisfactions in his life have been the beauties of his plantation, and the joys of observing the wonders of nature. He here tells us how he has come upon the greatest of all blessings, peace, and a firm assurance of the Creator's love.*

ᗡ

IF every human being could be asked what he would rather have in life than anything else, a composite of all the answers would probably show that *peace in the heart* is what we really want. Certainly that is what all intelligent, reflective people long for; and surely, is not the attainment of spiritual peace in a world of many discords the master human achievement?

By striving to read the First Gospel, which is the Book of Nature, I believe that I have come upon peace. Will you let me try to tell you of my discovery? Let us take hands and wander for a day, from sunrise to sunset, together; and for a year, from springtime to autumn. Nature is the art of God; and to enter this stupendous gallery of living masterpieces, all one needs is a willing and sensitive heart. Let us enter it together "without money and without price." Perhaps we shall discover in this universal Taj Mahal of God what all our searchings elsewhere can never secure for us—peace, perfect peace in the heart.

A sunrise has always been to me not alone a magnificent spectacle of Nature, having in it the grandeur of the mighty rhythm of the universe, serene and infallible; but invariably it suggests to me the presence of Him who planned it all. And I feel also, every time the morning comes, a sense of the forgiveness of God for all my short-comings and downright sins. Sunrise is to me a splendid pledge that God pardons me, and gives me another radiant chance at least three hundred and sixty-five times each year. We who speak of Creation as a wondrous work should give closer heed to the greater marvel of the continuance of the lordly achievement of Creation by the still more astonishing immortality conferred upon it. Whatever Man makes seems ephemeral; what God creates stays created. And every morning we are radiantly reminded by sunrise that "the hand that made us is divine." During the accepted span of a human life, the human heart has the privilege of being humbled and being cleansed through seeing more than twenty-five thousand sunrises.

Perhaps if I tell of certain of the sunrises that have meant most to me, I shall be the more able to convey clearly and adequately how much this daily recurring splendor has brought into my life. I ought to say that I am not one of those who believe that the mar-velous natural mechanism of our solar system is a mere matter of chance, or of the operation of unguided laws. My reason simply cannot leave God out. Granting that the sun does rise in obedience to law, it is a law established by Him "who pillared the blue firma-ment with light."

I recall a rather memorable experience with a sunrise that I had in the company of a plantation Negro named Sam Singleton. Aboriginal in thought and feeling, plantation Negroes are among the most authentic and interesting of human beings. They may be as yet far from what we proudly call civilization; but to me they seem very close to God. Their religious attitude is as unfeigned as that of children. To them the rain, the wind, the thunder, the stars, sunset, and sunrise are matters of great moment. I have many a treasured recollection of what I have heard Negroes say of these unfailingly recurrent waves in the vast sea of Nature's mighty symphony.

Sam and I left home at one o'clock one winter morning to paddle down the Santee River in South Carolina to a place appropriately called "Tranquillity," since it is as solitary as being in the heart of a wild delta can make it. Our plan was to drop down ten miles or so with the ebb tide, designing to reach at dawn the lonely hummock in the huge wasteland that stretches mistily between the two sea-reaching arms of the mighty river. We were to spend a few days duck shooting at Tranquillity, and we started at a time which would afford us sport with the morning flight.

A Southern river at night is a haunting thing, with great stars hanging like spangles in the dark pines and the ancient water oaks fringing the river shores. Wider flows the dim stream as it moves through the last reaches of the immense coastal plain. Baffling to navigate by broad daylight, the Santee at night is mysterious. And the peril of it undoubtedly was heightened by the kind of craft in which we were traveling. A dugout cypress canoe, it had as certain a tendency to roll as had its parent log, utterly lacking that virtue of stability that one relishes in a boat, especially when one is voyaging through the darkness of a huge river that seems to be wandering toward eternity.

But the stars that had been shining when we left home were soon obscured by a fog so dense that we could hardly see beyond the bow of our little boat. As we were going with the tide, we felt sure of our general direction, but when once or twice we came near looming shores, neither of us recognized the landscape as familiar. Then for an hour there was no land visible. I knew that we ought to be near our goal. But the waves that began to roll our canoe were suspiciously like sea waves. The roar of the surf that we had heard for a long time now became almost clamorous. Attempts to reach either shore were vain. The fact that the tide had now turned, or was about to turn, confused us still further. The canoe shipped water, gallons of it. The mist blinded us. There was no use blinking the truth, we were in immediate danger. I told Sam mildly that in case the canoe was swamped, we must turn it over and cling to it. How can I ever forget what he said?

"Never mind, Cap'n," that humble boatman told me; "it will be daybreak soon."

What was there in that plight of ours on which we could certainly count? Only one thing there was: the coming of light—daybreak, sunrise! It came in time to save us, though we were really on the brink of the sea when the rosy radiance over the delta disclosed our position to us. Yet it was not alone the coming of sunrise that rescued us; it was Sam's reminding me that it was *sure* to come, restoring thus my courage. And in all these years that have followed, whenever the shadows seem deepest and most impenetrable, I seem to hear, out of the dim celestial past, the quiet voice of Sam Singleton saying to my doubting and besieged heart, "Never mind, Cap'n; it will be daybreak soon."

As a personal experience, none of my own ever surpassed in moving power that beautiful and dramatic scene which, though it lies years back in the moonlit land of the past and of memory, is vividly alive to me now. It happened at sunrise, and it was of a sunrise.

One dearer to me than all else in life had, for days, lain helpless, speechless. Consciousness was gone. We knew that the mortal mists were fast gathering; that the irremediable river must soon be crossed. The last morning of our watching was misty; the day emerged so wanly that we hardly knew that it had come. Suddenly the one we loved so dearly sat up in bed, a strange light on her face of a happiness past all our mortal joy. She stretched abroad her arms, crying in the radiant abandon of spiritual certainty, "The Dawn! The beautiful Dawn!"

Those were her dying words—glad, triumphant. And for me they hold the eternal promise of the sunrise. They glow with immortality. In every sense, our mortal dawn that day was anything but beautiful; but she saw the beginning of an immortal day. Believing in a God of infinite love and of infinite power, I find it natural to believe that death is not a disastrous sundown but rather a spiritual sunrise, ushering in the unconjectured splendors of immortality.

I remember a marvelous dawn in Pennsylvania that filled me with a sense of shame. The night preceding had been filled with the tumult of a wintry storm. Snow and sleet had been driven madly against the streaming panes. The house creaked and swayed. Under the eaves the freezing wind hooted, thrusting its icy snout into every crack. As I looked out, I could barely see the dark trees, tossing their wild arms despairingly. I could not sleep for thinking of the quail, smothered by the snow in some fence corner; the deer, shivering in their search for browsing; the hapless grouse, trying to dive perchance beneath some treacherously shifting drift of snow to keep from freezing to death. A resentment against nature stirred in me. Why should there be tempests and blizzards?

Toward dawn I slept; and when I woke, golden light was streaming over my bed. Not a breath of wind was stirring. Dressing quickly, I went out into the grove of young white pines near my house. When I saw what I did, I was ashamed of my feeling during the storm of the night before. Here were the trees hanging, as Whittier beautifully says, "like crystal chandeliers," the snow and sleet on their brown branches softly taking fire in the calm sunrise. Here was breathless beauty, an innocence and a loveliness that shone with virtue. On no two kinds of trees did the snow cling the same way: the swarthy, heavy-foliaged white pines bent to the ground with their burdens; the silvery branches of the birches were delicately ridged with fairy hills and valleys of snow; the shagbark hickories had caught and were wearing on their windward sides shining garments. The old rail fence that sagged down toward the frozen pasture had arrayed itself in ermine, tinged rosily where the level sunbeams glistened upon it. In the air was a delicious sense of relenting, the thrilling certainty of returning love. Sparkling gladness surrounded me, called into being by the wild storm. However grim the tempest, it passes, and peace ensues, a peace that is impressive because it follows war. After a storm, always a calm; after darkness, light; after the mournful shadows and the berserk wind, sunrise again—not only over the earth but also in the heart.

One night I slept among the sand dunes of a wild southern sea island. I happened to be the only human being in that solitary beautiful wilderness. Deer roamed those tropical woods by hundreds; long lines of wild ducks sped veeringly into its Lethe-like streams; wild turkeys raked the pine straw under the huge yellow pines and fed ravenously upon the acorns of the live oaks.

The place was as perfectly wild as it had been before the days of Columbus. In such a place a man is likely to be keenly aware of all that is about him; yet I had expected to be impressed chiefly by the wild life. It was not so. A sunrise over the lonely ocean stirred me far more than the sight of huge stags, shockingly tame; monstrous pines literally draped with wild turkeys gone to roost; and incredibly placid ponds swarming with wild fowl.

The deep woods of the island marched down to the rolling dunes; beyond the dunes was a fine stretch of beach, tirelessly trampled by the Atlantic. In a hollow between the dunes I slept, rolled in a blanket. Over me blazed the stars, tremulous with beauty. What woke me was the morning flight of the mallards and the black ducks and the teal; with glad cries they left the lagoons of the island for a sunny day among the sea marshes. I lay looking at them in the pearly morning heavens; like them, what was I but a child of Nature rejoicing in the return of day? Then I turned to face the sea and the sunrise.

The tide was flooding; and as the shoals before me extended for more than a mile, the playing of the white horses was spectral and spectacular. Tossed and snowy beauty, dimly illumined now, made the sea a visionary loveliness. The deep rose of the eastern sky turned scarlet, while long blushes of crimson stole softly to the heavens' high arch; a misty amethyst tinge came over the waters.

Now came the sun, its gorgeous shafts of fire reddening the rolling foam of ten thousand waves. Was there ever so gorgeous an arrival? The whole ocean was burning unconsumed before me, and upon the glossy shore there was not a shell that did not gleam and blossom with radiance. The sea and the sun! I gazed spellbound at these majestic forces, formed I know not by what amazing process of evolution; now harnessed, obedient—the sea keeping his bounds and the sun his destined course. The sea at sunrise! I searched my heart for words to express my feelings at sight of it. The words of the Shepherd King came to me, and they seemed adequate: "The sea is His, and He made it."

Then there was that sunrise that I spent with old Asher, a hunter; a man of sinister reputation; something of a feudist; but in appearance a patriarch of his clan. Tall and full-bearded he was, with a craggy face bronzed by the outdoor life of seventy years. Renowned as a hunter, he was also a leader of the people of the woods; and as such he was frequently in personal encounters. He and I had long been friends; and when I met him at dawn on that fateful morning in Hell Hole Swamp, we naturally fell to talking. I asked him where he was going.

"I got to see a man," he said; and he said it in such a way as to promise no good to the man to be visited. I could see from his expression that the subject was a delicate one. As we stood on the old bank, with the wild greenwood awakening around us, I heard the joyous sweet call of the Carolina wren ringing with silver tones through the morning mist, and I called Asher's attention to it. Apparently, however, he was not interested. Then over us passed in gorgeous splendor a stately flight of snowy wood ibises, bound for the distant salt marshes. Both Asher and I watched them stream away over the lofty pines; and just as they were disappearing the first rays of the risen sun glinted refreshingly on their plumage. The tall beauty of the pines was soon flooded with light. Rapture was in the air, fragrance, serene joy, peace. We could not escape all this, Asher and I. But I did not realize its true effect upon him until, when we were about to part, I found him going my way. He said something about returning home. When we did part a half hour later at his gateway he said:

"I'm glad I run into you this morning. If we hadn't stopped to talk, I might not have noticed the sunrise. But for that, I might have kilt a man. Don't it beat all how hard it is to be mean at sunrise, if you once stop to look at it?"

"Hard to be mean at sunrise." To me they are memorable words; and they came spontaneously yet thoughtfully from the depths of a heart deeply moved. But for a sunrise, Asher might have "kilt a man." It is one of those things that goes with me down the long years, giving reassurance, tinging the commonplace with the mystic bloom of wonder, suggesting to the heart that the pageants of Nature always have in them spiritual power for us if we do not drive through life so fast that we are unwilling to give their silent splendor a chance to redeem our souls.

It is futile to deny that human nature does not crave the sensational; but are we not shortsighted in imagining that in the brief and busy mortal span that is ours we are dependent solely upon ourselves and upon others like us to supply us with thrills? Besides, human performances can be gauged, can be imitated; many of the most spectacular are mere tricks. They utterly lack the superb aura of mystery that invests myriads of the masterful achievements of nature, which are the achievements of God. If we love thrills are we not missing inimitable chances if we fail to perceive many of those spectacular pageants staged by Nature? For poetic beauty what scene presented by man can compare with a sea moon setting beyond white-rolling waves? What form of entertainment can man devise more splendid, more satisfying than a gorgeous sunrise in a mountain land? I especially remember a great pageant that I watched near Mount Mitchell, the loftiest crest in America east of the Rockies.

One of my harmless pastimes is searching for Indian arrowheads; and on this particular morning I had gone down an old mountain trail to investigate a reputed ancient Indian camp site, high on a flat-topped hill overlooking a wild gorge. I found the hill top to be an old pasture, so grown to heavy grass that I knew my search for relics would be vain. But my trip was not, for I met little Ben Lance, a mountain boy who had just driven his cows into that wild mountain pasture. He was shy but friendly; a lad only ten years old, yet he had about him an air of sturdy manliness and independence; a shy friendliness that immediately won my heart. I asked him his name, and he told me not only that but also much about his life in the mountains. He came of ancient English stock, though he did not know it; his manner betrayed a long inheritance; he had an aristocracy of manner that only one who is truly democratic of heart can assume. As we sat together on a gray boulder, facing Mount Mitchell, the awful and sublime rose of sunrise began to bloom for us behind the shoulder of that mighty mountain, momentous and huge and black against the eastern sky.

"Ben," I said to my small companion, "you often see the sunrise from this pasture, don't you?"

"I calculate," he said, with his quaint drawl, "that she will be here just the same time I is. I is late sometimes, but the sunrise she ain't never late. I guess that's because God manages that."

I pondered the child's words as we looked together at the flaming waves of heliotrope that were fringing the mountain crest. Every tree on the skyline of those tremendous slopes stood out vividly; dark lay the valleys beneath.

"What do you know about God, Ben?"

He looked at me with clear, intelligent eyes.

"I know He made everything," he said; "and He watches how we behave. I like to be here when the sun comes up," he went on; "it makes me feel how great God is, and then I ain't skeered of nothing."

Childish ramblings, some would call them; yet to me they brought a heartening message. Here was a lonely little lad who felt God in the sunrise; who knew in his own way the meaning of communion. Ben Lance had learned by himself the most interesting thing that all Nature has to teach us: that God is close to us, is all-powerful, is loving. He learned it from the sunrise.

But all the beauty and all the wonder of the dawn would mean little if they did not infallibly suggest to the heart a spiritual dawn beyond our mortal night. In all the vast realm of human concern nothing has any real importance beside the question of personal immortality. If this one immortal hope of man is vain, all other fulfilled hopes are well-nigh futile. Our trust in immortality is our chief bond to God; without immortality, our claim of divinity in our natures is both ludicrous and pathetic. But we feel that we are true children of God. Being primal and native, man's instincts are commonly right; and he has had, in all times and in all lands, the instinct for immortality. He believes that he shall survive the dark passage of the misty river of death. Nor, even to the most practical mind, need this survival seem incredible; for through what varying forms has a man not passed during his few years on earth! Conceived mysteriously, borne about by his mother in palpable darkness; living as an innocent and happy child; then as a youth, then as a man, then as an old man. He has been many persons, yet one person; and always in him, to distinguish him from the brute creation, he has felt the divine fire, the far kinship to the celestial.

Sunrise suggests to me not only the power of God grandly to continue what He has begun but it also conveys the reassurance of the Creator's love returning to us daily, bringing joy and forgiveness; and to any reflective heart it intimates that no night is final; for, since with God all things are possible, His almighty love has, I confidently believe, prepared for us a radiant future beyond the sundown of death. And if we meditate but momentarily upon what He has done and upon what He does do, confidence in immortality is natural, reasonable, and, to my way of believing, to be counted upon as infallibly as the sunrise.

ADVENTURES IN CONTENTMENT

David Grayson

What dweller in the city has not felt the desire for permanent escape to the quiet and peace of the countryside? Most of us never have our wish—it is too difficult a change, too chancy an adventure. Sometimes Fate takes a hand and makes the decision. Thus it was with David Grayson, who was forced to abandon the strain of city life because of

*illness. It was a hazardous move, but it meant a return to health and a
richer, fuller life. Over the years, many thousands of readers have found
enjoyment in Grayson's "Adventures in Contentment," from which the
following selection is taken.*

∽

I CAME here eight years ago as the renter of this farm, of which soon
afterward I became the owner. The time before that I like to forget.
The chief impression left upon my memory, now happily growing
indistinct, is of being hurried faster than I could well travel. From
the moment, as a boy of seventeen, I first began to pay my own
way, my days were ordered by an inscrutable power which drove me
hourly to my task. I was rarely allowed to look up or down, but
always forward, toward that vague Success which we Americans love
to glorify.

My senses, my nerves, even my muscles were continually strained
to the utmost of attainment. If I loitered or paused by the wayside,
as it seems natural for me to do, I soon heard the sharp crack of the
lash. For many years, and I can say it truthfully, I never rested. I
neither thought nor reflected. I had no pleasure, even though I
pursued it fiercely during the brief respite of vacations. Through
many feverish years I did not work: I merely produced.

The only real thing I did was to hurry as though every moment
were my last, as though the world, which now seems so rich in
everything, held only one prize which might be seized upon before
I arrived. Since then I have tried to recall, like one who struggles to
restore the visions of a fever, what it was that I ran to attain, or why
I should have borne without rebellion such indignities to soul and
body. That life seems now, of all illusions, the most distant and
unreal. It is like the unguessed eternity before we are born: not of
concern compared with that eternity upon which we are now em-
barked.

All these things happened in cities and among crowds. I like to
forget them. They smack of that slavery of the spirit which is so
much worse than any mere slavery of the body.

One day—it was in April, I remember, and the soft maples in the
city park were just beginning to blossom—I stopped suddenly. I did
not intend to stop. I confess in humiliation that it was no courage,
no will of my own. I intended to go on toward Success: but Fate
stopped me. It was as if I had been thrown violently from a moving

planet: all the universe streamed around me and past me. It seemed to me that of all animate creation, I was the only thing that was still or silent. Until I stopped I had not known the pace I ran; and I had a vague sympathy and understanding, never felt before, for those who left the running. I lay prostrate with fever and close to death for weeks and watched the world go by: the dust, the noise, the very color of haste. The only sharp pang that I suffered was the feeling that I should be broken-hearted and that I was not; that I should care and that I did not. It was as though I had died and escaped all further responsibility. I even watched with dim equanimity my friends racing past me, panting as they ran. Some of them paused an instant to comfort me where I lay, but I could see that their minds were still upon the running and I was glad when they went away. I cannot tell with what weariness their haste oppressed me. As for them, they somehow blamed me for dropping out. I knew. Until we ourselves understand, we accept no excuse from the man who stops. While I felt it all, I was not bitter. I did not seem to care. I said to myself: "This is Unfitness. I survive no longer. So be it."

Thus I lay, and presently I began to hunger and thirst. Desire rose within me: the indescribable longing of the convalescent for the food of recovery. So I lay, questioning wearily what it was that I required. One morning I wakened with a strange, new joy in my soul. It came to me at that moment with indescribable poignancy, the thought of walking barefoot in cool, fresh plow furrows as I had once done when a boy. So vividly the memory came to me— the high airy world as it was at that moment, and the boy I was walking free in the furrows—that the weak tears filled my eyes, the first I had shed in many years. Then I thought of sitting in quiet thickets in old fence corners, the wood behind me rising still, cool, mysterious, and the fields in front stretching away in illimitable pleasantness. I thought of the good smell of cows at milking—you do not know, if you do not know!—I thought of the sights and sounds, the heat and sweat of the hay fields. I thought of a certain brook I knew when a boy that flowed among alders and wild parsnips, where I waded with a three-foot rod for trout. I thought of all these things as a man thinks of his first love. Oh, I craved the soil. I hungered and thirsted for the earth. I was greedy for growing things.

And thus, eight years ago, I came here like one sore-wounded creeping from the field of battle. I remember walking in the sunshine, weak yet, but curiously satisfied. I that was dead lived again. It came to me then with a curious certainty, not since so assuring, that I understood the chief marvel of nature hidden within the Story of the Resurrection, the marvel of plant and seed, father and son, the wonder of the seasons, the miracle of life. I, too, had died: I had lain long in darkness, and now I had risen again upon the sweet earth. And I possessed beyond others a knowledge of a former existence, which I knew, even then, I could never return to.

For a time, in the new life, I was happy to drunkenness—working, eating, sleeping. I was an animal again, let out to run in green pastures. I was glad of the sunrise and the sunset. I was glad at noon. It delighted me when my muscles ached with work and when, after supper, I could not keep my eyes open for sheer weariness. And sometimes I was awakened in the night out of a sound sleep—seemingly by the very silences—and lay in a sort of bodily comfort impossible to describe.

I did not want to feel or to think: I merely wanted to live. In the sun or the rain I wanted to go out and come in, and never again know the pain of the unquiet spirit. I looked forward to an awakening not without dread for we are as helpless before birth as in the presence of death.

But like all birth, it came, at last, suddenly. All that summer I had worked in a sort of animal content. Autumn had now come, late autumn, with coolness in the evening air. I was plowing in my upper field—not then mine in fact—and it was a soft afternoon with the earth turning up moist and fragrant. I had been walking the furrows all day long. I had taken note, as though my life depended upon it, of the occasional stones or roots in my field, I made sure of the adjustment of the harness, I drove with peculiar care to save the horses. With such simple details of the work in hand I had found it my joy to occupy my mind. Up to that moment the most important things in the world had seemed a straight furrow and well-turned corners—to me, then, a profound accomplishment.

I cannot well describe it, save by the analogy of an opening door somewhere within the house of my consciousness. I had been in the dark: I seemed to emerge. I had been bound down: I seemed to leap up—and with a marvelous sudden sense of freedom and joy.

I stopped there in my field and looked up. And it was as if I had never looked up before. I discovered another world. It had been there before, for long and long, but I had never seen nor felt it. All discoveries are made in that way: a man finds the new thing, not in nature but in himself.

It was as though, concerned with plow and harness and furrow, I had never known that the world had height or color or sweet sounds, or that there was *feeling* in a hillside. I forgot myself, or where I was. I stood a long time motionless. My dominant feeling, if I can at all express it, was of a strange new friendliness, a warmth, as though these hills, this field about me, the woods, had suddenly spoken to me and caressed me. It was as though I had been accepted in membership, as though I was now recognized, after long trial, as belonging here.

Across the town road which separates my farm from my nearest neighbor's, I saw a field, familiar, yet strangely new and unfamiliar, lying up to the setting sun, all red with autumn, above it the incalculable heights of the sky, blue, but not quite clear, owing to the Indian summer haze. I cannot convey the sweetness and softness of that landscape, the airiness of it, the mystery of it, as it came to me at that moment. It was as though, looking at an acquaintance long known, I should discover that I loved him. As I stood there I was conscious of the cool tang of burning leaves and brush heaps, the lazy smoke of which floated down the long valley and found me in my field, and finally I heard, as though the sounds were then made for the first time, all the vague murmurs of the countryside—a cow-bell somewhere in the distance, the creak of a wagon, the blurred evening hum of birds, insects, frogs. So much it means for a man to stop and look up from his task. So I stood, and I looked up and down with a glow and a thrill which I cannot now look back upon without some envy and a little amusement at the very grandness and seriousness of it all. And I said aloud to myself:

"I will be as broad as the earth. I will not be limited."

Thus I was born into the present world, and here I continue, not knowing what other world I may yet achieve. I do not know, but I wait in expectancy, keeping my furrows straight and my corners well turned. Since that day in the field, though my fences include no more acres, and I still plow my own fields, my real domain has expanded until I crop wide fields and take the profit of many curious pastures. From my farm I can see most of the world; and if I wait here long enough all people pass this way.

And I look out upon them not in the surroundings which they have chosen for themselves, but from the vantage ground of my familiar world. The symbols which meant so much in cities mean little here. Sometimes it seems to me as though I saw men naked. They come and stand beside my oak, and the oak passes solemn judgment; they tread my furrows and the clods give silent evidence; they touch the green blades of my corn, the corn whispers its sure conclusions. Stern judgments that will be deceived by no symbols!

Thus I have delighted, secretly, in calling myself an unlimited farmer, and I make this confession in answer to the inner and truthful demand of the soul that we are not, after all, the slaves of things, whether corn, or banknotes, or spindles; that we are not the used, but the users; that life is more than profit and loss. And so I shall expect that while I am talking farm some of you may be thinking of dry goods, banking, literature, carpentry, or what-not. But if you can say: I am an unlimited dry goods merchant, I am an unlimited carpenter, I will give you an old-fashioned country hand-shake, strong and warm, we are friends; our orbits coincide.

When I first came to this farm, I came empty-handed. I was the veritable pattern of the city-made failure. I believed that life had nothing more in store for me. I was worn out physically, mentally and, indeed, morally. I had diligently planned for Success; and, I had reaped defeat. I came here without plans. I plowed and harrowed and planted, expecting nothing. In due time I began to reap. And it has been a growing marvel to me, the diverse and unexpected crops that I have produced within these uneven acres of earth. With sweat I planted corn, and I have here a crop not only of corn but of happiness and hope. My tilled fields have miraculously sprung up to friends!

This book is one of the unexpected products of my farm. It is this way with the farmer. After the work of planting and cultivating, after the rain has fallen in his fields, after the sun has warmed them, after the new green leaves have broken the earth—one day he stands looking out with a certain new joy across his acres (the wind bends and half turns the long blades of the corn) and there springs up within him a song of the fields. No matter how little poetic, how little articulate he is, the song rises irrepressibly in his heart, and he turns aside from his task with a new glow of fulfilment and contentment. At harvest time in our country I hear, or I imagine I hear, a sort of chorus rising over all the hills, and I meet no man who is not, deep down within him, a singer! So song follows work: so art grows out of life!

And the friends I have made! They have come to me naturally, as the corn grows in my fields or the wind blows in my trees. Some strange potency abides within the soil of this earth! When two men stoop (there must be stooping) and touch it together, a magnetic current is set up between them: a flow of common understanding and confidence. I would call the attention of all great Scientists, Philosophers, and Theologians to this phenomenon: it will repay investigation. It is at once the rarest and the commonest thing I know. It shows that down deep within us, where we really live, we are all a good deal alike. We have much the same instincts, hopes, joys, sorrows. If only it were not for the outward things that we commonly look upon as important (which are in reality not at all important) we might come together without fear, vanity, envy, or prejudice and be friends. And what a world it would be! If civilization means anything at all it means the increasing ability of men to look through material possessions, through clothing, through differences of speech and color of skin, and to see the genuine man that abides within each of us. It means an escape from symbols!

I tell this merely to show what surprising and unexpected things have grown out of my farm. All along I have had more than I bargained for. From now on I shall marvel at nothing! When I ordered my own life I failed; now that I work from day to day, doing that which I can do best and which most delights me, I am rewarded in ways that I could not have imagined. Why, it would not surprise me if heaven were at the end of all this!

Now, I am not so foolish as to imagine that a farm is a perfect place. My life has not been without discouragement and loss and loneliness (loneliness most of all). I have enjoyed the hard work; the little troubles have troubled me more than the big ones. I detest unharnessing a muddy horse in the rain! I don't like chickens in the barn. And somehow Harriet uses an inordinate amount of kindling wood. But once in the habit, unpleasant things have a way of fading quickly and quietly from the memory.

And you see after living so many years in the city the worst experience on the farm is a sort of joy!

In most men as I come to know them—I mean men who dare to look themselves in the eye—I find a deep desire for more naturalness, more directness. How weary we all grow of this fabric of deception which is called modern life. How passionately we desire to escape but cannot see the way! How our hearts beat with sympathy when we find a man who has turned his back upon it all and who says "I will live it no longer." How we flounder in possessions as in a dark and suffocating bog, wasting our energies not upon life but upon *things*. Instead of employing our houses, our cities, our gold, our clothing, we let these inanimate things possess and employ us— to what utter weariness. "Blessed be nothing," sighs a dear old lady of my knowledge.

Of all ways of escape I know, the best, though it is far from perfection, is the farm. There a man may yield himself most nearly to the quiet and orderly processes of nature. He may attain most nearly to that equilibrium between the material and spiritual, with time for the exactions of the first, and leisure for the growth of the second, which is the ideal of life.

A city hammers and polishes its denizens into a defined model: it worships standardization; but the country encourages differentiation, it loves new types. Thus it is that so many great and original men have lived their youth upon the land. It would be impossible to imagine Abraham Lincoln brought up in a street of tenements. Family life on the farm is highly educative; there is more discipline for a boy in the continuous care of a cow or a horse than in many a term of school. Industry, patience, perseverance are qualities inherent in the very atmosphere of country life. The so-called manual training of city schools is only a poor makeshift for developing in the city boy those habits which the country boy acquires naturally in his daily life. An honest, hard-working country training is the best inheritance a father can leave his son.

And yet a farm is only an opportunity, a tool. A cornfield, a plow, a woodpile, an oak tree, will cure no man unless he have it in himself to be cured. The truth is that no life, and least of all a farmer's life, is simple—unless it is simple. I know a man and his wife who came out here to the country with the avowed purpose of becoming, forthwith, simple. They were unable to keep the chickens out of their summer kitchen. They discovered microbes in the well, and mosquitoes in the cistern, and wasps in the garret. Owing to the resemblance of the seeds, their radishes turned out to be turnips! The last I heard of them they were living snugly in a flat in Sixteenth Street—all their troubles solved by a dumb-waiter.

The great point of advantage in the life of the country is that if a man is in reality simple, if he love true contentment, it is the place of all places where he can live his life most freely and fully, where he can *grow*. The city affords no such opportunity; indeed, it often destroys, by the seductiveness with which it flaunts its carnal graces, the desire for the higher life which animates every good man.

After my experience in the country, if I were to be cross-examined as to the requisites of a farm, I should say that the chief thing to be desired in any sort of agriculture, is good health in the farmer. What, after all, can touch that! How many of our joys that we think intellectual are purely physical! This joy o' the morning that the poet carols about so cheerfully is often nothing more than the exuberance produced by a good hot breakfast. Going out of my kitchen door some mornings and standing for a moment, while I survey the green and spreading fields of my farm, it seems to me truly as if all nature were making a bow to me. It seems to me that there never was a better cow than mine, never a more really perfect horse, and as for pigs, could any in this world herald my approach with more cheerful gruntings and squealings!

But there are other requisites for a farm. It must not be too large, else it will keep you away from your friends. Provide a town not too far off (and yet not too near) where you can buy your flour and sell your grain. Demand a few good old oak trees, or walnuts, or even elms will do. No well-regulated farm should be without trees.

As for neighbors, accept those nearest at hand; you will find them surprisingly human, like yourself. If you like them you will be surprised to find how much they all like you (and will upon occasion lend you a spring-tooth harrow or a butter tub, or help you with your plowing); but if you hate them they will return your hatred with interest. I have discovered that those who travel in pursuit of better neighbors never find them.

Somewhere on every farm, along with the other implements, there should be a row of good books, which should not be allowed to rust with disuse: a book, like a hoe, grows brighter with employment. And no farm, even in this country where we enjoy the even balance of the seasons, rain and shine, shine and rain, should be devoid of that irrigation from the currents of the world's thought which is so essential to the complete life. From the papers which the postman puts in the box flow the true waters of civilization. You will find within their columns how to be good or how to make pies: you will get out of them what you look for! And finally, down the road from your farm, so that you can hear the bell on Sunday mornings, there should be a little church. It will do you good even though, like me, you do not often attend. It's a sort of Ark of the Covenant; and when you get to it, you will find therein the True Spirit—if you take it with you when you leave home. Of course you will look for good land and comfortable buildings when you buy your farm: they are, indeed, prime requisites. I have put them last for the reason that they are so often first. I have observed, however, that the joy of the farmer is by no means in proportion to the area of his arable land. It is often a nice matter to decide between acres and contentment: men perish from too much as well as from too little. And if it be possible there should be a long table in the dining-room and little chairs around it, and small beds upstairs, and young voices calling at their play in the fields—if it be possible.

Sometimes I say to myself: I have grasped happiness! Here it is; I have it. And yet, it always seems at that moment of complete fulfillment as though my hand trembled, that I might not take it!

I wonder if you recall the story of Christian and Hopeful, how, standing on the hill Clear (as we do sometimes—at our best) they looked for the gates of the Celestial City (as we look—how fondly!):

Then they essayed to look, but the remembrance of that last thing that the shepherds had showed them made their heads shake, by means of which impediment they could not look steadily through the glass: yet they thought they saw something like the gate, and also some of the glory of the place.

How often I have thought that I saw some of the glory of the place (looking from the hill Clear) and how often, lifting the glass, my hand has trembled!

HOME AGAIN

T'ao Yüan Ming

TRANSLATED BY H. A. GILES

The owner of the delightful garden described below was a Chinese gentleman who was born in A.D. *365. He had been appointed a magis-*

trate but served for only eighty-three days. At the end of that time he decided, in a way which Thoreau would have thoroughly approved, that his salary of rice was not a sufficient inducement for him "to crook the hinges of his knee" to his superiors. With joy he abandoned political maneuvering, with pleasure he returned to his house and garden. His essay is one of the most famous in Chinese literature.

~

HOMEWARDS I bend my steps. My fields, my gardens, are choked with weeds: should I not go? My soul has led a bondsman's life: why should I remain to pine? But I will waste no grief upon the past: I will devote my energies to the future. I have not wandered far astray. I feel that I am on the right track once again.

Lightly, lightly, speeds my boat along, my garments fluttering to the gentle breeze. I inquire my route as I go. I grudge the slowness of the dawning day. From afar I descry my old home, and joyfully press onwards in my haste. The servants rush forth to meet me: my children cluster at the gate. The place is a wilderness; but there is the old pine-tree and my chrysanthemums. I take the little ones by the hand, and pass in. I gaze out at my favorite branches. I loll against the window in my new-found freedom. I look at the sweet children on my knee.

And now I take my pleasure in my garden. There is a gate, but it is rarely opened. I lean on my staff as I wander about or sit down to rest. I raise my head and contemplate the lovely scene. Clouds rise, unwilling, from the bottom of the hills: the weary bird seeks its nest again. Shadows vanish, but still I linger round my lonely pine. Home once more! I'll have no friendships to distract me hence. The times are out of joint for me; and what have I to seek from men? In the pure enjoyment of the family circle I will pass my days, cheering my idle hours with lute and book. My husbandmen will tell me when spring-time is nigh, and when there will be work in the furrowed fields. Thither I shall repair by cart or by boat, through the deep gorge, over the dizzy cliff, trees bursting merrily into leaf, the stream-let swelling from its tiny source. Glad is this renewal of life in due season: but for me, I rejoice that my journey is over. Ah! how short a time it is that we are here! Why then not set our hearts at rest, ceasing to trouble whether we remain or go? What boots it to wear out the soul with anxious thoughts? I want not wealth: I want not power: heaven is beyond my hopes. Then let me stroll through the

bright hours as they pass, in my garden, among my flowers; or I will
mount the hill and sing my song, or weave my verse beside the
limpid brook. Thus will I work out my allotted span, content with
the appointments of Fate, my spirit free from care.

THE DOCTOR CHANGES HIS MIND

——————— *Leonard Dubkin* ———————

*The enjoyment of Nature need not always be confined to country life.
For Nature is more than rugged landscapes and green pastures. It can
assert itself in something as fragile and delicate as a butterfly's wing.
Leonard Dubkin was a young reporter in a big city, out of work and
with no opportunity to enjoy the pleasures of country life. But Nature
to him was a thing of fascination. Later in life, he was to write a book
called* White Lady, *a delightful volume about an unusual heroine—a
tiny white bat. Even before then, he understood much about the ways
of moths and butterflies. He discovered a beautiful specimen in the
yard of one Dr. Miroff, a man who had little use for Nature and none
for the democratic way. Surprise of surprises, even Dr. Miroff proved
not insensible to the beauties of Nature and the joys of observing its
ways.*

I SUPPOSE on a farm or in a small town people refer to the calendar
to keep track of the seasons, to tell them when it is time to start
plowing, or plant seeds, or weather-strip the windows against the
approaching frosts. But in the city the calendar is only convenient in
determining on what day of the week a certain date will fall, and
that is about the extent of its usefulness. Spring slides into summer,
summer becomes fall, fall declines and it is winter, and winter gives
way to spring; and what difference does all this make to us? We go
about our business as unconcernedly as though we were not inhabitants of the earth—and, strictly speaking, many of us are not.
Our days are spent in air-conditioned offices and our nights in
heated rooms, and we travel from one to the other in enclosed cars or
busses or trolleys. Except for a few minor details, as between our
homes and the garage or bus stop, we have succeeded in banishing
climate and weather from our lives, and so there is no need to keep

track of the seasons. We will know it is spring when we read in our morning papers that today is officially the first day of spring; and if we miss the item (it is on page 3, accompanied by a picture of a girl in a bathing suit throwing a snowball) someone down at the office will be sure to mention it.

Are we to be censured for living in a man-made climate, and ignoring the changes from one season to another? If one must work in an office, and most of us in the city must, is it not more comfortable that the office should have a constant, healthful temperature? And of what possible value could it be to us to know that spring is approaching, what meaning could that fact have in our lives? Sentimental people who live in the country, especially editorial writers, say that in the early spring the sap is beginning to flow in the trees, that plants are coming to life after their long winter sleep, that violets are blooming under the snow. But not in the city. Here the few trees are as bare and lifeless as in December, and no one is curious enough to look under their bark to see what is happening there. There are no plants yet, and under the snow there is only the hard pavement.

But that year as I wandered about the city I could tell that spring was approaching; I think I would have felt it even if I had not known it was March. There was an indefinable something in the air, the sky seemed more often blue, the wind less sharp and biting, and sounds rang out clearly, without the muffledness of winter. Then one day, on a lawn, I saw a forsythia bush with the little yellow blossoms newly opened, and a few days later a robin hopped across the sidewalk in front of me, a large, fat robin that looked almost as gaudy as an illustration of a robin in a bird guide. What a beautiful, brightly colored, graceful bird it was, I thought as I watched it. But I knew that in another month, when the city was full of robins, their nests in every tree and the air ringing with their calls, I would cease to be aware of their beauty and their grace, they would just be the common robins that I had known all my life.

One morning the sun shone down brightly on the city, the streets were dry, and there was a soft summer warmth in the air. The afternoon papers said the temperature, 69 degrees, had set a new record for that day, but we did not need the papers to tell us it was unseasonably warm. Impetuous young men appeared on the streets without topcoats or hats, and already a few people sat on the ground beside the Art Institute during their lunch hour, feeding scraps of bread to the pigeons.

I walked north beside the lake, gazing out at the calm water that stretched to the thin line where it met the blue sky. . . . I left the lake, crossed the boulevard, and walked west on one of the near north side streets. . . . I heard someone shouting, and turned my head to see Dr. Miroff hurrying down the steps of his house waving his arms. I had passed his house without remembering that he lived there— perhaps, I thought, I had passed it half a dozen times since our first meeting without recognizing it. And why should I remember it, why should I think of Dr. Miroff when I walked down that street? The truth of the matter was that I wanted to forget it, the sight of his house, and the remembrance of the miserable half hour I had spent there could only make me uncomfortable. Now he was coming down the walk toward me—for what purpose? Probably to ask me in again, so he could give me another lecture on the superiority of the Communist state, and the futility of being interested in nature. I would refuse.

"Young man," he said, his round, pink face beaming, "I want you to come in my house, I have something to show you."

I started to protest, but he took my arm and led me down the walk and up the flight of steps. On the porch outside the door he stopped and, still holding my arm as though he expected me to try to run away, put his face close to mine.

"Do you remember that cocoon you left with me, the one you picked from the tree down there in the yard?"

I nodded my head.

"Well, after you gave it to me I put it on the mantelpiece and forgot about it. Then one evening last week, Wednesday it was, I was sitting in my easy chair reading, and I looked up and saw this horrible-looking wet bug crawling from it. It crawled to the edge of the mantelpiece and began waving those two dripping things along its sides until they developed into a pair of magnificent wings. It was remarkable, it was positively extraordinary. You would not believe how beautiful that moth is. I sit by the hour watching it fly around my house! By the way, what did you say its name was?"

"It's a Polyphemus moth," I said.

"Polyphemus, I must remember that. But what are we standing here for? Come in and see it."

We went into the house, and he pointed out the moth to me. It was hanging onto the molding just under the ceiling of his living room, its wings spread open. It was a fine specimen, larger than most, its wings a darker brown than any I remembered seeing.

"What a lovely thing it is," Dr. Miroff said. "It has given me a great deal of pleasure, and I am delighted with it. But tell me honestly, where did you get it, and where does it come from?"

I looked at him increduously. "What do you mean?" I asked. "You saw me pick the cocoon from that tree in your yard."

He smiled shyly, then peered at me out of the corners of his eyes, like a fellow conspirator. "Yes, yes, I saw you pick something from my tree, but it was not this cocoon. These moths do not live in big cities."

So, I thought, he thinks this is all part of a carefully laid plot to subvert him, to bring him around to an interest in nature. He has the suspicious mind of a true Communist. Aloud I said, "You're quite sure of that, are you?"

"No, I am not sure of it, I know too little of nature, unfortunately. But if they live here in Chicago, how does it happen that I have never seen one before, that none of my friends has ever seen one? Surely such a large, brilliant moth would be conspicuous in the city."

"I'll tell you why you have never seen one before," I said. "Because you have never been interested enough to look for one. You probably would not see it if a Polyphemus moth flew past you." This was not strictly true, but I was having my revenge for the lecture he had given me at our first meeting. I had never seen one out in the open either, but I didn't have to tell him that.

"Yes," he said, nodding his head meditatively, "I suppose you are right. One must be receptive to an object before it can impress itself on one's attention. But I shall look for them now; I would like to see one here in the city this summer."

"Oh, come now, Doctor," I said, "don't tell me that you have become a nature lover? What's going to become of all those problems crying for solution—the diseases, and the wars, and the cosmic forces?"

He grinned broadly, a shy, embarrassed gin, and for the first time I liked him; he was like an overgrown boy. "You make no allowance for development in a man," he said. "One learns, is it not true?"

"I'm sorry, Doctor," I said, "forgive me." Then I looked up at the moth hanging from the molding. "What are you going to do with it?" "I intend to keep it," he said. "Come over here, I will show you something."

He led me to the mantelpiece, where the empty cocoon still lay, and beside it was a dish with a little water in it.

"Here in this dish I have some water with sugar dissolved in it. The moth already knows it is here, every few hours it comes down and sucks up a little sweet water. Tell me, does it require anything else—leaves, or flowers, perhaps?"

"No, it doesn't need anything else," I said. Then an idea struck me. "Say, I'll tell you what I'll do. This is a female; they're always larger and more brightly colored. I have five or six Polyphemus cocoons at home, and the first time a male comes out I'll bring it here and give it to you. I don't know whether she'll lay her eggs here in the house, but I don't see why not, if you bring the right kind of leaves in. If she doesn't, you can put her out in your yard after she's mated, and next winter you'll have a mess of cocoons."

He slapped me on the back jovially. "An excellent idea, young man. Thank you. It will be a pleasure to become a breeder of Polyphemus moths."

After I left I could not help thinking what a strange convert that Polyphemus moth had made. How would Dr. Miroff reconcile his interest in nature with his belief in Communism, how would he fit his new hobby into the framework of dialectic materialism? Perhaps on a farm, or if he were still living in a small town in Russia, the study of nature might have some pragmatic value; but here in the city, where nature consisted only of harmless, useless plants and insects and birds and small animals, he would have a hard time convincing anyone that his interest in them would bring any material benefits. And, if he was not careful to keep his hobby in its place, he would find his interest in nature usurping the time that should be devoted to his profession, just as, in my case, it had lost me one job and prevented me from getting others.

But then Dr. Miroff was not I. He would know what place to assign nature in the scheme of his life.

A DAY OF DISCOVERY

Mary Ellen Chase

Many others have experienced Thoreau's feeling of the presence of a higher Being in nature. One of them was a little Maine schoolgirl named Mary Ellen Chase. When she had the adventure which she describes in "A Day of Discovery," she was incapable of putting her feelings down in words. She hardly understood them herself, and yet they were so real that she was astonished when her family saw no change in the child they had always known. Years later, when she became a Professor of English at Smith College and wrote such best-selling novels as Dawn in Lyonesse *and* Mary Peters, *the experience remained with her. But now she was better able to analyze her emotions and put them into a form which we who read can comprehend.*

᧭

INTANGIBLE and yet real in its effect was that day in my childhood which I have never forgotten. I have often wondered why it has lingered in my mind through all these many years; but there it is, distinct, luminous, and inviolable.

It was a day in spring, and it must have been in early spring, for we had not as yet been allowed to cast off our winter underwear, and as the warmth of the morning increased, it felt cumbersome and uncomfortable. I have no remembrance of where I had been when the peculiar and essential meaning of the day stole over me, but probably on some errand to the village. I know that I was coming up the board sidewalk which led past the picket fence surrounding our orchard when all at once I felt an odd quickening within me.

There had been a white mist in the early morning from a heavy rainfall during the night, and the sun was just then breaking through it in long rays of light. I felt suddenly surrounded by light and half frightened by the equally sudden perception of it. I walked slowly up the sidewalk until I reached the white gate, where I stopped, for I was puzzled and bewildered.

Light to me before this had been the absence of darkness, the assurance of safety, of the ordinary and the familiar; and I could not understand why these rays of light dispelling the mist, this unexpected, sudden effulgence, seemed so different from daylight in its usual sense. I felt as though something were happening inside me, for I seemed all at once incomprehensibly alive and new, even as if I had just been born.

I did not open the gate and enter the driveway, for my home was at that moment unfamiliar, intrusive, unwelcome, and singularly far removed from me. I stood instead with my back against the gate. I had the curious thought that I was waiting for something to happen, for something to be explained to me, although I had no notion of what that something was. There was no one coming or going along the muddy road. I was alone with my mystery, which disturbed and troubled me.

Then I saw how the sunlight was irradiating everything, how the weather vane on the church steeple gleamed with it, how the brown puddles in the road glistened, how the sodden grasses in the field opposite sparkled from millions of shining drops. I became aware of the sound of water everywhere, dripping from the bare branches of the orchard trees, running through the grassy ditch on either side of the gate, falling from the eaves of the house into the pools below with round musical notes. In the stillness of the air I could hear the freed, full water of the brook beyond our field, falling over the dam and rushing through the millrace. All my small world was transfigured by light, motion, and sound; and I in my worn old reefer and stocking-cap seemed to be in some odd way transfigured also.

I do not know how long I stood outside the gate, watching and listening, waiting for something strange and overwhelming to become clear; for I felt as though I myself were filled with light and motion, as though I had never before been truly awake. I was suddenly afraid of the familiar, commonplace things in the house and of my family, who must, I thought, see at once that I was somehow different and ask to my embarrassment whatever had happened to me.

Needless to say, no one in the household was in the least aware of my transfiguration. To them I was as ordinary and usual as I had always been. Yet the meaning of the day never entirely left me, becoming like the frail tracks in the unbroken snow a secret—guarded, inexplainable, but forever real.

THE VISION OF THE ALPS

Hilaire Belloc

*The following moving description, by a famous English novelist
and poet, shows how nature can stimulate an observant mind to a feeling
of wonder and awareness of the glory of God. Belloc was born in France
and educated in England, and became a member of the House of
Commons. He wrote such diverse books as* The Modern Traveller,
Robespierre, Pongo and the Bull, The Servile State *and a four-volume*
History of England. *His temperament was strongly religious and mystical
and in his vision of the Alps, he saw not only jutting masses of stone
and earth but "magnificent creatures of God."*

∽

THE wood went up darkly and the path branched here and there
so that I was soon uncertain of my way, but I followed generally
what seemed to me the most southerly course, and so came at last
up steeply through a dip or ravine that ended high on the crest of
the ridge.

Just as I came to the end of the rise, after perhaps an hour, perhaps two, of that great curtain of forest which had held the mountain side, the trees fell away to brushwood, there was a gate, and
then the path was lost upon a fine open sward which was the very
top of the Jura and the coping of that multiple wall which defends
the Swiss Plain. I had crossed it straight from edge to edge, never
turning out of my way.

It was too marshy to lie down on it, so I stood a moment to
breathe and look about me.

It was evident that nothing higher remained, for though a new
line of wood—firs and beeches—stood before me, yet nothing appeared above them, and I knew that they must be the fringe of the
descent. I approached this edge of wood, and saw that it had a
rough fence of post and rails bounding it, and as I was looking for
the entry of a path (for my original path was lost, as such tracks are,
in the damp grass of the little down) there came to me one of those
great revelations which betray to us suddenly the higher things and
stand afterwards firm in our minds.

There, on this upper meadow, where so far I had felt nothing but the ordinary gladness of The Summit, I had a vision.

What was it I saw? If you think I saw this or that, and if you think I am inventing the words, you know nothing of men.

I saw between the branches of the trees in front of me a sight in the sky that made me stop breathing, just as great danger at sea, or great surprise in love, or a great deliverance will make a man stop breathing. I saw something I had known in the West as a boy, something I had never seen so grandly discovered as was this. In between the branches of the trees was a great promise of unexpected lights beyond.

I pushed left and right along that edge of the forest and along the fence that bound it, until I found a place where the pine-trees stopped, leaving a gap, and where on the right, beyond the gap, was a tree whose leaves had failed; there the ground broke away steeply below me, and the beeches fell, one below the other, like a vast cascade, towards the limestone cliffs that dipped down still further, beyond my sight. I looked through this framing hollow and praised God. For there before me, thousands of feet below me, was what seemed an illimitable plain; at the end of that world was an horizon, and the dim bluish sky that overhangs an horizon.

There was brume in it and thickness. One saw the sky beyond the edge of the world getting purer as the vault rose. But right up—a belt in that empyrean—ran peak and field and needle of intense ice, remote, remote from the world. Sky beneath them and sky above them, a steadfast legion, they glittered as though with the armor of the immovable armies of Heaven. Two days' march, three days' march away, they stood up like the walls of Eden. I say it again, they stopped my breath. I had seen them.

So little are we, we men: so much are we immersed in our muddy and immediate interests that we think, by numbers and recitals, to comprehend distance or time, or any of our limiting infinities. Here were these magnificent creatures of God, I mean the Alps, which now for the first time I saw from the height of the Jura; and because they were fifty or sixty miles away, and because they were a mile or two high, they were become something different from us others, and could strike one motionless with the awe of supernatural things. Up there in the sky, to which only clouds belong and birds and the last trembling colors of pure light, they stood fast and hard; not moving as do the things of the sky. They were as distant as the little upper clouds of summer, as fine and tenuous; but in their reflection and in their quality as it were of weapons (like spears and shields of an unknown array) they occupied the sky with a sublime invasion: and the things proper to the sky were forgotten by me in their presence as I gazed.

To what emotion shall I compare this astonishment? So, in first love one finds that *this* can belong to me.

Their sharp steadfastness and their clean uplifted lines compelled my adoration. Up there, the sky above and below them, part of the sky, but part of us, the great peaks made communion between that homing creeping part of me which loves vineyards and dances and a slow movement among pastures, and that other part which is only properly at home in Heaven. I say that this kind of description is useless, and that it is better to address prayers to such things than to attempt to interpret them for others.

These, the great Alps, seen thus, link one in some way to one's immortality. Nor is it possible to convey, or even to suggest, those few fifty miles, and those few thousand feet; there is something more. Let me put it thus: that from the height of Weissenstein I saw, as it were, my religion. I mean, humility, the fear of death, the terror of height and of distance, the glory of God, the infinite potentiality of reception whence springs that divine thirst of the soul; my aspiration also towards completion, and my confidence in the dual destiny. For I know that we laughers have a gross cousinship with the most high, and it is this contrast and perpetual quarrel which feeds a spring of merriment in the soul of a sane man.

Since I could now see such a wonder and it could work such things in my mind, therefore, some day I should be part of it. That is what I felt.

BEAUTY

Kahlil Gibran

*The appreciation of beauty is in many of us an undeveloped art. We
see a sunset and may make a casual remark about it. A symphony may
thrill us if we take the trouble to tune it in, but too frequently we feel
that listening is not worth the trouble involved. But note the hush that
settles over an audience as some superb dancer moves across the stage.
Watch the faces of visitors to an art gallery as they gaze at a masterpiece
of painting or sculpture. The appreciation of art, too often neglected in
our busy lives, can bring us rich rewards.*

*Such appreciation need not be limited to the fine arts. It can be had
in many moments of our days. A mystic, a poet and an artist, Kahlil
Gibran could see in the experiences of everyday living spiritual values
which spoke to millions. He was an artist with an extraordinary sensitivity
and insight. Here he shows that to each of us beauty speaks in a different
language, according to our needs. For each it represents our innermost
hopes and aspirations.*

AND a poet said, Speak to us of Beauty.

And he answered:

Where shall you seek beauty, and how shall you find her unless
she herself be your way and your guide?

And how shall you speak of her except she be the weaver of
your speech?

The aggrieved and the injured say, "Beauty is kind and gentle.
Like a young mother half-shy of her own glory she walks among
us."

And the passionate say, "Nay, beauty is a thing of might and
dread.

Like the tempest she shakes the earth beneath us and the sky
above us."

The tired and the weary say, "Beauty is of soft whisperings. She speaks in our spirit.

Her voice yields to our silences like a faint light that quivers in fear of the shadow."

But the restless say, "We have heard her shouting among the mountains,

And with her cries came the sound of hoofs, and the beating of wings and the roaring of lions."

At night the watchmen of the city say, "Beauty shall rise with the dawn from the east."

And at noontide the toilers and the wayfarers say, "We have seen her leaning over the earth from the windows of the sunset."

In winter say the snow-bound, "She shall come with the spring leaping upon the hills."

And in the summer heat the reapers say, "We have seen her dancing with the autumn leaves, and we saw a drift of snow in her hair."

All these things have you said of beauty,

Yet in truth you spoke not of her but of needs unsatisfied.

And beauty is not a need but an ecstasy.

It is not a mouth thirsting nor an empty hand stretched forth,

But rather a heart enflamed and a soul enchanted.

It is not the image you would see nor the song you would hear,

But rather an image you see though you close your eyes and a song you hear though you shut your ears.

It is not the sap within the furrowed bark, nor a wing attached to a claw,

But rather a garden for ever in bloom and a flock of angels for ever in flight.

People of Orphalese, beauty is life when life unveils her holy face.

But you are life and you are the veil.

Beauty is eternity gazing at itself in a mirror.

But you are eternity and you are the mirror.

BEING ALIVE TO POETRY

—— *Walter Russell Bowie* ——

Like Harry Emerson Fosdick, Walter Russell Bowie is one of America's most distinguished ministers. And like Dr. Fosdick, he is a man of wide-ranging knowledge. His book On Being Alive *tells us that to live life to the fullest, we must be intensely aware of the values not only of religion and God, but also of nature, poetry and the arts. Dr. Bowie thinks of poetry as typifying a whole attitude toward life, an attitude which can open doors to sunlight and serenity.*

⎯⎯

"But I do not like poetry"—a reader of this chapter heading may object. "To have to read a book of poetry would be a bore. Poetry twists simple things into fantastic exaggerations. I like plain facts, and plain ways of telling about them. Poetry insists that I walk around three sides of a square in order to go where I might have gone in one straight line."

Part of which is true. For poetry does lead simple things into a hall of mirrors which to the practical mind seems nothing but a maze. Poetry does beguile one's thoughts away from plain paths into all sorts of up-hill and down-dale excursionings. And poetry may even beckon us to come round three sides of a square instead of marching in a brisk hurry across its front.

"Then that proves exactly what I always thought," say the practical man. "Poetry has no common sense." But, in reply, the poetic spirit has certain serene but insistent questions which it presses. What is sense, and what is sensibility? And what, if you please, is life?

Now the individuals among us who have no use for poetry, and the mood of an age itself which tends to be indifferent to it, are not particularly given to definitions. Their forte is in action, not in expression. But they can meet the question asked of them with at least a rule-of-thumb reply. What is life? Well, life is activity. Life means getting on. The man who is alive is the man who sees the end he wants to reach, and then proceeds to clear a straight road by which to reach it.

Crowds of people in our time believe that. The concrete rewards of action have been great and glittering. A man must press ahead in order to win. He has no time for idle reflections upon the scenery at the side of the road. If he stops to dream, somebody will out-distance him. Everything he covets is up ahead, and the one condition of success is to arrive. The result is that for innumerable individuals life is a continual pushing past the crowd. There on the hilltop far out in front is the end of the rainbow which is supposed to mark the pot of gold. Keep going, therefore. Whatever distracts from the straight direction is silliness. Stick to the road and step lively. That is common sense.

But is it? Even our practical age is beginning to wonder. For sometimes when men go to the end of the rainbow of all their hard-headed strivings, the pot of gold is not there; and if it is there, they may find to their dismay that they do not know what to do with it now that it is in their hands. What enjoyments can they buy with it when they have lost all their fresh power to enjoy? What is the use of having arrived at the end of the road, if neither the road nor the end of it brings them any satisfaction when the blood stops beating in their ears and for the first time they can take breath and reckon with their surroundings?

In that moment, the too-long-forgotten spirit of poetry may be heard. And this is what it says: It was not good sense to imagine that life means a fierce postponement of the experience of living. To be aiming at coveted ends with such obsession as to neglect the here-and-now is to starve the spirit so long that it will never be able to taste anything with zest. Life is not meant to be a hectic scramble for a prize which is given only to the one who gets there first. Rather it has the quality of some infinitely abundant treasure hunt in which the things worth having are near at hand and only enough half-hidden to stimulate the thrill of search. Open your eyes, says the spirit of poetry, that you may see.

How have the poets of every land begun but by this mere fact of seeing—seeing what every eye may see, of object, or event, or cir-cumstance, if it will take the pains to look? They register what most of us are only vaguely aware of—register so sensitively that in their description the whole picture which they have seen reappears in form and color and distinctive atmosphere.

Consider, for example, these matchless opening lines of Gray's *Elegy in a Country Churchyard*. Except for the one monosyllable at the end of the second line, every word in the verse is a term of common use. Not upon any artificiality whatever, but only upon the vividness of his original perception and upon the simple rightness of common nouns and a few adjectives does the poet depend to reproduce the breathing reality of the scene upon which he had looked:

> The curfew tolls the knell of parting day,
> The lowing herd winds slowly o'er the lea,
> The ploughman homeward plods his weary way,
> And leaves the world to darkness and to me.

Or listen to the haunting cadences of William Butler Yeats, and under the spell of them watch the swift deftness of his suggestion recreate for us his picture of Innisfree.

> I will arise and go now, and go to Innisfree,
> And a small cabin build there, of clay and wattles made;
> Nine bean rows will I have there, a hive for the honey-bee,
> And live alone in the bee-loud glade.
> And I shall have some peace there, for peace comes dropping slow,
> Dropping from the veils of the morning to where the cricket sings;
> There midnight's all a-glimmer, and noon a purple glow,
> And evening full of the linnet's wings.

Robert Burns became the poet laureate of a nation's affection because he possessed in a rare degree this power to see and to describe what all men took delight in contemplating when he had roused them to perceive. From the "banks and braes o' bonny Doon," to the field-mouse in the furrow where the plough had rooted up its nest, from tipsy Tam o'Shanter to the Cotter going home on Saturday night, his eyes caught the swift impression of whatever was distinctive and significant; and it was because he first so lovingly had observed that he could so livingly describe. His expansive sympathies were as wide as life, so that with the same instinctive understanding he could describe the Cotter, "the cheerfu' supper done, wi' serious face," taking the family Bible and reading it in the firelight as the children gather round the hearth; or introduce in this fashion the exceedingly different but beguiling Tam:

> When chapman billies leave the street,
> And drouthy neibors, neibors meet,
> As market days are wearing late,
> And folk begin to tak the gate;

While we sit bousing at the nappy,
An' gettin' fou and unco happy,
We thinkna on the lang Scots miles,
The mosses, waters, slaps, and stiles,
That lie between us and our hame,
Whare sits our sulky sullen dame,
Gathering her brows like gathering storm,
Nursing her wrath to keep it warm.

But there is a poet nearer to our own time who illustrates even more abundantly than his great forerunners this capacity for unresting observation by which at least the raw materials for poetry are assembled. I mean Walt Whitman. Walt Whitman did not have the constructive genius of the supreme poetic masters. He fell short of that divine alchemy of touch which can transform the commonplace into something so ineffably significant that its whole nature becomes more golden and more glorious. But as a lover of the world and of life and of all their manifoldness, as a reveler in all that stirred sensation and aroused delight, no person of his own time— and scarce of any time—has equaled him. In his unleashed and exuberant spirit there was something which acted as a playful retriever acts, ranging the whole countryside with eyes and ears and nose alert, and bringing whatever he fancies back to his master's feet. So to Whitman the omnivorous love of life which was within him, and which went forth from him, brought back its spoil of a whole universe of sensation. He exulted in everything he could see or hear or smell or touch—in the human body and all its parts and exercise, in crowds of people on streets and omnibuses and ferries, in the odor of lilacs and grasses and apples and cedars and corn, "in the briny and damp smell, the shores, the salt weeds exposed at low water," in the movement of ships, in foam and the feel of the wind, and in all the tang of the sea. He wished to "absorb" all things, to feel with them and in them, and so to experience the infinite variety and fullness of life. In this immense objectivity he did certainly reveal the limitless stimulus to poetic emotion which the world contains; and it is by him that many of our most characteristic modern poets have been influenced. Carl Sandburg, for example, is like Whitman in his ability to extract the golden grains of poetry from the most crude and raw perceptions. Edgar Lee Masters and Robert Frost reflect him in their unvarnished mirroring of homely things. The whole trend of most modern poetry, away from the sophisticated and back toward the more primitive sensations, repeats the powerful impulse which Whitman gave.

This has its deficiencies, as we shall see; but it has the great value of making clear that poetry need not be an esoteric experience, but that it can grow out of contact with our ordinary and common earth. We do not have to wait until we climb some cloudy Olympus before we can feel poetic appreciation; we can feel it, if we are sensitive, down in the midst of familiar things. The chief worth of reading what the poets have written lies not in marveling at the vivid sufficiency of what they have said; it lies in realizing that in the midst of the same environment we may learn to feel as they have felt because our eyes are opened to see what they have seen.

Thus far we have thought of poetry as dependent upon the freshness and directness of our perceptions. But of course that is not all. One might perceive with utter clarity all that objectively appears in a given object, and be an admirable scientific observer, but not a poet. The poet sees in the object of his experience not only all that is there, but something more. In this aspect also are children often instinctively poetic beyond the grasp of their uncomprehending elders.

Here, of course, we enter into the realm of the imagination. Observation tells us what an idea or an object is; imagination tells us what it is like. It brings to the bare fact its overtones of meaning. It enriches it with innumerable clustering suggestions. The native experience is like an empty dove-cote stark against the sky; but when imagination calls, the atmosphere around it is filled with the hovering of a hundred wings.

This quickening imagination which is the soul of all true poetry is a much more primal and instinctive thing than we generally understand. We are prone to think of poets as individuals apart, rare exotics wholly different from ordinary people; and we think of poetry as compositions of intricate language and ingenious rhyme, written by men whose eyes were "in a fine frenzy rolling," and printed in books which only the very cultivated will actually read. But as a matter of fact, the poetic impulse is almost as old and as artless as life itself. It is part of the nature of the mind to find delight in comparing a new object of experience with one already familiar, and in clothing the new thing therefore with associations which give it interest and enrichment. This happy play of the imagination, instead of being a product of sophisticated culture as we sometimes foolishly suppose, belongs instead to our unspoiled original inheritance; and when we reach back through our clattering practicalities to possess ourselves again of the sensitive imagination which broods and listens and wonders and widely understands, we are regaining that which always can be ours.

Our human nature is a dual thing, and the world in which we live therefore is capable of a dual aspect. We may move upon the level of our uninspired senses, and perceive nothing except what the eyes and ears of any other unreflecting creature could equally well perceive. If there is a field of dumped red earth and pools of rain, then clay and puddles are all that we may see. If there are shabby houses round us, and people going about their humdrum business, then shabbiness and stodginess may seem to us to be all there is to life. That sort of perception is called realism; and there are some who think that realism is identical with reality. But it is not. The sort of realism which registers the stark facts of our environment with no appreciation of those rich, unseen suggestions which can cluster round them, does not represent our real earth. It represents only the shell of it—stripped of its atmosphere, and dead and barren as the moon. The full reality of our world appears only when the sunlight of our higher wondering falls upon it, and brings its hidden significance to light. *Then* the red clay may become castles, and the people who outwardly seem to be nothing but figures of earth may become invested with a divine flame.

The importance of reading poetry, and the penalty of ignoring it, has found perhaps its classic expression in the words not of a poet but of a scientist—that greatest scientist, Charles Darwin. In his autobiography he tells how, for the first thirty years of his life, poetry and music were a delight to him, but "now for many years I cannot endure to read a line of poetry. I have tried lately to read Shakespeare, and found it so intolerably dull that it nauseated me. I have also lost my taste for pictures or music." Then upon "this curious and lamentable loss of the higher æsthetic tastes" he goes on to comment in these memorable words:

My mind seems to have become a kind of machine for grinding general laws out of large collections of facts, but why this should have caused the atrophy of that part of the brain alone, on which the higher tastes depend, I cannot conceive. . . . If I had to live my life again, I would have made a rule to read some poetry and listen to some music at least once every week; for perhaps the part of my brain now atrophied would thus have been kept active through use. The loss of these tastes is a loss of happiness, and may possibly be injurious to the intellect, and more probably to the moral character, by enfeebling the emotional part of our nature.

The poets offer us not merely an æsthetic experience. They become to us the authentic interpreters of life. They push back our horizons; and they invest the near and the familiar with a richer light. The way by which they accomplish this is of course not by argument. They do it by that intangible magic of suggestion which leads the imagination on into a wider space. Could anything seem more simple than these three lines of Whitman, or could anything be more commonplace than his immediate theme? A barn door— that is what he is writing about—nothing more romantic or unusual than that. But mark the mood which he conveys.

Through the ample open door of the peaceful country barn
A sunlit pasture field with cattle and horses feeding,
And haze and vista, and the far horizon fading away—

Who can see that picture and not feel somehow that the doors of life can open, if we choose, upon sunlight and serenity, and that there is a meaning of things which stretches into the far distance, yet is not dissolved? And always the effect of poetry can be like that. It can heighten the values of everything. It can touch the common and make it uncommon. Nothing would come nearer to lifting this whole existence of ours to a new plane of interest and wondering delight than the deliberate experiment of trying to think of our own environment, or to speak of it inwardly, in the most poetic terms we can command. When friendship becomes a routine contact, and love sinks into a dull monotony, and work becomes a wretched grind, the reason is that the poetry of their possible suggestion has been lost, or has never consciously been there. But it can be won. This day-to-day existence may not always be the utmost we would choose: it has contradictions in it, and tragedies too. But as long as we can lighten it with imagination, it need never degenerate into a farce.

For there is a source of poetry which every life, no matter what its circumstances be, can always draw upon. That source is religion. Religion is often wrongly thought of as though it were a heavy dogmatism, a burden laid upon men's backs, a weight to bear instead of wings to rise by. But it is nothing of the sort. It is the message of life's immortal poetry, and the lift of an exhaustless inspiration. It brings lives into conscious relation with one another, with the past and with the future, and gives therefore to what might be a narrow lot a sense of wider dignity. The words of Jesus are full of this creative poetry. "Ye are the light of the world. A city that is set on an hill cannot be hid. . . . Ye are the salt of the earth. . . . Ye are my friends. Henceforth I call you not servants, but I have called you friends." Human existence is not measured by mortality; it comes of a divine heritage and therefore, with divinity in its consciousness, it must live in "the power of an endless life." It was this interpretation of existence which sent Paul the Apostle on his epic way. It was this that put a song upon the lips of Francis of Assisi and wrote the heroic story of a Father Damien in the leper colony of Molokai. It is this which for innumerable lesser souls has set up even in the barren places a ladder of life's meaning that reaches to the sky. This is the poetry of religion, and when men's hearts respond to that poetry's great bells, they know they have discovered that with which they were meant to be in tune.

THE HEROIC MUSICIAN: BEETHOVEN

——— *Romain Rolland* ———

It is generally recognized that Beethoven is one of the world's greatest composers, and that the French novelist and critic Romain Rolland is his foremost interpreter. Rolland's biographies of Beethoven, of Michelangelo and Tolstoy are literary masterpieces. But his greatest work is undoubtedly his multi-volume Jean Christophe. *This superb novel, for which he was awarded the Nobel Prize in 1915, is the story of a great composer who bears strong resemblances to Beethoven. Beethoven's life was indeed worthy of a talent as great as Rolland's. A consummate genius, recognized as such during his lifetime, he was nevertheless plagued by money worries, by lack of any real affection in his life, by overpowering emotions which he found it difficult to control, and by the deafness which came when he was in his thirties and which, for a composer, was a truly ironic affliction. Out of this tortured existence came an outpouring of music which speaks of the most intense and passionate human feelings. Here is love of nature and love of mankind. Here is*

*heroism and delicate soaring beauty. From Rolland's many writings about
Beethoven we have selected this short but impassioned tribute.*

BELOVED Beethoven! He is the most heroic soul in modern art. He is
the grandest and best friend of those who suffer and struggle. When
we are saddened by worldly miseries, it is he who comes near to us,
as he used to go and play to a mother in grief, and, without uttering
a word, thus console her by the song of his own plaintive resignation. And when we are utterly exhausted in the eternal battle use-
lessly waged against mediocrity, vice, and virtue, it is an unspeakable
boon to find fresh strength in this great ocean-torrent of strong will
and faith. An atmosphere of courage emanates from his personality,
a love of battle, the exultation of a conscious feeling of the God
within. It seems that in his constant communion with nature he had
ended by assimilating its deep and mighty powers. Grillparzer, who
admired Beethoven with a kind of awe, said of him, "He penetrated
into regions where art melts away and unites with the wild and ca-
pricious elements." Schumann wrote similarly of his *Symphony in C
Minor*: "Every time it is performed it exercises an unvarying power
on us, like natural phenomena which fill us with awe and amazement every time they occur." And Schindler, his confidential friend,
says, "He possessed the spirit of nature." It is true, "Beethoven is a
force of nature; and this battle of elemental power against the rest
of nature is a spectacle of truly Homeric grandeur."

His whole life is like a stormy day. At the begining—a fresh, clear
morning, perhaps a languid breeze, scarcely a breath of air. But
there is already in the still air a secret menace, a dark foreboding.
Large shadows loom and pass; tragic rumblings; murmuring awesome
silences; the furious gusts of the winds of the *Eroica* and the *C
Minor*. However, the freshness of the day is not yet gone. Joy remains
joy; the brightness of the sky is not overcast; sadness is never without
a ray of hope.

But after 1810 the poise of the soul is disturbed. A strange light
glows. Mists obscured his deepest thoughts; some of the clearer
thoughts appear as vapor rising; they disappear, are dispelled, yet
form anew; they obscure the heart with their melancholy and ca-
pricious gloom; often the musical idea seems to vanish entirely,
to be submerged, but only to reappear again at the end of a piece in
a veritable storm of melody. Even joy has assumed a rough and

riotus character. A bitter feeling becomes mingled in all his sentiments. Storms gather as evening comes on. Heavy clouds are big with tempests. Lightning flashes o'er the black of night. The climax of the hurricane is approaching. Suddenly, at the height of the tempest, the darkness is dispersed. Night is driven away and the clear, tranquil atmosphere is restored by a sheer act of will power. What a conquest was this! What Napoleonic battle can be likened to it? What was Austerlitz glory to the radiance of this superhuman effort, this victory, the most brilliant that has ever been won by an infirm and lonely spirit? Sorrow personified, to whom the world refused joy, created joy himself to give to the world. He forged it from his own misery, as he proudly said in reviewing his life. And indeed it was the motto of his whole heroic soul: Joy through suffering.

THE MIRACLE OF AN ARTIST

Dorothy Thompson

We read in a previous selection of a moment which contributed to Dorothy Thompson's education. Here she describes a different sort of experience, but one which she felt just as keenly. This is the story of that star-crossed genius Vincent Van Gogh. Like Beethoven, "beginning somberly, in darkness, and moving steadily into light," he was able to convey through his art the meaning which he found in life. It is this meaning, transfused into light and color, which has appealed so profoundly to viewers of his paintings. As Dorothy Thompson states, Van Gogh was a man who wanted to see God as He appears in Nature and in the faces of humankind.

DURING the past fall and winter, tens of thousands of New Yorkers and visitors from outside passed through the Metropolitan Museum of Art to see an extraordinary exhibition of drawings and paintings by a man who died in France over sixty years ago. On the walls of the Metropolitan Museum hung the story of a life and the expression of a human passion, the impact of it so terrific that after two hours of gazing, one's heart palpitated and one's knees trembled. The paintings are the record of a man beginning somberly, in darkness, and moving steadily into light, until, gazing straight into the sun, he tore the veil from nature to present an incandescent world of almost unbearable glory and beauty, in which all form is movement and all things are energy, a world where nature palpitates and sings.

The paintings of Vincent Van Gogh are a miracle. No one before him saw the world as he saw it, and no one having seen it through his eyes can ever see it in the same way again. He was, perhaps, all unconsciously, the first painter of the atomic age. He knew nothing of physics or of mathematics. His knowledge of the world came not through the brain but through the eye. Yet he certainly saw a world in which a chair, a flower, a plowed field, a tree, were not stable matter but vibrant neutrons of energy and light. If one looks at his greatest paintings close to the canvas they are a formless chaos. When one moves back the forms leap forward, forms of a nature caught in movement, no moment being like the preceding one or the one to follow. No one before Van Gogh caught in painting, I think, the fourth dimension of time.

What he saw destroyed him. Standing in a plowed field at the age of thirty-seven, ill, and mad, he put a bullet through his heart. No doubt he saw more than ever he could paint, and more than it is permitted man to see. Only a fragment of his vision is transmitted to us. But it is a vision beginning in sorrow and rising into joy—joy beyond happiness, joy exciting, disturbing, awesome, beautiful, and with an undertow of terror.

Vincent Van Gogh wanted to see God. Deeply religious, parsonage-born, in a Dutch Protestant family who had connections to the art world through members who were dealers, and who for generations had never been without a pastor member, he first sought God through the Bible and through theological training, in preparation for the ministry, and in work among the poorest and lowliest Flemish miners and weavers. Of this period, before he had realized himself as a painter, he leaves a pictorial *de profundis* of patient, long-suffering human misery. He paints with pity to dissolve his colors and they are the colors of the static earth.

But Vincent Van Gogh did not find God in humanity as such, though he found Him in the human mystery. God, he found, was life. He was in all living things, and above all in nature. And Van Gogh's eye saw, for all the pain and suffering of humanity, the glory of life and the truth of the glory. And that is what he has transmitted to us.

His own life was a record of personal frustration, material wretchedness, and universal misunderstanding. From the time he left his father's house to the day he ended his life, he never earned even pocket money. His entire family, with one exception—his brother Theo—regarded him as a black sheep and useless dreamer. And even Theo, as we see from Vincent's letters, often wavered in his faith. The artist did not accept their judgment debonairly, and for most of his life their judgment of him was his own. His teachers— when he was able to get them through Theo—scolded him that what he did was neither "charming" nor "salable." He never had money enough to marry, though he longed for a home. He was often ill, perpetually humiliated, frightfully lonely, and in the last years of his life quite incurably mad. Although he lived in the vast museum of art treasures which Europe was and is, he never saw Greece or Rome, or the glorious paintings of the Renaissance in Florence and Venice.

The great burst of his genius—and his whole life as a painter was compressed into ten years—came when he removed to the sleepy town of Arles, in the French Provence country of color and sun, and there he painted his greatest pictures, living after a time in a hospital, painting what he saw through his window, until finally he was transferred to the insane asylum at St. Rémy, twenty miles away, occasionally let out to paint the surrounding orchards and fields, living the rest of his life in recovery and relapse, and painting when well, in a sort of trance. All that he painted in this period is alive and growing. His trees are not standing but growing or fading like his wheat fields and his people. He needed to search nowhere for things to paint—he painted what was all around him.

His view of the world has been called romantic. But his letters reveal great refinement of intellect and no painter ever put himself through more austere disciplines, attaching enormous importance to drawing, if it only were drawing from living models. Poverty, indifference to convention, and lack of capacity to cope with everyday life made his personal life disorderly, but he was not disorderly in his work, though he pursued it with febrile intensity, in a conscious race against time.

He hated his dependency on his brother, who was not very well off himself. There was never enough money for both the most primitive comforts and the materials of his art, and he starved himself to buy paint and canvas. From critics, art dealers, and the public he received no encouragement. When he died he had sold only one painting. His total earnings from ten years of the most intense and inhuman effort were about one hundred dollars. But the exhibition assembled in New York by the Metropolitan Museum of Art and the Art Institute of Chicago from museums and private collectors all over the Western world, is valued at $3,000,000, and by no means contains all his great works.

But I am not writing a posthumous success story, but trying rather to inquire into what constitutes a great life. Vincent Van Gogh not only left the record of himself in his paintings, but he left a complete autobiography in his extraordinary letters to Theo, published last year for the first time in America, and edited by Irving Stone. These letters express almost unutterable anguish. But they also express almost unutterable aspiration and ecstatic joy. Minutely he describes to his brother the color, shape, and sounds of things. A walk, in an undistinguished landscape, fills him with rhapsody. And incredible patience possesses him, and he is always humble. Although he cries, "I want more soul, more love, more heart!" (in life and in his work), he feels that in spite of all his misery, life has granted him the *privilege* to be an artist. He commiserates with his brother that he does not paint and therefore misses so much! He tries to communicate to him, not only his material anguish but his spiritual joy. Not for an instant does he rail against God. He affirms His existence; he sees nobility in the poorest and most fallen creatures, who "cannot," he declares, "be destined for the worms."

What is happiness? In our own age we think of it as comfort and the sum of material things.

Happiness is difficult without some comfort. Van Gogh would not, I believe, have been a less great artist had he had enough to eat. But happiness is *not* joy. Joy springs *only* from creative activity, and by some mystery we do not understand creation is almost always integrated with pain. All intense effort—the effort of the mother in childbirth, of the athlete, of the scholar, working in intense intellectual concentration, or of the saint in his intense spiritual concentration, of the artist, of the craftsman—has in it an element of pain, for effort stems from the urge to rise above one's own limitations, to do what is beyond one's strength and capacities. Effort is by nature *uncomfortable*. Yet only through effort does anyone find exhilaration and joy.

To men and women of genius, Van Gogh among them, who died before I was born, I owe vicarious joy and an intensification of experience, and therefore of life. Because they lived, and suffered, and worked, all men after them can, if they will, live more than they would otherwise have done. And that, too, is part of the miracle.

PAINTING AS A PASTIME

——— *Winston S. Churchill* ———

It is not only through appreciation that we can take pleasure in the arts. All of us, even the most unskilled, can enjoy active participation in them. The child sings as he engages in an impromptu dance with his playmates; the woman takes pleasure in the design of a dress, or even of a table setting; the man whistles as he works at his scroll saw. There are higher reaches too. At the mere thought of practicing one of the fine arts, most of us automatically quail, with "I've never painted a stroke in my life," or "I can barely tell the difference between a violin and a piano." No matter; almost all of us can learn, not with the hope of attaining professional skill, but purely for the joy in the endeavor. The author of the following selection is of course one of the greatest figures of the twentieth century.

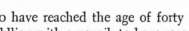

To have reached the age of forty without ever handling a brush or fiddling with a pencil, to have regarded with mature eye the painting of pictures of any kind as a mystery, to have stood agape before the chalk of the pavement artist, and then suddenly to find oneself plunged in the middle of a new and intense form of interest and action with paints and palettes and canvases, and not to be discouraged by results, is an astonishing and enriching experience. I hope it may be shared by others. I should be glad if these lines induced others to try the experiment which I have tried, and if some at least were to find themselves dowered with an absorbing new amusement delightful to themselves, and at any rate not violently harmful to man or beast.

I hope this is modest enough: because there is no subject on which I feel more humble or yet at the same time more natural. I do not presume to explain how to paint, but only how to get enjoyment. Do not turn the superior eye of critical passivity upon these efforts. Buy a paint-box and have a try. If you need something to occupy your leisure, to divert your mind from the daily round, to illuminate your holidays, do not be too ready to believe that you cannot find what you want here. Even at the advanced age of forty! It would be a sad pity to shuffle or scramble along through one's playtime with golf and bridge, pottering, loitering, shifting from one heel to the other, wondering what on earth to do—as perhaps is the fate of some unhappy beings—when all the while, if you only knew, there is close at hand a wonderful new world of thought and craft, a sunlit garden gleaming with light and color of which you have the key in your waistcoat-pocket. Inexpensive independence, a mobile and perennial pleasure apparatus, new mental food and exercise, the old harmonies and symmetries in an entirely different language, an added interest to every common scene, an occupation for every idle hour, an unceasing voyage of entrancing discovery— these are high prizes. Make quite sure they are not yours. After all, if you try, and fail, there is not much harm done, the nursery will grab what the studio has rejected. And then you can always go out and kill some animal, humilate some rival on the links, or despoil some friend across the green table. You will not be worse off in any way. In fact you will be better off. You will know "beyond a peradventure," to quote a phrase disagreeably reminiscent, that that is really what you were meant to do in your hours of relaxation.

But if, on the contrary, you are inclined—late in life though it be —to reconnoiter a foreign sphere of limitless extent, then be persuaded that the first quality that is needed is Audacity. There really is no time for the deliberate approach. Two years of drawing-lessons, three years of copying woodcuts, five years of plaster casts—these are for the young. They have enough to bear. And this thorough grounding is for those who, hearing the call in the morning of their days, are able to make painting their paramount lifelong vocation. The truth and beauty of line and form which by the slightest touch or twist of the brush a real artist imparts to every feature of his design must be founded on long, hard, persevering apprenticeship and a practice so habitual that it has become instinctive. We must not be too ambitious. We cannot aspire to masterpieces. We may content ourselves with a joy ride in a paint-box. And for this Audacity is the only ticket.

I shall now relate my personal experience. When I left the Admiralty at the end of May, 1915, I still remained a member of the Cabinet and of the War Council. In this position I knew everything and could do nothing. The change from the intense executive activities of each day's work at the Admiralty to the narrowly-measured duties of a counselor left me gasping. Like a sea-beast fished up from the depths, or a diver too suddenly hoisted, my veins threatened to burst from the fall in pressure. I had great anxiety and no means of relieving it; I had vehement convictions and small power to give effect to them. I had to watch the unhappy casting-away of great opportunities, and the feeble execution of plans which I had launched and in which I heartily believed. I had long hours of utterly unwonted leisure in which to contemplate the frightful unfolding of the War. At a moment when every fiber of my being was inflamed to action, I was forced to remain a spectator of the tragedy, placed cruelly in a front seat. And then it was that the Muse of Painting came to my rescue—out of charity and out of chivalry, because after all she had nothing to do with me—and said, "Are these toys any good to you? They amuse some people."

Some experiments one Sunday in the country with the children's paint-box led me to procure the next morning a complete outfit for painting in oils.

Having bought the colors, an easel, and a canvas, the next step was to begin. But what a step to take! The palette gleamed with beads of color; fair and white rose the canvas; the empty brush hung poised, heavy with destiny, irresolute in the air. My hand seemed arrested by a silent veto. But after all the sky on this occasion was unquestionably blue, and a pale blue at that. There could be no doubt that blue paint mixed with white should be put on the top part of the canvas. One really does not need to have had an artist's training to see that. It is a starting-point open to all. So very gingerly I mixed a little blue paint on the palette with a very small brush, and then with infinite precaution made a mark about as big as a bean upon the affronted snow-white shield. It was a challenge, a deliberate challenge; but so subdued, so halting, indeed so cataleptic, that it deserved no response. At that moment the loud approaching sound of a motor-car was heard in the drive. From this chariot there stepped swiftly and lightly none other than the gifted wife of Sir John Lavery. "Painting! But what are you hesitating about? Let me have a brush—the big one." Splash into the turpentine, wallop into the blue and the white, frantic flourish on the palette—clean no longer—and then several large, fierce strokes and slashes of blue on the absolutely cowering canvas. Anyone could see that it could not hit back. No evil fate avenged the jaunty violence. The canvas grinned in helplessness before me. The spell was broken. The sickly inhibitions rolled away. I seized the largest brush and fell upon my victim with berserk fury. I have never felt any awe of a canvas since.

Everyone knows the feelings with which one stands shivering on a spring-board, the shock when a friendly foe steals up behind and hurls you into the flood, and the ardent glow which thrills you as you emerge breathless from the plunge.

This beginning with Audacity, or being thrown into the middle of it, is already a very great part of the art of painting. But there is more in it than that.

> La peinture à l'huile
> Est bien difficile,
> Mais c'est beaucoup plus beau
> Que la peinture à l'eau.

I write no word in disparagement of water-colors. But there really is nothing like oils. You have a medium at your disposal which offers real power, if you only can find out how to use it. Moreover, it is easier to get a certain distance along the road by its means than by water-color. First of all, you can correct mistakes much more easily. One sweep of the palette-knife "lifts" the blood and tears of a morning from the canvas and enables a fresh start to be made; indeed the canvas is all the better for past impressions. Secondly, you can approach your problem from any direction. You need not build downwards awkwardly from white paper to your darkest dark. You may strike where you please, beginning if you will with a moderate central arrangement of middle tones, and then hurling in the extremes when the psychological moment comes. Lastly, the pigment itself is such nice stuff to handle (if it does not retaliate). You can build it on layer after layer if you like. You can keep on experimenting. You can change your plan to meet the exigencies of time or weather. And always remember you can scrape it all away.

Just to paint is great fun. The colors are lovely to look at and delicious to squeeze out. Matching them, however crudely, with what you see is fascinating and absolutely absorbing. Try it if you have not done so—before you die. As one slowly begins to escape from the difficulties of choosing the right colors and laying them on in the right places and in the right way, wider considerations come into view. One begins to see, for instance, that painting a picture is like fighting a battle; and trying to paint a picture is, I suppose, like trying to fight a battle. It is, if anything, more exciting than fighting it successfully. But the principle is the same. It is the same kind of problem, as unfolding a long, sustained, interlocked argument. It is a proposition which, whether of few or numberless parts, is commanded by a single unity of conception. And we think—though I cannot tell—that painting a great picture must require an intellect on the grand scale. There must be that all-embracing view which presents the beginning and the end, the whole and each part, as one instantaneous impression retentively and untiringly held in the mind. When we look at the larger Turners—canvases yards wide and tall—and observe that they are all done in one piece and represent one single second of time, and that every innumerable detail, however small, however distant, however subordinate, is set forth naturally and in its true proportion and relation, without effort, without failure, we must feel in presence of an intellectual manifestation the equal in quality and intensity of the finest achievements of warlike action, of forensic argument, or of scientific or philosophical adjudication.

In all battles two things are usually required of the Commander-in-Chief: to make a good plan for his army and, secondly, to keep a strong reserve. Both these are also obligatory upon the painter. To make a plan, thorough reconnaissance of the country where the battle is to be fought is needed. Its fields, its mountains, its rivers, its bridges, its trees, its flowers, its atmosphere—all require and repay attentive observation from a special point of view. One is quite astonished to find how many things there are in the landscape, and in every object in it, one never noticed before. And this is a tremendous new pleasure and interest which invests every walk or drive with an added object. So many colors on the hillside, each different in shadow and in sunlight; such brilliant reflections in the pool, each a key lower than what they repeat; such lovely lights gilding or silvering surface or outline, all tinted exquisitely with pale color, rose, orange, green, or violet. I found myself instinctively as I walked noting the tint and character of a leaf, the dreamy purple shades of mountains, the exquisite lacery of winter branches, the dim pale silhouettes of far horizons. And I had lived for over forty years without ever noticing any of them except in a general way, as one might look at a crowd and say, "What a lot of people!"

I think this heightened sense of observation of Nature is one of the chief delights that have come to me through trying to paint. No doubt many people who are lovers of art have acquired it in a high degree without actually practicing. But I expect that nothing will make one observe more quickly or more thoroughly than having to face the difficulty of representing the thing observed. And mind you, if you do observe accurately and with refinement, and if you do record what you have seen with tolerable correspondence, the result follows on the canvas with startling obedience. Even if only four or five main features are seized and truly recorded, these by themselves will carry a lot of ill-success or half-success. Answer five big questions out of all the hundreds in the examination paper correctly and well, and though you may not win a prize, at any rate you will not be absolutely plowed.

But in order to make his plan, the General must not only reconnoiter the battle-ground, he must also study the achievements of the great Captains of the past. He must bring the observations he has collected in the field into comparison with the treatment of similar incidents by famous chiefs. Then the galleries of Europe take on a new—and to me at least a severely practical—interest. "This, then, is how————painted a cataract. Exactly, and there is that same light I noticed last week in the waterfall at————." And so on. You see the difficulty that baffled you yestreday; and you see how easily it has been overcome by a great or even by a skillful painter. Not only is your observation of Nature sensibly improved and developed, but you look at the masterpieces of art with an analyzing and a comprehending eye.

The whole world is open with all its treasures. The simplest objects have their beauty. Every garden presents innumerable fascinating problems. Every land, every parish, has its own tale to tell. And there are many lands differing from each other in countless ways, and each presenting delicious variants of color, light, form, and definition. Obviously, then, armed with a paint-box, one cannot be bored, one cannot be left at a loose end, one cannot "have several days on one's hands." Good gracious! What there is to admire and how little time there is to see it in! For the first time one begins to envy Methuselah. No doubt he made a very indifferent use of his opportunities.

But it is in the use and withholding of their reserves that the great commanders have generally excelled. After all, when once the last reserve has been thrown in, the commander's part is played. If that does not win the battle, he has nothing else to give. The event must be left to luck and to the fighting troops. But these last, in the absence of high direction, are apt to get into sad confusion, all mixed together in a nasty mess, without order or plan—and consequently without effect. Mere masses count no more. The largest brush, the brightest colors cannot even make an impression. The pictorial battlefield becomes a sea of mud mercifully veiled by the fog of war. It is evident there has been a serious defeat. Even though the General plunges in himself and emerges bespattered, as he sometimes does, he will not retrieve the day.

In painting, the reserves consist in Proportion or Relation. And it is here that the art of the painter marches along the road which is traversed by all the greatest harmonies in thought. At one side of the palette there is white, at the other black; and neither is ever used "neat." Between these two rigid limits all the action must lie, all the power required must be generated. Black and white themselves placed in juxtaposition make no great impression; and yet they are the most that you can do in pure contrast. It is wonderful— after one has tried and failed often—to see how easily and surely the true artist is able to produce every effect of light and shade, of sunshine and shadow, of distance or nearness, simply by expressing justly the relations between the different planes and surfaces with which he is dealing. We think that this is founded upon a sense of proportion, trained no doubt by practice, but which in its essence is a frigid manifestation of mental power and size. We think that the same mind's eye that can justly survey and appraise and prescribe beforehand the values of a truly great picture in one all-embracing regard, in one flash of simultaneous and homogeneous comprehension, would also with a certain acquaintance with the special technique be able to pronounce with sureness upon any other high activity of the human intellect. This was certainly true of the great Italians.

I have written in this way to show how varied are the delights which may be gained by those who enter hopefully and thoughtfully upon the pathway of painting; how enriched they will be in their daily vision, how fortified in their independence, how happy in their leisure. Whether you feel that your soul is pleased by the conception or contemplation of harmonies, or that your mind is stimulated by the aspect of magnificent problems, or whether you are content to find fun in trying to observe and depict the jolly things you see, the vistas of possibility are limited only by the shortness of life. Every day you may make progress. Every step may be fruitful. Yet there will stretch out before you an ever-lengthening, ever-ascending, ever-improving path. You know you will never get to the end of the journey. But this, so far from discouraging, only adds to the joy and glory of the climb.

Try it, then, before it is too late and before you mock at me. Try it while there is time to overcome the preliminary difficulties. Learn enough of the language in your prime to open this new literature to your age. Plant a garden in which you can sit when digging days are done. It may be only a small garden, but you will see it grow. Year by year it will bloom and ripen. Year by year it will be better cultivated. The weeds will be cast out. The fruit-trees will be pruned and trained. The flowers will bloom in more beautiful combinations. There will be sunshine there even in the winter-time, and cool shade, and the play of shadow on the pathway in the shining days of June.

Once you begin to study it, all Nature is equally interesting and equally charged with beauty. I was shown a picture by Cézanne of a blank wall of a house, which he had made instinct with the most delicate lights and colors. Now I often amuse myself when I am looking at a wall or a flat surface of any kind by trying to distinguish all the different colors and tints which can be discerned upon it, and considering whether these arise from reflections or from natural hue. You would be astonished the first time you tried this to see how many and what beautiful colors there are even in the most commonplace objects, and the more carefully and frequently you look the more variations do you perceive.

But these are no reasons for limiting oneself to the plainest and most ordinary objects and scenes. Mere prettiness of scene, to be sure, is not needed for a beautiful picture. In fact, artifically-made pretty places are very often a hindrance to a good picture. Nature will hardly stand a double process of beautification: one layer of idealism on top of another is too much of a good thing. But a vivid scene, a brilliant atmosphere, novel and charming lights, impressive contrast, if they strike the eye all at once, arouse an interest and an ardor which will certainly be reflected in the work which you try to do, and will make it seem easier.

It would be interesting if some real authority investigated carefully the part which memory plays in painting. We look at the object with an intent regard, then at the palette, and thirdly at the canvas. The canvas receives a message dispatched usually a few seconds before from the natural object. But it has come through a post-office *en route*. It has been transmitted in code. It has been turned from light into paint. It reaches the canvas a cryptogram. Not until it has been placed in its correct relation to everything else that is on the canvas can it be deciphered, is its meaning apparent, is it translated once again from mere pigment into light. And the light this time is not of Nature but of Art. The whole of this considerable process is carried through on the wings or the wheels of memory. In most cases we think it is the wings—airy and quick like a butterfly from flower to flower. But all heavy traffic and all that has to go a long journey must travel on wheels.

In painting in the open air the sequence of actions is so rapid that the process of translation into and out of pigment may seem to be unconscious. But all the greatest landscapes have been painted indoors, and often long after the first impressions were gathered. In a dim cellar the Dutch or Italian master recreated the gleaming ice of a Netherlands carnival or the lustrous sunshine of Venice or the Campagna. Here, then, is required a formidable memory of the visual kind. Not only do we develop our powers of observation, but also those of carrying the record—of carrying it through an extraneous medium and of reproducing it, hours, days, or even months after the scene has vanished or the sunlight died.

I was told by a friend that when Whistler guided a school in Paris he made his pupils observe their model on the ground floor, and then run upstairs and paint their picture piece by piece on the floor above. As they became more proficient he put their easels up a story higher, till at last the *élite* were scampering with their decision up six flights into the attic—praying it would not evaporate on the way. This is, perhaps, only a tale. But it shows effectively of what enormous importance a trained, accurate, retentive memory must be to an artist; and conversely what a useful exercise painting may be for the development of an accurate and retentive memory.

There is no better exercise for the would-be artist than to study and devour a picture, and then, without looking at it again, to attempt the next day to reproduce it. Nothing can more exactly measure the progress both of observation and memory. It is still harder to compose out of many separate, well-retained impressions, aided though they be by sketches and color notes, a new complete conception. But this is the only way in which great landscapes have been painted—or can be painted. The size of the canvas alone precludes its being handled out of doors. The fleeting light imposes a rigid time-limit. The same light never returns. One cannot go back day after day without the picture getting stale. The painter must choose between a rapid impression, fresh and warm and living, but probably deserving only of a short life, and the cold, profound, intense effort of memory, knowledge, and will-power, prolonged perhaps for weeks, from which a masterpiece can alone result. It is much better not to fret too much about the latter. Leave to the masters of art trained by a lifetime of devotion the wonderful process of picture-building and picture-creation. Go out into the sunlight and be happy with what you see.

Painting is complete as a distraction. I know of nothing which, without exhausting the body, more entirely absorbs the mind. Whatever the worries of the hour or the threats of the future, once the picture has begun to flow along, there is no room for them in the mental screen. They pass out into shadow and darkness. All one's mental light, such as it is, becomes concentrated on the task. Time stands respectfully aside, and it is only after many hesitations that luncheon knocks gruffly at the door. When I have had to stand up on parade, or even, I regret to say, in church, for half an hour at a time, I have always felt that the erect position is not natural to man, has only been painfully acquired, and is only with fatigue and difficulty maintained. But no one who is fond of painting finds the slightest inconvenience, as long as the interest holds, in standing to paint for three or four hours at a stretch.

Lastly, let me say a word on painting as a spur to travel. There is really nothing like it. Every day and all day is provided with its expedition and its occupation—cheap, attainable, innocent, absorbing, recuperative. The vain racket of the tourist gives place to the calm enjoyment of the philosopher, intensified by an enthralling sense of action and endeavor. Every country where the sun shines and every district in it has a theme of its own. The lights, the atmosphere, the aspect, the spirit, are all different; but each has its native charm. Even if you are only a poor painter you can feel the influence of the scene, guiding your brush, selecting the tubes you squeeze on to the palette. Even if you cannot portray it as you see it, you feel it, you know it, and you admire it for ever. When people rush about Europe in the train from one glittering center of work or pleasure to another, passing—at enormous expense—through a series of mammoth hotels and blatant carnivals, they little know what they are missing, and how cheaply priceless things can be obtained. The painter wanders and loiters contentedly from place to place, always on the look out for some brilliant butterfly of a picture which can be caught and set up and carried safely home.

Now I am learning to like painting even on dull days. But in my hot youth I demanded sunshine. Sir William Orpen advised me to visit Avignon on account of its wonderful light, and certainly there is no more delightful center for a would-be painter's activities: then Egypt, fierce and brilliant, presenting in infinite variety the single triplex theme of the Nile, the desert, and the sun; or Palestine, a land of rare beauty—the beauty of the turquoise and the opal—which well deserves the attention of some real artist, and has never been portrayed to the extent that is its due. And what of India? Who has ever interpreted its lurid splendors? But after all, if only the sun will shine, one does not need to go beyond one's own country. There is nothing more intense than the burnished steel and gold of a Highland stream; and at the beginning and close of almost every day the Thames displays to the citizens of London glories and delights which one must travel far to rival.

VI. The Gifts of Religion and God

WHERE LOVE IS, GOD IS

Leo Tolstoy

We come to our final section, on "The Gifts of Religion and God."
As the first selection in it we have chosen a story by a great Russian
who ranks with Beethoven in artistry. He was born in Tula in 1828, served
in the Crimean War and at the end of the campaign retired to his
estates. There he devoted himself to work, study and the betterment
of his peasant serfs. With the publication of his monumental War and
Peace, *a novel about Russian society at the time of the French Revolution*
and the invasion of Russia by Napoleon, he became one of the foremost
intellectual spokesmen of his generation. Instead of resisting evil, he
said, we should accept it and turn it into love. His doctrine is the basis
for "Where Love Is, God Is." This and other of his writings had a
profound effect on his contemporaries. They added a leavening of gentle-
ness to the harsh and brutal society of nineteenth-century Czarist Russia.
They continue to have a message for today's world, with its ever-increasing
dedication to violence.

IN a certain town there lived a cobbler, Martin Avdeich by name.
He had a tiny room in a basement, the one window of which looked
out on to the street. Through it one could only see the feet of
those who passed by, but Martin recognized the people by their boots.

He had lived long in the place and had many acquaintances. There was hardly a pair of boots in the neighborhood that had not been once or twice through his hands, so he often saw his own handiwork through the window. Some he had resoled, some patched, some stitched up, and to some he had even put fresh uppers. He had plenty to do, for he worked well, used good material, did not charge too much, and could be relied on. If he could do a job by the day required, he undertook it; if not, he told the truth and gave no false promises; so he was well known and never short of work.

Martin had always been a good man, but in his old age he began to think more about his soul and to draw nearer to God. While he still worked for a master, before he set up on his own account, his wife had died, leaving him with a three-year-old son. None of his elder children had lived, they had all died in infancy. At first Martin thought of sending his little son to his sister's in the country, but then he felt sorry to part with the boy, thinking: "It would be hard for my little Kapiton to have to grow up in a strange family, I will keep him with me."

Martin left his master and went into lodgings with his little son. But he had no luck with his children. No sooner had the boy reached an age when he could help his father and be a support as well as a joy to him, than he fell ill and, after being laid up for a week with a burning fever, died. Martin buried his son, and gave way to despair so great and overwhelming that he murmured against God. In his sorrow he prayed again and again that he too might die, reproaching God for having taken the son he loved, his only son, while he, old as he was, remained alive. After that Martin left off going to church.

One day an old man from Martin's native village, who had been a pilgrim for the last eight years, called in on his way from the Troitsa Monastery. Martin opened his heart to him and told him of his sorrow.

"I no longer even wish to live, holy man," he said. "All I ask of God is that I soon may die. I am now quite without hope in the world."

The old man replied: "You have no right to say such things, Martin. We cannot judge God's ways. Not our reasoning, but God's will, decides. If God willed that your son should die and you should live, it must be best so. As to your despair—that comes because you wish to live for your own happiness."

"What else should one live for?" asked Martin.

"For God, Martin," said the old man. "He gives you life, and you must live for Him. When you have learnt to live for Him, you will grieve no more, and all will seem easy to you."

Martin was silent awhile, and then asked: "But how is one to live for God?"

The old man answered: "How one may live for God has been shown us by Christ. Can you read? Then buy the Gospels and read them: there you will see how God would have you live. You have it all there."

These words sank deep into Martin's heart, and that same day he went and bought himself a Testament in large print, and began to read.

At first he meant only to read on holidays, but having once begun he found it made his heart so light that he read every day. Sometimes he was so absorbed in his reading that the oil in his lamp burnt out before he could tear himself away from the book. He continued to read every night, and the more he read the more clearly he understood what God required of him, and how he might live for God. And his heart grew lighter and lighter. Before, when he went to bed he used to lie with a heavy heart, moaning as he thought of his little Kapiton; but now he only repeated again and again: "Glory to Thee, glory to Thee, O Lord! Thy will be done!"

From that time Martin's whole life changed. Formerly, on holidays he used to go and have tea at the public-house and did not even refuse a glass or two of vodka. Sometimes, after having had a drop with a friend, he left the public-house not drunk, but rather merry, and would say foolish things: shout at a man, or abuse him. Now all that sort of thing passed away from him. His life became peaceful and joyful. He sat down to his work in the morning, and when he had finished his day's work he took the lamp down from the wall, stood it on the table, fetched his book from the shelf, opened it, and sat down to read. The more he read the better he understood and the clearer and happier he felt in his mind.

It happened once that Martin sat up late, absorbed in his book. He was reading Luke's Gospel; and in the sixth chapter he came upon the verses:

To him that smiteth thee on the one cheek offer also the other; and from him that taketh away thy cloak withhold not thy coat also. Give to every man that asketh thee; and of him that taketh away thy goods ask them not again. And as ye would that men should do to you, do ye also to them likewise.

He also read the verses where our Lord says:

And why call ye me, Lord, Lord, and do not the things which I say? Whosoever cometh to me, and heareth my sayings, and doeth them, I will shew you to whom he is like: He is like a man which built an house, and digged deep, and laid the foundation on a rock: and when the flood arose, the stream beat vehemently upon that house, and could not shake it: for it was founded upon a rock. But he that heareth, and doeth not, is like a man that without a foundation built an house upon the earth, against which the stream did beat vehemently, and immediately it fell; and the ruin of that house was great.

When Martin read these words his soul was glad within him. He took off his spectacles and laid them on the book, and leaning his elbows on the table pondered over what he had read. He tried his own life by the standard of those words, asking himself:

"Is my house built on the rock, or on sand? If it stands on the rock, it is well. It seems easy enough while one sits here alone, and one thinks one has done all that God commands; but as soon as I cease to be on my guard, I sin again. Still I will persevere. It brings such joy. Help me, O Lord!"

He thought all this, and was about to go to bed, but was loth to leave his book. So he went on reading the seventh chapter—about the centurion, the widow's son, and the answer to John's disciples—and he came to the part where a rich Pharisee invited the Lord to his house; and he read how the woman who was a sinner anointed his feet and washed them with her tears, and how he justified her. Coming to the forty-fourth verse, he read:

And turning to the woman, he said unto Simon, Seest thou this woman? I entered into thine house, thou gavest me no water for my feet: but she hath wetted my feet with her tears, and wiped them with her hair. Thou gavest me no kiss; but she, since the time I came in, hath not ceased to kiss my feet. My head with oil thou dist not anoint: but she hath anointed my feet with ointment.

He read these verses and thought: "He gave no water for his feet, gave no kiss, his head with oil he did not anoint. . . ." And Martin took off his spectacles once more, laid them on his book, and pondered.

"He must have been like me, that Pharisee. He too thought only of himself—how to get a cup of tea, how to keep warm and comfortable; never a thought of his guest. He took care of himself, but for his guest he cared nothing at all. Yet who was the guest? The Lord himself! If he came to me, should I behave like that?"

Then Martin laid his head upon both his arms and, before he was aware of it, he fell asleep.

"Martin!" he suddenly heard a voice, as if someone had breathed the word above his ear.

He started from his sleep. "Who's there?" he asked.

He turned round and looked at the door; no one was there. He called again. Then he heard quite distinctly: "Martin, Martin! Look out into the street tomorrow, for I shall come."

Martin roused himself, rose from his chair and rubbed his eyes, but did not know whether he had heard these words in a dream or awake. He put out the lamp and lay down to sleep.

Next morning he rose before daylight and after saying his prayers he lit the fire and prepared his cabbage soup and buckwheat porridge. Then he lit the samovar, put on his apron, and sat down by the window to his work. As he sat working Martin thought over what had happened the night before. At times it seemed to him like a dream, and at times he thought that he had really heard the voice. "Such things have happened before now," thought he.

So he sat by the window, looking out into the street more than he worked, and whenever any one passed in unfamiliar boots he would stoop and look up, so as to see not the feet only but the face of the passer-by as well. A house-porter passed in new felt boots; then a water-carrier. Presently an old soldier of Nicholas' reign came near the window, spade in hand. Martin knew him by his boots, which were shabby old felt ones, goloshed with leather. The old man was called Stepanich: a neighboring tradesman kept him in his house for charity, and his duty was to help the house-porter. He began to clear away the snow before Martin's window. Martin glanced at him and then went on with his work.

"I must be growing crazy with age," said Martin, laughing at his fancy. "Stepanich comes to clear away the snow, and I must needs imagine it's Christ coming to visit me. Old dotard that I am!"

Yet after he had made a dozen stitches he felt drawn to look out of the window again. He saw that Stepanich had leaned his spade against the wall and was either resting himself or trying to get warm. The man was old and broken down, and had evidently not enough strength even to clear away the snow.

"What if I called him in and gave him some tea?" thought Martin. "The samovar is just on the boil."

He stuck his awl in its place, and rose; and putting the samovar on the table, made tea. Then he tapped the window with his fingers. Stepanich turned and came to the window. Martin beckoned to him to come in and went himself to open the door.

"Come in," he said, "and warm yourself a bit. I'm sure you must be cold."

"May God bless you!" Stepanich answered. "My bones do ache to be sure." He came in, first shaking off the snow, and lest he should leave marks on the floor he began wiping his feet, but as he did so he tottered and nearly fell.

"Don't trouble to wipe your feet," said Martin; "I'll wipe up the floor—it's all in the day's work. Come, friend, sit down and have some tea."

Filling two tumblers, he passed one to his visitor, and pouring his own out into the saucer, began to blow on it.

Stepanich emptied his glass, and, turning it upside down, put the remains of his piece of sugar on the top. He began to express his thanks, but it was plain that he would be glad of some more.

"Have another glass," said Martin, refilling the visitor's tumbler and his own. But while he drank his tea Martin kept looking out into the street.

"Are you expecting anyone?" asked the visitor.

"Am I expecting anyone? Well now, I'm ashamed to tell you. It isn't that I really expect anyone; but I heard something last night which I can't get out of my mind. Whether it was a vision, or only a fancy, I can't tell. You see, friend, last night I was reading the Gospel, about Christ the Lord, how he suffered and how he walked on earth. You have heard tell of it, I dare say."

"I have heard tell of it," answered Stepanich; "but I'm an ignorant man and not able to read."

"Well, you see, I was reading of how he walked on earth. I came to that part, you know, where he went to a Pharisee who did not receive him well. Well, friend, as I read about it, I thought how that man did not receive Christ the Lord with proper honor. Suppose such a thing could happen to such a man as myself, I thought, what would I not do to receive him! But that man gave him no reception at all. Well, friend, as I was thinking of this I began to doze, and as I dozed I heard someone call me by name. I got up, and thought I heard some one whispering, 'Expect me; I will come tomorrow.' This happened twice over. And to tell you the truth, it sank so into my mind that, though I am ashamed of it myself, I keep on expecting him, the dear Lord!"

Stepanich shook his head in silence, finished his tumbler and laid it on its side; but Martin stood it up again and refilled it for him.

"Here, drink another glass, bless you! And I was thinking, too, how he walked on earth and despised no one, but went mostly among common folk. He went with plain people, and chose his disciples from among the likes of us, from workmen like us, sinners that we are. 'He who raises himself,' he said, 'shall be humbled; and he who humbles himself shall be raised.' 'You call me Lord,' he said, 'and I will wash your feet.' 'He who would be first,' he said, 'let him be the servant of all; because,' he said, 'blessed are the poor, the humble, the meek, and the merciful.' "

Stepanich forgot his tea. He was an old man, easily moved to tears, and as he sat and listened the tears ran down his cheeks.

"Come, drink some more," said Martin. But Stepanich crossed himself, thanked him, moved away his tumbler, and rose.

"Thank you, Martin Avdeich," he said, "you have given me food and comfort both for soul and body."

"You're very welcome. Come again another time. I am glad to have a guest," said Martin.

Stepanich went away; and Martin poured out the last of the tea and drank it up. Then he put away the tea things and sat down to his work, stitching the back seam of a boot. And as he stitched he kept looking out of the window, waiting for Christ and thinking about him and his doings. And his head was full of Christ's sayings.

Two soldiers went by: one in Government boots, the other in boots of his own; then the master of a neighboring house, in shining goloshes; then a baker carrying a basket. All these passed on. Then a woman came up in worsted stockings and peasant-made shoes. She passed the window, but stopped by the wall. Martin glanced up at her through the window and saw that she was a stranger, poorly dressed and with a baby in her arms. She stopped by the wall with her back to the wind, trying to wrap the baby up though she had hardly anything to wrap it in. The woman had only summer clothes on, and even they were shabby and worn. Through the window Martin heard the baby crying, and the woman trying to soothe it but unable to do so. Martin rose, and going out of the door and up the steps he called to her.

"My dear, I say, my dear!"

The woman heard and turned round.

"Why do you stand out there with the baby in the cold? Come inside. You can wrap him up better in a warm place. Come this way!"

The woman was surprised to see an old man in an apron, with spectacles on his nose, calling to her, but she followed him in.

They went down the steps, entered the little room, and the old man led her to the bed.

"There, sit down, my dear, near the stove. Warm yourself and feed the baby."

"Haven't any milk. I have eaten nothing myself since early morning," said the woman, but still she took the baby to her breast.

Martin shook his head. He brought out a basin and some bread. Then he opened the oven door and poured some cabbage soup into the basin. He took out the porridge pot also, but the porridge was not yet ready, so he spread a cloth on the table and served only the soup and bread.

"Sit down and eat, my dear, and I'll mind the baby. Why, bless me, I've had children of my own; I know how to manage them."

The woman crossed herself, and sitting down at the table began to eat, while Martin put the baby on the bed and sat down by it. He chucked and chucked, but having no teeth he could not do it well and the baby continued to cry. Then Martin tried poking at him with his finger; he drove his finger straight at the baby's mouth and then quickly drew it back, and did this again and again. He did not let the baby take his finger in its mouth, because it was all black with cobbler's wax. But the baby first grew quiet watching the finger, and then began to laugh. And Martin felt quite pleased.

The woman sat eating and talking, and told him who she was, and where she had been.

"I'm a soldier's wife," said she. "They sent my husband somewhere, far away, eight months ago, and I have heard nothing of him since. I had a place as cook till my baby was born, but then they would not keep me with a child. For three months now I have been struggling, unable to find a place, and I've had to sell all I had for food. I tried to go as a wet-nurse, but no one would have me; they said I was too starved-looking and thin. Now I have just been to see a tradesman's wife (a woman from our village is in service with her) and she has promised to take me. I thought it was all settled at last, but she tells me not to come till next week. It is far to her place, and I am fagged out, and baby is quite starved, poor mite. Fortunately our landlady has pity on us, and lets us lodge free, else I don't know what we should do."

Martin sighed. "Haven't you any warmer clothing?" he asked.

"How could I get warm clothing?" said she. "Why, I pawned my last shawl for sixpence yesterday."

Then the woman came and took the child, and Martin got up. He went and looked among some things that were hanging on the wall, and brought back an old cloak.

"Here," he said, "though it's a worn-out old thing, it will do to wrap him up in."

The woman looked at the cloak, then at the old man, and taking it, burst into tears. Martin turned away, and groping under the bed brought out a small trunk. He fumbled about in it, and again sat down opposite the woman. And the woman said:

"The Lord bless you, friend. Surely Christ must have sent me to your window, else the child would have frozen. It was mild when I started, but now see how cold it has turned. Surely it must have been Christ who made you look out of your window and take pity on me, poor wretch!"

Martin smiled and said, "It is quite true; it was He made me do it. It was no mere chance made me look out."

And he told the woman his dream, and how he had heard the Lord's voice promising to visit him that day.

"Who knows? All things are possible," said the woman. And she got up and threw the cloak over her shoulders, wrapping it round herself and round the baby. Then she bowed, and thanked Martin once more.

"Take this for Christ's sake," said Martin, and gave her sixpence to get her shawl out of pawn. The woman crossed herself, and Martin did the same, and then he saw her out.

After the woman had gone, Martin ate some cabbage soup, cleared the things away, and sat down to work again. He sat and worked, but did not forget the window, and every time a shadow fell on it he looked up at once to see who was passing. People he knew and strangers passed by, but no one remarkable.

After a while Martin saw an apple-woman stop just in front of his window. She had a large basket, but there did not seem to be many apples left in it; she had evidently sold most of her stock. On her back she had a sack full of chips, which she was taking home. No doubt she had gathered them at some place where building was going on. The sack evidently hurt her and she wanted to shift it from one shoulder to the other, so she put it down on the footpath and, placing her basket on a post, began to shake down the chips in the sack. While she was doing this a boy in a tattered cap ran up, snatched an apple out of the basket and tried to slip away; but the old woman noticed it and, turning, caught the boy by his sleeve. He began to struggle, trying to free himself, but the old woman held on with both hands, knocked his cap off his head, and seized hold of his hair. The boy screamed and the old woman scolded. Martin dropped his awl, not waiting to stick it in its place, and rushed out of the door. Stumbling up the steps, and dropping his spectacles in his hurry, he ran out into the street. The old woman was pulling the boy's hair and scolding him, and threatening to take him to the police. The lad was struggling and protesting, saying, "I did not take it. What are you beating me for? Let me go!"

Martin separated them. He took the boy by the hand and said, "Let him go, Granny. Forgive him for Christ's sake."

"I'll pay him out, so that he won't forget it for a year! I'll take the rascal to the police!"

Martin began entreating the old woman.

"Let him go, Granny. He won't do it again. Let him go for Christ's sake!"

The old woman let go, and the boy wished to run away, but Martin stopped him.

"Ask the Granny's forgiveness!" said he. "And don't do it another time. I saw you take the apple."

The boy began to cry and to beg pardon.

"That's right. And now here's an apple for you," and Martin took an apple from the basket and gave it to the boy, saying, "I will pay you, Granny."

"You will spoil them that way, the young rascals," said the old woman. "He ought to be whipped so that he should remember it for a week."

"Oh, Granny, Granny," said Martin, "that's our way—but it's not God's way. If he should be whipped for stealing an apple, what should be done to us for our sins?"

The old woman was silent.

And Martin told her the parable of the lord who forgave his servant a large debt, and how the servant went out and seized his debtor by the throat. The old woman listened to it all, and the boy, too, stood by and listened.

"God bids us forgive," said Martin, "or else we shall not be forgiven. Forgive everyone, and a thoughtless youngster most of all."

The old woman wagged her head and sighed.

"It's true enough," said she, "but they are getting terribly spoilt."

"Then we old ones must show them better ways," Martin replied.

"That's just what I say," said the old woman. "I have had seven of them myself, and only one daughter is left." And the old woman began to tell how and where she was living with her daughter, and how many grandchildren she had. "There now," she said, "I have but little strength left, yet I work hard for the sake of my grandchildren; and nice children they are, too. No one comes out to meet me but the children. Little Annie, now, won't leave me for anyone. 'It's grandmother, dear grandmother, darling grandmother.' " And the old woman completely softened at the thought.

"Of course it was only his childishness, God help him," said she, referring to the boy.

As the old woman was about to hoist her sack on her back, the lad sprang forward to her, saying, "Let me carry it for you, Granny, I'm going that way."

The old woman nodded her head, and put the sack on the boy's back, and they went down the street together, the old woman quite forgetting to ask Martin to pay for the apple. Martin stood and watched them as they went along talking to each other.

When they were out of sight Martin went back to the house. Having found his spectacles unbroken on the steps, he picked up his awl and sat down again to work. He worked a little, but could soon not see to pass the bristle through the holes in the leather; and presently he noticed the lamplighter passing on his way to light the street lamps.

"Seems it's time to light up," thought he. So he trimmed his lamp, hung it up, and sat down again to work. He finished off one boot and, turning it about, examined it. It was all right. Then he gathered his tools together, swept up the cuttings, put away the bristles and the thread and the awls, and, taking down the lamp, placed it on the table. Then he took the Gospels from the shelf.

He meant to open them at the place he had marked the day before with a bit of morocco, but the book opened at another place. As Martin opened it, his yesterday's dream came back to his mind, and no sooner had he thought of it than he seemed to hear footsteps, as though someone were moving behind him. Martin turned round, and it seemed to him as if people were standing in the dark corner, but he could not make out who they were. And a voice whispered in his ear: "Martin, Martin, don't you know me?"

"Who is it?" muttered Martin.

"It is I," said the voice. And out of the dark corner stepped Stepanich, who smiled, and vanishing like a cloud was seen no more.

"It is I," said the voice again. And out of the darkness stepped the woman with the baby in her arms, and the woman smiled and the baby laughed, and they too vanished.

"It is I," said the voice once more. And the old woman and the boy with the apple stepped out and both smiled, and then they too vanished.

And Martin's soul grew glad. He crossed himself, put on his spectacles, and began reading the Gospel just where it had opened; and at the top of the page he read:

I was an hungered, and ye gave me meat: I was thirsty, and ye gave me drink: I was a stranger, and ye took me in.

And at the bottom of the page he read:

Inasmuch as ye did it unto one of these my brethren, even these least, ye did it unto me (*Matt.* xxv).

And Martin understood that his dream had come true; and that the Savior had really come to him that day, and he had welcomed him.

THIS I BELIEVE

A Letter to My Son

———— *Robert O. Ballou* ————

There are men, puzzled by our universal modern problem of morals and religion, unwilling to subscribe to any particular faith or creed, who nevertheless are firm believers in a Deity and are sincerely anxious to walk righteously before Him. One of the most eloquent spokesmen for this group is Robert O. Ballou, who feels that the most important job everyone has in life is the search for God. Such a person deserves to be heard, even though his opinions may clash with those of individuals holding more orthodox beliefs. Mr. Ballou, a publishing executive in New York City, wrote a book expounding his beliefs which he subtitled "A Letter to My Seven-year-old Son," and in which he held up standards for guiding the boy in the path of morality and decency. It is a lovely book, in which the author affirms his belief in the goodness of the world and in the fact that truth and wisdom are the essence of the Universe. From it we have taken the following selection.

✍

Now this is what I would say to you particularly: The search for God seems to me to be the most important job every man and every woman has in life. And the acceptance of the rules and tenets of any church or creed and calling those rules and tenets your religion will limit your search. I would not have you be a Buddhist, but this is not because I do not believe in many of the truths Gautama uttered. I would not have you be a Zoroastrian, but this is not because I do not believe in many of the truths which Zoroaster uttered. I would not have you be a Taoist, but this is not because I do not believe in the truths Lao-tze uttered. I would not have you be a Jew (in the religious sense) but this is not because I do not believe in the truths which Moses and Isaiah and Amos and the writers of the Talmud uttered. And I would not have you be a Christian (in the sense in which the Christian church uses the word), but this is surely not because I do not believe in the truths which Jesus of Nazareth uttered.

Rather it is because I believe in the wisdom and greatness of all of these, in the uncompromising and constant search for God which all of these great religious leaders exemplified, and especially in the truths Jesus spoke and lived, and in the loving wisdom and beauty of his search, that I would not have you limit yourself to any set of specific rules, but rather to conduct your search for God by trying as they did to go beyond the words of the prophets to the sources of all knowledge. I would have you proceed in the light of knowledge which the wisdom of all of them and all that have come since make available to you, climbing upward toward what will be the ultimate truth for you on the good words of every prophet and every seer you encounter (whether he calls himself a religious man or a scientist or scholar or none of these) and the deep perception and courage which was placed in your own soul and mind by the force of God which created you.

You will find truth and wisdom that will be helpful to you in all true religions and in all truly religious persons. You will find truth and wisdom and knowledge of God in all that true science has to tell you. You will find these things in art and music and in all those who see things and hear them and speak of them with sensitiveness and understanding. Often you will find them in places where you least expect them. . . .

To every man his own prophets. To the Buddhists, Gautama, for in his utterances they found truth; to the Taoists, Lao-tze, for in his utterances they found truth; to the Jews, Moses and Isaiah and Hosea, for in their utterances they found truth; to the Christians, Jesus, for in his utterances they found truth; to the sincere churchly persons, the church, for in it they find something which satisfies their need; to Richard Wagner, Beethoven, for in his utterances he found truth. And to you, not only one but all of these and many more so long as life shall last, for you have inherited the wisdom of thousands of years and you will be less than a man if you refuse to take it.

Thus you must do your seeking, taking that which will help you wherever you find it, rejecting that which is of no use to you. You yourself must be the judge.

So far I have written only of the way I feel about this great force which moves in everything, and the need to recognize it and know it in Nature, and follow its laws, and have said nothing about what I believe about human beings (save that they, as well as other animals and plants and rocks and rivers and mountains and all things, are subject to the laws of this force) or about what I think my conduct should be in relation to them, or what part this plays in what I call my religion. But before this I have intimated that I felt good rules of human conduct constituted at least half of any good religion. Now I must try to explain to you why I believe that this is so.

I am a human being. Though I have in me the same stuff and must obey the same basic laws as a tree, a blade of grass, a worm, a bee, a dog, I am not tree, nor blade of grass nor worm nor bee nor dog. I am related to them closely, but I have another form and there are differences in that of which I am made, differences which make me a human being. I am one of over 2,000,000,000 human beings living together on the earth. While I have a dim understanding of the life of a tree, a blade of grass, a worm, a bee, a dog, and through increasing this understanding I increase my understanding of the force of life in all of us, I cannot understand the processes of life in these things as well as I can the same processes which are at work in human beings, for I see the latter express my own feelings, see them seek the satisfaction of my own desires, see them struggling under the same difficulties, suffering under the same sorrows, feeling the same joys as my own. And because of this, knowledge of them becomes to me a clearer knowledge of the great force which is my chief interest.

But only by living well with them, by brotherliness, kindness, honesty, trying to do my part of the work of the world, being tolerant and as understanding as I can, helping someone else whenever I can, keeping my heart and mind open to love of others, rejecting as well as I can feelings of jealousy and meanness toward others, trying to be considerate of them, obeying as well as I can what seem to me to be the best social laws, trying to avoid and trying to influence others to avoid those things which are harmful to others, such as waste, cruelty, war, taking things which belong to others, harmful lies, loving money more than truth and kindness, can I learn to know human beings well, and through this knowledge gain a greater knowledge of the central force of life on which I depend, and a greater sense of identification with it. This is my religious reason for believing that I ought to treat all people honestly and kindly and as helpfully as I can. And only by living helpfully as a part of the great unit in Nature which the human race is, can I help to further the welfare of that unit through following the laws of Nature—that is, the laws of God. (There is another, more immediate and practical reason which is that only by treating others well can I expect to be treated well by them. This is not, for me, a religious reason, though it is also a good and a sound reason for treating others well. But here we are concerned with religion.)

You have seen how carefully I take care of my grapevines. You have heard me scold you for rushing into the young vines in the spring and breaking off some of the tender young shoots. You know that I watch the peach trees in the spring and try to help them by removing tent caterpillars from them. I cannot find out about these things, the grapevines and the peach tree, I cannot learn as much as I want to know from them about the force which gives them life if they are destroyed. Instead of letting them be destroyed I try to help them to live as well as they can, for thus I can learn more of them and through them of the force I want to know so much about because it is that force which I have recognized as God and on which I depend for all of my life and for all of the peace and comfort I can ever know. (And besides I can get more peaches and grapes in this way!) I want to know as many of the laws of this God as I can and obey as many of them as I am able, so that I may live a happy and satisfying life.

And as it is with the grapevine and with the peach tree, so also is it with human beings.

It is because I have found these things true for myself that I believe that you will also find them true for you. It is because I have needed desperately at times to feel the strength of a greater power than is in man alone (as have all men) that I know you also will face this need. Just as you now depend upon your mother and upon me for a great many things, because we are stronger than you are, just as you always need us when you are in trouble, so will you always need something which is stronger than you. You will outgrow your need for us for the time will come when you will be stronger than we are and we cannot help you as we do now. But you will never be so strong that you will always feel adequate for all the things which life will do to you. There will be times when you will feel helpless and terribly alone and know pain for which there seems, at the moment, no relief. And it will be at times like this that knowledge of and faith in something which you know is much stronger than your mother or I ever were and much stronger than yourself will help you. This is why I am concerned now with whether or not you find a religion in which you can believe as firmly as people of older times believed in their gods.

There are these primary differences between the life of your grandmother, who first taught me about religion, my life, and yours, and these differences are important to your consideration of how much, if any, you will take of your grandmother's religion (a part of which the church is now trying to teach you), how much, if any, you will take of mine, and how much you must make for yourself.

Between the time when your grandmother learned about religion as a child, and the time when she became adult, there had been few changes of any great importance in the way people lived and thought.

The world in which she lived as she became adult was, generally speaking, the world she had been taught, as a child, to expect. And it was of this world that she taught me. Most of the important inventions and discoveries of science which have made great differences in the way people live and in the things they know, have come into existence, or at least into general use, since I was born. And so, by the time I had grown up, the world has changed so much that it was very different from the world your grandmother had been able to teach me to expect. Many of the things I have told you about the religions of people long long ago were unknown until after I had grown up. Many of the things now known about the way the mysterious force of God works in Nature were not known until recently. Many of the things we know about human beings (both good things and bad things) were unknown until recently.

Those born at about the time when I was, and still living, have seen greater changes take place than any other people born at any other time in the history of the world. Many have lived good lives, as their religious training taught them to do. Many have believed in the God of the Bible, yet this has not spared them from the suffering which the world has gone through in this time. The world, since 1914, has seemed to many a place inhabited by a race of madmen, who are bent on destroying themselves. And the church, still repeating the Ten Commandments (as though their very repetition constituted a sort of magic which would accomplish miracles) and the words of Jesus, while within their membership and without few are practicing the principles of Jesus, has been utterly powerless to check the onrushing forces of destruction. The leaders of the church, who have always been considered the religious leaders of the world, have had no lasting peace, and no enduring comfort to give to the world. And so people have turned away from religion.

Yet the world daily proclaims its need for the basic approach to life which religion has furnished to the truly religious in all ages. It is sick in mind and body. Economically, socially, politically, mentally, chemically, it is in a state of illness which at times threatens the collapse of all civilization. A thousand formulas for curing it have been offered and many more will be offered during your lifetime. None so far offered or tried have changed its prospects materially. The human race has well risked the charge of failure. And its failure (if it be finally demonstrated) in all its details, economic, social, political, mental, chemical, is at base a spiritual failure, a failure to know the laws of God and to follow them.

In the early days of the life of mankind it was less essential that man know all of these laws. When there were fewer people on earth and there were vast surfaces of land which no human foot had ever trod, when groups of people were smaller, and there were fewer groups, it was enough for men and women to learn how to live well within themselves and with each other, kindly and justly and understandingly. And if members of the same group disagreed among themselves some could leave the group and go to another place to live as they wished, as the Pilgrim Fathers did when they left England to find freedom of worship in the new land of America. They did not have to fight with each other (unless they were terribly greedy or quarrelsome) for there was room for all and good fresh land for all. It was necessary then for men to learn only a few of the laws of God—those which taught them how to live well within their hearts, how to think well and wisely, and how to live justly and kindly and understandingly with other people. These laws— only a few of the laws of God—were those with which the early religions concerned themselves. They are vastly important laws, but they are not all of the important ones, and it is necessary now to know many of the other laws.

For today the numbers of people have increased so that they overrun the face of the earth. There is not room any more for them to move on after they have used a part of the world nor are there unoccupied places to which those who disagree with other members of their groups may move. Practically speaking the human race is using all of the earth now and finding in many places that it is using it up so rapidly that it faces starvation. And when men and their children and their women begin to get hungry they will steal and murder, taking land away from others in order to get food, trying to drive some members of their groups out of their countries, or murdering them, as the Jews in Germany. Yet even when they have done this they have only postponed their day of starvation for a little while, unless they live more wisely in the future than they have lived in the past.

For if the human race is to survive it must know now not only those laws of God which pertain to the heart of man but also those which pertain to the heart of the earth itself, and to its body and all that grows and crawls and creeps upon its surface, and ferments underground, and flies in the air above it or swims under its waters.

Knowing these laws, living in harmony with them as they apply to all forms of life, are as essential spiritual duties of man today as are those of purifying the heart and dealing in love and justice with one's neighbor.

This is not the whole of religion. It is not enough for you, my son, or for those who grow beside you into the human future which lies just ahead in the coming years of your maturity. You must have a better, a fuller religion than this to support you and render you capable of living the life of a man in the world as it is now and is to be. It will not cure itself. It needs all the help which the best that is in you and the best that is in all of your generation can give it.

For there is no real assurance yet that human beings are learning how to live more peacefully and sanely or that they have learned and accepted enough of the laws of Nature to save them from tremendous suffering still to come. What hope the world has is for future generations. You must help to make that hope greater. There can be no sound expectation that wars and murder will be done with or that greed and violence and hatred will be lessened in your life-time. Life will hurt you with these things. You must find something which will give you strength with which to bear your pain and comfort against it and the satisfaction of knowing that you have done your part in trying to make the human future a little better. I believe that the only thing which can possibly help you is religion, a true and sound religion, a religion the content of which is a constant seeking after truth, a constant awareness of the universal force of life and its laws, a constant need for a greater knowledge of and a greater closeness to this force, a constant faith in its rightness, regardless of how wrong much of human life may be, and a constant effort to relate yourself to all human beings, and all other creatures, whether plant or animal, or insentient, with as deep understanding as it is possible for you to gain through knowledge, following as closely as you can learn to follow them, the great unswerving laws of the God which moves in all creation.

In urging you to achieve such a religion I offer you the hope of finding a God not for a child-world, but for a world become old, which must now also become wise.

How shall you find him?

Strictly speaking you must find the way yourself. I have tried in this letter to give you some hints and a few rules by which to live and learn. Yet the best rules which I can give you, you may have eventually to discard. Use them while they are useful to you. Do not hesitate to deny their truth when they are no longer true for you. The truth must come from within you, from your own comprehension. That which I, or any other man or woman gives you, you must use only as a stimulant to your own processes of seeking the truth, not as the truth itself.

Yet you must never discard the words or help of any person or anything without consideration. Take that which you can wherever you can find it, from the sky, from the sun, from the good life which has its roots in the earth and thrusts eager stalks into the air of your garden, from your mother and from me, from your school teachers and your Sunday School teachers, from your playmates, and later those with whom you associate at work, from your dog or cat (which have wisdom and knowledge in them of a kind unknown to human beings), from great books and art and music, from the mountains which thrust their serene heads above the river and plain, mighty monuments to the strength of that power which pushed them upwards, from trees, and from the roots of trees and grasses, from newspapers even. Let your five senses be eager in their search. Let your fingers burrow into the earth, that you may learn by touch as well as by the sight of your eyes, the greediness of lilac roots, the delicacy of the tubered tentacles of lilies of the valley, the tenacity of grass roots, the far-reaching search of the root of the grape. Let your sense of smell help you to understand the seeking of the bee for the flower, nor let it run away from those less pleasant (but no less truthful) messages which tell of death and the return of elements to the soil from which they came, nor ever close your mind to similarly true implications. Let your ears hear all good words and all sounds in Nature and music, and the voices of animals in pleasure or distress and all audible evidence of life above and below the surface of the earth, that your mind may ponder these things. Let your eyes see all that passes before them and search for those things which seem hidden from you. Fear no knowledge, but be eager in every moment of your life—above all things be eager for the truth regardless of whether in prospect it seems pleasant or unpleasant to you.

Retain respect for the uses of your own mind and its ability to grasp intimations of the truth. Take the judgments of no man nor any group of men unless, through subjecting them to the honest and respectful processes of your mind you can make them your own judgments. Yet give the sincere words of all men your ear and your examination. Trust, too, those perceptions within you which are more of the heart than of the mind. Know that the mind is not all wise or all capable, that true knowledge is a nicely balanced mixture of intellectual and emotional perception.

Because of this value the words of every true mystic, of every artist, of all the ages. Learn to know the significance of this fact: that mystics thousands of years ago uttered (with no greater proof than the knowledge within them) truths which scientists are only now enunciating on the basis of intellectual findings.

Yet you must have the detailed and specific knowledge and proofs which only science can give you. Through those branches of science called astronomy, geology, soil chemistry, meteorology, learn all that you can of the natural laws which govern universal bodies and the soil which nourishes you. Through biology learn all that you can of plants and animals. Through general history learn the story of mankind, of which you are so intimately a part. Study the social theories of the great revolutionists and the great humanists. Learn something of the history and content of all the great religions and take as many as you can of the truths they have to offer you. Concern yourself with the social and political problems of your time, but accept no theory, no policy of government or social conduct simply because it is the theory or policy of a group of the moment. If it cannot seem true and good to the honest processes of your mind and heart, reject it and continue your search.

Get as much good formal education as you can, but however little or much this is, know that neither can many years spent in classrooms of themselves make you an educated man, nor few make it impossible for you to gain an education. Books and life and art and work and thought—in these your education awaits. You must take it greedily, whether in or out of classrooms. Your taking must never cease. And in every bit of truth which you gain about anything, you will have added to your knowledge of God.

Learn to order your ways so that the hours of your life (which you will find all too short) are not wasted in your search for the universality of God. Learn as Ecclesiastes did:

To everything there is a season and a time to every purpose under the heaven:
A time to be born, and a time to die; a time to plant, and a time to pluck up that which is planted;

A time to kill, and a time to heal; a time to break down, and a time to build up;

A time to weep, and a time to laugh; a time to mourn, and a time to dance;

A time to cast away stones, and a time to gather stones together; a time to embrace, and a time to refrain from embracing;

A time to get, and a time to lose; a time to keep, and a time to cast away;

A time to rend, and a time to sew; a time to keep silence, and a time to speak;

A time to love, and a time to hate; a time of war, and a time of peace.

Know the truth of these things and do not avoid knowledge of the universal character of God any more than knowledge of the varied impulses of man. Know that the prophets had it as did Isaiah:

I girded thee, though thou hast not known me:

That they may know from the rising of the sun, and from the west, that there is none beside me. I am the Lord, and there is none else.

I form the light and create darkness: I make peace, and create evil: I the Lord, do all these things.

I would say to you (and could wish that most of them were my own) these words of Paul, the Christian apostle, which I copy for you here out of a book your grandmother gave me on my sixth birthday. ("With Mamma's love" is written in the front of it, and that love is yours too, now, and is of value to you, and it has the glory of God in it.)

Ye are all the children of light, and the children of the day: we are not of the night, nor of darkness.

Therefore let us not sleep . . . but let us watch and be sober.

For they that sleep, sleep in the night; and they that be drunken are drunken in the night.

But let us, who are of the day, be sober, putting on the breastplate of faith and love; and for an helmet, the hope of salvation.

For God hath not appointed us to wrath, but to obtain salvation. . . .

Wherefore comfort yourselves together, and edify one another, even as also ye do.

And we beseech you, brethren, to know them which labor among you. . . .

And to esteem them very highly in love for their work's sake. And be at peace among yourselves.

Now we exhort you, brethren, warn them that are unruly, comfort the feeble-minded, support the weak, be patient toward all men.

See that none render evil for evil unto any man; but ever follow that which is good, both among yourselves and to all men.

Rejoice evermore. . . .

In everything give thanks, for this is the will of God. . . .

Quench not the spirit.

Despise not prophesyings.

Prove all things; hold fast that which is good. . . .

And the very God of peace sanctify you wholly; and I pray God your spirit and soul and body be preserved blameless. . . .

Seek your God quickly, my dear son. Never cease in your search —you, and all of your generation and those who are to come after you. Let you find quickly the glory of God which will lighten the world before it is too late, lest the spirit of man perish and the human race, proved futile, shall be wiped from the face of the earth by the God of Moses and Elijah, the God of Gautama Buddha, the God of Jesus, the God of St. Francis, the God of your grandmother, the God of Richard Wagner and Beethoven and Toscanini, the God of Zoroaster, the God of Vardhamana, the God of Lao-tze, the God of Paul B. Sears, the God of gentle spring rains, of growing flowers and singing birds, the God of flood and drought and earthquake, the God which is in the electric light and the telephone, the God of earthquake, the torpedo, and the volcano, the God of plenty and of famine, the God of the building up of soil and of its tearing down, the God of peace and of war, of harmony and of discord, the one true God who is within your soul.

My love for you and my faith in you be with you always in your search.

YOUR FATHER

WHY I KNOW THERE IS A GOD

Fulton Oursler

A man whose interpretations of the personality of Jesus have been read by millions here offers his own testament of faith. In it he tells of the spiritual experience of another writer, Franz Werfel, who wrote The Song of Bernadette. He might, with equal justification, have drawn the example from his own life. Fulton Oursler as a younger man had been extremely successful as both a writer and a magazine editor. There came a time when his powers seemed to fail him. The magazine of which he was chief editor required his services no longer and he found himself unable to put pen to paper. Now, finding himself deep in material and spiritual depression, he turned almost unwillingly to God and religion. It was this experience which gave him the courage to go on and to achieve heights of success which he had never even aspired to as a younger man.

✍

MY SEARCH began more than fifty years ago. One morning in April my colored nurse led me to the door of a gray-stone chapel at Twenty-third Street and Guilford Avenue, in Baltimore. Welcoming me inside, a Sunday-school teacher awesomely informed me that I was now in God's house.

"Whereabouts," I asked, "is God?"

"God," the lady assured me, "is everywhere."

But I wanted Him to be somewhere. Like the little girl in the fable, I did not want Him to be invisible; I wanted Him "with skin on." That was why I refused to sit still on my little oaken chair, but ran about the room during the singing of "Little Drops of Water." I peeked under the pew and in a broom closet, only to be rescued finally, breathless and dusty, from behind the pipe organ, weeping because I had not found God.

Thus my quest began, and through half a century I never entirely abandoned it. Even in childhood the reality or non-reality of the Creator seemed to me the most important matter in life; nor can I understand today how any intelligent person can think otherwise. It is the one supreme matter on which a man has to be sure, for every decision he makes hinges upon it.

But can anyone really know? Lanland said: "I have swept the heavens with my telescope and have not found God." While other scientists testify: "We have examined the brain with our microscopes and have not found the soul!"

Yet I begin every day by speaking the words of the ancient creed: "I believe in God, the Father Almighty, Maker of Heaven and Earth. . ."

I recite it all because I believe it all, even though some of my nearest and most intelligent friends challenge my belief.

"We know that you believe, all right," they say. "But you can't really know, now can you?"

"I do know," I assure them, and sometimes quote the Old Testament direction: "Be still, and know that I am God." However, in such friendly discussions it is much easier to know God than it is to keep still; that is the time when arguments begin.

And yet, a man has got to feel that he knows. A creed, a belief, can be of no lasting value if it does not prove itself. The great St. Paul tells us that those are blessed who believe although they have not seen. The blind man of Galilee believed first; not until then were his eyes opened and he saw men as trees walking. Faith comes first; but make no mistake about it, the man of faith does not linger in credulity; it is by his faith that he is led into the full light of knowledge. That is the divine paradox; we come to know when we believe, and not before.

Only those who have never known God will call this transcendental experience an illusion. It is not wishful thinking; it is a sublime reality. But it is difficult to convey to others. The man who tries to confide the experience of hearing Beethoven's Fifth Symphony to a deaf man has a much easier task. Still, the deaf man's misfortune does not make the music an illusion; it is, instead, a vivid fact and a blessing upon the man whose ears and soul are open to its beauty. Now arises a magnificent difference: not everyone can hear an orchestra, but everyone can hear the voice of the Father. The supreme franchise of the human soul is that it can know God. The supreme tragedy of today's tormented world is that so many do not know Him.

When I say such things to some of my friends, who are earnest doubters, they demand to know how anyone can ever prove that God exists. To that question there are two answers, two keys to the most exciting mystery of life.

The first way to know God is by sheer reason, through the brain. That was my first way. Surely, I told myself, if logic is a science, then one should be able to prove or disprove the existence of God scientifically. I knew that physicists had often established beyond dispute the reality of things which could neither be seen nor heard, nor ever known by other senses. Has any eye ever seen an atom? Yet the survivors of Hiroshima and Nagasaki know its terrible actuality. Again, all the billions upon billions of genes in the world could be contained in one child's thimble. Beyond vision or touch, these particles have, nevertheless, been demonstrated; they exist, reservoirs of incredible power.

Every high school student knows how, once upon a time, an astronomer discovered a star without ever having looked upon it. So exact was his knowledge of stellar mathematics that he calculated—he did not have to believe; he *knew*—that there must be another planet in our solar system or else the whole celestial circus would fly apart. Later on, when larger telescopes were built, astronomers could actually see that planet. But it had already been discovered by sheer reason. So, through the same mechanism of the intellect, our Father in Heaven also clearly reveals Himself to the logical mind.

But many another person like myself recoils from skull-busting theological complexities. I preferred firsthand knowledge. While it was possible, I told myself, for a man to read a textbook on swimming and come to know aquatics thoroughly, solely by diagrams and theory, I would rather plunge in a pool and swim. We all exult in the joy of experience, free motion, the splendor of survival in another element.

That is the second way to know God—by personal experience. That was my second way.

In my search for truth I had already explored many different fields. A study of comparative religions over a decade of years led me from Buddhism, and its Western translation called Theosophy, all the way to Bahaism and Zoroastrianism, with many stops between. As a reporter for the Baltimore *American*, I had also attended many religious conferences, and for three months I covered evangelistic meetings of Billy Sunday. I had been immersed in doctrine. I had even waited for specters in dark-room séances of spiritualist mediums. Out of all this I emerged, at the age of thirty, a self-styled agnostic. In those days I considered myself a liberal person, emancipated from superstition, although still genially loyal to ethical values—when they did not interfere too much with what I wanted to do.

I declared that I believed in live and let live. Circumstances, I felt, altered not some cases, but all. There were no absolutes. No more right or wrong. And—for me—no more authority, and no more revelation. Certainly no more supernaturalism. All these things were anathema to my emancipated and rational mind. I couldn't be like Christ, I told myself, I would just be myself.

Such tolerance and emancipation and what I considered common sense and good will should have brought me happiness but did not. Nor did they bring happiness to anyone I knew. Most of my friends felt as I did; none of us better or worse than the other, I suppose;

all very independent and self-reliant and disdainful of the old-fashioned faith of our fathers. We all had a great deal of fun, too, but somehow our hilarities left us dispirited. No part of life was ever really satisfying. With our freedom *and* our liberal principles we should have known a high sense of spiritual well-being, of contented integrity. But was it true freedom? It was certainly not true liberalism. Not one of us knew any real security. Instead, we all had an inner restlessness of disappointment and discontent. Nothing was ever as sweet to see, hear, taste, touch, or feel as we, in our expectations, hoped it would be. At every pay-off we were always let down —and, one way or another, there was always a hang-over.

This inner sulkiness and depression had nothing to do with material success. Among my friends were many who had achived fame and riches, or, at least, a lot of money in the bank. But no matter how much more wealth they piled up, how often their pictures were on the front page, their new possessions, their new wives—nothing was ever enough. After they got what they wanted, they didn't want it. Without avail, they haunted doctors and psychiatrists and yogis.

The world in which I lived was a world of self-pity, self-justification, alibis, envies, jealousies, greeds, fears, resentments, grudges, and hatreds. Today was never good enough, but tomorrow they hoped to be glad. I say they, but I mean we. Today there are eight million men and women quite like us, who are under mental care. There will be, psychiatrists tell us, ten million more in a year or so. People who find the burden of life too much for them; their brain rebels and seeks escape in fantasy.

I shall be forever grateful that in the midst of mental bleakness I found the way out. It is not easy to tell how this happened; I cannot bring myself to open old wounds to public gaze. But you may remember the true story of the illustrious refugee at Lourdes, a famous liberal writer who, with his wife, had slipped through the Nazi frontier. They were working their way southward from Germany through France. The Gestapo was after them, and capture meant the concentration camp or worse. Their hope was to cross the Spanish border and sail for the United States. But they were stopped by Spanish officials. Bribes and entreaty alike failed; they were turned back and found a lodging in the little town in the Pyrenees called Lourdes. On his first night there the fugitive writer stood in front of the famous shrine and made a prayer, a cry from the heart.

"I do not believe in you," he said, in effect, "and I must be honest and say so. But my danger is great, and in my extremity, on the chance that you might after all be real, I ask your help. See my wife and me safely across the barrier, and when I get to the United States I will write the story of this place for all the world to read."

Having finished his prayer, he returned to his hotel. Never, he told me later, had he known a calm so deep; it was pure peace reaching him from beyond; he had touched something beyond the prison of the five senses.

Strange as it sounds, Franz Werfel and his wife got safely through, within the week. The first thing he did, once safe in our land, was to write *The Song of Bernadette*. In our day no more popular tribute to faith was ever penned than the story written by the refugee novelist. Before he died he told me that in the terror of his plight he had come to know God and thereafter had never lost the sense of His presence.

Now something akin to that happened to me. It was nothing so spectacular as a flight from Hitler's agents, but within my own modest sphere I, too, felt surrounded and in danger and afraid. My agnostic self-reliance was no longer helpful; trouble came and littered on my doorstep. Not only I but those nearest and dearest to me were in trouble with me, until I felt I really needed God's help. Yet even then I could not, as an intelligent man, command myself to believe, or pretend to obey—for a man is a fool who tries to deceive either God or himself. The most—the best that I could manage was to admit to myself that I wished I could believe.

And that was enough!

Faith is a gift—but you can ask for it! "O Lord," prayed a man in the Bible, "I believe; help Thou mine unbelief." As he laid his situation before God, and as Werfel did, so did I. Not in Palestine, nor in the Pyrenees, but close to the fashionable parade on Fifth Avenue. On a blustery day, with dark clouds lowering, I turned suddenly into a house of God and asked for the gift of faith. And in the chapel, I took one more vital step.

"In ten minutes or less I may change my mind," I prayed. "I may scoff at all this—and love error again. Pay no attention to me then. For this little time I am in my right mind and heart. This is my best. Take it and forget the rest; and, if You are really there, help me."

It was a striking omen to me that when I came out on the steps the sun had crashed through the dark skies and the lordly avenue was full of color and light. There was a curious feeling of hope in my heart; not peace, but the confident expectancy of peace.

Merely for the record, and not to prove anything whatever, let me say that as Werfel was brought safely to the United States, so the perplexities of my problem were most remarkably and swiftly disposed of. Only chance would explain it to the unbelieving, because no human agency contrived the events. The complication dissolved itself by the oncoming of a series of what the rationalist would call beautiful coincidences. In two weeks I no longer had a serious problem.

In that result, of course, I was most fortunate. It might easily have been otherwise. Yet do not mistake me. Even so, as I know now, my petition would have been heard. Millions of prayers go up every instant, and every one is answered—but sometimes the answer is no.

The Old Greeks had a saying that when the gods were angry with a man they answered his prayers. A little boy implores his father for a bicycle. There is nothing inherently wrong with such a request. But if the neighborhood is dangerous because of traffic, the wise father has to refuse. It is hard for the child to grasp that wisdom. In perfect trust one learns to say, "Thy will be done," knowing that whatever answer comes, is best.

But for me the real knowing of God was just beginning on that day. Only incidentally is prayer asking for help. One should have to ask favors of God no oftener than a sensible child asks favors of his father on earth. Prayer is not a slot machine, where you drop in a request and a boon comes tumbling out of the bottom. We do pray for help, but oftener we pray for help for others, and even oftener we pray our thanks for blessings already received. Above everything else, we pray daily in sheer felicity, in communion, in close contact with the Father, asking nothing whatever but the joy of knowing Him.

It is through prayer that we know there is a God, that God is there; through prayer that we know Him—as Father and friend.

Now here the skeptics turn away in disdain. I can never figure out why. If they admit that they have never known God, and I maintain that I have known and do continue to know Him, and that the path to that knowing is through prayer, then why, in the name of God, do they not pray, just to test it? Why don't they find out by personal experience?

The materialist will deride prayer as a superstitious practice, a psychological hoax, a self-hypnosis, an illogical conception, a childish folly—but never will he put his prejudice to the test in his own discontented life. Tell him that prayer is the only way to God, and he will reject that way. "Bring Him on, face to face," he demands. "Nothing else will do for me."

He wants to rewrite the universal law to meet his own requirements. He is like a man from Mars who is suspicious of photography, sure that it is some kind of trick. "Why," he demands, "do you have to go into that darkroom and do things? That's where the trick is. Let's see you develop and print a picture right out here in the broad light of day. That can't be done, now can it?

No, you have to have darkness to find a picture on the sensitive plate, and you have to have prayer to bring out the invisible presence of God.

But once a man can lift from his soul old Adam's curse of pride, once he finds the humility to ask himself: "Where was I when Thou laidst the foundations of the world?"—once he can, with the perfect trust of a child, reach out to the invisible Father—then comes grace abounding, and a man knows God most intimately; nearer than breathing, closer than the hands and feet.

God meant it, too, when He said in the first commandment that He was jealous and would have no others before Him. He wants you —all of you. You have opened the door; He will come in and take possession. And at once you find yourself plagued with a vague unease that comes equally with His peace. Your daily life becomes a whole series of paradoxes like that.

Possessed of a new feeling of profound tranquillity, nevertheless, you want to be active. Your kind instincts will no longer be satisfied with sending checks to worthy charities; you will be ashamed to buy yourself off. That is like the old Civil War custom whereby a draftee, if he had the money, could hire a substitute to do his fighting for him. It is hiring others to serve God for you. Such gifts to charity are necessary, but never enough. We have to do the corporal works of mercy ourselves; and, as we come to know God, the urge to serve Him personally becomes overpowering. We must feed the hungry, visit the sick, comfort the widow and orphan, clothe the naked, shelter the shelterless—under our own roof, with our own bare hands.

That is when a human being comes closest to God and knows Him best.

Isn't it strange that it should have taken me fifty years to find that simple key to the mystery? Ten thousand times in ten thousand days of that half century, God walked with me to school, rode with me in the bus, held out a beggar's hand at the corner alley, roared at me in the very blasphemy of a reeling old sot from whom all had fled. So many times He was at my elbow, and I pushed on, unaware. Fifty years of never noticing! I have much lost time to make up for.

The skeptic deserves to be assured that all that faith will bring a man can also be justified by his intellect. But that process, I dare to think, can wait. If a man would find God, let him humbly ask for a chance to believe; and, meanwhile, let him go personally and not by delegate to his less fortunate brothers—and sisters—helping the needy of body and soul. He will presently find what he seeks. For when a man can leave himself and enter the lives of others, he leaves his own heart open so that God may enter and dwell with him. This blessing I wish on every reader of these lines.

HOW DO YOU PICTURE GOD?

Harry Emerson Fosdick

Again we turn to Dr. Fosdick for a discussion of what is perhaps the crucial problem of all—the nature of the Deity whom we worship. Is God the patriarchal bearded figure many of us envisioned in our childhoods? Or is God an all-prevading Being far more difficult to envision? No wonder so many people have difficulty believing in God, says Dr. Fosdick, when it is so difficult for them to know just what they are being asked to believe in. In this, one of his most distinguished and perceptive essays, he tries to show us the meaning and essence of a higher Power, the rational basis for a belief in such a Power, and the enormous spiritual rewards which come to us with acceptance of such a belief. We quote Dr. Fosdick's final sentence: "And if you say that this is too good to be true, I am sure of the answer: it is too good not to be true."

ᔍ

DEAR MR. BROWN:

I am glad that, in my last letter, I happened to remark that some people who disbelieve in God are really disbelievers in some particular idea of God. You write now, wondering whether this may not be your trouble—that you have in your mind a picture of God which makes belief in him difficult, if not impossible. This may very probably be a major factor in your problem. Men use the word "God" continually, but what varied pictures of him and ideas about him are in their minds! Whitehead, the philosopher, calls God "the Principle of Concretion" in the universe; and a young girl, surprised at first hearing that Jesus was a Jew, says, "Jesus may have been a Jew, but God is a Baptist." Between such extremes an endless variety of images occupy men's minds when they think of God.

Inevitably, in this world of cause and consequence, we feel that there must be something casual behind existence. Canon Streeter of Oxford used to tell a story about a country mouse and a city mouse arguing about God, with the more sophisticated and skeptical city mouse getting the country mouse completely confused, until at last, trying to save some shreds of its faith, the country mouse exclaimed, "But, dash it all, there must be a sort of something!" Many people never get any clearer idea of God than that—"a vague oblong blur," as one churchman described him. At the other extreme many retain into maturity the most vivid, detailed and picturesque portraits of God which their childhood's imaginations knew. One college student wrote, "I have always pictured him according to a description in *Paradise Lost* as seated upon a throne, while around are angels playing on harps and singing hymns." No wonder that many people—perhaps you yourself—face as their central problem, not is there a God, but what idea of God am I either believing or disbelieving?

In considering this problem one basic fact confronts us: we cannot possibly jump outside of our human experience and find any terms with which to describe God except such terms as our day-by-day living provides. All our thinking about God has to be done with pictures, symbols, images, drawn from human experience. As a result, can anything we say about God be adequate to take him all in and describe him fully? Of course not! Since when has the Pacific Ocean been poured into a pint cup, that the God of this vast universe should be fully comprehended in human words? Nevertheless, even a pint cupful of the Pacific Ocean reveals its quality. So we go on trying to express what we think is true about God's quality in symbols drawn from our experiences. In the Bible God is a rock, a fortress, a high tower; he is father, mother, husband, friend. Go to church any Sunday and what varied pictures of God are presented to us! The first hymn may be, "O worship the King, all glorious above." The second hymn may be, "Spirit of God, descend upon my heart."

The third hymn may be, "The Lord's my shepherd, I'll not want." This use of human symbols in describing God calls out the derision of the unbelievers. Watch these Christians, they say, trying to catch the sun at noon in their verbal butterfly nets! But the fact is that the unbelievers are doing exactly the same thing. They too are trying to describe the basic, creative fact behind the universe, and they too have to say: it is most like—and then they have no choice except to us a symbol drawn from human experience. The cosmos is most like a machine, say the mechanistic materialists. Or, as Haeckel put it, the ultimate reality is most like "a chemical substance of a viscous character, having albuminous matter and water as its chief constituents."

So, we all alike confront the same necessity. As Goethe said, "The highest cannot be spoken." If we think at all about life's underlying reality, we have to think in limited human terms. The question is: Which elements in our experience best express the truth? "Dynamic dirt going it blind," say the materialists. "The Great Architect of the Universe now begins to appear as a pure mathematician," says Sir James Jeans, the scientist. "Our Father, who art in heaven," says the Christian.

No wonder that many people have difficulty believing in God! Like all the rest of us, they start with childish ideas of God—a venerable bookkeeper, with white flowing beard, standing behind a high desk and writing down everybody's bad deeds, was the way Professor John Fiske of Harvard in his boyhood pictured God. All maturing minds, therefore, face this dilemma: either they must give up their belief in God or else they must get a worthier concept of him. So many "atheists" are not really atheists at all. Whenever I have the chance I ask them to describe the God they do not believe in and, when they have done so, I generally can say that I do not believe in that God either, but that we still have the universe on our hands, and do they really think that the cosmic scheme of things is mindless and purposeless, without meaning or destiny, that

> The world rolls round forever like a mill;
> It grinds out death and life and good and ill;
> It has no purpose, heart or mind or will.

That is what genuine atheists do think, but, in my judgment, there are not many such. I corresponded recently with a man who had sent me a manuscript in which he was plainly scornful of faith in

God, but when I asked him whether he did not believe in Mind behind and in the universe, and Purpose running through it, he answered that of course he believed that. He was denying, not God, but some picture of God that insulted his intelligence.

Take Shelley, for example. He signed himself "Percy Bysshe Shelley, atheist." But, when John Keats died and Shelley was stirred to the depths, his faith in Eternal Beauty poured out of him in inspired verse, as though he had clean forgotten he had ever called himself an atheist.

> The One remains, the many change and pass;
> Heaven's light forever shines, Earth's shadows fly;
> Life, like a dome of many-coloured glass,
> Stains the white radiance of Eternity, . . .
> That Light whose smile kindles the Universe,
> That Beauty in which all things work and move.

What picture of God Shelley was denying, when he called himself an atheist, I do not know, but obviously he was a worshiper of "One" eternally beautiful.

You touch the very nub of the difficulty, which troubles many people, when you say that you find it hard to think of God as "a person." I quite agree with you. To say that God is "a person" seems to imply that a human personality is being used as a mold into which the idea of God is poured. That is what scholars call "anthropomorphism"—making a man-sized God. Long ago the Psalmist rebuked that kind of idolatrous thinking, when he pictured God as saying, "You thought that I was one like yourself." Take one look at this immeasurable universe, and obviously no intelligent mind can believe in any such picture of the Eternal.

The real problem calls for another kind of approach. Granted that the whole truth about God is infinitely beyond our comprehension —as the Bible says,

> higher than heaven—what can you do?
> Deeper than Sheol—what can you know?

—the question still remains: starting as we must with our limited human experience, what is the road our thoughts ought to travel out toward the truth about God? Shall we take the lowest roadway, matter, and say that down in that direction through protons and neutrons lies the course our thinking should travel? Or shall we takes the best we know, personality—consciousness, intelligence, purposefulness, good-will—and say that up that road, infinitely beyond our understanding, lies the truth about God? Well, you know what I think. God is not "a person" in any man-sized sense, but I am sure that he is personal, in the sense that only up the highway of man's best can our thinking rightly travel toward the ultimate truth about the Eternal. And because man's best is so marvelously revealed in Jesus Christ, he is my picture, my symbol, my image of God—"the light of the knowledge of the glory of God in the face of Christ."

When I deal with a young man like you, doubting God, I always think of George Matheson. His faith and courage inspired multitudes, and two of his hymns we are singing yet: "O Love That Wilt Not Let Me Go," and

> Make me a captive, Lord,
> And then I shall be free.

In his early ministry he had a parish in the Scottish highlands. He resigned it. He had lost his faith. He could no longer believe in God as he had always conceived him. He decided to leave the ministry. But, though his kirk was in the Scottish highlands, they would not let him go. The Presbytery told him that he was a young man and would yet solve his theological problems. He did. He remained in the church, preaching as much vital Christianity as he could believe in, until his ideas of God expanded,

> And, as the universe grew great,
> He dreamed for it a greater God.

That kind of experience is normal. The greatest men of faith have always had to work their way out of old concepts, truthfully dealing with their doubts, and winning through at last to convictions honestly their own because they had to fight for them.

This is true of the Bible itself. God, at the beginning of the Bible, walking in a garden in the cool of the day, making a woman from a man's rib, confounding men's speech lest they build a tower too high, trying to slay a man at a wayside inn because his child was not circumcised, or dwelling on Mt. Sinai, where he says to Moses, "You shall see my back, but my face shall not be seen," is a very different deity from the one you find at the Bible's end, "God is spirit, and those who worship him must worship in spirit and in truth." The story goes that a young girl was very much troubled by some passages in the Old Testament where God, for example, commanded Saul to smite the Amalekites, and "not spare them, but kill both man and woman, infant and suckling, ox and sheep, camel and ass." So the girl's father read to her some passages from the later Hebrew prophets—such as "What does the Lord require of you but to do justice, and to love kindness, and to walk humbly with your God?" —and from the New Testament: "Beloved, let us love one another, for love is of God, and he who loves is born of God and knows God." The girl was silent for a moment and then said, "Daddy, God grew better as he got older, didn't he?" Well, that is one way of putting it! Certainly no intelligent man can retain his faith in God unless his God does grow better as he, the man, gets older.

Let me try another approach to your problem. Many people, puzzled about God, keep asking, Who is God? What kind of being is he? Another question, however, goes much more closely to the heart of the matter: *Where* is God? We do not want merely to believe theoretically that God is; we want to find him, experience him. Where, then, do we expect to find him? Where is he? The thoughts of many, when they face that question, do not turn inward to the depths of their own souls, but go out into the physical universe. God, they think, is a dim figure behind the universe. Vague and gigantic, he is off somewhere, the one who created the cosmos, omnipotent, omniscient, omnipresent, and when in religious poetry they try to picture him, they sing,

Ancient of Days, who sittest throned in glory.

Now, we may believe in the existence of a being like that, but certainly Christian faith at its best has always meant more than that. What possible meaning could ever get into the idea of loving such a gigantic cosmic sovereign? One might fear such a God, stand in awe of him—but love him? When, however, one turns to the New Testament one finds those first Christians talking, not simply about belief in God, but about loving him. Their language is lyric. Their faith in the Divine is no cool or fearful credence, but a passionate devotion. And the reason for this goes back to their answer to the question, Where is God? Listen to them! "Do you not know that you are God's temple and that God's spirit dwells in you?" You see, ask them where God is and their thought does not shoot off among the stars but goes deep down within human life—there is God. "Behold, I stand at the door and knock; if any one hears my voice and opens the door, I will come to him and eat with him, and he with me."

That is where God is, in all beauty and excellence inspired by his presence within man's life. "God is love, and he who abides in love abides in God, and God abides in him." That is where we discover the Divine, wherever love illumines life.

Over thirty years ago I preached a sermon in which I used this analogy:

Recently I visited once more my island off the coast of Maine and fell in love again with the sea. Now, I do not know the whole sea. It is very great. I never sailed the tropic ocean where the Orinoco and the Amazon pour out their floods through primeval woods. I never watched the Antarctic sea where today pioneers press their perilous way over the polar ice pack. Wide areas of the sea are to me unknown, but I know the sea. It has a near end. It washes my island. I can sit beside it and bathe in it and sail over it, and be sung to sleep by the music of it.

So is God. He is so great that in his vastness we can think of him only in symbolic terms, but he has a near end. Indeed, the nub of the whole inquiry about the nature of Deity lies in the answer to this question: Where do we think in our experience we touch the near end of God? Do we think that only matter is the near end of him and that all the God there is is simply physical, or do we think that in spiritual life at its best we have touched the near end of Deity, and that when we start with that and think out through that as far as we can go, we are thinking most truly about him?

I still believe that to be a true analogy. The cosmic end of God I marvel at, but the near end of God I love—the Divine close to us wherever there is beauty, love, integrity, truth. No one ever can believe in *all* of God. He is too great for even our faith to grasp. Believe in as much of God as you can—that is the way to start. Begin with the near end of God and think your way out through that toward the whole of him.

Begin, for example, with the moral order where "whatever a man sows, that he will also reap." We live not simply in a law-abiding physical system but in a moral order also. Pilate sat in judgment on Jesus, but now Jesus sits in judgment on Pilate. In the long run the Bible is right: "Be sure your sin will find you out." How ever could a chaos of aimless atoms eventuate in a system of moral cause and consequence?

Or begin with the mathematics in the universe. Einstein condenses the truth about cosmic energy into a mathematical formula, $E:MC^2$. Man did not create this mathematical order; he discovered it. Mind meets mind at every step in our exploration of the world we live in. How can aimless, purposeless chance be the explanation of such a system?

Or begin with the beauty that Shelley sang about. There is plenty of ugliness here, but why should "dynamic dirt going it blind" make symmetry and rhythm and light and color and the endless charm of their variety? How can such an explanation account for a scarlet tanager playing in a dogwood tree, or Chopin's nocturnes and Beethoven's symphonies? Sometimes I think that if all other evidence for the Divine should vanish, I still should have to believe that there is an artist somewhere at the heart of things.

Or begin with great character in persons who have made this world a more decent place for the human family to live in. If you have a father and mother such as I had, if through the reading of biography you have fallen in love with history's transcendent souls, if Jesus Christ has captured your imagination and devotion, you simply cannot believe that blind, aimless matter can explain them. No! They are the near end of God.

Or begin with your own inspired hours, when you experienced what Hugh Walpole, the novelist, once described: "I affirm that I have become aware, not by my own wish, almost against my will, of an existence of another life of far, far greater importance and beauty than this physical one." You must have had hours like that. When John wrote about "the true light that enlightens every man," he was talking about all of us. There is a spark of the Divine in each of us, and sometimes it surprises us with an hour of insight, vision, and faith.

See all these near ends of God with which we can start and think our way out through them toward the whole of him. And if you say that this is too good to be true, I am sure of the answer: it is too good *not* to be true.

FAITHFULLY YOURS,

PRAYER

Alexis Carrel

Long before his famous best-seller Man, the Unknown *made his name
a household word, Alexis Carrel occupied a distinguished place in the
field of science. He was a great surgeon and research biologist. The
Carrel-Dakin solution for the treatment of wounds, of which he was
co-discoverer, is credited with having saved thousands of lives in World
War I. He was awarded the Nobel Prize for medical research in 1912.
Later, in 1938, he collaborated with Charles A. Lindberg in writing*
The Culture of Organs. Man, the Unknown *was published in 1935 and
became one of the best-selling books of the century. In it he challenged
many orthodox views of science, upholding among other things the power
of prayer. This thesis, which he described briefly in* Man, the Unknown,
was later elaborated in his small book entitled Prayer. *It is here presented
as the mature thought of an eminent philosopher.*

✧

Definition of Prayer

PRAYER seems to be essentially a tension of the spirit towards the
immaterial substratum of the world. In general, it consists in a complaint, a cry of anguish, a demand for succour. Sometimes it becomes
a serene contemplation of the immanent and transcendent principle
of all things. One can define it equally as an uplifting of the soul to
God. As an act of love and adoration towards Him from Whom
comes the wonder which is life. In fact, prayer represents the effort
of man to communicate with an invisible being, creator of all that
exists, supreme wisdom, strength and beauty, father and saviour of
each one of us. Far from consisting in a simple recitation of formulas,
true prayer represents a mystic state when the consciousness is absorbed in God. This state is not of an intellectual nature. Also it remains as inaccessible, as incomprehensible to the philosophers and to
the learned. Just as with the sense of beauty and of love, it demands
no book knowledge. The simple are conscious of God as naturally as
of the warmth of the sun, or the perfume of a flower. But this God,
so approachable by him who knows how to love, is hidden from him
who knows only how to understand. Thought and word are at fault

321

when it is a matter of describing this state. That is why prayer finds its highest expression in a soaring of love through the obscure night of the intelligence.

Its Technique—How to Pray

How must one pray? We have learned the technique of prayer from Christian mystics from St. Paul up to St. Benedict and to the crowd of anonymous apostles who for twenty centuries have initiated the peoples of the West to the religious life. The God of Plato was inaccessible in his grandeur. That of Epictetus was confused with the soul of things. Christianity on the contrary has brought God within the reach of man. It has given Him a countenance. It has made of Him our Father, our Brother, our Saviour. To reach God there is no longer need of a complex ceremonial or of bloody sacrifices. Prayer has become easy and its technique simple.

To pray it is only necessary to make the effort of reaching out towards God. This effort must be affective and not intellectual. For example, a meditation on the greatness of God is not a prayer, unless it is at the same time an expression of love and of faith. Thus the spoken prayer, following the method of La Salle, leaves the domain of intellectual attention in order to reach that of immediate feeling. Whether short or long, whether vocal or only mental, prayer should be like the conversation of a child with its father. "We come as we are," said one day a little Sister of Charity who for thirty years had been consuming her life in the service of the poor. In fine, one prays as one loves, with one's whole being.

As to the form of prayer, it varies from the short aspiration towards God, up to contemplation, from the simple words spoken by a country woman before The Calvary at the cross road, up to the magnificent Gregorian chanting under the arches of the cathedral. Solemnity, grandeur and beauty are not necessary to the efficacy of prayer. Very few men have known how to pray like St. John of the Cross, or St. Bernard of Clairvaux. But there is no need to be eloquent in order to be heard. In judging the value of prayer by its results, our most humble words of supplication and praise seem as acceptable to the Master of all beings, as the most beautiful invocations. Formulas mechanically recited are in some wise a prayer, even as the flame of a Church candle. It is sufficient that these inert formulas and this material flame should symbolise the flight towards God of a human being. One prays also by action. St. Louis de

Gonzague said that the accomplishment of duty is equivalent to prayer. The best way of communing with God is without doubt fully to accomplish His will. "Our Father, Thy Kingdom come, Thy will be done on earth as it is in Heaven." And doing God's will manifestly consists in obeying the laws of life, as they are inscribed in our tissues, our blood and our spirit.

Prayers, which rise like a great cloud from the surface of the earth, differ from each other as much as the personalities of those who pray. But they consist of variations on two main themes: distress and love. It is entirely legitimate to implore the help of God to obtain what we need. Yet it would be absurd to ask for the gratification of a whim or for what our own effort would procure. The importunate, obstinate, aggressive petition is heard. A blind man, seated by the wayside, shouted his supplications more and more loudly in spite of those who wanted to silence him. "Thy faith hath made thee whole," said Jesus, who was passing that way. At its loftiest, prayer ceases to be a petition. Man lays bare to the Master of all things, that he loves Him, that he thanks Him for His gifts, that he is ready to accomplish His Will, whatever it is. Prayer becomes contemplation. On old peasant was sitting alone in the back pew of an empty church. "What are you waiting for?" he was asked. "I am looking at Him," he answered, "and He is looking at me." The value of a technique is measured by its results. Every technique of prayer is good which draws man nearer to God.

Where and When to Pray

Where and when to pray? One can pray anywhere. In the road, in a car, in a railway carriage, in the office, in the school, in the factory. But one prays better in the fields, the mountains and the woods, or in the solitude of one's own room. There are also the liturgical prayers offered in church. But whatever the place of prayer, God only speaks to the man who has established calm within himself. Inward calm depends at the same time on our organic and mental state and on the milieu in which we are plunged. Peace of body and spirit is difficult to obtain in the confusion, the bustle and the dispersion of the modern city. There is need today of places for prayer, preferably churches where the towns-people can find, if only for a brief moment, the physical and psychological conditions indispensable to their inward tranquillity. It would neither be difficult nor costly to create thus little islets of peace, attractive and beautiful in the centre of the uproar of the city. In the silence of these refuges, men could, in lifting up their thoughts to God, rest their muscles and their organs, relax their spirit, clarify their judgment and receive the strength to support the hard life under which our civilisation crushes them.

It is when prayer becomes a habit that it operates on the character. It is necessary therefore to pray frequently. "Think of God more often than you breathe," said Epictetus. To pray on rising and then to behave the rest of the day like a pagan is absurd. Very brief thoughts or mental invocations can hold a man in the presence of God. All conduct is then inspired by prayer. Thus understood, prayer becames a way of life.

Effects of Prayer

Prayer is always followed by a result if made under proper conditions. "No man has ever prayed without learning something" wrote Ralph Waldo Emerson. Nevertheless prayer is looked upon by modern men as a useless habit, a vain superstition, a remnant of an uncivilised existence. In truth, we are almost completely ignorant of its effects.

What are the causes of our ignorance? First, the rarity of prayer. The sense of the holy is on the way to disappearance among civilised people. It is probable that the number of Frenchmen who pray habitually does not exceed more than four or five per cent of the population. Further, prayer is often sterile. For most of those who pray are egoistic, lying, proud, pharisees incapable of faith and love. Finally, its effects, when they occur, very often escape us. The reply to our demands and to our love is usually given in a slow, insensible and almost inaudible way. The little voice which murmurs this reply in the depths of our souls is easily smothered by the clamour of the world. The material results of prayer, they too are obscure. They are generally confounded with other phenomena. Few people, even among priests, have thus had the chance of observing them in a precise way. And doctors, through lack of interest, often allow cases within their reach to pass without study. Further, the observers are often baffled by the fact that the reply is far from being always the one expected. For example, he who seeks to be cured of an organic malady remains uncured, but experiences a profound and inexplicable moral transformation. Nevertheless, the habit of prayer, though exceptional amongst the whole population, is relatively frequent among the groups that have remained faithful to the ancestral religion. It is within these groups that it is still possible today to study its influence. Among its innumerable effects, the doctor above all has the opportunity of observing those we call psycho-physiological and curative.

Psycho-physiological Effects

Prayer acts on the spirit and on the body in a way which seems to depend on its quality, its intensity and its frequency. It is easy to perceive the frequency of prayer, and to a certain extent its intensity. Its quality remains unknown, for we have not the means of measuring others' faith and their capacity for love. Yet, the way in which he who prays lives can enlighten us on the quality of the invocations he puts up to God. Even when prayer is weak and consists mainly of mechanical recitations, it exerts an effect on the behaviour. It strengthens at the same time the sense of the holy and the moral sense. In the centres where prayer is wont to be made, there is a certain persistence in the sentiment of duty and of responsibility, less jealousy and wickedness, a certain kindness toward others. It appears manifest that with equal intellectual development, character and moral value are higher among individuals who pray, even in a mediocre way, than among those who do not pray.

When prayer is habitual and really fervent, its influence becomes very clear. It is slightly comparable to that of an internal secretion gland, as for example the thyroid gland or the suprarenal gland. It consists in a kind of mental and organic transformation. This transformation operates in a progressive way. One might say that in the depths of consciousness a flame is kindled. Man sees himself as he is. He discovers his egoism, his cupidity, his errors of judgment, his pride. He bends himself to the accomplishment of moral duty. He endeavours to acquire intellectual humility. Thus there opens before him the Kingdom of Grace . . . little by little an inward appeasement is produced, a harmony of the nervous and moral activities, a greater endurance in regard to poverty, slander, worries, the capacity for enduring without enfeeblement the loss of dear ones, pain, illness, death. A doctor who sees a patient give himself to prayer, can indeed rejoice. The calm engendered by prayer is a powerful aid to healing.

However, prayer must not be likened to morphia. For it leads, at the same time as to tranquillity, to an integration of the mental activities, a sort of flowering of the personality. Sometimes heroism. It stamps its believers with a peculiar seal. The purity of the glance, the tranquillity of the bearing, the serene joy of the expression, the virility of the conduct, and when necessary, the simple acceptance of the soldier's or martyr's death, betray the presence of the treasure hidden in the depths of the organs and the spirit. Under this influence, even the ignorant, the backward, the feeble, the poorly endowed make better use of their intellectual and moral forces. Prayer, it seems, lifts men above the mental stature which belongs to them by their heredity and their education. This contact with God impregnates them with peace. And peace radiates from them. And they carry peace wherever they go. Unhappily there is at present in the world a very small number of people who know how to pray in an effective way.

Curative Effects

It is the curative effects of prayer which in all epochs have chiefly attracted the attention of men. Even to-day, among people who pray, one speaks fairly frequently of healings obtained in answer to supplications addressed to God and His saints. But when it is a matter of illnesses susceptible of spontaneous cure, or from the help of ordinary medications, it is difficult to know which has been the real agent of healing. It is only in the cases where all therapeutics are inapplicable or have failed, that the results of prayer can be surely proved. The medical board of Lourdes has rendered a great service to science in demonstrating the reality of the cures. Prayer has sometimes, so to speak, an explosive effect. Patients have been cured almost instantaneously of affections such as lupus of the face, cancer, kidney troubles, ulcers, tuberculosis of the lungs, of the bones or peritoneum. The phenomenon is produced nearly always in the same way. Great pain, then the feeling of being cured. In a few seconds, at most a few hours, the symptoms disappear and the anatomic lesions mend. The miracle is characterised by extreme acceleration of the normal processes of healing. Never has such an acceleration been observed up till now in the course of their experiences by surgeons and physiologists.

For these phenomena to take place, it is not necessary for the patient to pray. Little children still unable to speak and unbelievers have been cured at Lourdes. But near them, some one prayed. Prayer made for another is always more fruitful than when made for oneself. It is on the intensity and the quality of the prayer that its effect seems to depend. At Lourdes miracles are much less frequent than they were forty or fifty years ago. For the sick no longer find there the atmosphere of profound contemplation which formerly reigned there. The pilgrims have become tourists and their prayers inefficacious.

Such are the results of prayer of which I have a sure knowledge. Alongside these, there is a multitude of others. The history of saints, even of modern saints, mentions many marvellous cases. It is unquestionable that most of the miracles attributed, for example, to the Curé d'Ars, are veridical. This mass of phenomena introduces us into a new world, the exploration of which has not begun and will be fertile in surprises. What we already know for certain is that prayer produces tangible effects. However strange this may appear, we must consider as true, that whosoever asks receives, and that the door is opened to him who knocks.

Meaning of Prayer

To sum up, everything happens as if God listened to man and answered him. The effects of prayer are not an illusion. One must not reduce the sense of the holy to the anguish experienced by man before the dangers which encompass him and before the mystery of the universe. Nor must one make simply of prayer a sedative, a remedy against our fear of suffering, of illness and of death. What then is the meaning of the sense of the holy? And what place does nature itself assign to prayer in our life? Truly, this place is very important. In nearly all ages the men of the West have prayed. The ancient city was principally a religious institution. The Romans erected temples everywhere. Our ancestors of the middle ages covered with cathedrals and gothic chapels the soil of Christendom. In our own times, above each village rises a belfry. It was by churches, as by universities and factories, that the pilgrims who came from Europe set up in the new world the civilisation of the West. In the course of our history, prayer has been a need as elemental as that of conquering, of working, of building, or of loving. In truth, the sense of the holy appears to be an impulse from the very depths of our nature, a fundamental activity. Its variations in a human group are nearly always bound to those of other basic activities, the moral sense and character, and sometimes the sense of the beautiful. It is this so important side of ourselves that we have allowed to become atrophied, and often to disappear.

It must be remembered, that man cannot without danger behave according to his whim. To succeed, life must be led following invariable rules which depend on its very structure. We run a grave risk when we allow to die in ourselves some fundamental activity, whether it be of the physiological, intellectual or spiritual order. For example, the neglect of the development of the muscles, of the bodily frame and of the non-rational activities of the spirit among certain intellectuals is as disastrous as the atrophy of the intelligence and of the moral sense among certain athletes. There are innumerable examples of prolific and strong families which produce only degenerates or die out, after the disappearance of ancestral beliefs and the cult of honour. We have learnt from hard experience that the loss of the moral sense and of the sense of the holy in the majority of the active elements of a nation leads to the downfall of that nation and its subjection to the foreigner. The downfall of ancient Greece was preceded by an analogous phenomenon. From all the evidence, the suppression of mental activities required by nature is incompatible with the fulfilment of life.

In practice, the moral and religious activities are bound together. The moral sense vanishes soon after the sense of the holy. Man has not succeeded in building, as Socrates desired, a moral system independent of all religious doctrine. Societies in which the need for prayer has disappeared are generally not far from degeneracy. That is why all civilised peoples—unbelievers as well as believers—must be concerned with this grave problem of the development of every basic activity of which the human being is capable.

For what reason does the sense of the holy play such an important role in the fulfilment of life? By what mechanism does prayer operate upon us? Here we leave the domain of observation for that of hypothesis. But hypothesis, though risky, is necessary to the progress of knowledge. We must remember, first of all, that man is an indivisible whole composed of tissues, organic liquids and of consciousness. He is not therefore entirely contained within the four dimensions of time and space. For consciousness, if it dwells in our organs, at the same time extends beyond the physical continuum. On the other hand, the living body which seems to us independent of its material environment, that is to say of the physical universe, is in reality inseparable from it. For it is intimately bound to this milieu by its incessant need of the oxygen of the air and the foods provided

by the earth. Are we not permitted to believe that we are plunged
into a spiritual milieu which we could no more do without than the
material universe, that is to say the earth and the air? And this
milieu would be none other than the Immanent Being, in all beings
and transcending them all, whom we call God. Prayer could then be
considered as the agent of natural relations between consciousness
and its own milieu. As a biological activity dependent upon our
structure. In other words, like a normal function of our body and
of our spirit.

Conclusion

To sum up, the sense of the holy takes on, in relation to the other
activities of the spirit, a singular importance. For it puts us in communication with the mysterious immensity of the spiritual world.
It is by prayer that man reaches God and that God enters into him.
Prayer appears to be indispensable to our highest development. We
should not look upon prayer as an act in which only the weak-
minded, the beggars or cowards indulge. "It is a shameful thing to
pray" wrote Nietzche. In fact, it is no more shameful to pray than to
drink or to breathe. Man needs God as he needs water and oxygen.
Joined to intuition, to the moral sense, to the sense of the beautiful
and to the light of intelligence, the sense of the holy gives to the
personality its full flowering. There is no doubt that fulfilment of
life demands the integral development of each of our activities,
physiological, intellectual, affective and spiritual. Spirit is at the same
time reason and sentiment. We must therefore love the beauty of
science and also the beauty of God. We must listen to Pascal with
as much fervour as we listen to Descartes.

TWENTY-THIRD PSALM

The Lord is my shepherd; I shall not want.

He maketh me to lie down in green pastures: he leadeth me beside the still waters.

He restoreth my soul: he leadeth me in the paths of righteousness for his name's sake.

Yea, though I walk through the valley of the shadow of death, I will fear no evil: for thou art with me; thy rod and thy staff they comfort me.

Thou preparest a table before me in the presence of mine enemies: thou anointest my head with oil; my cup runneth over.

Surely goodness and mercy shall follow me all the days of my life: and I will dwell in the house of the Lord for ever.